HISTORY OF THE
VIOLIN

WILLIAM SANDYS
SIMON ANDREW FORSTER

DOVER PUBLICATIONS, INC.
Mineola, New York

Bibliographical Note

This Dover edition, first published in 2006, is an unabridged republication of *The History of the Violin, and Other Instruments Played On with the Bow from the Remotest Times to the Present,* originally published by William Reeves Bookseller, Ltd., London, in 1864.

International Standard Book Number: 0-486-45269-7

Manufactured in the United States of America
Dover Publications, Inc., 31 East 2nd Street, Mineola, N.Y. 11501

HISTORY OF THE
VIOLIN

FROM PETERBOROUGH CATHEDRAL
12th Century

[Original Frontispiece]

THE

HISTORY OF THE VIOLIN,

AND OTHER INSTRUMENTS PLAYED ON WITH THE

BOW FROM THE REMOTEST TIMES

TO THE PRESENT.

ALSO, AN ACCOUNT OF THE PRINCIPAL MAKERS, ENGLISH AND
FOREIGN, WITH NUMEROUS ILLUSTRATIONS.

BY WILLIAM SANDYS, F.S.A.

AND

SIMON ANDREW FORSTER.

" Omnium rerum principia parva sunt, sed suis progressionibus
usu augentur."—*Cic. De Fin. Bon. et Mal.*

LONDON
WILLIAM REEVES
1864.

[Original Title Page]

DEDICATED

(WITH PERMISSION)

TO

LORD GERALD FITZ-GERALD,

AND THE

NOBILITY AND GENTRY OF THE SOCIETY OF

WANDERING MINSTRELS.

PREFACE.

HAVING for many years past been in the habit of making collections respecting (among many other things) violins and instruments played on with .the bow, we have ventured to lay the result of our labours before such portion of society as may feel an interest in the subject; and, as the taste for music has of late years so much increased, we may hope this may not be a small portion. Our work should strictly have been called, " Collections towards the History of the Violin," as we ourselves have not only been obliged to omit many things connected with this history, to avoid making the book too bulky and too expensive, but are fully aware that there must be many facts connected with it with which we have not been fortunate enough to meet. We may observe here, that what we have omitted, would only have been additional illustrations, or evidences in support of what we have already stated in the work, and we should be well pleased if any one competent to the task, and with better opportunity and leisure than we have had, would undertake the History in a more enlarged and important shape. In the meantime we trust this work may be received in the kindly spirit in which it is offered to the musical world. Throughout a long extent of time we have been thrown in the society of many professors (some of the highest talent and genius) and amateurs, and among both have numbered some of our dearest friends, and we would willingly consider our book as a slight mark of regard and affectionate memory to those dear friends departed before us, and of esteem and brotherhood to those still remaining; and we must be allowed to express our satisfaction at having the permission to inscribe it to the Wandering Minstrels.

We have stated nothing without authority, though we have not in every instance given it, it seeming scarcely necessary, as all the important ones are given, and we shall be happy on application to supply the particulars of any others in our possession. The index will refer to several, but this is itself only intended to enable the reader to find the principal subjects, as many perhaps as may be requisite, but is by no means presented as a complete index.

In every case where practicable we have referred to the original authorities, and have taken every care to have the illustrations accurate. The lithographs of the Viol da Gamba are taken from excellent photographs of the instrument by Mr. Robert C. May, of Sloane Terrace. We have read with attention and derived information from the numerous works of the well-known author, Mons. Fetis, as far as they relate to the subject of our work, and, in common with all lovers of music, must express the obligation we are under to him for his interesting publications; and have to thank Mons. Vuillaume, the celebrated French maker, for a copy of "Antoine Stradivari." We have also, especially, to give our thanks to that distinguished writer, Mons. de Coussemaker, for the interest he has shown in our undertaking, and the leave he has kindly given us to copy or trace all or any of the illustrations to his valuable " Essai sur les Instruments de Musique au Moyen Age," in " Annales Archeologiques." We have been able to introduce some original letters of Haydn, which we think will be of interest.

We have endeavoured to give our opinion of the origin of the bow impartially, and if any differ from us we would gladly hear their proofs and reasons, our object being to get at the truth. The origin of many well known things is difficult of proof—

" Felix qui potuit rerum cognoscere causas."

CONTENTS.

CHAPTER I.

Page

HE Violin—Effects of Music—Eastern Instruments—
Greek and Roman Instruments — Spurious Roman
Examples—Conductor—Notation   1

CHAPTER II.

Egyptian Instruments—Ninevites—The Bow—Rote—Crwth   .   18

CHAPTER III.

Fiddle—Rote—Rebec—Gigue.   36

CHAPTER IV.

The Bow—Viol—Notation   49

CHAPTER V.

The Viol in Twelfth and Thirteenth Centuries—Early Makers—
Viol in Fourteenth Century—Minstrel Galleries—Conductors Bâton
—Troubadours   61

CHAPTER VI.

Minstrels—Corporation of Minstrels—Kings of Minstrels   . .   72

CHAPTER VII.

Page

Viol in the Fifteenth Century—Early Makers—Kerlin—Notation 83

CHAPTER VIII.

Viol and Violin in the Sixteenth Century—Tuning of Viols—
Viols in French Festivals ; in English Royal Bands—Ancient Viol
da Gamba—Viols in Early Dramas—Musical Publications—
Notation 90

CHAPTER IX.

Viols and Violins in Early Musical Dramas—Tuning of Viols—
Viols in Seventeenth Century—Instruments described—Performers
—Musical Publications 114

CHAPTER X.

Viols and Violins in English Dramatic Writers of Seventeenth
Century—Instruments in Court Masques—Payments to Performers
—Musical Publications 132

CHAPTER XI.

Time of Charles II.—Anthony Wood—Pepys—Baltzar—
Matteis—Simpson—Mace—Publications—The Bow 145

CHAPTER XII.

The Eighteenth Century—Violoncello—Bonanni—Laborde—
Performers 161

CHAPTER XIII.

Orchestras—Performers 176

CHAPTER XIV.

Nineteenth Century—Performers—Paganini—Lindley—Dragonetti 186

CHAPTER XV.

Page

Makers—Early English—Duiffoprugcar—Early Italian Makers
—Amati Family 196

CHAPTER XVI.

Makers in Seventeenth Century—French—Italian—German—
Klotz—Steiner 211

CHAPTER XVII.

Stradiuarius—Guarnerius 224

CHAPTER XVIII.

Italian Makers—German—French—Vuillaume 235

CHAPTER XIX.

English Makers, from Rayman to Betts 248

CHAPTER XX.

English Makers 274

CHAPTER XXI.

The Forster Family 284

CHAPTER XXII.

William Forster (2) 296

CHAPTER XXIII.

The Forster Family and School, continued 333

CHAPTER XXIV.

Page
English Makers, continued 352

CHAPTER XXV.

The Banks Family 359

CHAPTER XXVI.

English Makers, continued 367

CHAPTER XXVII.

Recent English Makers—Resident Foreign Makers 377

HISTORY OF THE VIOLIN.

CHAPTER I.

SMITH says, at the commencement of his "Harmonics," that "Sound is caused by the vibrations of elastic bodies, which communicate the like vibrations to the air, and these the like again to our organs of hearing." "For instance, the vibrating motion of a musical string puts others in motion, whose tension and quantity of matter dispose their vibrations to keep time with the pulses of air, propagated from the string that was struck." The sound of the violin, and instruments of that class, arises from the vibrations of the strings produced by the friction of the bow communicating with the air, the power being increased by means of the two vibrating plates of the instrument, generally called the back and the belly, connected with each other by the sound post, and with the strings by means of the bridge.

The greatest care is necessary in the construction of these instruments; to ensure the proper elasticity of the vibrating plates, to settle the model or form of the body, the position of the sound-holes; and, in fact, the whole structure is the result of long experience and skill. The

pitch depends on the length, thickness, and tension of
the strings, and the quality, on the shape, proportions,
and materials of the instrument; and, also, on the purity
of the strings, and the power, taste, and talent of the
performer; the difference between the delightful tones of
a performer of the first class, and the twang of a crowdero vile, being such that we can scarcely realize them as
proceeding from the same instrument.   By one we are
soothed until for a time the cares of the world are forgotten, whilst the other seems to rasp against the nerves,
and scrapes us to the quick.   We are here speaking of
the majority of mankind, for there are some few who
seem insensible to the charms of music; and among
these, even excellent good people, quite unfit for "trea-
sons, stratagems, and spoils," but probably defective in
organization.   King George III. said to Madame D'Arblay (then Miss Burney), that Lady Bell Finch once
told him that she had heard there was some difference
between a psalm, a minuet, and a country dance, but
they all sounded alike to her.   On the other hand,
there have been excellent musicians who have been excellent in little else.   The celebrated Lord Chesterfield
told his son that fiddling "puts a gentleman in a very
frivolous and contemptible light, and brings him into a
good deal of bad company, and takes up a good deal of
time which might be much better employed."   Considering, however, the nature of Lord Chesterfield's advice to
his son in some other respects, we may discard him as
any authority.   He would probably have approved of
the Gentoo Law, which prescribed that the king or rajah
should not always be employed in dancing, singing, and
playing on musical instruments.

Curious effects have been produced on animals by
music.   Fetis mentions a dog, which had such a dislike

to the sound of a violin, that he began to howl in antici-
pation as soon as he saw it touched. He gives an account
of a lizard, which would come out of an old wall, where
he had established a domicile, on hearing the adagio to
Mozart's quartett in C, but would not pay the same com-
pliment to any other piece. The little reptile's musical
taste must have been limited as well as scientific. The
same remark may apply to the pigeon mentioned by Mr.
John Lockman, as cited by Hawkins, which would fly
down from his dove-house, and perch on the parlour
window, to hear Handel's air of " Spera si, mio caro,"
played on the harpsichord, and return when the tune was
finished. Lenz, in his anecdotes of animals, relates one
of an elephant, who paid no attention to the performances
of an orchestra in his vicinity, until they played " Char-
mante Gabrielle," when he appeared much pleased,
keeping time with his trunk, and was particularly
attracted by M. Duvernais, who played the horn.
Vigneul Marville, whose real name was Noël Bonaven-
ture d'Argonne, and who lived in the latter half of the
seventeenth century, in his " Mélanges d'Histoire," &c.,
and Bonnet, in his " Histoire de la Musique," give some
examples. On hearing a trumpet marine, a dog sat on
his hind legs, like a monkey, fixing his eyes on the performer, and remained so for more than an hour. An
ass continued to eat his thistles with sublime indifference.
Domestic poultry seemed to pay no attention, while the
smaller birds around sang in rivalry as if they would
burst. Cows stopped, looked up a little, and then walked
on. A hind raised her ears, and seemed attentive. A
horse raised his head from time to time while feeding;
and horses generally are attracted by the sound of the
trumpet, and other warlike instruments; we have seen
them attentive to the sound of a gong. A cat seemed

to pay no attention to the trumpet marine, and looked as if he would give all the instruments in the world for a mouse.   Cats, however, are capricious, for while some that we have known have remained stretched on the rug in a state of the utmost indifference to the sound of the violoncello, others have shown the greatest objection to it (perhaps the fault of the performer), particularly to those notes producing what is called the wolf. A gentleman frequently practising on the instrument, observed that if those notes often occurred, the cat then reposing on the rug became restless, and gave indications of displeasure, but if he dwelt on the note the animal would look up at him with anger, and if he persisted would begin to growl, and finally spit and hiss, and run away in violent indignation.   There is a singular but well authenticated anecdote related of an officer of the regiment of Navarre, confined in the Bastille for six months for having spoken too freely of M. de Louvois.   He was allowed the use of his lute, but on beginning to play he was surprised to see the mice come out of their holes, and the spiders descend from their webs. The intendant of Madame de Vendôme assured M. Bonnet that he had tried the same experiment himself with a violin, and that within a quarter of an hour a great number of spiders had descended towards his table.   Playford, in his "Introduction to the Skill of Musick," says, that as he was once travelling near Royston he met a herd of about twenty stags following the sounds of a bagpipe and a violin, walking on while the music was played, but stopping when it ceased; and in this manner they were brought from Yorkshire to Hampton Court; a dance that beats Kempe's "nine daies morris daunce" from Norfolk.

One of the most ludicrous anecdotes, however, of the

power of music, is that related by Howell, in a letter to Sir James Crofts, 6th September, 1624, where he calls it a pleasant tale of Sir Thomas Fairfax, of a soldier with his bagpipes, who, after a weary walk in Ireland, sat down to enjoy his frugal meal of bread and cheese. While so employed, two or three gaunt and hungry wolves approached, and the soldier, somewhat dismayed, first threw them a bit of cheese, and then a bit of bread, till his stock was exhausted, but the fierce animals still seemed unsatisfied, and approached nearer. The soldier then took up his bagpipes in despair, and treated the animals with some choice bits on this ancient instrument, on which they turned tail, and trotted off, howling in unison. "A plague on it," says the soldier; "if I had known you loved music so well, you should have had it before dinner."

It may seem to those but imperfectly acquainted with the subject that not much can be said respecting the history of the violin. Fiddles were played on, they suppose, some time back, perhaps by the Greeks and Romans; they have heard of Nero playing the fiddle while Rome was burning, and have been told that the best fiddles are called Cremonas, and, indeed, even in the present day, some have asked whether Cremona is the name of a maker or a performer.

In truth, however, the history of the violin—meaning thereby stringed instruments played on with a bow—is a subject of great difficulty, and the origin, like that of many other well known things, seems lost in obscurity, especially the commencement of the use of the bow. Considerable labour and attention are required to give even a reasonable account; and, though we do not seek to rival the research and perseverance of Father Ocampo, who began his intended history of the emperor Charles V.

with the Creation, and after thirty years' labour was surprised by death, when he had only reached the time of
the Sabine War, yet we have honestly endeavoured to
give such a chronicle as may prove useful and interesting
not only to the musician but to the general reader, so
that we may not be asked, as Ariosto was by the Cardinal
d'Este, "Dove diavolo avete pigliato tante coglionerie?"

Jean Rousseau, the great violist of his age, in his
"Traité de la Viole," 1687, seeking to prove the antiquity and excellence of his instrument, says, that as
Adam was acquainted with all arts and sciences, and the
viol is the most perfect instrument, if he had any instrument, it must have been that.   We may, however, refer
to Jubal as the father of all such as handle the harp
(*i.e.* the kinnor) and organ; or, in the quaint words of
Capgrave, "Jubal, he was fader to alle hem that singe
in the orgoun, or in the crowde."—"He was fynder of
musick, not of the very instrumentis which be used now,
for thei were founde long after."

The words translated into harp and organ in the Old
Testament may probably be considered as representing
the stringed and wind instruments, and though the
learned Kircher describes the kinnor, or harp, as something like a dulcimer with thirty strings, he cannot be
relied on.   Peter Walker may as well be taken for an
authority for ancient fiddles, where, in his "Life and
Death of Three Famous Worthies," referring to the destruction of Sodom and the surrounding country by fire
and brimstone from heaven, while the wicked people
were enjoying "fulness of bread and idleness," he says,
"their fiddle strings and hands went all in a flame; and
the whole people in thirty miles of length, and ten of
breadth, as historians say, were all made to fry in their
skins."   Kircher describes several others of the ancient

Jewish instruments, as supposed by him, mentioning that some were played on with a bow, but there is no authority for this. Rousseau, eager to prove the antiquity of the viol, refers to Kircher's description of the neghinoth, as being similar to it, having three gut strings, and played on with a horse-hair bow; and Baptiste Folengius considers the nablum, or psalterium, to have been the same as the viol. The passage in the old play of "Lingua" may be considered of equal authenticity.

> " 'Tis true the finding of a dead horse-head
> Was the first invention of string instruments,
> Whence rose the gitterne, viol, and the lute."

Numerous musical instruments are mentioned in the Old Testament, and in the early times, as now, the Jews were skilled in the science; but it would be foreign to our purpose to enter into any account of these instruments, as there is no proof, or even a probability, of any of them having been of the violin or bowed class. It is true, according to our version, Isaiah says, speaking of the feasts of Israel, "the harp and the viol, the tabret, and pipe, and wine, are in their feasts;" and Amos speaks of the melody of viols, and says, "they chant to the sound of the viol, and invent to themselves instruments of music like David;" but the word viol was only used by the translators as the name of an instrument known to them, to express the Hebrew word *nebel*, of which instrument nothing distinctly was known.

The kinnor, translated harp, was probably like the portable harp, or lyre, used by the early Egyptians and Ninevites, to which we shall presently refer; and thus David could play on it, even while dancing before the ark, and the Jewish captives could readily hang it up by the waters of Babylon.

Julius Bartoloccius, cited by Gerbert, in his valuable

work, "De Cantu et Musicâ Sacrâ," mentions among
the instruments of the Hebrews the viola, or chelys, and
many other stringed instruments, but he makes no advance in identifying them; and as, amongst other instruments, he mentions the "spinettæ," the integrity of his
list cannot much be depended on. He divides the instruments into three classes, and thus describes what he calls
fidicina: "Secundi generis sunt omnia instrumenta quæ
chordis seu nervis instructa, digitis vel pinnis vel etiam
plectris in harmonicos motus artificiose incitantur, et
sonum suavem reddunt; ut sunt, citharæ, testudines,
theorbæ, nablia, harpæ, lyræ, viola seu chelys, sambucæ,
pectides, pandoræ, clavicymbala, clavichordæ, spinettæ,
barbita, aliaque his similia, et omnis generis citharæ
vulgo chitarre."

The Eastern nations had, probably, from an early
period stringed instruments, but principally of the lute or
guitar class. There is no early record or representation of
the use of the bow; and when it does appear, it may have
had its origin from a more frequent intercourse with the
Western and Northern countries. We do not, therefore,
look for the introduction of the bow from the East, though
we may be indebted remotely to the ancient Egyptians,
as hereafter mentioned, for an instrument that, with
some modification, may have afterwards become one of
the earliest bowed instruments. The bowed instruments
most in use in the Eastern countries were generally made
of a cylinder of sycamore, or other suitable wood, or
sometimes a cocoa-nut, hollowed out and polished, a
prepared skin, or a slip of fine satin-wood, being placed
over the cavity. The neck was very long and slender,
and the strings two or three in number, with a bridge;
the bow of bamboo and hair. Varieties of these are still
in use in India, Persia, Arabia, China, and other coun-

tries. Captain Saris, who was at Japan in 1613, says
the ladies played on an instrument like the theorbo (a
species of lute), but having only four strings, which they
fingered very nimbly with the left hand, having an ivory
plectrum in the other.

Several early instruments of the East are named, varying in number of strings and details, as the serinda,
omerti, rouana, and ravanàstron, and others ; the latter,
according to the exaggerated Oriental tradition, having
been invented by Ravona, king of Ceylon, 5000 years
before the Christian æra.

The Indian mythology has some curious legends about
music, which may be seen more at length in Creuzer's
" Religions de l'Antiquité," vol. i. Hanouman, a faithful
follower of Vishnu, was a skilful musician, and the inventor of one of the four systems of Indian musiċ that
keeps his name. He with his lyre, and Crichna with his
flute, conducted the dance of the spheres, the stars, the
months, and the seasons, accompanied by the raguinis,
and other musicians of the court of India. Saraswati
was the goddess of music, and her son Naesda invented
the lyre. The six ragas who presided over the six musical modes were also her children, and each of these had
thirteen assistants of an inferior class, so that there were
eighty-four modes of the Indian mythological system of
music connected with their astronomy, namely, six pri-
mitive and seventy-eight derivative. The power of these
ancient modes, called the ragas, was very great, placing
Orpheus quite in the background. A celebrated musician once sang that called the night raga, before the
Emperor Akber at mid-day, and caused night within the
sound of his voice. Another raga had the quality of
destroying by fire any one who sung it; but the same
emperor, notwithstanding, compelled an unfortunate

vocalist to sing it, when, although every precaution was taken, and he was plunged up to the neck in the river Jumna, the flames burst out and destroyed him. A female singer was more happy, for in a time of famine from want of rain, she sung the rain-producing raga, and seasonable showers followed and revived the parched rice crops.

Many have seen the anecdote given by Olaus Magnus, of Eric, king of Denmark, who was excited to madness by the performance of a celebrated musician. First he produced grief, then joy, and then fury, to such an extent that Eric destroyed some of those who endeavoured to restrain him. We can only say that we have seen this account in the work of Olaus, and that Kircher believed it. However, he also believed the story of the magic piper of Hammelin, who in the year 460, in revenge at not being paid for piping away the mice of the place, piped away all the boys from four to twelve years of age, and disappeared with them in the side of a hill. Verstegan says the year was 1376, and that the boys were 130 in number, of whom one who was lame escaped by lagging behind. Kircher must be right, for he had seen the hill, and a picture representing the fact.

The fancy of the music of the spheres is not confined to India—

> " The music of the spheres,
> So loud it deafens mortal ears,
> As wise philosophers have thought,
> And that's the cause we hear it not."—*Hudibras.*

The celebrated astronomer Kepler, had a fanciful notion about this music of the spheres, making Mercury the treble, Venus and the Earth the counter-tenors, Mars the tenor, and Jupiter and Saturn the basses. If he had lived to this time, he might have established a very imposing choir with the numerous additional planets.

Stringed and bowed instruments are mentioned by travellers in many countries, but they are generally of a simple, and often of a rude form, and to none can we look for the origin of our violin. The Tatars, the modern Greeks and Egyptians, even the Africans have them. Bowditch, in his " Mission to Ashantee," describes one used by the natives from the interior, made from a calabash, with a deer-skin at the top, having two large sound-holes, one broad string made of cow-hair, and the bow strung with the same material. Layard mentions the Bedouins who attended him chanting verses to the monotonous tones of a one-stringed fiddle, made of a gourd covered with sheepskin. Prince Youssoupow also, in his " Luthomonographie," relates having met with travelling orchestras of Persians, Turks, and Armenians, in which there were instruments of the violin class, but without its tone or regular form, being commonly made of half a gourd, or sometimes hollowed wood covered with a piece of bladder, having three or four strings. The prince is in favour of the Eastern origin of the violin, thinking it was brought to Spain by the Moors in the eighth century, but whatever instruments they had were probably more of the guitar or lute kind. Du Halde refers to a kind of violin with three silken strings, in China, used by the common people ; and Sir Joseph Banks saw one in Iceland of a clumsy form, with four copper strings and frets; this, however, might have been adopted from Norway or Sweden. Sir Edward Belcher mentions those of the Asiatic Esquimaux, and their skill on violins of their own manufacture.

The Arabs, besides their lute, or guitar, or mandolin, of which Laborde, in his somewhat fanciful " History of Music," mentions a species having no less than a hundred frets, and the neck of which must, therefore, have rivalled

that of the giraffe, had a bowed instrument that may
have been similar to one frequently named by the old
poets and romance writers.   This was the rebab, or
rebec, with two or three strings, which is supposed by
some to have been brought into Europe by the Crusaders;
but as at the time of the Crusades the viol had been for
a very long time well established in England and many
parts of the Continent, it is more probable that the Sara-
cens adopted it originally from the Crusaders. Monsieur
Fetis, whose extensive musical research is well known,
considers that the bow was not derived from the East,
but from some of the Northern people, from whom it
travelled southward, and passed into the East at a very
early date.

The Russian peasants have a rude sort of violin without any inward curvatures, called the goudok : it has
three strings, of which the first is touched with the finger,
while the other two are sounded at the same time by a
short, clumsy bow.   They have also an instrument of
the guitar kind, called the balalaika, with two or three
strings and a very long neck, which is mentioned by
Laborde, and also by De Passenans in " La Russie et
l'Esclavage," 1822.

Neither the Greeks or Romans appear to have any
authentic representations of a bowed instrument; they
had principally different kinds of lyres and flutes, together
with the ancient syrinx or Pan's pipes, now degraded
into a common street instrument, and indeed, seldom
heard at all. Mersennus and other writers of the middle
ages, use the word barbiton for instruments of the fiddle
class, but the barbiton that Anacreon complains of, as
preferring love-strains to singing of Atreides and Cadmus,
was a species of lyre, the ode being addressed to his lyre.
We should have said Anacreon, or whoever wrote the

poems generally attributed to him, as modern progress supposes them to be of a later date; just as Babrius supplants our old friend Æsop. Horace also mentions the barbiton.

The epigonium and magadis have been named as the originals of the viol and violin, but the former appears to have been of the lute or harp class, having forty strings, and an instrument called the simicon had thirty-five; while, as to the magadis, according to the Supplement to Montfaucon, it is not even agreed what the instrument was; whether a flute, or of the guitar class, and if so, whether it had twenty strings or less—that the pectis was the same as the magadis, and the dicord the same as the pectis; but that the matter was altogether uncertain. Apollodorus says it was the same as the psalterium. Some further particulars will be found in " Musonii Philosophi Opus de Luxu Græcorum," in the eighth volume of Gronovius's " Thesaurus," including the scindaphos, pariambos, clepsiambos, lyrophœnicion, spadix, phorminges, trigona, chelys, cithara, lyra, "et alia fortasse quamplurima, quorum investigationem aliis relinquamus." A representation is given in the Supplement, of the dicord, and also of a cithara, taken from an old Roman sculpture, which seems to have eight strings, though there are but five screws. It is like the old viol in shape, and has no appearance of frets, bridge, or finger-board, but is not adapted to the use of the bow. Anacreon mentions playing on a magadis with twenty strings (this puts an end to the flute question), and in another ode names the pectis, which has been translated cithara. Aristotle also calls these the same instruments. Montfaucon gives a representation of a procession of Isis taken from an old sculpture, where one of the figures —probably a priestess—is playing on a large triangular

or harp-shaped instrument, having twenty strings, held
under the right arm, on which she plays with a plectrum,
and which may have been a magadis. He has also a
representation of Apollo (supposed to have been intended
for Nero), with a lyre in his left hand and a long plectrum in the right.

There are numerous representations of the plectrum
used with the ancient lyre and lute, many of which, with
the authorities, may be found in Montfaucon, and in
Millin's "Galerie Mythologique." In the latter work
there is a figure of Polyphemus in a state of musical and
jealous excitement, holding an enormous lyre, made of
the trunk of a tree with two branches, having four strings,
and played on with a plectrum. Among the fictile vases
in the British Museum, there is a figure of Anacreon
playing on a lyre with seven strings, which has a plectrum attached to it by a string, and is played on with
the right hand, while the fingers of the left hand touch
the strings ; the instrument is somewhat like the lyre
du Nord, referred to hereafter.

Some supposed old Roman sculptures or medals are
mentioned with representations of something like a
violin, but these are not considered genuine. The
following is Spence's account of the detection of some
that were once considered proofs of the early use of the
bow, commencing with the figure of Apollo in the Grand
Duke's Tribuna at Florence, supposed by Addison to
have been genuine, but proved by Winckelman to be
comparatively modern. "The little figure in the Tribuna, with a musical instrument like a violin, is left
rough and unfinished by the artist, particularly the
violin and the stick to play on it. It is held as we hold
our violins." Mr. T. — Spence adds, "I have met but
with two figures besides this with the modern violin.

One of them is in a relievo on the death of Orpheus, in the University at Turin; and the other is a statue either of Orpheus or Apollo, in the Montalta Gardens at Rome. It is unlucky that all three have something to be said against them. That at Florence is an unfinished piece, and perhaps not quite indisputable; that at Turin of a very bad taste, or of a low age; and in that at Rome, the fiddle at least is evidently modern." Mr. Singer, the editor of "Spence's Anecdotes," from which these extracts are taken, being part of the valuable " Library of Old Authors" published by Mr. J. Russell Smith, thought that Mr. T. was probably Mr. Townley, (who, in his account of some ancient gems, mentions a curious figure of a centaur, with a whip in his hand to lash himself!)

Rousseau refers to an account given by Achilles Tatius of a banquet, where a youth came forward with a cythara, on which he first played with his fingers, and then used a bow, and sang to it: also to a description of Orpheus by Philostratus in the time of Nero, who supports the lyre on his thigh, striking the strings with his left hand, whilst his right holds a bow. Rousseau uses the words viole and archet, but the Latin words are cythara and plectrum, which do not warrant his translation; nor can we agree with him in his application of a quotation from Ovid's third book " De Arte Amandi "—

" Nec plectrum dextrâ cytharam tenuisse sinistrâ
Nesciat arbitrio fœmina docta meo."

The plectrum and cythara here neither mean a viol or a bow, but the former was occasionally long, such as that represented by Montfaucon in the figure of Apollo before mentioned. In the early ages of Christianity, the word cythara was frequently used to designate any stringed instrument; as, cythara Barbara, cythara Teutonica, cythara Anglica (which seems to have been a harp).

Hawkins cites Nichomachus Gerasenus, who in his account of stringed instruments A. D. 60, does not name the bow. Blanchinus, in his history of the instruments of the ancients, gives a figure called the chelys (a term in after-times applied to the viol class) or, as he adds, " seu lyra Mercurii reformata." It is of the lute kind, and has neither bridge, sound-holes, neck, or finger-board, and is played on with a plectrum.

If, however, these nations, whose languages and customs were instilled into us during our eight years' residence at our venerable old school at Westminster, had not violins and bows, they forestalled us in the appointment of a coryphæus or conductor, who kept time either with his foot, armed with a wooden or iron sandal, or with his hands, having shells or bones of animals in them to increase the sound. How would a modern audience like such a conductor, performing thus a sort of sabotier dance, or rivalling the " bones " of the American minstrels?

With our comparatively simple system of notation, it seems scarcely credible how the complicated and cumbrous system of the Greeks could ever be properly understood; it must alone have proved a great check to anything like rapid execution, from want of capability to express such passages. Or, if once such execution had been attempted and introduced, the necessity of the case would have advanced the notation. Their characters, though comparatively few at first, and formed from the letters of their alphabet, increased so much that they were obliged to vary the position of these letters in various ways, and to introduce numerous arbitrary signs, every mode requiring a new arrangement; and in the time of Alypius, 115 B.C. the characters amounted to more than 1600. A very laboriously constructed table of them may be seen in the first volume of Laborde's History. The Romans also used the letters of the alphabet. It is, however, foreign to our purpose to do anything more than refer slightly and occasionally to the systems of notation, as it would require a volume with numerous illustrations to treat the subject properly.

CHAPTER II.

THE Egyptians were musical from the earliest times, but their usual stringed instruments appear to have been the harp and lyre, or of that class. They are repeatedly found in their sculptures, and Sir Gardner Wilkinson, in his "Ancient Egyptians," mentions a harp as old as Osirtasen I. who was the Pharaoh of Joseph, and therefore lived about 1700 years before our Saviour. The harps were generally of a portable shape, the strings varying in number from four to twenty-two, and made of what is commonly called catgut. They were occasionally made of costly materials and richly ornamented, and sometimes were played on with a plectrum; but there is no appearance of any bowed instrument. Burney gives a figure of an instrument of the guitar class, with a long neck and two strings, sculptured on a broken obelisk supposed to have been brought from Heliopolis by Sesostris, but this does not appear to have been played on with a bow. Rousseau, however, in his enthusiasm for the viol, says the Egyptians had one with one or two horsehair strings, played on with a bow strung with similar materials; it had a long neck, and was supported on the ground by an iron rest. As before mentioned, he thought Adam might have played on the viol, and he might therefore have deduced its descent through Noah to the Egyptians. He does, however, give its travels from Egypt to the Greeks, then to the Italians, then to the English, who first composed and played pieces of harmony for the instrument; from them it passed to the Germans and Spaniards, and finally, as he says, to the French, to whom it owes its perfection.

Passing by Rousseau's theory, which has not the proof of any Egyptian viol to support it, the Egyptians had an instrument with considerable affinity to the crwth, and to which we shall presently refer again, wishing first to make a few observations on the musical instruments on the sculptures at Nineveh made known to the world by the skill and enterprise of Mr. Layard. Some of these are supposed to be at least as old as any mentioned by Sir G. Wilkinson, and among them there is no appearance of the bow. There is the representation of a very ancient one on an engraved scarabæus, where it is called a nable or guitar, and there are figures of a portable lyre or harp struck by a plectrum. In one bas-relief from Konyunjik there is a representation of musicians going to meet the Assyrian conquerors—three men carry harps with many strings; another has a stringed instrument like the modern sautour of the Egyptians, with a number of strings stretched over a hollow case or sounding-board; the strings are pressed with the fingers of the left hand, and struck by a small wand or hammer in the right; there are also four women playing harps.

The Egyptians and Ninevites, as before observed, had in the earliest ages an instrument somewhat similar to the crwth, which was not played on with a bow, but sometimes with a plectrum, sometimes only with the fingers; the strings varying from three to thirteen (Fig. 1). When the tide of population flowed westward and northward, the descendants of Japhet took this crwth-shaped instrument with them, and in very early ages were established in our country. The bow, we

consider, was afterwards introduced or invented here, for we find here the earliest trace of it, and none of any antiquity in the East. The wand or plectrum was an approach to the bow; the beating on the tightened strings inducing the experiment of the effect of friction, and thus leading to its use.

Long before the time of Cæsar there were inhabitants in our land who had made considerable progress in the arts and learning of the early ages, as the Celtic records remaining prove; and the earliest of

FIG. 1.

these show their love for music. It is supposed by scholars of high repute, that Ireland and the south-western parts of England were in very early ages peopled from the peninsula of Spain, where the Phœnicians had formed a colony or settlement; and many parts of the south coast may have been probably peopled from the opposite coast of Gaul. In other parts, settlers came over from Scandinavia and Germany—for the first visit of the Saxons or Northmen was long previous to Hengist and Horsa—and they appear to have had at an early age an instrument of the fiddle or viol class.

The crwth of the Britons resembles to a considerable extent the Egyptian and Ninevite instrument before referred to, and was well known to the Continent in very early times. Venantius Fortunatus, Bishop of Poitiers, who lived about the end of the sixth century, says—

" Romanusque lyra plaudat tibi, Barbarus harpa,
Græcus Achilliaca, chrotta Britanna canat."

The chrotta must have been known on the Continent as a British instrument long before this, or it would scarcely have been so distinguished by a foreign author. Notker, in the ninth century, says that the rotta (or chrotta) was derived from the psalterion—the ancient psalterion, as he even at that early time calls it. This instrument had some similarity to the Egyptian or Ninevite instrument before referred to, and was sometimes of a triangular form, sometimes square or rectangular, with occasional varieties of form. Notker says that the ancient psalterion had ten strings, and that the form, the Greek delta (Δ), had a mystical signification; but after it became in use by common or secular performers, they added strings to it, and made the shape more convenient (by rounding the angles), and called it the rotta, thus changing the mystical form of the Trinity. The mysticism, however, of the form, probably only existed in the imagination of Notker, and the passage is in an article "In Symbolum Athanasii." This rotta, as appears from the lines just quoted, was known long before Notker, but we have cited him as an authority for its derivation from the ancient psalterion. In a letter from Cuthbert, cotemporary with Bede, to Lullus, successor of St. Boniface, Archbishop of Mayence, written about 755, he says, " Delectat me quoque cytharistam habere qui possit cytharizare in cythara quam nos appellamus rottæ, quia citharam habeo et artificem non habeo." M. Fetis considers this to have been the cithara Teutonica, formed from the rounded psalterion ; and with him Mr. W. Chappell, whose opinion on everything connected with music is entitled to much attention, concurs. M. de Coussemaker, to whose learned " Essai

sur les Instruments de Musique au Moyen Age," we are
much indebted, and with whom M. Bottée de Toulmon
agrees in his " Dissertation sur les Instruments de
Musique employés au Moyen Age " (Mémoires de la
Société Royale des Antiquaires de France, vol. xvii. p.
95), considers that the rote was derived from the chrotta
or crwth in the following manner :—It was found after
a time (and after the introduction of the bow) that the
hand was embarrassed in its movements by the shape of
the instrument, as the bow must necessarily have struck
several strings together.   To obtain greater facility, the
external parts surrounding the neck, which had been
introduced, were removed, and the shape became gradually something like the bass-viol, and played in the same
way, between the legs, or on the knee.   The rote, then,
according to this opinion, was a modification of the
original chrotta or rotta, and this does not seem inconsistent with the derivation of the early instrument given
by Notker, and Gerbert gives two representations of the
cythara Teutonica (Figs. 2 and 3) from MSS. of probably about the eighth century, though he considers one
to be older.   From the epithet " Teutonica," they were
evidently instruments derived from or belonging to the
northern countries, and similar to the chrotta Britannica,
and not at this time played on with the bow.   The word
cythara seems to have been used by the early writers as
a general expression for many classes of stringed instruments : the cythara Anglica, for instance, was a harp,
another example of a northern instrument.   Cassiodorus,
in the sixth century, includes among stringed instruments,
and which he says were struck with a plectrum, " species
cithararum diversarum."
    These instruments, including the ancient psalterion,
were not viewed by the Churchmen with favour for

ecclesiastical use. In the Council of Cloveshoe, 747, it was decreed that "ex monasteriis citharistæ aliique fidicines expellerentur;" and St. Jerome says, "fidicinas et psaltrias et hujusmodi chorum diaboli quasi mortifera sirenarum carmina proturba ex ædibus tuis."   The

Cythara teutonica

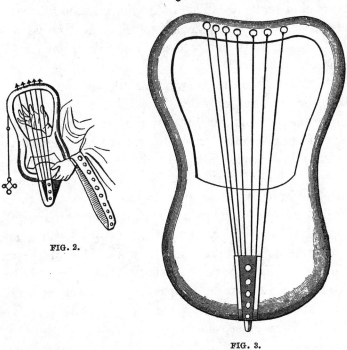

FIG. 2.

FIG. 3.

Abbot Amalarius, in the early part of the ninth century as cited by Gerbert, referring to the expression required in singers, says—implying the absence of any instruments,—" Nostri cantores non tenent cymbala, neque lyram, neque citharam manibus, neque cætera genera musicorum, sed corde. Quanto cor maius est corpore, tanto Deo devotius exhibetur, quod per cor fit, quam per corpus, ipsi cantores sunt tuba, ipsi psalterium, ipsi cithara, ipsi tympanum, ipsi chorus, ipsi chordæ, ipsi organum, ipsi cymbala." John of Salisbury, in the twelfth century, writing on the use of music in churches, says: "Sumite psalmum, date tympanum, psalterium iocundum cum cithara." In an old French Bible of the same date, the third verse of the 149th Psalm is rendered, "Loent-il son noun en crouth, si chantent-il à lui en tympan et psaltruy." Thomas Aquinas, in the thirteenth century, says, "Instrumenta musica, sicut citharas et psalteria, non assumit ecclesia in divinas laudes, ne videatur iudaizare."

Although the rotta, rota, or chrotta, was thus derived, according to Notker, from the psalterion, yet it did not supersede that instrument, but they gradually differed more from each other in shape, and the rote adopted the bow, while the psalterion, about the fifteenth century, was known as the dulcimer. They are frequently mentioned together in old writers, and also in conjunction with the vielle, or viola. The pseudo-Bede mentions together the organum, viola, and cithara, atola, and psalterium; and Constantinus Africanus, in his work "De Morborum Curatione," says that soft music should be played before the invalid, as from the campanula, vitula, rota et similibus; and Sanutus, amongst other sweet music, names "violæ, citharæ, et rotæ."

Gerson, of a later date (about the fourteenth century), whom we also cite from the valuable work of Gerbert, in reference to the passage in the Psalms, "laudate eum in chordis et organo," says, "Chordæ secundum glossas positæ sunt pro quibuslibet instrumentis, aliis a psalterio et cithara quæ chordis sonat (sic) repercussis, sit viella, sit symphonia, sit lyra, sit rota, sit guiterna," &c.; and in another part he says, "Canticum cum pulsu fit tripliciter; aut in rotatu, ut in symphonia; aut tractu aut retractu, sicut in viella aut rebella ; sive cum impulsu vel impulsivo quodam tractu cum unguibus vel plectro, cum virgula, ut in cithara et guiterna, lituo, psalterio quoque et tympano, atque campanulis." In these passages he refers to the rota as a bowed instrument, and to the psalterion as not being bowed.

Many examples may be given from the ancient poets and romance-writers to the same effect, of which we will cite a few, and they may also be taken to show the use of the instruments, the vielle, or viol, and the gighe ; and to prove that the vielle, gighe, rote, psalterion, and symphonie, or chyfonie, and rubebe (rebec), were different instruments. In the Roman de Brut, about the end of the twelfth century, we find—

> " Lais de vieles et de rotes,
> Lais de harpes et de fretiaux,
> Lyres, tymbres, et chalumiaux,
> Symphonies, salterions,
> Monocordes, tymbres, corrons."

In another part, relating the skill and talents of the celebrated king Blegabres (or Blæthgabreat, as he is called in the version of Lazamon), who flourished, according to Stow, 104 A.C., was the god of jongleurs and singers, and played on every instrument, he is thus described :—

> " Blegabres regna après li,
> Cil sot de nature de cant,
> Oncques nus n'en sot plus, ne tant.
> De tos estruments sot maistrie,
> Et de diverse canterie ;
> Et mult sot de lais et de note,
> De vièle sot et de rote,
> De lire et de salterion,
> De harpe sot et de choron,
> De gighe sot, de symphonie.
> Si savoit assés d'armonie.

De tous giex sot a grant plenté ;
Plein fu de debonnaireté,
Por ce qui il est de si bons sens,
Disoient li gent à son tens,
Que il ert dex des jugléors
Et dex de tos les chantéors."

In or about the thirteenth and fourteenth centuries there are numerous examples. From the "Estoire de Troie le Grant," Roquefort, "De la Poesie Françoise," &c. quotes :—

" N'orgue, harpe, ne chyfonie,
Rote, vielle, et armonie,
Sautier, cymbale et tympanon,
Monocorde, lire et coron,
Ses sont li xii instrument
Que il sonne si doucement."

Also from " Roman de la Poire,"—

" Et si i ot à grant planté
Estrument de divers mestiers,
Estives, harpes, et sautiers,
Vieles, gygues, et rotes,
Qui chantoient diverses notes."

In a romance by Guiraud de Cabrera, the following instruments are mentioned together :—

" L'us menet arpa, l'autre viula,
L'us flautella, l'autre siula ;
L'us mena giga, l'autre rota."

In the "Romance of Cleomades,"—

" Plenté d'estrumens y avoit ;
Vieles et salterions,
Harpes et rotes et canons
Et estives de Cornouaille."

Guillaume de Machault, of the fourteenth century, in "Le Tems Pastour," has a very long list of instruments :—

" Mais qui véist après mangier
Venir menestreux sans dangier

Pignez et mis en pure corps.
Là furent meints divers acors
Car je vis là tout en un cerne
Viole, rubebe, guiterne;
L'enmorache, le micamon,
Citole et le psalterion;
Harpes, tabours, trompes, nacaires,
Orgues, cornes plus de dix paires;
Cornemuses, flajos et chevrèttes,
Douceines, simbales, clochettes,
Tymbre, la flauste Brehaingne
Et le grand cornet d'Allemaingue,
Flajos de Saus, fistule, pipe,
Muse d'Aussay, trompe petite,
Buisines, eles, monicorde,
Ou il n'a qu'une seule corde,
Et muse de blet, tout ensamble;
Et certainement il me semble
Qu'oncques mais tele mélodie
Ne fut oncques veue ne oye."

In the "Prise d'Alexandrie," by the same author, many of the same instruments are mentioned together, among which are the following which relate to our subject:—
"Vielles, rubebes et psalterion, gingues, rotes, monocòrde, chifonie."

Eustace Deschamps, in his poem on the death of Machaut, introduces together,—

" Rubebes, leuths, vielles, syphonie,
Psalterions, trestous instrumens coys,
Rothes, guiterne, flaustres, chalemie."

In the "Romance of Sir Degrevant," of about the fourteenth century, printed by the Camden Society, it is said,—

"·He was ffayre mane and ffree,
And gretlech yaff hym to gle,
To harp and to sautré,
And geterne ffull gay;
Well to play in a rote."

In a note, a passage from an unpublished poem by

Lydgate is given, where the following instruments are named,—

> " Harpys, fythels, and eke rotys,
> 　Wel accordyng with her notys,
> 　Lutys, rubibis, and geterns,
> 　More for estatys than taverns:
> 　Orguys, cytolys, monacordys."

Here we have the word fythel introduced. Gower says,—

> " He taught her, till she was certene
> 　Of harpe, citole, and of riote,
> 　With many a tewne, and many a note."

And Chaucer's "frere,"—

> " ———— Certainly he had a merry note,
> 　Wel coude he singe and plain on a rote."

Very long before the time of these latter examples the rote had received various modifications and improvements in form, and the bow had been introduced. M. de Coussemaker has given the figure of a rote or crwth of the eleventh century, with three strings, and played on with a clumsy bow (Fig. 4). This has quite the character of the old crwth, and the method of using the fingers is shown. Another, given by him from the Cathedral of Amiens, of the thirteenth century, with six strings, has also many of the distinctive

FIG. 4.

marks of the crwth; and the similarity of the sound-holes to the modern ones will be observed (Fig. 5).

FIG. 5.

Carter, in his "Ancient Sculpture," gives the figure of an angel playing a crwth, in Worcester Cathedral, of about the twelfth century, under part of the seats of the choir. It has five strings, a tail-piece, and two sound-holes; no neck, no bridge, the left hand being placed through the hole at the lower end to manage the strings. The bow is short, and in form like the modern double-bass bow; it is a characteristic example, but in this instance the instrument was held like the viol (Fig. 6).

FIG. 6.

The word crwth was occasionally used for the violin and viol down to a recent time, and is still so applied in some parts of the country, most commonly to the violoncello, or bass-viol, as it is also called. A curious example may be given from a work not likely to be much known to our readers; an old Cornish drama of the date probably of the fourteenth century, called "Ordinale de Origine Mundi." The ancient Cornish language was akin to the Welsh, both having the same origin, and this extract will show that the words "crowd" and "fylh" were applied to different instruments. King David is giving directions to his minstrels—

> " Whethong menstrels ha tabours
> trey-hans harpes ha trompours
> cythol crowd fylh ha savtry
> psalmus gyttrens ha nakrys
> organs in weth cymbalys
> reçordys ha symphony."

Thus translated by the able editor, Mr. Edwin Norris—

> " Blow, minstrels, and tabours;
>   Three hundred harps and trumpets;
>   Dulcimer, fiddle, viol, and psaltery;
>   Shawms, lutes, and kettle drums;
>   Organs, also cymbals,
>   Recorders and symphony."

The crwth was of early date in Scotland, as well as in England and Wales, and an instrument of this nature was among the ornaments on the outside of Melross Church, founded in 1136.

Dauney, in his " Ancient Scottish Melodies," quotes from an old poem called the " Houlate," 1450, where are mentioned—

> " The psaltry, the citholis, the soft atharift,
>   The croude and the monycordis, the gythornis gay;
>   The rote and the recordour, the ribus, the rift," &c.

Edward Jones, in the " Relics of the Welsh Bards," gives a poetical description of the crwth, written in the fifteenth century by Gruffydd Davydd ab Howel, with a translation. It agrees very much with that given by Daines Barrington, to which we shall presently refer. It is said that Bishop Morgan, in his translation of the New Testament into Welsh, printed in 1567, translated "vials of wrath" by crythan, that is, crwds or fiddles. Hawes, in his " Pastime of Pleasure," of nearly the same date, thus describes the attendants of Dame Music :—

> " There sat dame Musyke, with all her mynstrasy;
>   As tabours, trumpettes, with pipes melodious,
>   Sakbuttes, organs, and the recorder swetely,
>   Harpes, lutes, and crouddes right delycyous;
>   Cymphans, clarycordes, eche in theyr degre,
>   Did sytte aboute theyr ladyes mageste."

We find the word crowd used for fiddle by the dramatic writers of the seventeenth century. For instance, in

"The Old Law," by Middleton, fiddlers are introduced to play at an expected wedding, a ceremony where they were always in requisition : Gnatho, the servant, says: "Fiddlers, crowd on, crowd on ; let no man lay a block in your way; crowd on, I say!" The wedding being broken off, the unlucky fiddlers are sent off without their fee : "Case up your fruitless strings, no penny, no wedding." In Marston's "What you will" they are mentioned in a somewhat disparaging way :—

> "—— Now the musicians
> Hover with nimble sticks o'er squeaking crowds,
> Tickling the dried guts of a mewing cat."

Their constant resort to convivial meetings is frequently alluded to, as—

> "The fiddler's croud now squeaks aloud,
> His fidlinge stringes begin to trole ;
> He loves a wake and a wedding cake,
> A bride-house and a brave May-pole."
> *Cupid's Banishment*, 1617.

Ben Jonson and Drayton each name the crowd, as an instrument to dance to ; and Sir W. Leighton, in "Teares or Lamentations of a Sorrowfull Soule" (1613), where a curious list of musical instruments is given to sound the praises of the Almighty, mentions crowdes and vialls. In the "Diary of John Richards," printed in the "Retrospective Review," published by Mr. J. Russell Smith, there is an entry on 5th July, 1699, of Mr. Mallerd coming to finish Jack's crowd, and taking away his own bass-viol to mend. This crowd was no doubt a fiddle, as part of Jack's outfit in 1700, on going to Wimborne School, was "1 violin." We are inclined to think that during our Westminster æra, a fiddle would have led a sad life amongst our three hundred companions ; we have heard, however, of one or two now of distinguished

rank who boldly persevered, but personally remember
no musical attempts, excepting some half-dozen flutes
and flageolets, in a greater or less state of perfection;
we confess to two joints of one of the former. We must
not omit some notice of Hudibras's Crowdero, said to
have been one Jackson, formerly a milliner, who lost a
leg in the service of the Roundheads, and was obliged to
get a precarious livelihood by fiddling from one tavern
to another.

> " I'th' head of all this warlike rabble
> Crowdero march'd expert and able,
> *   *   *   *
>
> A squeaking engine he applied
> Unto his neck on north-east side,
> *   *   *   *
>
> His warped ear hung o'er the strings,
> Which was but souse to chitterlings:
> His grizly beard was long and thick,
> With which he strung his fiddle-stick;
> For he to horse-tail scorn'd to owe
> For what on his own chin did grow."

After this digression on the application of the word
crowd to the violin, we must return for a short space to
the ancient crwth, which appears to have continued in
use in Wales until a comparatively recent time. Daines
Barrington, in 1770, says that the only person that could
then play on it was John Morgan of Newburgh in
Anglesey, then aged fifty-nine years; but Bingley, in
his account of North Wales, says he heard an old bard
play on the instrument at Carnarvon in 1801. We have
given a figure of one from Mr. Barrington's account in
the third volume of "Archæologia" (Fig. 7). It has
six strings placed in a peculiar way, with a flat bridge,
so that the bow must have struck several together, and
prevented any extent of execution. The bridge is curious,
as one leg goes through the sound-hole to the back of

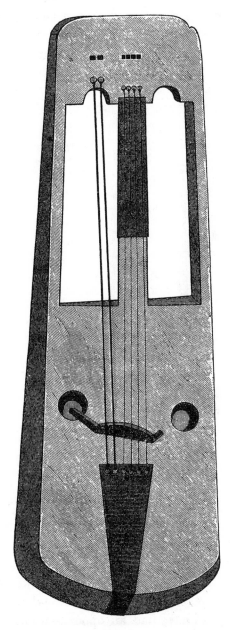

FIG. 7.

the instrument, thus serving also for a sound-post. There is no proof, however, of this example having been of ancient date. It is stated to have been thus tuned :—

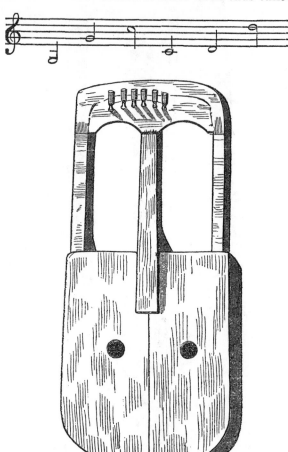

FIG. 8.

We have only been able to meet with one existing specimen, which by the kindness of Charles W. G. Wynne, Esq. we have had an opportunity of examining and of giving a drawing. The wood is worm-eaten and in tender condition, showing apparently greater age than the date of the ticket, and rendering it not improbable that it might have been only repaired at that time. It has no bridge, or tail-piece, or strings at present. It is 22 inches in length (about that of a violin), $9\frac{1}{2}$ in width, and 2 in depth at the deepest part; the finger-board being $10\frac{1}{4}$ inches long. It is a curious and interesting relic (Fig. 8). The following is a copy of the ticket:—

maid in the paris of
anirhengel by Richard
Evans Instruments maker
In the year 1742.

CHAPTER III.

THE names fiddle, or fythele (fydele), among the Anglo-Saxons, and fidula with the Latin writers, are of very early date; by some of the latter, the "cithara sive fidula" is classed with "vulgaris musica." Isidore, Bishop of Seville in the seventh century, uses the word cithara as a general name for stringed instruments, stating there were several sorts, as psalterium, lyra, barbiton, &c. Some have derived the Latin word vidula, or vitula, from vielle, but we do not see why it should not be derived direct from fythele. Mr. Wm. Chappell, in his valuable and interesting work on the "Popular Music of England," one that while it shows the research of its author, places our country in a high position in the early history of music, derives vielle from fythele in the following manner. The Normans, finding the Saxon ð or *th* not easy to pronounce, were in the habit of adapting it to their own pronunciation, and thus changed the word fythele to viele, or vielle, omitting the objectionable letters; but whether this derivation be correct or not, the term fydyll or fithele also continued in use. In the legendary life of St. Christopher, written about the year 1200, it is said the king "loved melodye of fithele, and of songe;" and in the version or edition of Lazamon's "Brut" (a work of the thirteenth century) by Sir F. Madden, the fythele

is named among the instruments of the accomplished
Blæthgabreat:—

> " Ne cude na mon swa muchel of song
> of harpe & of salteriun :
> of fidele & of coriun
> of timpe and of lire."

We have already referred to the lines of Lydgate—

> " Harpys, fitheles, and eke rotys,
> Wel according to ther notys."

In "The Vision of Piers Ploughman," of the middle of
the fourteenth century, the word is again introduced,—

> " I am a mynstrall," quod that man,
> " My name is Activa Vita ;
>
> * * * *
>
> . . I ken neither taboure ne trompe,
> Ne telle no gestes,
> . . ne fithelen
> At festes, ne harpen."

And in "Octouian Imperator," where the rote and
psalterion are mentioned together :—

> " Ther myghth men here menstraleye,
> Trompys, taborus and cornettys crye,
> Rowte, gyterne, lute, and sawtrye,
> Fydelys, and other mo :
> In Parys gret melodye
> They maden tho."

The admirers of Chaucer will remember that the
Clerk of Oxenford would rather have—

> " Twenty bookes, clothed in black and reed,
> Of Aristotil and of his philosophie,
> Then robus riche, or fithul, or sawtrie."

In the present day wiser scholars than he have proved
that a clerk may love his "fithul" without neglecting his

"philosophie." Queen Guenever, of scant fame, had at
her revels, as appears in the "Romance of Launfel,"—

> ". . . menstrales of moch honours,
> Fydelers, cytolyrs and trompours."

While Sir Thomas on his visit to the Fairy Queen finds
harp and fidul, getorn, sautry, lute, and rebybe, and "alle
maner of mynstralcy." So Sir Thomas was very well
pleased for a time, as may be seen in Halliwell's "Fairy
Mythology," which contains much interesting matter.
Many other examples might be given, if necessary, in
further proof of the frequent use of the word; we shall
bring forward some of them by and bye for a different
purpose. One or two references may be made to more
sober writers, as Geoffrey de Vinesauf, about the year
1200, who, after mentioning "somniferæ cytharæ," immediately afterwards introduces "vitulæ jocosæ." Gerbert adds, "Vitulæ an violæ? quæ passim inter instrumenta musica medii ævi censentur." John de Garlande,
in his vocabulary of the middle of the thirteenth century, has the word vidula amongst his musical instruments; and we are told that Isabella, Queen of Edward
II, had in her train, amongst others, two poor musicians,
"vidulatores," to play before her. The fiddle of these
early times, however, was the viol and not our modern
violin.

In the "Nibelungen Lied," of the twelfth century, a
celebrated warrior and minstrel is introduced, named
Volker; his fiddle-bow, or videl-bogen, appears to have
been a powerful weapon of offence; and he is called
videlære. A short but amusing account of Volker, and
some other ancient musical worthies, as Swemmel and
Werbel, "court fiddlers and minstrels" to King Etzel,
will be found in "A Few Notes on the Fiddle," by the

accomplished antiquary Mr. William J. Thoms, published
in No. 47 of the "Musical World," where, however, he
finishes by leaving his friend Volker in the lurch, admitting him to be a myth. As we, in common with
all who have the pleasure of knowing him, must hold his
learning and wit in high estimation, and, as in these "Few
Notes" he says, "No catalogue of fiddlers can be complete in which there does not appear the name of Lewis
van Vaelbeke as a player and maker," we must state from
his information that Lewis, or Lodéwyk van Vaelbeke,
of Brabant, who died at Antwerp in the very beginning
of the fourteenth century, was an eminent " vedelare,"
and, on the authority of a rhyming chronicle, written by
Nicolaus Clerk, was the first to stamp or beat time.
Mr. Thoms humorously commences his translation of the
lines applicable to Van Vaelbeke thus :—

> " About this time departed slick,
>   That good fiddler Lodewyk ;"

and finishes thus—

> " He was the first to find and show,
>   To stamp or beat the manner how,
>   Just as we hear it practised now."

We cannot, however, on the authority of the extract
given—and with the highest respect for the translator—
admit the name of Vaelbeke as a maker, without further
authority, and Mr. Thoms himself allows the obscurity
of the phrase cited for the purpose. We have already
shown that beating time was known to the Greeks.

Johannes de Muris, about the fourteenth century,
would seem to distinguish the vielle from the fiddle as a
variety.   In describing the class of instruments he calls
chordalia, he says, " Chordalia sunt ea, quæ per chordas
metallinas, intestinales vel sericinas exerceri videntur,

qualia sunt cytharæ, viellæ et phialæ, psalteria, chori, monochordum, symphonia seu organistrum et his similia." In "Promptorium Parvulorum" (about 1440), fydyll and fyyele (viol) are Latinized, viella, fidicina, vitula; while crowde is called chorus.

The viol, or vielle on the Continent, was the name most commonly used for instruments of this description, and viol, indeed, has descended to the present time, while vielle, about the fifteenth century, became applied to an instrument the parent of our hurdy-gurdy, which was originally called the organistrum, and symphonie, or ciphonie. This was clearly a different instrument from the rote, being frequently mentioned at the same time. The celebrated Blæthgabreat played on the rote and the symphonie, and in the "Romance d'Alexandre," quoted by Ducange (voce *rota*) "Rote, harpe, vielle et gigue et ciphonie," appear together. In that curious composition, "Les Deux Troveors Ribauz," of about the thirteenth century (which may be found in "Œuvres de Rutebeuf," i. 335-7), being a dispute between two trouveres, or minstrels, as to their qualifications; one of them says to his opponent,—

> "Sez-tu nule riens de citole,
> Ne de viele, ne de gigue?
> Tu ne sez vaillant une figue."

To which the answer is,—

> "Ge te dirai que je sai faire:
> Ge suis juglères de viele,
> Si sai de muse et de frestele,
> Et de harpe et de chifonie,
> De la gigue, de l'armonie,
> De l'salteire, et en la rote
> Sai-ge bien chanter une note."

He then goes on to say he can raise spirits, and perform

feats of magic, which are foreign to our purpose; the extract, however, shows the symphonie and rote to have been different, as well as the vielle and the gigue. This symphonie is also mentioned as the lyra mendicorum, and a figure of it is given by Mersennus and other writers, proving its similarity to the hurdy-gurdy. Happily this instrument is now very rarely heard in our streets since the departure of blind Sally of Westminster notoriety, whom many of our readers may remember; a slight suspicion of it only occasionally occurring in the hands of some wandering Italian boy.

In a MS. of the fourteenth century at Ghent, referred to by M. de Coussemaker, there is the figure of an instrument to which no name is attached, said to have been invented by one Albinus. The celebrated Alcuin, who died in 804, travelled on the Continent under that name, and was skilled in music, having written a treatise on the subject, although it is not now extant. It may not, perhaps, be assuming too much to consider him the Albinus referred to. The instrument is somewhat of guitar-shape, and has four strings marked c, g, d, c. There are considerable inward curvatures, but no bridge or finger-board; the tail-piece is broad, and there is a semi-lunar sound-hole on each side (Fig. 9). On a capital of the eleventh or

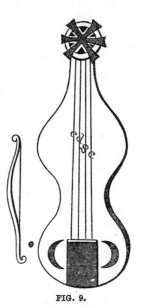

FIG. 9.

twelfth century, from Boscherville, stated to be in the Museum at Rouen, there are eleven figures playing on different instruments, while a twelfth is tumbling.

One of the instruments (Fig. 10) is held on or between
the knees · of the performer, and,
though of smaller size, is not unlike
the viol da gamba in shape. It has
four strings, and four semi-circular
sound-holes, but no appearance of a
bridge or finger-board. The absence,
however, of some of the details of an
instrument, either in sculpture or painting, must not be taken as a proof in
all cases that the parts omitted did not
exist; they might have been omitted by
the artist either from want of knowledge
of the instrument, or because he thought such details
unnecessary. It might also be possible, in some cases,
that a layer of hard wood was applied, as in the present
guitars, to avoid the indentations that would take place
in soft wood from constant use.

FIG. 10.

In the porch of Notre Dame de Chartres of the twelfth
century, is a representation of a curious instrument of this
class (see Fig. 11, from Potier's " Monumens Français,"
vol. i.). It is not unlike a cumbrous violoncello in shape,
but the apparent heaviness may be the effect of the
sculpture. The bridge in particular is thick, and deeply
grooved for the strings, which are three in number and
very large. The tail-piece is much ornamented, and
there are four sound-holes, two of quatrefoil shape, and
two much like the modern ones, but with both ends
turned the same way. There is another instrument of
this class of the same date, mentioned by M. de Coussemaker, from a marble statue in the Museum at Cologne.
The body is rather longer than usual, it has three strings,
and two wide sound-holes. This, with the examples 9
and 10, are of the class considered by M. de Cousse-

maker to be rotes, or viols of large size, and Potier's example is similar.

Shaw, in "Dresses and Decorations," gives an example of the thirteenth century from Arundel MS. 157, which has three strings and two round sound-holes (Fig. 12); the bow is much like the modern violoncello bow, but is held under-handed.

Another variety was called the rebec, sometimes the ribible or rebelle, and rubebe. It seems originally to have been of a trapezoid form, and afterwards oblong, with the angles cut, and had two or three strings. Roquefort says it was a sort of bastard violin, or "violin champêtre," and was a favourite among the rustic classes, but fell into disuse in the sixteenth century—probably in con-

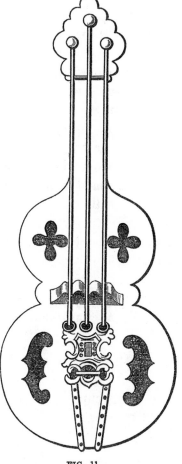

FIG. 11.

sequence of the introduction of the violin proper about this time. Laborde, in his "History," gives engravings of persons playing on the rebec, and on the violin, as he calls it, with three strings, of the thirteenth and fourteenth centuries; but the figures are evidently modernized, and little reliance can be placed

FIG. 12.

on the early part of his history.   He mentions the
figure of the celebrated Colin Muset at the porch of St.
Julien des Menestrier at Paris, of the date of 1240, playing on a rebec or violin ; but the hospital of St. Julien and
St. Genès (who was a Roman mime martyred in the
time of Dioclesian, and adopted as the patron saint of
his profession) was founded by the Corporation of Minstrels about the year 1330, and the figure called Colin
Muset by Laborde, is by others said to have been King
Chilperic, or St. Genès himself.   The church referred
to was destroyed in the time of the French Revolution.
The instrument is mentioned by Aimeric de Peyrac in
the thirteenth century, and is frequently named in the
fourteenth century.   It was played on by Absolon,
Chaucer's parish clerk, who appears also to have been a
distinguished dancer.

> " In twenty maners he coude skip and daunce,
> After the scole of Oxenforde tho,
> And with his legges casten to and fro ;
> And pleyen songes on a small rubible."

The instrument is named with the Idle Apprentice in
the " Cook's Tale."

A gay young clergyman of the time of Edward II.
when he goes out—

> " He putteth in his pawtener
> A kerchyf and a comb,
> A skewer and a coyf
> To bynd with hys loks,
> And ratyl in the rowbyble
> And in non other boks
>   Ne mos."

Gerbert quotes Gerson of the fifteenth century, who
names the viella, the rota, and the rebella (that is, the
rebec) together as bowed instruments.   We have given

a figure of one, which seems characteristic of the class, from a picture attributed by M. de Coussemaker to Hemling of the fifteenth century, where an angel is represented playing on it (Fig. 13).

FIG. 13.

Henry VIII. had three rebecs in his band, as well as two viols; and the same instruments appear in the bands of his three children, his successors. The three performers in the band of Henry VIII. in the seventeenth year of his reign, were John Severnake and John Pyrot, who had forty shillings monthly wages each, and Thomas Evans, who had only six shillings and eight pence. Severnake seems to have been continued in the three following reigns. In the privy purse expenses of Henry VIII. 1531, there is an entry of xx^s " paiede for a Rebecke for great guilliam ; " a considerable sum, taking into account the difference in the value of money ; it is unlucky that the name of the maker is not mentioned. There is a rebec mentioned in that valuable record, the " Northumberland Household Book," 1512, who had 33s. 4d., and it forms one of the " mynstrasy " of Dame Musyke, before mentioned.

Jerome de Moravia describes the instrument as having two strings, tuned by fifths, and extending from C (Ut grave) to the D octave, but it could not rise higher, proving that the shift was not then known : however, it frequently seems to have had three strings. Towards the sixteenth century it declined in favour, and became more particularly the instrument of the lower classes on the Continent, and was used to accompany the rustic dances. Artusi mentions it in 1600, together with the viol, the bastard-viol, and the violin, and many other instruments. It was evidently considered of an inferior rank in France in the seventeenth century, as in regulations made in 1628 and 1648, all minstrels not properly admitted as masters, are forbidden to play any violin except that with three strings, or the rebec, and it gradually got into disuse. M. Hersart de la Villemarqué, in the introduction to " Barzaz-Breiz populaires de la Bretagne," names it as in use there among the wandering minstrels, " bardes mendiants."

The rebec, as well as other varieties of the viol, occasionally had a head carved at the end of the neck, where the scroll now is, and generally a grotesque or fanciful one. Rabelais distinguishes Badebec, the mother of Pantagruel, by her likeness to one :—

> " Elle en mourut la noble Badebec
> Du mal d'enfant que tant me sembloyt nice
> Car elle avoyt visaige de rebec."

In an inventory of King Charles V. in the middle of the fourteenth century, several instruments are particularized, having carved heads, one with the head of a lady, another of a lion, &c.

Another variety, the gigue, is frequently mentioned in the thirteenth and fourteenth centuries, and is supposed to have been derived from the ancient form of the viol, which was originally of something like pear-shape ; that is, like the half of a pear, cut through longitudinally, and was made of one piece ; it gradually became of an oval shape, and the neck was detached. What was called the gigue, retained very much the old shape ; the back, however, becoming gradually rounded, the neck still being a prolongation of the body. It generally had three strings, and continued in use till towards the latter part of the sixteenth century, and occasionally was even of later date. It would seem to have been of German adoption, as the word geige is the German name for a viol or violin, and the performers were sometimes called "giguéours d'Allemagne." It was probably the instrument used in some of the curious early dramatic performances of Gros-Guillaume, Gautier Garguille, and Turlupin (or the comic actors who assumed those names), which were a strange medley of singing, recitation, and dancing. Something like them was afterwards introduced in England, and hence the name jig may have arisen. The three celebrated actors just mentioned met with a melancholy end after a successful career for fifty years. Gros-Guillaume was imprisoned for imitating the grimaces of some well-known magistrate, who was stupid enough to exercise his power to punish him. The

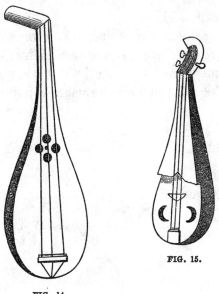

FIG. 15.

FIG. 14.

unfortunate man died from shame in consequence, and his two friends are said to have died from sympathy.

One of the figures of the elders at the cathedral at Amiens, of the thirteenth century, has in his hands a gigue with three strings and two sound-holes, but with no appearance of a bridge or distinct finger-board. M. de Coussemaker describes one from the Cathedral at Mans, of the fourteenth century, where the head is thrown back ; it has three strings, with the sound-holes placed in a peculiar manner, and the shape is elegant, but there is no appearance of a bridge (Fig. 14). In the same century, the top of the instrument was frequently rounded, and was not unlike the modern scroll. Martin Agricola, 1545, gives characteristic figures of four of these instruments, of different sizes ; Discantus, Altus, Tenor, and Bassus. They have three strings, bridge, tail-piece, and two crescent-shaped sound-holes. The peculiar shape will be seen from the representation of the Descantus (Fig. 15).

As we have before observed, the several instruments before referred to were distinct from each other, and are frequently mentioned together in the same passages of the early English and French romance writers.

CHAPTER IV.

HAVING shown the probability of the introduction or invention of the bow in this country in connection with the crwth or instruments of that class, and referred to the very early use of the instrument generally known as the viol, and also the absence of proof of the prior use of the bow elsewhere, we think we may fairly claim the origin of it for our own country. We were peopled in very early ages, and, although some of our ancient chronicles give rather fabulous accounts of the first settlers, yet they are generally not devoid of some foundation, however perverted and exaggerated the facts may have become. The Druids, in the time of Cæsar, were a learned body, and skilled in the arts of their age, which, from many of the existing Celtic remains, had made considerable advance. Some antiquaries, of deep research, believe they can see glimpses amongst our oldest remains or monuments of the past, of a state prior to the Druids, whether connected with the serpent worship, or with what else, is foreign to our purpose. The great antiquity of our island as an inhabited country is undoubted, and the early use, therefore, of the musical instruments of which it is our earnest wish to give a just and impartial, and we hope also an interesting account, though the undertaking may be difficult. We may observe that in our

very early history there are references to and statements
of visits to the neighbouring continent, and after the
arrival of the Romans there are many instances of emi-
gration there, and on one occasion a kind of colony was
established in Britanny, where there are still many marks
of resemblance to the Celtic portions of our country.
King Alfred even sent a mission to the far East; and on
all these occasions some of our arts and customs would
be carried over to, and, to some extent, be adopted by,
the countries visited.

The more ancient form of the viol, as before mentioned,
appears to have been of pear shape, that is, like a pear
divided longitudinally; but it afterwards became of a
more oval shape, and subsequently inward curvatures,
more or less defined, were introduced, and the instrument
in time became much in form like the modern violin,
though of heavier make; but this was after the lapse of
centuries.   Before the inward curvatures were introduced, the rounded sides must have interfered with anything like execution, and checked the action of the bow,
which, from the form of some of these instruments, must
have struck several strings together.   As increased execution, or the desire for it, occurred, the sides would be
curved inwards to meet the necessity, and frets were
afterwards introduced to guide the fingers.   These curvatures would also facilitate the holding of the larger
instruments between the knees. The strings varied from
one (but this is very rare, and we only find it in Gerbert's
example) to six, but rarely more.   At first there was no
detached finger board, but the neck was an elongation of
the body of the instrument; the sound-holes were generally two, but there are examples with four; there was a
bridge varying in size and position, and usually a tail-
piece of some sort.   There are instances of two bridges,

but these are quite exceptional, and probably arise from some error in the representation, as they would seem to be unmanageable.

The earliest representation we have been able to find is that in the learned work of Gerbert, "De Cantu," &c., plate 32, taken from a MS. supposed to be of the eighth or ninth century, and called "Lyra." It is of pear shape, and has but one string, but there are two semi-circular sound-holes, with a small bridge between them; the neck, although in shape like an elongation of the body, yet from the mark of division across it might have been of a separate piece (Fig. 16).

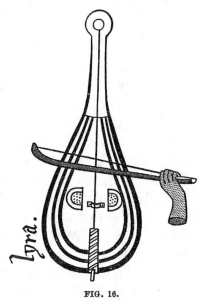

FIG. 16.

The Cotton MS. Tiberius, c. vi. of the tenth century, contains representations of several ancient instruments similar to those given by Gerbert, and De Coussemaker, but the most interesting one for our purpose is that of the performer on the viol, who is accompanying a juggler playing with three balls and three knives, and rivalling our modern wonders in this line. The figure has been often produced before, but we think it necessary to insert it here as a very early and distinct specimen (Fig. 17). It is of pear shape, with four strings, two round sound-holes, and a tail-piece, but with no appearance of bridge or finger-board. The

bow is somewhat of the form of our modern double-
bass bow. The performer looks
as serious as the man who does
Punch in the streets, looking at
his companion's skill as the mere
means of procuring a dinner.

In Gori's "Thesaurus Vete-
rum Diptychorum," there is a
representation, supposed to have
been taken from a MS. of the
ninth century, of David playing
on a sort of lyre, and four
musicians with him; one playing an organ, one a trumpet,
one on four bells, and the
fourth on a viol with three
strings, and two crescent-shaped
sound-holes, a finger-board, and,

FIG. 17.

apparently, a tail-piece, but no bridge. It is of oval, or
nearly circular shape, and the bow something between
the double-bass and violoncello bow. Ledwich describes,
among the figures in the crypt at Canterbury Cathedral,
a grotesque figure playing on the viol, which he ascribes
to the time of Alfred, but this crypt is not considered
to have been older than the twelfth century, and the
figure, therefore, is somewhat more recent than those in
Peterborough Cathedral, to which we shall soon refer.
The viol is mentioned in a "Treatise on Music," formerly attributed to the Venerable Bede, but now supposed to be of later date, by one who may be called
Pseudo-Bede.

From the earliest Anglo-Saxon times the viol and its
congeners appear to have been well established instruments at all festivals and social meetings, and so continued

downwards during the successive changes of dynasties, until superseded by the more lively violin. Played by the violars, frequently associated with jougleurs and minstrels, at the courts of the kings of the eight Saxon kingdoms, which we are instructed in youth to call the Saxon Heptarchy—afterwards at those of the Normans and their successors—in the bowers of the fair Saxon and proud Norman dames—at the country gatherings and fairs—and in the halls of the barons, where, as Whistlecraft (Frere) says—

> "They served up salmon, venison, and wild boars,
> By hundreds, and by dozens, and by scores,
> * * * * *
> With mead, and ale, and cider of our own,
> For porter, punch, and negus were not known."

To be sure these barons, notwithstanding their encouragement of minstrelsy, were sometimes troublesome neighbours; one would occasionally have a grand *battû*, when—

> " . . . omne vicinagium destruebat,
> Et nihil relinquebat de intacto,
> Ardens molinos, casas, messuagia,
> Et alia multa damna atque outragia," &c.

We have before observed that the instrument was frequently called the fythele. In Strutt's "Manners and Customs," there is a figure from a MS. in the Bodleian Library, of the twelfth century, of a performer on the viol of an oval shape, having five strings, without any appearance of sound-holes, bridge, or fingerboard, but with a tail-piece (Fig. 18).

FIG. 18.

The tail-piece in some instances may have been attached to the belly in the same manner as in our guitar, and therefore have partially served for a bridge. There is a

curious variety of the instrument, stated to be of the
end of the eleventh century, given in that richly em-
bellished work, Shaw's "Dresses and Decorations," from
additional MS. 11,695. It is of long oval shape, with five
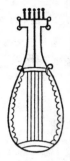
strings ; the neck is, perhaps, separate, and
it has no bridge or sound-holes.   It seems
to have been of large size.   The screws are
placed in a singular manner at the top (Fig.
19).   The bow is very much curved.   Figures
of about the same date, playing on the usual
oval-shaped viol, were on the door of the
ancient church of Barfreston, Kent, and on a
frieze at Adderbury Church, Oxfordshire, and

FIG. 19.   in other places, some of which of a later date
we shall mention afterwards.

We must not omit to notice one well worthy of honour
—Rahere, the king's minstrel, who founded St. Bartholomew's Hospital in 1103, and whose name is still attached
to a small street in the neighbourhood.   He is said to
have kept company with fiddlers who played with silver
bows ; but our authority, " The Pleasaunt History of
Thomas of Reading," is not convincing as to this latter
fact.   He appears, however, to have been a man of wit,
and to have been jester as well as minstrel, to Henry I.
and this before the court jester degenerated into the
mere buffoon.   He was one of the first known as "joculator regis ; " not the first, as has been stated, for William
the Conqueror had one who was probably on one occasion during his wars the means of saving his life. Berdic,
joculator regis, is also mentioned in Domesday Book, as
of the time of Edward the Confessor.

There are some very curious representations of the
viol and other instruments painted on the interior of the
roof of the fine old cathedral at Peterborough, which we

have seen, and are fortunate enough to possess a copy of
the coloured engraving of it by Mr. Strickland, by
whose permission we will introduce some of the figures.
This roof is considered to be of the date of 1194, or
a little earlier, when the work was completed by Abbot
Benedict, who presided from 1177 to 1194. The ceiling
was retouched a little previous to 1788, and repaired in
1835, but the greatest care was taken to retain every
part, or restore it to its original state, so that the figures
even where retouched are in effect the same as when
first painted. One is a grotesque figure playing on a

FIG. 21.   FIG. 22.

viol with three strings and four sound-holes (Fig. 20,
frontispiece); another is a crowned figure, perhaps to
signify a royal minstrel, playing on an instrument with
four strings and two sound-holes (Fig. 21); a third is a
female figure having the instrument on her lap with four
strings and four sound-holes (Fig. 22). Each figure on
the roof is placed in a separate lozenge-shaped ornamental compartment, differing occasionally in the style
of ornament, and in the colour of the ground. We have
represented that belonging to number 20. The instruments have inward curvatures at the sides, and are not

very unlike the modern violin in shape.　There is an appearance of finger-boards and tail-pieces, but none of bridges.　Other female figures are represented playing on the psalterion or dulcimer, and the symphonie, the parent of our hurdy-gurdy.　Grotesque figures in paintings and sculpture were not uncommon about this time, and many may be found in old manuscripts and in the wood carvings of ancient churches.　There is a curious representation on the Peterborough roof, of an ass playing on the harp, which may have some reference to the singular celebration of the Feast of the Ass, wherein part of the service was called " Asinus ad Lyram; " but it would occupy a chapter by itself to enter even slightly upon this interesting subject, and the numerous varieties of the Feast of Fools.　In " Monnaies des Fous," &c., mention is made of the figure of an ass on the old tower at Chartres, playing on a stringed instrument, which, from the account given, appears more like a harp than the vielle, but the figure had the name of " l'âne qui vielle."

In France, as in England, music was encouraged from an early period, having been introduced, as appears most probable, from the north; and the performers frequented the courts of the kings, from Clovis downwards.　There is a St. Arnold, who was a "joueur de violon," that is the viol, in the ninth century.　In the midst of the changes of the French monarchy and their constant warfares, petty and great, and notwithstanding the uncertain tempers of their royal and noble patrons, the minstrels kept their ground.　And a difficult task they must sometimes have had.　Take Sismondi's account of one, rather a quiet one, towards the end of the eleventh century, Philip I.　" Cependant, comme il n'avait point de volonté, il n'éprouvait point de contrariétés; comme il ne faisait jamais la guerre, il n'était point battu ; et comme il ne formait pas de projets, il ne les voyait jamais échouer : sa vie domestique était prospère, et sa santé résistait à sa longue intempérance."

Instruments played with the bow do not appear to have been numerous on the Continent before the eleventh century, but increased in number and variety towards the middle of it. The form at first was conical or pear-shaped, having the body and neck formed of one piece ; but soon assumed a more oval shape, with the neck and body separate. There is said to be a representation of an ancient French king in the church of Notre Dame, with a bow in one hand and a viol in the other, of about the last date ; but there is some doubt whether this is Chilperic or Robert, who commenced the building in the tenth century ; Montfaucon says it was the former. There is a curious figure of a performer on the viol on a medallion of the eleventh century at Boscherville. He holds it artistically under the chin, and appears to be singing at the same time, though his aspect is somewhat lacrymose, as if he were attempting for the first time the studies of the Paganini of the period. The instrument apparently has four strings, and is of oval shape, but has neither bridge, sound-holes, or finger-board in the representation. We have referred before to the figures on a capital at Boscherville of the twelfth century ; one of these is playing on a sort of viol of oval shape, having two semicircular sound-holes, but without any appearance of bridge or finger-board (Fig. 23). M. de Cousse-maker considers this instrument to be a gigue.

FIG. 23.

As far back as the thirteenth century we find the figure of a monochord of a rectangular, oblong, and narrow form, and taller than the performer; from this was probably derived that curious instrument, the trumpet marine. There was also an instrument somewhat smaller, having two strings, called the diacord or dicord.

The profession of a jougleur or trouvère of early times, was by no means an easy one, and comprised not only skill on several instruments, but juggling, sleight of hand, and many similar qualifications. We have already referred to some of these in our extract from " Les Deux Trovéors Ribaux."

Colin Muset, the celebrated minstrel of this date, according to Laborde, even exceeded the usual musical qualifications; but the song given by him as one of Muset's, is evidently modernized, and we will give but one verse, concluding with the bard's modest estimation of himself.

> " Il chante avec flûte ou trompette,
> Guitarre, harpe, flageolet,
> Tambourin, violon, clochette ;
> Il fait la basse et la fausset ;
> Il inventa vielle et musette :
> Pour la manivelle ou l'archet,
> Nul n'égale Colin Muset."

But even the great Colin Muset had sometimes to complain of neglect from the great. He thus speaks of one who had paid him nothing for his minstrelsy :—

> " Sire quens j'ai vielé
> Devant vos en vostre otel ;
> Si ne m'avez riens donné,
> Ne mes gages acquitez,
> C'est vilanie."

A great improvement had taken place in musical

notation by the time of the eleventh century, and the
name of Guido d'Aretin is well known for his exertions
in this respect, and indeed, as is frequently the case in
such matters, he has more credit given to him than he is
entitled to ; some of his supposed discoveries having been
previously known. For a considerable time prior to such
date, notation was by what were called neumes ; whence
Ducange says, " Neumare est notas verbis musicè decan-
tandis superaddere." These neumes were arbitrary
characters or accents, several in number, which superseded the letters previously in use, and were placed over
the words to be sung, a separate value, or power, or
pitch, being attached to each. Gerbert gives a table of
forty, with their names. At first, until about the end of
the ninth century, there were no lines or indications of
clefs, and there being no guide, it was difficult to assign
the value with any accuracy, and people differed as to
the relative pitch. About the tenth century a horizontal
line, either black or red, was placed over the words,
which marked the place of a fixed note, and the place
of the neumes over or under this line distinguished the
quality of the note much better than had previously
been the case. A song of the twelfth century on the
battle of Fontanet or Fontanay, with notation in the
style of the neumes, without the horizontal line, is supposed to be one of the earliest examples of secular music.
Afterwards, two lines were used, one red, which had the
letter F at the commencement, and the other yellow or
green, which had C. Subsequently two other lines were
added ; one between the two former ones, and the other
either above or below them ; the letters at the head of
the principal lines being the origin of the clefs of our
modern notation. The notes were named, ut, re, mi, fa,
sol, la, from the commencing syllables of the lines of a

Latin hymn, of which the corresponding musical notes were each a tone higher than that of the preceding syllable. They were afterwards called C ut, D re, &c. Howell, in one of his letters, October 7, 1634, mentions that the Germans, who were then great drinkers, would sometimes drink a health musically to each of the six notes, comprising them, together with the reasons for drinking, in the following hexameter :—

UT RE levet MI serum FA tum, SOL itosque LA bores.

The lines were afterwards increased to five : indeed, there are some ancient pieces of music with many more ; but still much—especially of the ecclesiastical music—continued to be written with four. In the twelfth century, the grave square notes still to be seen in the old church music, came into general use ; these gradually improved in appearance, and became less in size, as they became the representatives of greater celerity, until now they have reached that extreme railway speed and complication of figure scarcely to be managed in many cases but by musicians of the highest skill and practice, of whom, happily, we have many.

CHAPTER V.

IN the twelfth and thirteenth centuries, the representations of the viol differ much; the strings vary from two to six, but three and five are the usual numbers. Some have inward curvatures more or less defined; the majority have bridges; there is seldom any appearance of a detached finger-board, and the sound-holes are usually two, sometimes four, and occasionally there is one like that of the guitar. As before observed, the defects in the details may sometimes arise from omissions in the delineations.

Potier, in "Monumens Français," vol. i. says there are no representations of the viol before the tenth century, but frequent examples after the eleventh. M. de Coussemaker says the oldest representation is on a sculpture at the door of the church of St. Aventin, in the environs of Bagnères, of the eleventh century. Gerbert's representation, however, and that in Cotton MS. are older. Potier gives several examples of the twelfth century; some from the porch of St. Denis. A king, said to be David, who is often named when the identity of the monarch is doubtful, holds in his right hand a viol with five strings: the body is oval and somewhat of a guitar shape, with two sound-holes, and apparently a bridge, but no separate finger-board. The bow is short, and

like that of the double bass.   There are two other
instruments very similar, one of which has but three
strings, but by way of compensation has four large sound-
holes, two in each division.   He gives representations of
two viols of the same date from a MS. in the Bibliothèque Impériale, one of which is of oval shape, with
five strings, and one large round sound-hole like the
guitar in the centre.   The other has inward
curvatures, four strings, and two small sound-
holes (Fig. 24).   They both appear to have
bridges, but no distinct finger-boards.

M. de Coussemaker, in his learned and interesting account of ancient instruments so frequently referred to, mentions a viol of the
twelfth century, on a window at the royal chapel
of St. Denis.   It is of a long oval shape, much

FIG. 24.   more so than usual, with six strings and two
large semi-circular sound-holes.   There is no bridge, and
what we should call the tail-piece is in the middle of the
body, and the strings seem to be fastened to each end of
it.   The bow is like that of the double bass, a common
form in these times (Fig. 25).   There is also a grotesque
figure of Neptune of the same date playing on a viol
with three strings, and two semicircular sound-holes, with
a kind of tail-piece, but no appearance of a bridge or
separate finger-board (Fig. 26).

In Cotton MS. Nero. D. i. of about the same date,
there is a viol which shows the distinctive oval shape,
having the neck and body of one piece.   It has two
semicircular sound-holes, with four strings and a tail-
piece, but no appearance of a bridge (Fig. 27).   There
is a figure like this in the left hand of one of the elders
in the Cathedral of Amiens (Fig. 28).   Other representations of about the same date and much of the same

character may be found in MSS. at the British Museum and elsewhere, of which it does not seem necessary to multiply examples, and this remark will apply to subsequent times. We may observe that Jerome de Moravie, in his

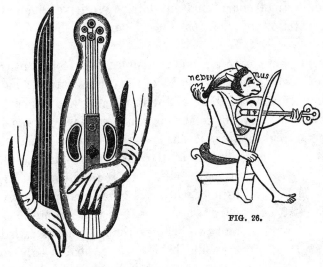

FIG. 26.

FIG. 25.

treatise on music, of the thirteenth century, mentions the vielle amongst instruments having four or five strings.

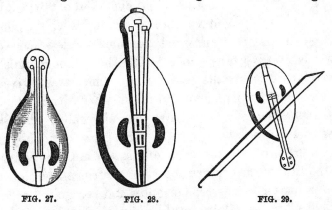

FIG. 27.　　　FIG. 28.　　　FIG. 29.

Among the sculptures at what is called the Musicians' House at Rheims, of the thirteenth century, there is a figure playing on an oval-shaped instrument with three strings, and two sound-holes nearly in the shape of ears. The attitude of the performer is very easy, and the bow is iron and of light construction, almost appearing to be an addition of more modern date. We have given a representation of the instrument and the bow (Fig. 29).

Burney notices an antique enamelled basin found near Soissons, which he states to be of the ninth century; but it is now considered to be of the thirteenth, and has been described both by Potier and de Coussemaker. Amongst other musical figures, it has two, apparently females, playing on the viol; one of the instruments has three

strings, with two sound-holes and a bridge, while the other has apparently only two strings, but four sound-holes and two bridges, though what is called a second bridge was probably only to denote the end of the finger-board, as two bridges would be objectionable in many respects (Fig. 30).

FIG. 30.

Towards the end of the thirteenth century the convex sides of the viol became by degrees indented, or more or less curved inwards, to give freer scope for the bow, though much time elapsed before the present finished form was arrived at, and many trials made, and failures experienced.

Catgut strings, as they are generally called, though now made from sheep, are of very great antiquity, as they were used for the harp of the ancient Egyptians. In the thirteenth century the sale of strings must have been a matter of some importance, and recognised as an article of trade, for in an old poem of this date called "Du Mercier," which may be considered as a sort of trade-song by a mercer, amongst other articles to entice customers, he says—

" J'ai bones cordes à violes."

If the prices had been affixed it would have been more interesting.

About the same time, in an account of Paris under Philippe le Bel, 1292, being the particulars of a tax of 100,000 livres levied on the inhabitants, there is probably the first notice of any makers of instruments, namely, " citoleurs 4," being strictly makers of citoles, a species of guitar; but no doubt they were also makers of the different sorts of viols, just as the term " luthiers " was applied afterwards not only to makers of lutes, &c., but also of viols and violins. There is another maker, however, who is still more defined, " Henri aus vièles," or Henry, the maker of viols, who may be considered the first of his art on record.

The representations and notices of the viol or vielle, and instruments of that class, are numerous in the fourteenth century. It was a favourite instrument with the minstrels, and the name of one is handed down as Arnold le Vielleux, and another in the service of the Emperor Conrad IV, called Jouglet, was distinguished as a performer. In an account of the Dukes of Burgundy from 1382 to 1481, there is an entry of musical instruments, from which it appears that the Duchess had two Spaniards, performers on the vielle or viol, called Juan de Cordova, and Juan Fernandez, of whom the former was blind. In the wardrobe accounts of Edward II, who was not sparing in his expenses, there is a payment of 5l. to " Robert Daverouns, violist of the Prince of Tarentum, performing his minstrelsy in the king's presence, of the king's gift at Neuburgh ; " a great sum in those days, probably equal to 70*l.* or 80*l.* at present. On the marriage of his sister Margaret, minstrels came from all parts, foreign as well as English, 426 in number, to whom 100*l.* were given in reward. We have already mentioned Queen Isabella's vidulatores. Edward III. in his band of nineteen musicians, had a fiddler (*i. e.* violist) with the pay, like his companions, of 12*d.* a day.

The sound-holes were usually two, semi-circular or ear-shaped, and placed nearly as at present; the strings varying from three to six. The instrument had now generally inward curvatures, more or less decided. There is not always the indication of a bridge, or detached finger-board, but, as before observed, the absence or imperfection of details cannot always be taken as proof of the state of the instrument. M. de Coussemaker gives a representation of one of the fourteenth century, the body of which does not differ much in shape from that of the modern violin. It has three

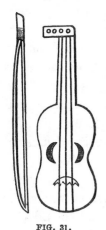

FIG. 31.

double strings, though the screws appear to be four, a rounded bridge, and two semi-circular sound-holes, but no distinct finger-board; and the top of the neck, or what would be our scroll, is turned at right angles (Fig. 31). He gives the representation of another from the Royal Library at Brussels, without curvatures, and with four strings that pass through a series of teeth with which the bridge is provided; it has a finger-board, and two sound-holes.

Potier has given a figure of an instrument of the fourteenth century, with three strings and a bridge, but no separate finger-board; the neck, if it may be so called, is large, and of a lozenge shape, found in the early forms of the instrument, but at this time going out. It has two sound-holes, and the bow like the double-bass bow (Fig. 32). D'Agincourt, in his "History of Art," has a representation from a painting by Barnabas de Modena, 1374, of the crowning of the Virgin by our Saviour in Heaven, where several figures are introduced playing on musical instruments. Amongst them is the viol, having five strings, with two semi-lunar sound-holes and a tail-piece, but no bridge or finger-board: the bow-hand has great ease in its position, and

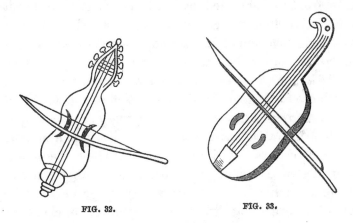

FIG. 32.   FIG. 33.

the bow is very like that known as the Corelli bow (Fig. 33). A small pair of double drums is introduced, placed on the back of one angel, and played on by another; also the musette or bagpipes.

The viol may frequently be found in the sculptures in our cathedrals and old churches. Carter has given some representations from Ely Cathedral of the early part of the fourteenth century. One appears to have five strings and a tail-piece, but with no appearance of bridge or sound-holes; the other has more the form of what has been called

FIG. 34.

the rebec, without inward curvatures, but the details are very imperfect (Figs. 34 and 35). The

FIG. 35.

superb screen in York Cathedral, separating the nave from the choir, has numerous figures of angels playing on musical instruments, and the viol among them. In Exeter Cathedral there is a small fabric of stone projecting from the north wall of the nave, of about the middle of the fourteenth century, supported by a cornice, and called the minstrels' gallery. The front is supported by thirteen pillars, dividing it into twelve niches, each containing an angel playing on a musical instrument, and among these is the viol. It is the custom for the choristers to go to this gallery on Christmas Day and sing a hymn. Carter represents the figure of an angel on the lower tier of the screen at the west front of this cathedral, playing on a pear-shaped viol. Minstrel galleries, with figures playing on musical instruments, are likewise mentioned at the cathedrals of Winchester, Lincoln, and Worcester. Dibdin, in his "Bibliographical Tour," gives engravings of what he calls "Drolleries at Strasbourg Cathedral," of about the date 1370; one of these grotesque figures is playing on a sort of pear-shaped viol, with apparently four strings, and two ear-shaped sound-holes, but no other details.

The *bâton* of the conductor is comparatively a modern introduction into our orchestras, and many of us still remember the tap of the leader in our concerts, for which the *bâton* has now been successfully substituted. It had, however, been known long previously on the Continent, and in a list of the orchestra of the Opera at Paris, in 1713, there appears at the head, " the Batteur de Mesure," with a salary of 1000 livres. The cantor's staff was known many centuries back in our ecclesiastical establishments, and in those on the Continent, and the custom is still preserved in many parts. Pugin, in his "Glossary of Ecclesiastical Ornament," gives an engraving of a highly decorated one, and describes others at St. George's, Windsor; York, St. Paul's, and Lincoln, naming at the latter cathedral "two staves of wood, having upon them little plates of silver, with branches of vines." Gerbert mentions some singers having silver wands and staffs about the sixteenth century.

There is a curious story or gossip about a *báton de chantre*, related in "Annales Archéologiques," iii. 266-7, which may not be generally known. When Napoleon I. was crowned, he intended, in order to have all the adjuncts as complete as possible, to carry in his hand the original sceptre of Charlemagne. It was resuscitated for the purpose from the treasures of the Abbey of St. Denis, and was to be repaired and put in order for the ceremony; most unexpectedly, on removing the old velvet with which it was covered, there appeared the date 1394, which the Committee of Antiquaries, to whom the matter had been intrusted, saw was inconsistent with the time of Charlemagne; and there was not only this date, but also an inscription, from which the following is an extract, proving the supposed sceptre to be simply a *báton de chantre :—*

> " Qu'il fust gardé,
> Et en grans festes regardé,
> Car pour loyaulte maintenir
> Le doibt chantre en la main tenir."

What was to be done? De Non was consulted, but he desired that the discovery should be kept secret. The *báton* was dressed up, and converted into the sceptre of Charlemagne (just as upon occasion a common working grub is converted into a queen bee), and performed its appointed part in the imposing ceremony.

The troubadours were accompanied by violars, or performers on the harp, or viol, or instruments of that class, and were frequently skilful performers themselves. Indeed Thibaut, Count of Champagne, towards the beginning of the thirteenth century is said to have taken up the study of the viol, to console himself in an unsuccessful attachment for Queen Blanche, the mother of Saint Louis, and became a skilful performer. We must, however, refer those who wish to learn more of the history of this distinguished race, from William, Count of Poitiers downwards, to Hawkins's "History of Music," and more especially to Raynouard, "Choix des Poésies Originales des Troubadours," and Fauriel, "Histoire de la Poésie Provençale," where many of the chanzos, sirventes, &c. will be found. The romantic histories connected with Châtelain de Courcy, Jauffred de Radel, Guillaume de Cabestaing, and others, afford curious examples of the manners of their age. The last-named of these troubadours, as is known to those versed in these chronicles, fell violently in love with Sermonde, the wife of Raymond of Roussillon; but the husband, instead of approving of this choice, slew the poet, and, having taken out his heart, had it served up at table before his wife, who, when she became informed of the fact, threw herself out of window and was killed. Her friends and those of Guillaume, assisted by other troubadours, took upon them to ravage the lands of Raymond, and destroy his castle; after which praiseworthy act they buried the unfortunate lovers in one grave. The husband was certainly a little brusque in his treatment of de Cabestaing, but we cannot help thinking that all the sympathy is not due to the lovers. Jauffred de Radel was still more

romantic ; he fell violently in love with the Countess of
Tripoli from mere description, and induced his friend
Bertrand d'Allamanon to accompany him to the Levant
in 1162, but fell ill during the passage, and, on his
arrival at Tripoli, just lived long enough to see the
countess, express his passion, and then die. In the
"Conte of Aucassin and Nicolette," Nicolette having
been made captive, is discovered to be the daughter of
the King of Carthage, and she wishes to return to Aucassin to avoid being married to a rich pagan king.
The difficulty is how to escape, but at last she contrives
to manage this in the garb of a minstrel: "Elle quist
une viele, s'aprist à vieler, et elle s'embla la nuit, si
s'atorna à guise de joglior;" and having thus arrived
safely in Provence, "si prist sa viele, si alla vielant par
le pays, tant qu'elle vint au castel de Biaucaire."

CHAPTER VI.

THE minstrels are so connected with the practical part of music, that a short notice of them appears requisite in a work of this nature, even at the risk of repeating in part what may be found elsewhere; but we hope, also, we may add some particulars that may not be generally known. The distinguished antiquary, Mr. Thomas Wright, F.S.A., has a chapter on minstrels and jougleurs in his interesting "History of Domestic Manners."

In the early times of our country the king's bard, or harper, was an officer' of high rank, and enjoyed many privileges; the king's minstrel was also an officer of distinction at the Saxon and Norman courts. The story of Taillefer, at the time of the Conquest, is well known; jumping on shore one of the foremost of the invaders, singing the war-song of the celebrated Rollo, and dying like the fabled swan, with a song in his mouth. We have no particular account of any such officer in the reigns immediately succeeding the Conquest, though every one, even without the benefit of a competitive examination, as fully believes the story of King Richard and Blondel as he does those relating to the bold Robin Hood, Little John, and Scathlock, or Scarlett, with Maid Marian, and that unlucky Bishop of Hereford. In the forty-first of Henry III, however, we find a payment of

4*l.* 7*s.* paid to Henry Abrinces, the king's versifier, by
some called his jester, who received 6*d.* a day. If there
may be some doubt as to his being a minstrel as well as
a poet, we may at any rate consider him as a sort of
proto-poet-laureate. He offended, on some occasion,
Master Michael Blaumpayne, the humorous Cornish
poet, who abused him in some very personal satirical
lines. At the installation feast of Ralf de Born, Prior
of St. Augustine, Canterbury, 1309, the minstrels present were paid 3*l.* 10*s.* for their reward. Edward II.
during his father's life was evidently fond of convivial
society, and payments are found to William Fox, and
Cradoc his companion, for singing before the prince and
other nobles; generally 20*s.* each time. After he succeeded to the throne, several minstrels are named, and
on the occasion of the marriage of Elizabeth, daughter
of Edward I. to John, Earl of Holland, every king's
minstrel received a fee of 40*s.*; and one at least, named
Robert, was in the habit of receiving regular pay. Ja-
nino le cheveretter, or bagpiper, at one time had 40*s.*
given to him, and at another 20*s.* The bagpiper, however, seems to have been in repute in these times, for in
the reign of Edward III. Barbor the bagpiper had licence
to go beyond the seas to visit the schools of minstrels,
with 30*s.* for his expenses; and Morlan the same leave,
with 40*s.* This was, no doubt, to enable them to see if
any advantages were to be derived from the study of
the Continental style of play. The musette, a very
ancient instrument, was popular on the Continent, and,
judging from the tone of the modern instruments, it is
softer and more melodious than that of the common
bagpipe. During the festivals on the crowning of Pope
John XXIII, about 1410, the Marquis of Ferrara brought
with him fifty-four knights, all clothed in scarlet and

blue, attended by five trumpets, and four companies of minstrels, each with different instruments; and, on the morrow of his coronation, the Pope was attended during his procession by thirty-six bagpipes and trumpets, and ten bands of minstrels playing on musical instruments, each band consisting of three performers. In that curious poem, " The Vows of the Heron," about 1338, where some strange examples of the vows of the knights, and even of the ladies, may be seen, Robert of Artois has the heron brought in between two dishes of silver, and compels two players on the viol, and one on the guitar, to introduce it—

> " Entre deux plats d'argent fu li hairons assis ;
> Deux maistres de viele a quens Robert saisis,
> Avec un quistreneus, accordant par devis ;"

afterwards they fiddle very sweetly,—

> " Et li dois menestral vielent douchement ;"

but subsequently, at his command, they have to come out *fortissimo*—

> " Il fait les menestreux de viele efforchier."

Many entries are found of payments to minstrels, and frequently large ones, considering the difference in the value of money, but generally the recipient is only called minstrel, and his particular instrument is not named. In the eleventh of Edward III, John de Hoglard, minstrel of John de Pulteney, was paid 40s. for exhibiting before the king at Hatfield and London ; and Roger the trumpeter, and the minstrels his associates, for performing at the feast at Hatfield, for the queen's delivery, had no less a sum than 10l. presented to them. At the feast of St. George at Windsor, in 1358, connected with the celebration of the Order of the Garter, the early history

of which will always be interesting, whether connected
with the Countess of Salisbury or not, Haukin Fitz-
Libbin and his twenty-three fellows, the king's minstrels,
had for their good services 16*l.*

During the compulsory visit of John, King of France,
here, after the battle of Poictiers, from 1357 to 1360,
there are several entries in his accounts of payments to
minstrels. In one case there is a payment of four nobles
to go and see some instruments for the king, and on
another occasion two nobles to buy a harp. The largest
appears to be forty nobles, or 13*l.* 6*s.* 8*d.* to the minstrels
of the King of England, the Prince of Wales, and the
Duke of Lancaster, who played before the king on the
feast of St. John, June 24, 1360. There is, however, an
unlucky note in the margin of the original account, implying that this money was not paid, though for what reason
does not appear. Payments to minstrels appear in the
time of Richard II, who was better suited to the luxuries
of a court than the cares of a crown. There are similar
payments in the time of Henry IV, among which there
is one to William Byngley, the king's minstrel, of
2*l.* 6*s.* 8*d.* to purchase apparel for his person, probably
for a sort of livery.

When Henry V. went over to France he was accompanied by several minstrels, Rymer mentions fifteen, and
among them was one Snyth Fydeler; their wages appear
to have been 12*d.* a day. They played for an hour
morning and evening at the king's head-quarters, and
on the eve of the battle of Agincourt, though the English were fatigued and oppressed with hunger, and
expected death on the morrow, yet they played on their
trumpets and various other instruments throughout the
night, and confessed their sins with tears, numbers of
them taking the sacrament. A song on the battle of

Agincourt is the oldest English song known with music. There is an order in the first of Henry VI. to pay several minstrels by name an annual pension of 100s. each, of whom the first seven had accompanied his father to France; and in the twelfth year of his reign there is an order for a payment which for procrastination may match any of modern times, being one to the representative of the representative of the man who earned it more than fourteen years previously. It is a payment of 10l. to Henry Jolipas Clerk, executor of Joan, wife of John Clyff, a minstrel, the executrix of the same John Clyff, who had gone over to France in the third year of Henry V. with seventeen other minstrels, at the rate of 12d. a day, and with whom certain jewels had been lodged as a security.

In the twenty-third of Henry VI. there were liberal payments made to some foreign minstrels, who came over to witness the state and grand solemnity of the coronation of the Queen, and make a report of the same abroad. Five minstrels of the King of Sicily had 10l. each, and two of the Duke of Milan 5 marks, or 3l. 6s. 8d. each; liberal payments, no doubt remembered on making the report. Edward IV, who in the early part of his kingly career alternated with Henry VI, according as the white or red rose was triumphant, paid by the hands of Thomas Vaughan 20l. to the heralds and minstrels on the day of the creation of the Lord the Prince at Westminster, in the eleventh year of his reign. Some unlicensed minstrels apparently gave trouble in his time, and got access to great houses and feasts under the pretence of being king's minstrels, which induced him in 1469 to grant a charter to Walter Halliday (a name which appears among the minstrels of Henry V.) as marshal, and seven others, establishing, or as some

called it, restoring a fraternity or guild, to be governed
by a marshal and two wardens, empowering them to
regulate the profession of minstrels, but it did not prove
of much benefit, and they contrived to lose their reputation by the time of Elizabeth. In her reign, 1581, we
find Thomas Lovell, in his "Dialogue betwene Custome
and Veritie concerning the use and abuse of Dauncing
and Mynstralsye," abusing the minstrels for not singing
godly songs, and proceeding,—

> " . . . He that cannot gibe and jest,
>   Ungodly scoff and frump,
> Is thought unmeet to play with pipe,
>   On tabret or to thump.
> The minstrels doo with instruments,
>   With songs, or els with jest,
> Maintain them selves, but as they use,
>   Of these naught is the best."

Henry VII. was a careful man, and may come under
Sydney Smith's definition of being fond of his specie, if
not of his species. In all his travels and progresses he
was met at different towns by minstrels, waits, and other
musicians, each town of note having then its own set.
There are numerous payments made to them, but in
general, less than 20s. For instance, the waits of Northampton had 13s. 4d. in reward, while those of Coventry,
Sandwich, and Canterbury, had but 10s., and those of
Dover only 6s. 8d. Even the minstrels who played in
his ship, the *Swan*, that took him from Sandwich to
Calais, were only paid 13s. 4d. for their performance,
notwithstanding they had to brave the perils and incon-
venience of the sea. Of the more regular performers,
Pudesay, the piper in bagpipes, had but 6s. 8d. for his
performance, whilst 5l. were paid to three string minstrels for wages ; and in a subsequent entry, 15s. is
given to one for a month's wages. In 1501, a sum of 2l.

is paid to the " Princesse stryngmynstrels at Westm^r ;" but in February, 1495, there is a most liberal payment of 30*l.* to the Queen of France's minstrels, it being politic to pay foreign performers of this class well.

Henry VIII. was fond of show and entertainments during the first twenty years of his reign, and not only encouraged minstrelsy, but was himself a good musician, and a gallant sort of personage ; many payments to minstrels are therefore found in his accounts.   In later times he suffered from an *embarras de richesses* in respect of his wives, and amused his leisure hours with polemical studies, ultimately becoming fat, argumentative, and ill-tempered, with the inconvenient power of cutting off his opponent's head, as well as crushing his argument.   As his size increased, minstrelsy decreased, and faded for the want of royal patronage.

In the " Northumberland Household Book," it is stated that my lord is accustomed to give yearly to every earl's minstrel, when they come to him yearly 3*s.* 4*d.*, but if they come only once in two or three years, then 6*s.* 8*d.* The gift to his own minstrels, when at home on New Year's Day, was 20*s.* for playing at his chamber door, being 13*s.* 4*d.* for himself, and 6*s.* 8*d.* for his lady, when she was at her lord's finding ; also 2*s.* for playing at Lord Percy's, and 8*d.* at each of the younger sons.   In the " Archives of Canterbury," 1523, there is an entry on the 1st of July of 6*s.* 8*d.* paid to the king's minstrels ; and in the twenty-second year of his reign, eighteen minstrels are appointed to the household at 4*d.* a day, most of them, from their names, appearing to be Italians. There is an anecdote of a famous player on the shalme, among the minstrels of Cardinal Wolsey, when he was in France in 1527.   He was much admired by the French king ; but, as Stow rather quaintly says, whether from extreme labour of blowing, or from poison (as some judged) he died within a day or two after playing all night, without resting, to the French king and others who were dancing. There does not appear to have been much necessity for presuming poison in this case.

There was a corporation of minstrels formed in Paris in the early part of the fourteenth century, which was of high repute, and possessed great power. An interesting account of it may be seen in " Bibliothèque de l'Ecole des Chartres," 1841-2, tom. 3, pp. 377-404, and vol. iv. pp. 524-48. It flourished till about the middle of the seventeenth century, when it began to decline, though orders were made for its government from time to time down to the eighteenth century.

Previous to this corporation, and towards the end of the twelfth century, many minstrels and players on instruments were accustomed to frequent Paris, and we find among the king's minstrels performers on the trumpets, timbales, and psalterion, being paid 3 sous a day, and their apparel and board. A sum of 60 sous is given by order of the king to Plumion, to buy " une flute dyvoire." In the middle of the thirteenth century, the minstrels enjoyed many privileges, and amongst them, that of exemption from a certain toll levied on entering Paris, provided they sung the couplet of a song to prove their right. Hence the expression, " Payer en gambades, et en monnoie de singe," as they frequently had monkeys with them, who exhibited their accomplishments in part payment. In the thirteenth century they had so increased, and were of such consequence, that they gave name to " La rue aus Jugléeurs," afterwards " Rue des Ménetriers," and in modern times, " Rue Rambuteau." At the time of the tax in 1292 before referred to, there were sixty-three persons assessed in this street.

In the year 1321, thirty-seven minstrels, at the head
of whom was Pariset, menestrel le roy, who was a player
on the "naquaires," or "tymbales," (and at one time
had 60 sous given him to get some timbales made), applied to have some statutes or regulations granted under
the sanction of the Prefect of Paris, and eleven were
granted them, by which they obtained a monopoly, that
enabled them to control the practice of their profession,
and to send away all strange minstrels. Among the
names affixed to these statutes are Jehannot l'Anglois,
and Adeline, fame G. l'Anglois.

In 1330 or 1331, they founded the hospital of St.
Julian, and St. Genès already referred to. It took its
rise, like our own Royal Society of Musicians, from the
charitable feelings of two of the profession. These are
said to have been Jacques Grave de Pistoye, otherwise
called Lappe, and Huet le Guette, who were moved with
compassion on seeing a poor paralytic woman, called
Fleurie de Chartres. She became one of the first patients
of the hospital, where she remained till her death. There
were several figures of angels in the church playing on
various instruments; and at the entrance were two sta-
tues, that of St. Julien on the left, and of St. Genès on
the right, in the costume of a minstrel, playing on a viole
with four strings. Laborde calls this figure Colin Muset,
who, however, was of later date. The viol, or vielle, was
a favourite instrument among them. In the account of
the appointment of masters or governors of the hospital
in October, 1343, the names appear of Jehan le Vidaulx
(player on the viol), and Guillaume de la Guietarne, with
others, who chose Henriet de Mondidier and Guillaume
Amy, "fleuteurs," masters and governors.

Among the minstrels who came to France in 1274
with Mary, daughter of Henry III. Duke of Brabant, on

her marriage with Philip III. of France, was Adenez le
Roi, or Le Roi Adenez, king of arms to the duke, who was
an excellent poet also, and may have been king of the
minstrels; but at all events Charmillon, who was chosen
as such king in 1295, is one of the earliest on record,
Robert, king of the minstrels to Louis X, being twenty
years later. Jean Poitevin was " roi des menestriers "
of France in 1392, and one called Hennequin Poitevin
held that title in 1409, and at the same time we find
mentioned " Jehan de Tonnelaur joueur de personnages
du roy," who is probably the earliest comedian of the
king mentioned, and " Gracieuse d'Espaigne menestrelle
de la royne," also has a gift made to her. Jean Farcien
the elder is said to have been king of the minstrels in
the early part of the fifteenth century, probably succeeding Poitevin; he was a performer on the viol. We
are not going to give a chronological list of these distinguished characters, but merely to name a few. There
was one called Nyon, commonly known as La Foundy,
who was remarkable for his skill on the violin; he was
made king of the violins, and died in 1641, having
abdicated however some years previously. In the time
of Louis XIII. in the first half of the seventeenth century, there was an able performer called Constantin,
who held this office and died at Paris in 1657. He was
succeeded in his lifetime by Guillaume Dumanoir in
1630, and after him came Guillaume Dumanoir the
second, who resigned in 1685. No successor was appointed to the office until 1741, when Guignon, remarkable for his execution, was installed, but subsequently
getting into disputes with his fellow-musicians, he found
the office so troublesome that he resigned it in a few
years, and in 1773 it was suppressed altogether.

Charles IX. of France granted by letters patent in

1570, to Jean Antoine de Baif and Joachim Thibaut de Courville the power to form an academy of music. Among the rules there was one admirable one which might be advantageously introduced in our times, particularly in amateur musical conversazione, namely, that none of the auditors should talk, or make any noise while there was any singing; we beg to add in defence of the instrumental performers, also while there was any playing. We should, however, call the attention of concert-givers to the observations supposed to have been made by a Chinese, as reported by Abbé Arnaud, in "Variétés Littéraires:" "Vos concerts, surtout s'ils sont un peu longs, sont des exercices violens pour ceux qui les exécutent, et de vrais supplices pour les personnes qui les écoutent."

CHAPTER VII.

IN the fifteenth century we meet with the names of some makers. The viol is represented with four or five strings, and frequently has inward curvatures, the old oval shape gradually becoming obsolete. The bridges and tail-pieces occasionally are wanting, which may be merely an omission in the representation, and frets are shown in some of the figures. The term vielle seems now superseded by viol, the former term being applied to an instrument like our modern hurdy-gurdy. The sound-holes, with occasional exceptions, became much like those in present use. Potier gives a representation of an instrument with three strings, and a bridge, having a large perforated sound-hole like the guitar, the head being bent back at a considerable angle : it has no inward curvatures, and the bow is much like that of the double-bass (Fig. 36). There is a figure given by M. de Coussemaker of a viol of this century from a painting by Hemling, which has five strings, with two sound-holes much like our modern ones reversed, with a tail-piece and finger-board ; it also has frets, but no appearance of a bridge, and is of guitar shape (Fig. 37). Another has inward curvatures, with four strings

FIG. 36.

fastened like those of the guitar, with a large round sound-hole in the centre, the head is a little reversed, with the pegs at the side as at present. D'Agincourt has a representation of a fresco painting of this age by Melozzo da Forli (the inventor of foreshortening,) at the staircase of the Palazzo Quirinale, where the figure of an angel is introduced playing on a viol with five strings, but there are no details. In the Minstrels' Pillar, at St. Mary's Church, Beverley, of the time of Henry VI, one of the five figures is playing on a viol of oblong shape with four strings and a short tail-piece; but no bridge, detached neck, or finger-board are shown in Carter's

delineation (Fig. 38). In the same church, over the column, are several figures playing on musical instruments, and among them an angel with a long oval or nearly pear-shaped viol with three strings; another male

FIG. 37.   FIG. 38.

figure with a large or tenor viol something in shape of a long modern tenor with angles rounded off; it has five strings, but no details are given of either instrument, except two small sound-holes in the last (Fig. 39).

FIG. 39.   FIG. 40.   FIG. 41.

Strutt has given several representations of musical instruments from the "Liber Regalis" of the time of
Richard II. of which we have reproduced four (Figs. 40,
41, 42, 43).

There was a curious application of a musical performance
in the early part of this century,
arising from one of those eccen-
tricities which occasionally vary
the common routine of life : it
took place on the death of Louis
Cortusio, a lawyer at Padua, who

FIG. 42.   FIG. 43.

died in 1418; he directed by his will that all the minstrels of the city should be invited to his funeral; fifty
were to walk with the clergy, some before and some
after the body, filling the air with the sound of lutes,
viols, flutes, hautbois, trumpets, tambourins, &c., and
chanting as at Easter. Each performer was to have a
demi-écu for his trouble ; and the body was to be carried
by twelve young girls engaged to be married, each of
whom had a sum of money by way of portion; they
were to sing joyous songs, and the whole ceremony was
to be conducted in the same cheerful manner. Any of
his relations who wept at his funeral were to have no
share of his property, and he that laughed most was to
have the largest share. It is not recorded that the tears
were abundant; but as his family grieved for the loss of
his money, if they did not mourn for him, they disputed
the will; however, the Paduan Court of Probate confirmed it. This hilarious funeral reminds us of an
amusing French proverb, where, in a country place, the
mayor and magistrates are in expectation of a visit from
some living great personage, a great event in the chronicles of their town, and also the passage through of the

body of a deceased dignitary. Councils are held, committees appointed, honorary secretaries installed; arrangements made to meet the living hero with songs, dances, and garlands of flowers, and the dead with overwhelming grief and sorrow, crape and cypress. Everything is rehearsed and the actors are perfect, or consider themselves so; but by some unlucky confusion, both the living and dead celebrities approach the town unexpectedly from different quarters at the same time. Away fly the magistrates, committee-men, honorary secretaries and all, eager to show their loyalty, and recite their speeches; but more eager than discreet, a sad blunder is made; all the songs, dances, and garlands, are bestowed on the dead, while the living grandee is met with every mark of the profoundest grief and woe, much to his disgust and astonishment.

Deviations from common forms, like those directed by Louis Cortusio, are not, however, confined to any age or time. The late Mr. Knill, who died in 1811, bequeathed some property to trustees, in order that every five years a matron and ten maidens, dressed in white, should walk in procession with music from the market-house at St. Ives in Cornwall, and dance round a granite pyramid erected by him, singing some lines in chorus.

The term fiddler is frequently found in the accounts of this time, as on February 17, 1497: "To the Quenes fideler in rewarde, 1*l*. 6*s*. 8*d*." A female performer, however, is very shabbily paid on November 2, 1495: "To a woman that singeth with a fidell, 2*s*." In the Scottish accounts, as given by Daunay, similar entries appear, as, 1490: to Benat, 18*s*., and to "ane oder fydlar," 5*s*. In 1496: "To the tua fithelaris that sang Graysteil to the king," 9*s*.

Fetis mentions two "luthiers," or makers of lutes and

other instruments, in the first half of the fifteenth century, namely, Jean Ott of Nuremberg, and Hans Frey of the same place, who was father-in-law of Albert Durer. The term "luthier" was, and still is, applied to makers of violins and other bowed instruments, and we may therefore reasonably suppose that these two "luthiers" made viols as well as other instruments. There was, however, a maker of this date, of whose instruments there can be no doubt. One of his viols was exhibited at Koliker's, in Paris, in the early part of the present century. The neck had been changed, and it was strung with four strings like a violin. It was of a high model, and had no tail-piece, but instead of it, an ivory nut at the bottom, with four holes for the strings. The quality of tone was low and sweet, and it had a ticket with the inscription, "Joan Kerlino, 1449." This maker is considered to have been the founder of the school of makers at Brescia, and is said to have been originally from Britanny.

About this time there was an improvement in the notation of music. Thomas of Walsyngham, in the beginning of the century, says that a new character called the crotchet had been introduced, but mentions the five characters, large, long, breve, semibreve, and minim; stating that musicians should remember there should be no division beyond the minim. Square or quadrate notes had been invented by John de Muris, in the middle of the previous century.

The introduction of printing improved the character of musical notation, and the increased requirements of music, and advancement in powers of execution would cause an extension of the signs. The first specimen of music printing is said to have been by Franchinus Gafurius, at Milan; and Jean Froschouer, at Augsbourg, engraved characters for plain-chant and music, on wood, towards the end of the century. Hawkins states the first music printed in England to have been in the "Polychronicon" of Ralph Higden, by Wynkyn de Worde, in 1495, and strange-looking it is. By the middle of the following century, however, characters were gradually introduced, approaching somewhat in form to those in modern use. Conrad Paulman, who was born blind, and died in 1473, is said to have invented the lute tablature, and to have excelled on all instruments.

Louis XI. was treated with a strange concert of music about this time. Having asked his master of music, the Abbé de Baigne, to give him a concert of pigs, the abbé assembled a number of those peculiarly unmusical animals, of different ages and sizes, and with variety of intonation, it is to be presumed, carefully selected, and placed them in a tent, having in front a table like the keyboard of a pianoforte. As the keys were touched they moved certain pins, which pricked the unfortunate pigs, who grunted and squeaked accordingly; we suppose there must have been somewhat too much sostenuto. This Louis was not much of a man of jokes, except in his own peculiar way, and some of his recorded amusements were not of a harmless description. According to Brantôme and others, he caused his brother the Duc de Guienne to be poisoned, as he feared he might become troublesome, and his crime was accidentally made known to his domestic fool in the following manner. The king was praying to his "bonne patronne," in the presence of his fool, who, he thought, was too imbecile to attend to or to understand him : "Ah ! ma bonne dame, ma petite maistresse, ma grand' amie, en qui j'ai eu toujours mon reconfort, je te prie de supplier Dieu pour

moi, et estre mon advocate envers luy, qu'il me pardonne
la mort de mon frere que j'ay fait empoisonner par ce
mechant abbé de Sainct Jean d'Angely," &c.   The fool
was less imbecile than his master had fancied, and repeated the whole matter for the edification of the king
and his court at dinner-time.

CHAPTER VIII.

IN the sixteenth century we arrive at the æra of the Amatis, and find the violin in its present form, when the details received the most careful attention, and everything connected with the instrument was calculated on scientific principles, and it possessed the power and tone which, after a lapse of 300 years, have not been surpassed. Many experiments have been made, to some of which we shall refer hereafter, in change of form and detail, material and disposition of strings; but none with any effect or improvement; more frequently, indeed, the reverse. Some alterations have been made in strengthening the centre, mostly of the upper vibrating plate; and a stronger sound-bar has been applied to resist the increased tension of a higher pitch; and trials have been made without any sound-posts or bars, and with short tail-pieces, and varied positions and number of sound-holes, but there has been no permanent or essential change since the latter part of the sixteenth century.

The violin is stated to have been first referred to in Zacconi's "Pratica di Musica," 1596, where it is mentioned with a compass precisely of the present extent, without the shift; but the instrument was known in our country, and in use in the royal band, prior to this date, and some of the Amatis also were previous to it.

The viol was still in great repute, and it was by slow degrees that the superiority of the violin was allowed; and this after skilful performers in the succeeding century, whose powers of execution were in advance of their time, had shown the increased facility afforded by the younger instrument, and the brilliancy of tone and sprightliness of effect of which it was capable, combined with sweetness, of less monotonous character than that of the viol. The viol had now from three to six strings, and a French player named Mauduit, of the time of Henry IV. of France, is said to have added the sixth string, but it appears to have been previously in use. It had frets—occasionally six or seven—to guide the fingers, made of small pieces of gut-string dipped in warm glue, and tied round the neck at proper intervals; sometimes they were inlaid in the neck or finger-board, and slightly in relief, and the practice was carried down to a comparatively recent period.

Franchinus Gafurius, before mentioned in connexion with music-printing, in "De Harmoniâ Musicorum Instrumentorum," 1518, has a plate showing the connéxion of harmony with the celestial bodies, &c. There is a figure playing on a sort of viol, with the neck turned back, having four strings, but no bridge or sound-holes; the bow something like that of the double-bass (Fig. 44). We have before observed on the probability of the absence of details, even of the bridges, arising occasionally from the omission of the

FIG. 44.

artist. Carter has a representation of a sculpture on the outside of St. John's Church, Cirencester, of the beginning of this century, where there are several figures playing on instruments; one has an oval viol, with four strings and a tail-piece, and four round sound-holes, but no appear-

ance of a bridge (Fig. 45). Potier describes a handsome instrument of the larger size of this class from a MS. of the sixteenth century. It has four strings, and the scroll is curved nearly into a semi-circle, having a boldly carved head at the top; the sound-hole is round, and perforated like that of a guitar, and there is no appear-ance of a separate finger-board or

FIG. 45.

bridge, though this would appear to be necessary on looking at the formidable bow (Fig. 46).

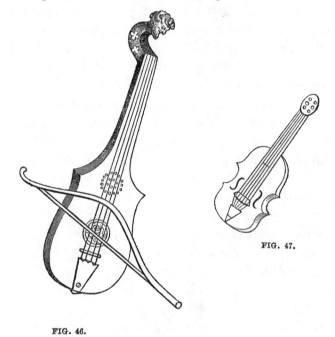

FIG. 46.

FIG. 47.

The celebrated printer John Oporinus, at Basle, about 1530, had for his device, Arion, sometimes standing on the dolphin with a small three-stringed instrument held reversed in his left hand, and the bow in his right; and sometimes playing on a large viol with six strings, which approaches the modern tenor in form (Fig. 47). Christopher Froschouer, a printer at Zurich of about the same date, also has a viol in some of his title-pages. In the several representations of the " Dances of Death " of this age, the figure of Death is occasionally represented playing on the viol and other instruments, while leading on his victims with grim satisfaction to their fate.

Mersennus gives a description of a bass-viol in the time of Charles IX. which was large enough to contain a young page inside, who sang the treble of some ravishing airs, while the performer, Granier, played the bass part on the huge instrument, and at the same time sung the tenor, thus completing the trio. There is a very large contre-basse represented in a picture of the " Marriage of Canaan," by Paul Veronese, which has nine strings and is apparently about nine feet high; but we must allow for pictorial license.

Martin Agricola, in " Musica Instrumentalis," 1545, on the back of his title-page represents the Fraw Musica, a smartly dressed female, playing on an instrument of the guitar class. In one corner of the engraving is an instrument of the bass-viol kind, with four strings and frets, a bridge, and a tail-piece, with considerable inward curvatures, and two semi-lunar sound-holes under the two outer strings; it has no appearance of a separate finger-board, and the bow is like a double-bass bow. He describes four instruments of different sizes, but all of the same unsightly shape : they are called respectively descantus, altus, tenor, bassus, each with four strings, a large round sound-hole in the centre, like that of the guitar, reaching from side to side, and two crescent-shaped sound-holes facing each other in the upper part

of the instrument, and frets, of which the
discant and bass have six, and the others
seven; the head is turned back, the curvatures are very abrupt and deep, and
extend down half the instrument; there is
no appearance of bridge, or tail-piece, or
detached finger-board; the bow, as usual,
is like that of the double bass. Our
figure is that of the discantus (Fig. 48).
We have already given the figure of the
gigue from the same work. He describes
the following as the method of tuning a
quartett of viols with four strings:—

FIG. 48.

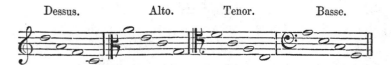

while for grand viols with five strings, and the bass with
six, the tuning is thus:—

The Italian viols, according to Ganasi del Fantego,
1542, had six strings and seven frets, and were tuned
thus:—

Rousseau, in his Treatise, written in the seventeenth century, says that the first viols used in France, meaning the class of instrument on which he was a celebrated performer, had five large strings, the bridge placed low and below the sound-holes, and were tuned in fourths from C down to E, and in figure were like what he calls the bass-violin. The viol afterwards, he says, became more like the violin in form, and a sixth string was added, when he describes the tuning as D, A, E, C, G, and D. After this a seventh string, A, was added by his master, St. Colombe. There were four sizes, answering to the four classes of voices; basse, taille, haute-contre, and dessus. Sometimes also a contre-basse was added.

The French tuned the taille a fourth higher than the bass, the haute-contre a fourth higher than the taille, and the dessus a fourth higher than that. Jerome de Moravia, three centuries before this, gives three different methods of tuning the vielle, but as the description is long and somewhat complicated, we did not think it necessary to insert it.

Luscinius, in 1536, mentions and gives a figure of a chelys or bass-viol, with nine strings and frets, with sides much curved in, and very similar to the figure given from Agricola; also the monochord, the rebec, the viol da gamba, the vielle or lyra mendicorum (that is, the hurdy-gurdy, to which the name vielle was now applied), and the violin or treble viol; but this is an instrument with three strings only, and more properly, perhaps, the gigue. Laborde gives a drawing of a large instrument of the double-bass class, with numerous strings, invented by Jean Doni, called the amphicordum or accord, which must have been very puzzling to play on, and was probably little more than an experiment.

The term chelys is introduced into the somewhat
pompous introduction of a curious poem called, " Canum
cum catis certamen," in which every word begins with
the letter C.

> " Cattorum canimus certamina clara canumque,
> Calliope concede chelyn ; clariæque Camœnæ
> Condite cum cytharis celso condigna cothurno
> Carmina."

Hucbald, the well-known writer on music in the ninth
century, wrote " Ecloga de Laudibus Calvitii," which,
besides a Proæmium and some lines at the end, as
" Clausula Carminis," has twelve chapters, each beginning with " Carmina clarisonæ calvis cantate Camœnæ,"
and consisting of ten lines, every word beginning with
C. There is a very rare work, " Carmen contra clypeum
Cyclopum concordiam," by John Nasus, a Franciscan
monk, about 1580. Other pieces are known, every
word beginning with P, as, " Pugna Porcorum," and
also with other letters.

Several fine performers on the viol are mentioned at
this time, as, Alphonse della Viola, Alessandro della
Viola, and Giovan-Battista del Violino (probably a violin-
player). Granier was one of the finest players of his
age, and died about 1600. He was attached to the
court of that singular character Queen Marguerite, who,
after the assassination of her husband, Henry IV, lived
in a strange mixture of pleasure and devotion, luxury
and literature, music, dancing, and charity ; and, according to Dreux du Radier, entertained a passion, when
past the age of fifty, for Comine, her master of music,
who was called, apparently in consequence, " le Roi
Margot." The celebrated female fool of the French
court, Mathurine, whose folly in her later years was
probably to some extent assumed, and under cover of

which she made a large fortune, had a son called Blanc-Rocher, who was an admirable player on the lute. When Henry IV. was stabbed by Jean Chastel, in 1594, he at first thought the act had been committed by Mathurine, who was in the carriage with him, and cried out, " Au diable soit la folle ; elle m'a blessé ! " but from her presence of mind she mainly contributed to the capture of the real criminal. The celebrated Zwinglius was an amateur performer, admitting to Faber, who had objected to his love of music, that he had learned to sing to the chelys, fidicula, tibia, and other instruments, and defended the art.

Claudio Monteverde, of Cremona, dwelling therefore among the Amatis, in the end of this century, was not only a distinguished performer on the tenor viol, but also a composer, and we shall have to refer to him again. Vincentio Galilei, the father of the great astronomer, was an able writer on music, and in 1582 names the viola da braccio, which he says was called the lira not many years previously, the viola da gamba, and the violono, but not the violino, which must, however, have been known before his time. He attributes the invention, erroneously, as we consider, to Italy.

Francis I. of France is said to have been the originator of a chamber-band, in addition to the music of his chapel, and to have had violins ; but there were musical establishments of this nature in the French court long previously. An anecdote is told of his sending a band of accomplished musicians to Solyman, the second Emperor of the Turks, in 1543, who, having heard them three times, caused all their instruments to be destroyed, and after making them handsome presents, sent them out of the country, on pain of death should they return ; fearing that his people might become enervated by hearing

them, and suspecting that Francis had sent them over
for political purposes, and to divert him from the
business of war.   There is a story of much more recent
date, where a band was sent over to some Eastern poten-
tate, and on their first proposed performance, began as
usual to tune, when the monarch and his grandees,
supposing this to be the commencement of the concert,
were so astonished and ear-struck, that they sent the
unconscious offenders back again as fast as they could,
without waiting for further proof of their skill.   Something like this would seem to be alluded to in the
" Knight of the Burning Pestle," " They say 'tis present
death for these fiddlers to tune their rebecks before the
great Turk's grace."

In the time of Henry IV. of France, there was a
dispute between his musicians and those of the Cathedral
of Notre Dame, as to the right of precedence before
him ; when the king decided that they should all sing,
but that the musicians of his chapel should begin.   He
had his band of " vingt-quatre violons du Roi," but
they seem only to have been used for dancing.

The statutes of the Corporation of the makers of
instruments, players, and professors, which had been
confirmed in 1454 by Charles VII, and enlarged by
François de Harlay, Archbishop of Rouen, in 1517,
were regulated in 1578 by Henry III.   Even Charles
IX. himself was fond of music, and played on the violin.
Poisot, in his " History of Music," recently published,
states that he had seen his instrument at the Bibliothèque de Cluny Saône et Loire ; but notwithstanding
this taste of the king, the composer Goudimel, the master
of the renowned Palestrina, was killed in the massacre
of St. Bartholomew's Day, which Charles is said to have

personally encouraged, and to have assisted in : but Nero himself was a patron of music.

The two following entries from the accounts of the expenses of Charles, taken from " Archives Curieuses de l'Histoire de France," are interesting, especially the latter, as it shows that Cremona was then famous for its instruments ; and, if the fifty livres tournois formed the price of one violin, the value would be high even at that time, as the livre tournois was worth five francs five centimes, and fifty would be equivalent to 252½, or probably about 1200 in present value. Part of the sum, however, may have been for the expenses of the journey :—

" 7 Novembre, 1572. A Baptiste Delphinon, violon ordinaire de la chambre dudict sieur, la somme de 75 livres tourn, dont Sa Majesté luy a faict don, pour luy aider a supporter les frais et despence qu'il luy convient faire s'en allant présentement à Millan, par commandement de Sa Majesté pour faire venir des musiciens pour son service et plaisir."

" 27 Octobre, 1572. A Nicolas Delinet, joueur de fluste et violon dudict sieur, la somme de 50 livres tourn, pour luy donner moyen d'achepter ung violon de Cremonne pour le service dudict sieur."

In the accounts of his successor, Henry III, from 1580 to 1588, violins are mentioned amongst other instruments, and as early as 1550 the name of Pierre de la Haye, joueur de violin, appears in the register of the performances of the ancient drama at Bethune. Violins, and instruments of this class, are mentioned frequently in the accounts of festivals in the French memoirs of this age, of which a few examples may suffice. There is an account given in the Memoirs of Marguerite de Valois, of a *fête* given at the interview of her mother, Catherine

de Medicis, with her son, King Charles IX. in 1565, at
Bayonne, where several provincial dances were introduced with the appropriate instruments, as, "les Poite-
vines avec le cornemuse, les Provençales la volte avec
les timballes, les Bourguignones et Champenoises avec le
petit hautbois, le dessus de violin, et tabourins de village; les Bretonnes dansans les passepieds et branles-
gais; et ainsi toutes les autres provinces." We think a
history of dancing by some properly qualified person
would prove an interesting, as well as an amusing work,
though we are not prepared to go as far as the Maître à
danser, in "Le Bourgeois Gentilhomme:" "Tous les
malheurs des hommes, tous les revers funestes, dont les
histoires sont remplies, les bévues des politiques, et les
manquements des grands capitaines, tout cela n'est venu
que faut de savoir danser."

According to a song made on the marriage of the
same monarch—

> " Tabourins et trompettes,
> Hautbois et violins,
> D'une haulteur parfaite
> Faisoient tantir leurs sons."

At a splendid *fête* given in 1579, on the marriage of
Margaret of Loraine, the sister of the queen of Henry
III, to the Duc de Joyeuse, several violins were introduced to play the dances, the whole being arranged by
the celebrated Baltazar, or Baltazarini, one of the first
famous violin-players on record. He was *valet de
chambre* and superintendent of music to Catherine de
Medicis, and also the chief of the king's band, and was
commonly called De Beaujoyeulx. After the nuptials of
Margaret, Queen of Austria, with Philip III. of Spain,
at Ferrara, in 1598, and those of the Duke Albert with the
Infanta Isabella, the king's sister, amongst other enter-

tainments a concert was given by the nuns of the Convent of St. Vito, wherein they played on violins and bastard viols, together with other instruments, intermingled with voices.

Having previously given an account of a concert of pigs, we may be allowed, perhaps, to vary our work a little by relating one where cats formed part of the orchestra, before Philip II. of Spain, at Brussels, in 1549. A bear was seated on a great car, at the figure of an organ, which instead of pipes had twenty cats, of different sizes and notes, shut up in small cages, with their tails out, and attached to the register of the organ, so that, as the bear pressed the keys, the tails of the unlucky cats were pulled, and, according to the chronicler, the cats began to squeal " des basses, des tailles et des dessus, selon la nature des airs que l'on voulait chanter, avec tant de proportion, que cette musique des bêtes ne faisait pas un faux ton." We should have suspected, but for this statement, some hanging of the notes occasionally. The description proceeds to state that, at the sound of this feline instrument, monkeys, bears, wolves, stags, and other animals danced about on an accompanying stage; but as from the context it appears that, with the exception of the cats and monkeys, the beasts were represented by children dressed up, we may almost fancy some tampering with the cats, though nothing of the sort is mentioned.

The viol appears in England in the royal bands in this century, as well as the rebec and fiddle, as before mentioned. In the seventeenth of Henry VIII. we find his band consisted of fifteen trumpeters, three lewters, three rebikes, three taberets, one harper, Andrew Newman the waite, two vialls, four drumslades, a phipher, and ten sagbuts; the wages varying from 4*l.* to 33*l.* 6*s.*, the

three principal sagbuts alone receiving the highest rate.
Nearly similar lists appear in subsequent years. In
September, 1532, there is a sum of 3*l*. 7*s*. 6*d*. charged
in the Privy Purse expenses, for the livery coats of three
of the " vyalls," showing that the members of the royal
band were provided with a dress at that time. In 1538
Henry had three " vyalls," named Hans Highbourn,
Hans Hossenet, and Thomas Highbourne, at salaries of
33*s*. 4*d*. per quarter; and three years after the number
was doubled, their names, as we learn from Mr. Collier's
" Annals of the Stage," being Vincent de Venitia, Alex.
de Venitia, Albertus de Venitia, Ambroso de Milano,
Joan Maria de Cremona, and Antony de Romano, all of
them foreigners, and one, it will be observed, from Cremona, now soon to take a distinguished place in the
annals of the violin; their salary was 4*l*. quarterly.
These performers were accustomed to participate in the
New Year's Gifts, then so liberally and regularly distri-
buted; for instance, on New Year's Day, 1542-3, they
received from the Princess Mary the sum of 20*s*., being
a larger sum than that given to any others of their own
class; many similar examples might be given.

In a curious inventory of the effects of Henry VIII,
taken immediately after his decease, there are no less
than nineteen " vialles," great and small, and four " git-
terons " (guitars), with four cases to them, called "Spanishe
vialles;" the catalogue comprises numerous instruments,
especially flutes, and finishes with " sondrie Bookes and
Skrolles of Songes and Ballattes."

The succeeding monarchs, Edward VI, and Mary and
Elizabeth, both of whom were skilful musicians themselves, had bands formed much in the same way as that
of their father. The viols in Edward's band, of whom
there were eight, were paid, six at the rate of 30*l*. 8*s*. 4*d*.

each, one at 20*l.*, and one at 18*l.* 5*s.* The first notice of violins by name in the royal bands appears to be in 1561, when the sum of 230*l.* 6*s.* 8*d.* was paid to them; in the same year we shall find them introduced in the tragedy of "Gorboduc." Ten years afterwards the queen had seven, who received 325*l.* 15*s.* One of the New Year's gifts given to her in 1577-8, was a viol by Marke Antony; these gifts were so regulated and graduated, that every one connected with the court was expected to give one, down to *Smyth*, dustman, who gave "two boltes of cameryck." There is an entry in the "Calendar of State Papers," 1569, of the names of the officers of the queen's household who were defaulters in payment of the subsidy, and all the musicians appear in this list, which does not speak well for their position, unless they were returned as defaulters as a matter of favour, for the purpose of being excused. In the Accounts of the Scotch Court, given by Dauney, in his "Ancient Scottish Melodies," are several entries relating to viols and "fithelars" of this century, as, in 1503, "To Adam Boyd, Bennet, and Jame Widderspune fithelaris xlij^s." 1505, "To Sir George Lawederis fithelar, ane fithelar of Striuelin, &c., ilk man ix^s. xlv^s." 1507, Jan. 1. "To divers menstrales, schawmeris, trumpetis, taubroneris, fithelaris, lutaris, harparis, clarscharis, piparis," extending to lxix persons "x^{li}. xj^s." In 1538, payments are made "To the foure menstralis that playis upon the veolis, for their yeirlie pensioun ij$^{c\,li}$," and also "To Jakkis Collumbell player upon the veolis."

The price of a common bass-viol was moderate enough, for there is an entry in the diary of Philip Henslowe, "Lent unto Richard Jonnes the 22 of desembr 1598, to bye a basse viall and other instrementes for the companey xxxx^s." In an inventory of Henslowe, of the same year, are included a trebel viall, a basse viall, a bandore, and a sytteren. In the accounts at Hengrave, in 1572, there is a charge of 20s. for a treble violin; and there seems little doubt but that the violin was now in requisition for dances, except perhaps for the stately pavan, or others of the grave and ceremonious class.

In an interesting "History of Horselydown," by Mr. Corner, F.S.A., to whom we are indebted for a copy, there is an engraving from an old picture in the possession of the Marquis of Salisbury, at Hatfield, the work of George Hofnagle, a Flemish artist. The date of this picture, which represents a fair at Horselydown, is 1590. On the right are some figures dancing; the musicians are, on one side a piper or flutist, and two playing on violins, much of the modern shape, and two other similar violin-players on the other side of the dancers.

The approach to the present shape of the violin was probably gradual; the first makers of violins being also makers of viols. Kerlin and Duiffoprugcar preserved much of the viol quality; but some instruments of Gaspar de Salo, especially tenors and double basses, are made quite in the present shape. At the time of the "Amatis" this shape seems to have been completely settled and perfected.

At the conversazione of the Musical Society of London, on the 29th of January, 1862, the curious old violin described in "Hawkins's History of Music," with an engraving, and stated to have been given by Queen Elizabeth to the Earl of Leicester, was exhibited. It is of the date of 1578, and is of heavy make, the upper part of the body being much deeper than the lower; there is a great deal of ornament and carving about it, and we should expect the tone would be nasal and sluggish. It is now kept at Warwick Castle. Burney.

mentions Corelli's violin, then the property of Giardini, after whose death we believe the well-known Mr. Salomon became its possessor; it was made in 1578, and the case is said to have been painted by Annibal Caracci.

One of the writers of this work has in his possession a very handsome viol da gamba of about this date, richly inlaid and ornamented, purchased from the late Mr. John Cawse, the artist, but we have been unable to ascertain the previous owners. The body is about the size of a modern violoncello, and it has frets. It is altogether so fine a specimen of this class of instruments, that we have had photographs, from which our illustrations are taken. (Figs. 49, 50.) When the lamented Prince Consort, on the 16th of April, 1845, being the director for the evening of the Ancient Concert, had some music of the 16th century performed on instruments of that period, some of which were sent over by M. Fetis from Brussels for the purpose, Mr. Cawse lent this viol da gamba, which was played on by Mr. Richard Hatton. In the course of the evening he was desired to attend and show the instrument to the Queen, who examined it carefully, and expressed herself much pleased with it. We may remember that Sir Andrew Aguecheek, amongst other accomplishments, was a performer, " he plays o' the viol-de-gamboys."

Viols, violins, and fiddles, are mentioned in early dramatic works of this age, and in the " Interlude of the Four Elements," in 1510, one character says,—

> " This daunce wold do mych better yet,
> Yf we had a kyt or taberet,
> But alas! ther is none here."

He is answered by another, who proposes to go to a tavern, where they will be sure to find one or two minstrels. In that quaint production, "Gammer Gurton's Needle," our oldest comedy, except "Ralph Roister Doister," and which is said to have been written as far back as 1551, Diccon, the mischief-maker between Gammer Gurton and Dame Chat, says at the end of the second act—

> " Into the town will I, my frendes to vysit there,
> 　And hether straight again to see th' end of this gere ;
> 　In the mean time, felowes, pype up your fidles, I say, take them,
> 　And let your friendes here such mirth as ye can make them."

In our earliest tragedy, "Gorboduc," which was acted in 1561, we have the first specimen of music between the acts, the choice of the airs being probably left to the performers. There is a dumb-show at the beginning of each act, taking the place of chorus, and foretelling the subject of the following division of the play, each accompanied by appropriate music. At the commencement of the dumb-show to the first act it is stated, "Firste the Musicke of Violenze began to play, durynge whiche came in vppon the Stage sixe wilde men clothed in leaues." Previous to the other acts, musical instruments of different classes are introduced.

In the banquet scene in the "Lamentable Tragedy, mixed ful of pleasant mirth, of King Cambises," of the same date, being that alluded to by Shakespeare when referring to speaking in King Cambises' vein, the king says :—

> " Me think, mine eares dooth wish the sound
> 　of musicks harmony ;
> 　Heer for to play before my grace,
> 　in place I would them spy."

Ambidexter, the vice of the piece, replies,—

> " They be at hand, sir, with stick and fidle ;
> 　They can play a new daunce called, *Hey, didle didle.*"

He seems to have been hard pressed for a rhyme, but he

is the buffoon of the play, and on his first appearance
comes in dressed with " an old capcase on his hed, an
olde pail about his hips for harnes, a scummer and a
potlid by his side, and a rake on his shoulder."

In Gascoyne's " Jocasta," nearly of the same date, each
act is preceded by a dumb show, accompanied by viols,
cythren, bandores, and other instruments. At the end
of the play of " Wyt and Science," " cumth in foure with
violes and syng, Remembre me, and at the last quere
all make cursye, and so goe forth syngyng." Katherine,
in " Taming the Shrew," calls her supposed music-master
rascal fidler, and twangling Jack; and in the old play
on which Shakespeare is supposed to have founded his,
Valeria, who personates the music-master, exçlaims,
" Hold, mistresse, souns will you breake my lute?"

> " *Kate.*   I on thy head, and if thou speake to me,
>   There take it vp, and fiddle some where else.
>   (*She throwes it downe.*)
>   And see you come no more into this place,
>   Least that I clap your fiddle on your face."

In the old play of " Timon " (not Shakespeare's), one of
the hangers-on is Hermogenes, a fiddler, and the fiddle
and fiddling are frequently referred to in connection
with him. In one of the songs during Queen Elizabeth's
royal progresses, being Rowland's song in praise of the
Fairest Beta, by Drayton, about 1590, we find the following collection of instruments :—

> " Sound out your trumpets then from London's stately towers,
>   To beate the stormie winds a-backe, and calme the raging showers.
>   Set to the cornet and the flute,
>   The orpharion and the lute ;
>   And tune the tabor and the pipe to the sweet violons ;
>   And moove the thunder in the ayre with lowdest clarions."

The common fiddlers at this time, if not attached to the
court, or to the establishment of some great person, pro-

bably led a rambling life, inducing too often habits of intemperance, especially as they frequently had to attend taverns and social meetings, where, if they possessed tolerable skill, and were able to sing a good song, their companionship was courted, especially about Christmas time. "Faith, fellow fiddlers," says one of the characters in the "Returne from Pernassus," "here's no silver found in this place; no, not so much as the usuall Christmas entertainment of musitians, a black Jack of beare, and a Christmas pye."

One of Tarlton's jests is connected with two musicians (most probably fiddlers) called Fancy and Nancy, who used with their boys often to visit Tarlton, he being one of their best friends, at the sign of the Saba, in "Gracious Street." One summer morning they came to play him "The Hunt's up," (a tune for playing which adapted to some political song on the "crowd or fyddyll," one John Hogon had got into difficulties in 1537,) with other music; when he came out of his room in his shirt and night-gown to drink some muscadine with them. In the meantime, a rogue steps in and steals his apparel, which seems to be the point of the joke; and many of these jests are much of the same quality.

Armin, in his "Nest of Ninnies," gives an account of a mischance that befel a fiddler, in collision with Jack Oates, the domestic fool of Sir William Hollis. One Christmas-time, Oates being out of sorts, his master told him to go home, as he would get another fool; upon which Jack began to cry, and went down to the great hall, where, being strong of arm, he snatched the pipes out of the piper's hands and broke them over the unoffending fellow's head, putting a stop to the dancing. Sir William was very angry at this, and offered a gold noble for another fool, on which an unlucky fiddler, who was present, proposed to take the place, and was approved of. He was so pleased that he threw his fiddle one way and broke it, his bow another, and his case another, and went out to dress. In the meantime Jack returned, having recovered his good humour, and began his gibes and jokes, of which an average specimen may be given in his stating that there was a wench in the hall who had eaten garlic, and seventeen men were poisoned from kissing her. His rival, or intended substitute, now entered the room dancing and grimacing, and dressed in one of Jack's dresses; but the practised fool flew at the interloper and beat him severely, so that the unfortunate fellow not only lost his fiddle, but also, as the story says, the use of his left eye. Those who wish to learn more of the interesting and curious history of court and domestic fools, will find much entertainment and information in Dr. Doran's work on the subject.

Two celebrated fiddlers, called Out Roaringe Dicke and Wat Wimbars, are named about this time, who could make their 20s. a-day at Braintree Fair, a great resort for these characters. Anthony Now-now, and Blind Moon, were also well known. The former is thus introduced in Chettle's " Kind Hart's Dream," 1592 :— " The first of the first three was an od old fellow, low of stature; his head was couered with a round cap, his body with a side skirted tawney coate, his legs and feete trust vppe in leather buskins, his gray haires and furrowed face witnessed his age, his treble violl in his hande, assured me of his profession. On which (by his continuall sawing having left but one string) after his best manner, hee gaue me a huntsvp: whome, after a little musing, I assuredly remembred to be no other but old Anthony Now-now." In some parts of the work the instrument is called a crowd. Anthony Munday is said to have been the person intended to be ridiculed by Anthony Now-now, and he obtained his name from singing a song in which each verse ended with Anthony now, now ; one verse may suffice for an example :—

> " When is the best time to drinke with a friend?
> When is the meetest my money to spend?
> O Anthony, now, now, now,
> O Anthony, now, now, now."

The instrument was, however, also admitted into good society, for Selden's father, who was passing rich with forty pounds a-year, delighted in the violin, on which he played well, and would play to his neighbours at Christmas-time while they danced.   Chests of viols were also kept in many families, as we shall presently describe, and therefore we may assume that violins were also.

Towards the end of this century publications began to appear of songs adapted to various instruments, which, in the succeeding century, were very numerous.   In 1558 our acquaintance, Anthony Munday, published " A Banquet of Daintie Conceits," to sing to the lute, bandora, virginalls, or any other instrument.   In 1593, William Barley published " A New Booke of Tablature, containing Instructions to guide and dispose the hand, to play on sundry Instruments, as the Lute, Orpharion, and Bandora," &c.   John Dowland, the composer of some excellent madrigals, and himself a distinguished performer on the lute, whom Fuller calls the rarest musician that his age did behold, published in 1597, "The First Booke of Songes or Ayres of foure parts with Tablature for the Lute.   So made that all the partes together, or either of them severally may be song to the Lute, Orpherion, or Viol de Gambo."   In 1599, Richard Allison published the Psalms of David " in Meter, to be sung and played on the lute, orpharyon, citterne, or base violl;" and in the same year Morley printed a work of still more instrumental character, the "First Booke of Consorte Lessons," for six instruments to play together, namely, the treble lute, the pandora, the cittern, the flute, and the treble and bass viols. At the same time, Anthony Holborne published a collection of pavans, galliards, almaines, and other short airs, for viols and other instruments. William Lawes wrote some fantasias for viols, which it might be curious to compare with some of our modern fantasias.

There are several payments for strings charged in the accounts from which we have previously given extracts, generally called lute strings, but viol and violin strings may be considered to be included. Some of the payments were large, as for instance : Thomas Lytchfield, one of the grooms of the Privy Chamber in the time of Elizabeth, was paid at the rate of 13*l*. 6*s*. 8*d*. a-year for lute strings ; but except in one case, mentioned by Dauney, of 6*s*. paid in 1533 for "one dozen luyt stringis send to the kinge's grace in Glasgow," we do not find the actual value of the strings. There was a Custom-House duty in 1545 of 22*d*. the grose on "Lute Strynges called Mynikins."

Mersennus says that strings for fiddles and other stringed instruments were made from the intestines of sheep ; a practice as ancient as the early Egyptians. Baptista Porta gives some fanciful effects of strings made from various materials, which we introduce on his authority, not having had time to try the experiments ourselves ; but will recommend them to any of our readers having plenty of patience and a good stock of credulity. Strings made from sheep and wolf combined produce no music, but jar, and cause discords ; while the sounds of those made from serpents, and especially

vipers, cause women to miscarry. So drums made of
elephants', camels', or wolfs' skins, will frighten horses,
and one of horses' skin is literally a bugbear to the
ursine race, from the antipathy the living animals have
to each other. For a similar reason, Culpepper says
that a cobweb will stop the bleeding of a wound. We
should observe in reference to our recommendation to
make these experiments, that the learned Kircher, in
perfect simplicity and good faith, says, that having seen
the account of Porta, and some similar remarks of
Pythagoras and others, he got two polychords, and
strung one with sheep-strings, and the other with wolf;
but on trying the latter in a sheep-fold, the insensible
animals refused to be frightened, and no breaking of
strings was caused from the antipathy.

The notation of music in the present century is somewhat repulsive to a modern reader, from its angular and
frequently crowded characters ; but it was considerably
advanced from former times, and capable of expressing
passages that required much execution; in effect it
comprised our present notation in a ruder form and
without the smaller notes.   The first music-printing,
which was from blocks, is said to have been in the works
of Franchinus ; and the Germans exhibited much skill
in printing music with letter-press types.   There is
some account in Hawkins of musical notes of this time
from Andreas Ornithoparcus, khaw, Wilphlingsederus,
and Lucas Lossius, and he says that music from metal
types was invented by Ottavio de Petrucci, about
1515.   Grafton, in the Book of Common Prayer noted,
composed by John Marbeck, and published in 1550,
improved the notes of Higden, and his own characters
were improved by Day in 1560.

Marnef, a printer at Paris in the beginning of this

VIOL DE GAMBA
In the possession of S. A. Forster

FIG. 49

VIOL DE GAMBA
In the possession of S. A. Forster

FIG. 50

century, was one of the first who printed the plain-chant
in moveable characters with the signs of the ligatures,
and about the same time Oglin, at Augsbourg, was the
first who printed music from copper-plates; Hautin, at
Paris, being the first who engraved music in France.
The Ballards had a monopoly there in 1540, which
somewhat delayed the improvement, as they used the
old characters. Adrian le Roy, an eminent lutenist,
was afterwards associated with them, and the type was
improved. He published, about 1570, the precepts for
the tablature of the lute, an inconvenient method of
notation, that was occasionally applied even to the
different classes of the viol and violin, and did not wear
itself out until a comparatively recent period. Granjon,
who formed his notes rounded instead of lozenge-shaped,
Attaignant, Guillaume de Bé, Branton, and Sanlecque
and his son, were other clever printers of music of this
age. For the account of the notes from Gam ut, to
E la, from the semiquaver to the large, with all the
mysteries of moode, time, and prolation, perfect or imperfect, great or less; with the intricacies of black full,
and black void, red full, and red void, we must refer to
Morley's " Introduction to Practical Music," 1597, ob-
serving, that notwithstanding the various names and
characters in his work, they may be readily understood
with a moderate degree of attention; and such a study
might be as useful—perhaps more so—than the restoration of some of our supposed old ecclesiastical modes,
where many of the combinations and sequences sound
strange to the modern educated ear, and seem to belong
to bygone days; but of which the theory also is very
simple, and the knowledge of it to be attained by any
one with a moderate knowledge of music in a short time.

CHAPTER IX.

IN one of the first musical dramas, " L'Anima e del Corpo," 1597, no instruments are mentioned of the viol or violin class, excepting the lira doppia, which has been supposed to be the viol da gamba. In the opera of " Orfeo," 1607, the following instruments were used :— " duoi contrabassi di viola, dieci viole de brazzo, duoi violini piccioli alla Francese," and " tre bassi da gamba." As before observed, the violin was well known both in England nearly half a century previously, and in France before this date, and the use of the term " Francese," does not imply the French origin of the violin, but may show that it was popular, and serve as a distinction from the viols; and M. Bottée de Toulmon, in his " Dissertation," before referred to, states that he has not been able to find any authorities for the superior claim of the French violin at this time. However, violins were now regularly established in orchestras. In 1634 Stephen Lundi, in his musical drama called " Il S. Alessio," had violins, harps, lutes, theorbes, bass-viols, and clavecins, to accompany the vocal parts. The oratorio " di S. Gio. Battista," by the celebrated Stradella, who was himself a great performer on the violin, was accompanied by two violins and violoncello del concertino, and two violins, tenor and bass, del concerto grosso.

Burney says the first attempt of accompaniments by two violins, tenor and bass, our modern quartett, was in the oratorio "di Santa Cristina," by Federici, in 1676. The orchestras for the compositions of Cavalli, Lulli, and Carissimi (whose "Stabat Mater" is said to have been one of the first pieces in which orchestral accompaniments were introduced into churches), comprised principally violins and viols of different sizes, bass viols, and double bass-viols, called by the Italians violone, in distinction to the violins, which were called by the diminutive violini, the parent name being the viola. The music for the violins was written in the G clef, as at present; and for the viols for the C clef, on the first, second, or third lines, according to the size of the instrument, or soprano, mezzo-soprano, and alto clefs.

In 1637, at Venice, theatrical action, dancing, and the art of dramatic decoration were brought in aid of song and music, and from 1645 operas were occasionally tried in France. In 1671 a theatre was opened in Paris for the lyric drama, under letters patent from Louis XIV, dated the 28th of June, 1669, wherein it was inserted that gentlemen and ladies might sing at the operas without such an act being considered derogatory to their title of nobility, or their aristocratic privileges. Of course whatever Louis said was right; and there is an anecdote of flattery towards him which certainly throws most others in the shade. A preacher, in his discourse before him and his court, made use of the expression, "We are all mortal," a natural remark, considering that Louis himself had descended from a long line of mortal ancestors, and might be expected, notwithstanding his threescore and ten years' reign, to follow them to the grave. However, the incautious preacher found from the looks of some of the courtiers that he had made a blunder, and promptly recovered himself by exclaiming, "Nous sommes tous mortels—ou presque tous."

The viol continued in constant use in England in the seventeenth, as well as in the previous century, together with the violin, and it was common in musical families to have a chest of viols, containing two trebles, a tenor, and a bass-viol, and occasionally there were duplicates of some of the instruments; at Hengrave, for instance, there was a chest of six viols. Sir Thomas More, who was fond of music, kept viols and an organ in his house. Burney gives the following as the mode of tuning a chest of viols, containing three sorts with six strings :—

The bass-viol, or viol da gamba.

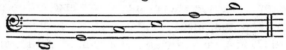

The tenor-viol, or viol da braccio.

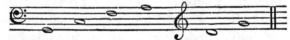

The treble-viol.

Cerreto, in his work "Della Prattica Musica," Naples, 1601, has his own portrait on the frontispiece, with an angel at each corner playing on a stringed instrument; two have them of the guitar sort, with five strings and seven frets; the other two have them of the class of viol da gamba, having five strings, with a circular sound-hole in the centre; their necks are long, and one of them has five frets; their forms are like the modern violoncello, with bows similar to double-bass bows. He names four gradations of the viola d'arco, the bass, tenor, alto, and soprano, and gives the compass of the six strings of each, stating that in playing together, the tenor and alto are tuned a fifth above the bass, and the soprano a fourth above them. He gives the names of several Neapolitan performers of the viola d'arco, and the lira, but none on the violin, which, therefore, was apparently of no high repute in Naples at that time. Cerone, a Spanish writer, in "El Melopæo y Maestro," 1613, names as stringed instruments, sistro comun, psalterio, acetabulo, pandura, dulcemiel, rebequina, or rabel, vihuela, violon, lyra, cythara or citola, quitarra, laud, tiorba, arpa, monochordio, clavichordio, cymbelo, and spineta; thus including some of the violin class.

Prætorius, in "Theatrum Instrumentorum," Wolffenbuttel, 1620, gives several curious figures of musical instruments, which may be considered as more particularly representing those then in use in Germany. Among them is the *gross contra-bassgeig*, much like a modern double-bass, with five strings, two S S sound-holes, a bridge, a finger-board, and a tail-piece, somewhat of a fanciful form, no frets, and the scroll like the modern; the bow, also, is similar to the present double-bass bow. The *violone* is much like the violoncello, and has six strings, two S S sound-holes, a bridge, finger-board, tail-piece, scroll like the modern, and six frets; the bow somewhat like a heavy or clumsy violoncello bow. The *Italianische lyra de gamba* is like a thick violoncello, with twelve strings, two S S sound-holes, a finger-board, a tail-piece, a bridge, no scroll, but a flat board, or plate, at the top of the finger-board, in which the screws are fixed; the neck is very short, and there are five frets. The bow is like that of the violoncello, and it would appear from the figure that several of the inner strings must have been struck together. There are three *violen*

de gamba, somewhat in shape like the violone just mentioned, with six strings, a bridge, a finger-board, a tail-
piece, a sound-hole like a crescent, a scroll with a figure
of a lion's head, or something similar at the top, and
each with seven frets.   The *viol bastarda* is also much
of the same shape as the violone, has six strings, bridge,
finger-board, tail-piece, plain scroll, two crescent-shaped
sound-holes, and also a round one above them.   The
Italianische lyra de bracio is like the *lyra de gamba,*
but smaller, and has only seven strings.   The *geig* is of
long pear-shape, with three strings, bridge, tail-piece, and
circular sound-hole, and very similar to our Fig. 15,

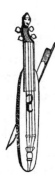

taken from Agricola.   The *klein posche*
is a small instrument, somewhat of the
same class, but of oblong shape, and narrow, with the neck apparently detached,
and one S sound-hole at the end of the
finger-board (Fig. 51) ; we have a similar
one in our possession.   The *discant-geig*
is of violin shape, but with a waving line
in the bouts, four strings, a bridge, a finger-
board, detached neck, S S sound-holes,

FIG. 51.

tail-piece, and scrolls.   The *rechte dis-*
cant-geig is much like the modern violin in every
respect.   The *tenor-geig,* like a modern viola, with
a short neck.   The *bas-geig de bracio,* like a clumsy
shaped violoncello, but with five strings, and a short neck ;
none of the last six instruments have frets.   He gives
the figure of the *trumscheide,* in the shape of a trumpet-
marine, but with four strings ; also the *scheidholt,* which
is a sort of oblong narrow box with three strings (there
are, however, four screws), and seems to have eighteen
frets, with a kind of double-bass bow, and would appear
to be more adapted for experiments than anything else.

There are figures of the *schlussel-fiddel*, and *stroh-fiddel*, which are of peculiar shape, and probably were never in general use. One of them has four strings, bridge, &c., but no inward curvatures at the side; the other has four strings, bridge, &c., but has an appendage at the neck, which is too obscure in the figure to be made out. The *alte-fiddel*, or old fiddle, has five strings, though there are ten screws, seven frets, two crescent-shaped sound-holes, and a round one below them, no bridge, and no scroll, but a head-piece turning back; it is much like our Fig. 48, from Agricola. He gives several representations of the varieties of the lute and guitar, harp, and wind instruments.

Mersennus, " De Instrumentis Harmonicis," has numerous representations of the stringed and bowed instruments of his age, the early part of the seventeenth century. He seems to distinguish the violin class as barbiton minor, and the viol class as barbiton major. In describing the first, he says it is much used for dancing, and that the professors of that art used a small one that they could carry in their pocket, called pera, or poche; he has three figures of them, of which we give one (Fig. 52); the others are similar, but of a longer and narrower make, and they all have an additional sound-hole in the shape of a heart, under the notion of thus obtaining more power. The necks are of one piece with the body, and they all have four strings and no frets. This instrument was somewhat akin to the old gigue, and also the precursor of the modern kit. He has figures of two large instruments of the barbiton minor, one of which may be considered as identical with a modern violoncello of very broad model, and the other has the corners at the inward curvatures, very distinct and angular, with the sound-holes larger than in the

modern instrument, the neck also is thicker and heavier
(Fig. 53). The strings were tuned in fifths, but the

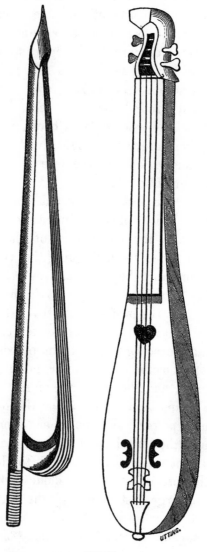

FIG. 52.

lowest string was G, a fifth, therefore, higher than the

FIG. 53.

violoncello. The representation he gives of another barbiton minor, or treble violin,
might easily be taken for a
modern fiddle (Fig. 54). The
sound of this class of instrument, he says, is stronger than
that of the barbiton major,
or viol; amongst other distinc-
tions he mentions the viols having six strings instead of four,
and frets; but these frets appear to have been occasionally
applied to the violin; we have
given a representation of one of
his figures of the barbiton major (Fig. 55). From his account
of the fingering of the violin,
it would seem as if the shift
was not then known; but in
describing the barbiton major he says the frets do
not exceed eight, which would imply that it was in
use. When it was first ventured on it was considered a
triumph of skill, and the performer did not attempt
beyond the C, or ut, on the first string, and if such a
passage was expected, the audience would say softly,
"*Gare l'ut;*" if the performer failed he was hissed, but if
successful was greeted with bravos and acclamations.
Mersennus gives a description with a figure of what he
calls the lyre, having eight frets and fifteen strings, of
which the bow must necessarily have struck several at
the same time. The shape is somewhat unmanageable,
being like a violoncello with an additional part at the
lower end; probably it was not much in use. He describes the monochord, and that singular instrument, now

FIG. 54.

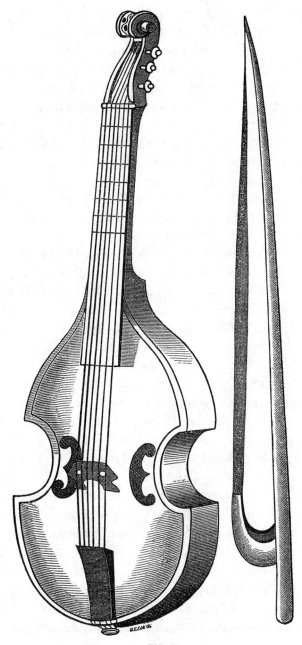

FIG. 55.

obsolete, the trumpet marine, the favourite instrument of
M. Jourdain, in "Le Bourgeois Gentilhomme;" also
the lyra mendicorum, like the hurdy-gurdy, which he
says some call the symphony, and the French the vielle.
The principal materials of strings he states were the intestines of sheep and other animals, brass and iron (used
for the clavicymbala), flax, and silk. Rome and other
cities produced the best strings, and some of the larger
ones were composed of from fifty to sixty guts twined
together.

Kircher, in his "Musurgia," 1650, describes and
gives figures of several instruments bearing, as it might
be expected, great similarity to those in the work of
Mersennus, calling the viols and violins by the name of
chelys, and the poche by that of linterculus.

In a curious book, "Symbola Divina et Humana
Pontificum, Imperatorum, Regum," &c. by John Frede-
ricus Hagen, 1666, which contains hieroglyphics of the
popes and monarchs, there are several of the kings of
England; and in that applicable to Henry VIII. is a
large instrument of the fiddle make, with six strings and
frets, but with no distinct finger-board; the head turning
forward. From the description, this is intended for the
pandura, though different in make and in number of
strings from that described by Mersennus, and was not
intended to be played on with a bow. In the accompanying explanation, Henry's usage of his wives is
referred to, and the fact stated that Ann of Cleves, after
her divorce, amused herself by playing on this instrument.

In 1611, Louis XIII. granted several new privileges
to the Corporation of Musicians. Two of the musicians
belonging to this monarch's chapel got into disgrace on
some occasion, and were curtailed of half their appointments. In their distress they applied to Marais, his

buffoon, who devised the following plan to relieve them. He went with them to dance in a masquerade before the king, each of them being only half dressed. "What does this mean?" said the monarch. "Sire," they replied, "it is because those who have only half their appointments, can only go half dressed!" Louis laughed, and restored them to favour and to full dress. A story of somewhat similar class is told of Haydn respecting his candle overture or symphony (letter B). Prince Esterhazy having for some reason dismissed all his band except Haydn; the composer, not liking to part with his old associates, composed the above piece of music, in the last movement of which, each performer as he completed the music allotted to him, put out his candle and quitted the orchestra, leaving the first violin to play about twenty-two bars by himself. The Prince was angry at this curious arrangement, and sent for Haydn to inquire into the meaning of it. Haydn bowed submissively, and said he wished to show of what little use one performer was, and the band were accordingly restored to their appointments.

Mersennus mentions some of the most distinguished performers of the seventeenth century, and in referring to the harmony produced by the twenty-four royal fiddlers, who consisted of six treble violins, six counter-tenors, six tenors, and six basses, says nothing could be sweeter or more pleasing; and as to the players, who more elegant than Constantine on the treble, more enthusiastic than Bocan, more delicate than Lazarine and Foucard, and Leger on the bass? There is a story told of this band of twenty-four going round as usual on New Year's Day, to play to the grandees and officers of the court, and obtain the gifts of the season in return. They went to the Marshal Duke de Grammont amongst others, when, after a little time, he put his head out of window and said, "Combien êtes-vous, messieurs?" "Nous sommes vingt, monsieur." "Je vous remercie tous vingt bien humblement," says the Marshal to the expectant musicians, shutting his window.

Bocan was the musician selected by Cardinal Richelieu in the following singular scene, related in the "Mémoires de Brienne," and elsewhere. The Cardinal, in the height of his power, had ventured to address the Queen, Anne of Austria, in the language of love. She, disguising her feelings at his boldness, informed him by her confidant, Madame de Chevreuse, that she required as a proof of his sincerity that he should appear before her in Spanish costume, and dance a saraband, never supposing that he, a high Churchman, and occupied with the state affairs of the country, would condescend to such a course. To her surprise, however, supposing that he had succeeded in his suit, he consented, merely stipulating that none should be present except her Majesty and his musician Bocan, who, however, is said to have betrayed him. The queen, notwithstanding, placed her favourite, Madame de Chevreuse, and two of her gentlemen, Vautier and Beringhen, behind a screen. At the appointed time Richelieu entered dressed in a tight-fitting suit of green velvet, with silver bells at his knees and castagnets in his hands, and began his task in sober earnest, until the queen could preserve her gravity no longer, and burst into a fit of laughter, which was repeated by her attendants behind the screen. The Cardinal left the room in great anger, and from that time became the enemy of the queen and her favourite.

Our Queen Elizabeth was fond of dancing, and when advanced in years seems to have used it politically; as Weldon mentions, that when any messenger came to her from King James, on lifting up the hangings, he was sure to find her dancing to a little fiddle " affectedly," that he might tell James her youthful disposition, and how unlikely it was he should come to the coveted throne.

Mersennus names Maugard and Hotman as extra-ordinary performers on the violin and viol; Rousseau says they were the first men who excelled on the viol in France, the former having great science and execution, and facility of working on a given subject ; while the latter had a beautiful tone. He names also Père André, a Benedictine, as a perfect master of the instrument, and Marais as a scientific player ; but the best pupil of Hotman was Sainte-Colombe, who surpassed his master, and is said, as before mentioned, to have added a seventh string to the instrument, and to have introduced lapped silver wires, but this is doubtful, as the same is said of Marais.

Amongst other players of this age, the most distin-guished were Biber, who was also a difficult and fanciful composer ; Michel Angelo Rossi, who played Apollo in his own opera of "Erminio sul Giardino," 1637, and proved his title to the name by his sweet and graceful melody ; Marco Fraticelli, who surpassed all previous performers on the viol da gamba; and Carlo Ambrosio Lunati, of Milan, commonly called Il Gobbo della Regina, who went to England in the time of James II. The celebrated singer Leonora Baroni was also an excellent player on the theorbo and viol. Pierre Pièche, who was appointed "musicien et garde des instrumens de la musique de la chambre du roi," on March 3, 1672, may be named for another reason, connected with an ancient custom of the French court. Previous to this time it had been customary to keep dwarfs as well as fools as court appendages, but the practice was now abolished, and the salary that had been given to Baltzard Pinson, nain, was transferred to Pièche. Ernest Henri Hesse, born in 1676, became one of the best players on the bass-viol in Germany. It is said he went to Paris in 1698, where he stayed three years, and took lessons at the same time from Marais and De Torqueray, unknown to each other. Each boasted of the superiority of his pupil, and they determined to test the merits of their respective scholars at a public concert, when, to their surprise and disappointment, they discovered the identity. Schnittelbach, of Lubeck, about 1660, was a fine performer, and the teacher of Strungk, one of the greatest players of his age. His visit to Corelli is no doubt known to many of our readers. In answer to Corelli's inquiry if he could play, he said he could do so a little, but should wish to hear Corelli, who accordingly gratified him. Strungk then took up the instrument and ran carelessly over the strings, upon which Corelli complimented him, and said that with practice he would make an excellent player. Strungk then altered the pitch of all the strings, and played with such skill that Corelli exclaimed, " They call me Arcangelo, but by heavens, sir, you must be Archidiavolo." Corelli, who was born in 1653, was a fine player himself, with a clear sweet tone ; his celebrated compositions may be studied and practised with much advantage even at the present day. His quiet and retiring behaviour when present at a large assembly where there was much talking, and therefore much interruption, was somewhat different to that of Viotti in a similar position. The latter, when about to play a concerto at the French court, had just commenced, when a cry was raised of " Place à monseigneur le Comte d'Artois!" The usual bustle ensued, in the midst of which Viotti placed his fiddle under his arm and walked off, to the great astonishment of the company, nor would he play in public again for a considerable time. Corelli, in his case, put his fiddle quietly on the table, saying he was afraid he disturbed the conversation.

The musician Maugard was an abbe, and formed one of the band of the Cardinal Richelieu. He played very finely on the bass-viol, but was deficient in other respects, and ill-conducted ; his forehead was particularly narrow in shape. He in some way or other offended the Abbé de Bois-Robert, who, however, professed to be reconciled, and recommended him to apply to the cardinal for the Abbaye de Crâne-étroit, which he told him was about to become vacant. The unconscious victim accordingly went to his great master to beg the vacant benefice. The cardinal, suspecting the author of the joke, could hardly refrain from laughter, but told him he should have the appointment, which he would no doubt retain for the rest of his life. Maugard went directly to the cardinal's secretary, a grave, solemn personage, to arrange, as he supposed, the formal part with him ; but the secretary, looking at him in a contemptuous manner, asked him how he dared come about the Abbaye de Crâne-etroit, which existed nowhere except in his face. The disappointed abbe then began to suspect the hoax, and kept out of the way for some time, to escape the jokes against him.

Corelli's concertos, trios, and solos have been frequently played in public, until within the last few years, especially during the existence of the Ancient Concerts ; and the delightful performance of the ninth solo, and in the eleventh trio of the second set by Lindley and Dragonetti, will never be forgotten by those who heard them. One of the last performances in public of the inimitable

Lindley was in that trio at the Philharmonic concert. Torelli's concertos appeared three years before those of Corelli, and he is therefore called the inventor of the concerto grosso.   Burney says the first trios for two violins and a bass, were by Turini, in 1624; and in 1652 Gregorio Allegri published some quartetts for two violins, tenor and bass.   There were also other writers for these instruments in different manners. We may refer, though the want of competent performers seems strange, to the anecdote in Mr. Chappell's work from Corette, that when the Regent Duke of Orleans wished to hear Corelli's sonatas, he was obliged to employ three singers, as no performers of sufficient skill could be procured.   Those who know these trios will think there are some queer passages for the voice.

In Brossard's Dictionary the following varieties of the viol are named at the end of the seventeenth century :— Viola d'amor, with six wire strings ; viola de bardone, a large viol, reaching to as many as forty-four strings, and a strange instrument therefore ; viola basso, viola bastardo, viola da braccio, or bratz, viola da gamba ; viola 1ma, haute-contre de violon ; viola 2da, taille de violon ; viola 3tia, quinte de violon ; viola 4ta, alto viola, or haute-contre ; tenore viola, or taille ; violetta, diminutive of viola, violono, violoncello, properly the quinte de violon, or petite basse de violon, with five or six strings ; violone, the basse de violon, or double-bass.

Michel Todini, an ingenious person and a skilful player on the musette, born at Saluzzo about 1625, invented several curious instruments, and amongst them was a viol da gamba which comprised all the four gradations of the viol. He is also said—but we should think this doubtful—to have been the inventor of the double-bass, to which he gave four strings. In Bonanni's

" Gabinetto Armonico," 1722, there is a representation of a curious instrument of the organ class invented by him, which had four distinct sets of keys, so placed that if required they could be played on by four different players at the same time, or one alone could manage the instrument. It was stated to be at the palace of Signor Verospi at Rome.

Mr. Lidel on the 22nd Nov. 1849, exhibited at a meeting of the Society of Antiquaries a viol-shaped instrument made by Tielke, 1687, which he called a barytone. It had six gut strings passing over a bridge, and fastened to an ebony tail-piece, that were played on with the bow; and eleven steel strings, which went under the bridge and were fastened to an ebony bar placed there obliquely. The steel wires vibrated from sympathy with the gut strings when the latter were struck with the bow, and the round and mellow tones of the one set of strings mingled with the crisp and metallic sound of the other, and produced a peculiarly pleasing effect, well adapted to soft music, as notturnos, &c. This instrument was exhibited as a viol d'amour at the conversazione of the Musical Society of London, July 2, 1862, and Mr. Lidel informed us that it had been given by the then Bishop of Salzburg to his grandfather, who was the composer of Lidel's " Duetts for Violin and Tenor," and other music where the viola is brought prominently forward.

CHAPTER X.

HERE are constant allusions to the violin and viol, and even to the name of crowd as previously mentioned, as well as to other instruments, in the English writers, dramatic and otherwise, in the seventeenth century; and the violin begins to obtain the favour over its older kin. In Ben Jonson's "Bartholomew Fair," Lanthorn Leatherhead, the hobby-horse man, offers amongst other toys, "What do you lack? what is't you buy? what do you lack? rattles, drums, halberts, horses, babies o' the best, fiddles of the finest." Afterwards he offers for the son of one of his customers a fiddle to make him a reveller. In the same author's "Sad Shepherd," Robin Hood says—

> "The woodman met the damsels and the swaines,
> The neatherds, plowmen, and the pipers loud,
> And each did dance, some to the kit or crowd,
> Some to the bagpipe, some the tabret mov'd."

Here we have the kit and crowd, and also the bagpipe, probably one like the musette, as instruments to dance to; and in Drayton's "Fairy Wedding" crowds and bagpipes are both introduced, the commencing word violins being probably addressed to the performers.

> "Violins, strike up aloud,
> Ply the gittern, scour the crowd!"

Let the nimble hand belabour
The whistling pipe, and drumbling tabor ;
To the full the bagpipe rack,
Till the swelling leather crack."

In his " Polyolbion," in the description of a musical contest between the English and Britons, he names many instruments then in common use, of which the following are connected with our subject:—

" The trembling lute some touch, some straine the violl best,
In sets which there were seene, the musick wondrous choice :
Some likewise there affect the gamba with the voice,
To show that England could varietie afford,
Some that delight to touch the sterner wyerie chord ;
The cythron, the pandore, and the theorbo strike :
The gittern and the kit, the wandring fidlers like."

Earle, in his " Microcosmography," 1728, says of a poor fiddler, he " is a man and a fiddle out of case, and he in worse case than his fiddle." " A country wedding and Whitsun-ale are the two main places he domineers in, where he goes for a musician, and overlooks the bagpipe." Stephens, in his " Essays and Characters," 1615, gives the following account : " A fiddler is, when he plays well, a delight only for them who have their hearing ; but is, when he plays ill, a delight only for those who have not their hearing." Many will agree with this opinion now.

A company or party of fiddlers was frequently called a noise. One of the characters in " The Dutch Courtezan," by Marston, with the unpoetic name of Mulligrubbe, says, " O, wife ! O, wife ! O, Jacke ! how does thy mother ?   Is there any fidlers in the house ? " *Mrs. Mul.* " Yes, Mr. Creakes noyse." *Mul.* " Bid 'em play, laugh, make merry." They not only frequented houses of resort, but different sets seem to have attended particular houses, and they were frequently treated with very little ceremony. An illustration of this will be found in " Westward Hoe," by Webster and Dekker, in the beginning of this century. A character called Monopoly says, " Where's this noise? what a lousy town's this! Has Brainford no music in it? " *Chamberlain* (of the Sun). " They are but rosining, sir, and they'll scrape themselves into your company presently." *Mon.* " Plague a' their cat's-guts and their scraping : dost not see women here, and can we, thinkst thou, be without a noise then ? " Soon afterwards the fiddlers appear on the stage, and Sir Gosling Glowworm, a spendthrift, says to them in the style of the gallants of those days, " What set of villains are you, you perpetual ragamuffins? " to which they quietly answer, as if used to such manners, " The town consort, sir." He takes them out with him and says, " — the chamberlain shall put a crown for you into his bill of items." The rosining or tuning referred to was probably a subject of complaint in those times, just as at present in a band not sufficiently well regulated, as Massinger says in " The Guardian "—

" Wire-string and cat-gut men, and strong-breath'd hoboys,
    For the credit of your calling have not your instruments
    To tune when you should strike up."

In former times, as occasionally in the present, usurers or money-lenders used to require the borrower to take as part of the loan, certain articles of which the value was appraised by the benevolent lender, such as choice pictures, fine wines, and sometimes much more homely articles. In " The Miser," by Shadwell, the character who gives the name to the play, treats his borrower harmoniously, including in his advance, " a Bolonia lute, a Roman arch-lute, two gittars, a Cremonia violin, 1 lyra viol, 1 viol de gambo, and a trump marin." Middleton, in his play of " The Witch," in one of the scenes of conjuring or enchantment introduces a cat playing on the fiddle; but the well-known nursery rhyme is older than this, and the fact of equal authenticity in both. We have a curious old French print, where there is a cat playing on the fiddle, and a dog with a fool's-cap, dancing; a pantaloon is also playing on the guitar; there are the figures of two fools in the engraving, one with a fool's-cap looking in through a sort of window, the other is having his head washed by a female figure called La Folie; in a chimney corner is a fat unwieldy figure with Mardy Gras as his legend, whilst an old woman is preparing cakes. Pussy's fiddle is of the viol character, with four strings and no frets. The print is called " Le Diuertissement de Mardy Gras." It has twelve lines at the bottom, of which the following four are connected with our subject :—

> " La grotesque rejouissance
> Du chat jouant du violon,
> et du chien qui dance en cadence
> de la guitarre a pantalon."

Many allusions are made to females playing on the viol da gamba, but we will only refer here to a ballad of the time of Charles I. in Mr. Chappell's book, called " Keep a good tongue in your head," where a wife is described as having numerous good qualities.

> " She sings and she plays
> And she knows all the keys
> of the viol de gambo, or lute,"

but,

> " She cannot rule her tongue."

Now, we are told that " The tongue is a little member, and boasteth great things;" " But the tongue can no man tame." As an old carol says—

> " off al the enmys that I can fynd,
> The tong is most enmy to mankynd."

Remember, however, that the tongue masculine is also here comprised ; for who is there that cannot appreciate and has not rejoiced at the gentle voice of woman?—the first that enlivens us in the opening morning of life, and frequently the last that soothes us in the hour of death. In the hours of sickness, the hours of sadness, the hours of deep trial and affliction—which have or will come to all—the hours when the mind dwells impatiently on lost opportunities, and long practised errors, and futile sacrifices to the glare and vanities of the world, how often does the soft, kind voice of woman cheer the oppressed mind, and restore its lost power and vigour.

The directions given for music in the different dramas and masques of the age, the latter of which were frequent at court, will show how the viols and violins were used indiscriminately; the juxtaposition of some of the instruments will appear strange to our modern arrangements.   In Marston's "Sophonisba," about 1606, the music of the fourth act is composed of organs, viols, and voices; and towards the end of the act "a treble viall, &c. a base lute, play softly within the canopy," and just previously there is "infernall music playing softly." At the opening of the fifth act the music is confined to "a base lute and a treble violl."   In Campion's masque at Lord Hay's marriage, of the same date, on one side are mentioned ten musicians with bass and mean lutes, a bandora, a double sack-bote, and an harpsichord, with two treble violins ; and on the other side, nine violins and three lutes.   In the masque of "Silenus," 1613, Silenus has for his music, a tabor and pipe, a base violin, a treble violin, a sackbut, and a mandora ; while Kawasha has a bobtail, a blind harper and his boy, a base violin, a tenor cornet, and a sackbut.   We find in some of the accounts the payments made to the violins and others connected with these masques, and otherwise engaged by the court, and the names of the leading persons. As in 1610, at a masque given by Queen Anne, Thomas Lupo, who was a distinguished performer on the instrument, had 5*l*. for setting the dances to the violins; the ten violins that continually practised to the queen, 20*l*., and four more that were added at the masque, 4*l*. In the Prince's Masque and Barriers, 1611, the same Thomas Lupo again had 5*l*. for setting the dances; the company of violins, 32*l*., and Thomas Lupo the elder, Alexander Chisan, and Rowland Rubidge, violins, 10*l*. In a court masque in 1613, where the celebrated Inigo Jones had 50*l*. for superintending, the same Thomas Lupo had 10*l*. and John Coperary, who we may assume was the skilful John Coperario, or Cooper, was paid 20*l*.; and ten of the king's violins received 10*l*. On the 23rd Nov. 1607, there is a warrant to pay Daniel Farrant, one of the king's musicians, for the violins, 46*l*. per annum. On the 22nd March, 1608, Alex. Chesham (the same, no doubt, as Alexander Chisan) was appointed one of his Majesty's musicians for the violins; and on the 6th February, 1612, Horatio Lupo had a grant of the place of the musician on the violin for life. Charles Guerolt and Thomas Giles appear at different times as instructors in music of Prince Henry, with annuities of 100 marks each. This prince, it is known, died young; but whether in consequence of a cold taken at the time of the visit of the Count Palatine to marry his sister Elizabeth, or from other causes hinted at, it is foreign to our purpose to inquire into.

Charles I. was not only a great patron of music, but also a fine player on the bass-viol or viol da gamba himself, especially in " those incomparable phantasies of Mr. Coperario to the organ," which had an accompaniment for one violin and a bass-viol. Charles was a pupil of Coperario, who himself excelled as a performer on the viol da gamba. Charles's band in 1625 consisted of eight players on the hautboys and sackbuts, and among them Richard Blagrave ; six players on the flute ; six players on recorders ; eleven players on violins, including Thomas Lupo, who is termed composer ; six players on lutes, and among them Nicholas Lanier ; four players on viols, including Alphonso Ferrabosco ; one player on the harp ; one keeper of the organs, and fifteen musicians for the lutes and voices, including Coperario, besides trumpeters, drummers, and fifers. On December 22, 1625, there is a discharge to his Majesty's musicians from payment of the two subsidies granted by parliament ; but it does not appear whether this was from inability to pay, or in reward ; but as all are included we may consider it to have been the latter. On the 20th July, 1628, there was a similar discharge from five subsidies. By warrant, dated July 11, 1626, the following payments were directed to be made :— To Nicholas Lanier, Master of the King's Music, 200*l.* per annum ; Thomas Foord, 120*l.* ; Robert Johnson, 60*l.* ; Thomas Day, 64*l.* ; and to Alfonso Ferrabosco, Thomas Lupo, and ten others, 40*l.* ; and to two others, 20*l.* each. On the 7th of the same month Ferrabosco was appointed composer of music in ordinary for life, with a yearly fee of 40*l.*, in the place of John Coperario, deceased. Many similar examples might be cited, and liveries were also given, as for instance, Oct. 22, 1628 : Warrant to the wardrobe for liveries to Alfonso Ferrabosco, musician for the viols, and Henry Ferrabosco, musician for the voices and wind instruments ; and Nov. 22 in the same year, a warrant to the Treasurer of the Chamber, to pay Nicholas Pieart, one of his Majesty's musicians of the violins, for his wages, 30*l.* per annum, and 16*l.* 2*s.* 6*d.* per annum for his entertainment, apparel, and livery, for life.

The name of Blagrave or Blagrove was connected with the court entertainments, and distinguished in music, at a very early period, as it is at the present time. Thomas Blagrove was Master of the Revels in the time of Queen Elizabeth, and William Blagrove was Master of the Children of the Revels in the reign of Charles I. Richard Blagrove and Thomas Blagrove were successively in the same king's band of musicians for wind instruments, the latter having been appointed in 1642, in the room of his father, deceased. He had 20*d.* per diem as salary, and 16*l.* 2*s.* 6*d.* for livery, being the same as his father, and money being worth nearly five times what it is now. There was a Thomas Blagrove of a Berkshire family, who was a gentleman of the chapel of Charles II, and a player on the cornet there; he was probably the Thomas Blagrove of Charles I.'s band. He, with a Robert Blagrove, were members of Charles II.'s celebrated private band, the first with a salary of 40*l.* 9*s.* 2*d.*, and the last with 58*l.* 4*s.* 2*d.*

In the accounts of James I. there is a charge of 40*l.* for a set (probably a chest) of viols for the king, and 32*l.* for another set, and a base-vyoll for the prince; a high price, considering the value of money before referred to. Alphonso Ferrabosco had a warrant on Nov. 27, 1604, for 20*l.* to buy two viols with cases, and one box of strings, for the use and service of the prince. About 1610, two great viols for him are charged 40*l.* while a lute and viol and other necessaries for a singing-boy are only 5*l.* 18*s.* 4*d.*

James I. incorporated the musicians of London, when

they had for arms, Azure, a swan argent within a tressure counter-flure, or ; in a chief, gules, a rose between lions, or ; for crest, the celestial sign Lyra, called by astronomers, the Orphean Lyre. Charles I. in his eleventh year (confirmed in his fourteenth) granted a charter to Nicholas Laniere and others, incorporating them by the style of "Marshall Wardens and Cominalty of the Arte and Science of Musick in Westminster, in the county of Middlesex," and gave them many privileges. They seem to have been in abeyance during the civil commotions and the rule of the Puritans, but were revived in 1661. Their rules from October 22, 1661, to July 20, 1679, are preserved in Harleian MS. 1911. They claimed considerable control over musicians ; for instance, on January 20, 1662, "It is ordered that Edward Sadler for his insufficiency be silenced and disabled from the exercise of any kind in publique houses or meetings." In the following month, perhaps to prevent their exceeding their powers, Mr. Richard Graham was "entertained their solicitor at law."

Braithwaite, in his "Rules for the Government of the House of an Earl," in the time of James I, says he should keep five musicians, who should play on the bass-viol, the virginals, the lute, and the bandora or cittern. At the time of any great feast, the service was to be accompanied by sackbuts, cornets, shawms, and other instruments, while during the repast, viols and violins were to be played. There is a representation given by Strutt ("Manners and Customs," vol. iii. plate 11) of a music party of about this date, consisting of six male figures at a table, playing from music books ; three have instruments of the guitar kind, one the flute, one a violin, held low against his breast, having four strings, S S sound-holes, a bridge, tail-piece, and finger-board ;

no frets. The remaining performer plays on a viol da gamba laid across his thighs, having five strings but seven pegs, S S sound-holes, and finger-board; but there is no appearance of frets, bridge, or tail-piece, which, as to the two latter, may be a mere omission in the original picture. The instrument itself is thick and short.

The quaint writer Tom Coryat, who is said to have introduced the use of forks into this country, for which reason he was called Furcifer, gives an amusing account of music at Venice on August 5, 1608, "especially that of a treble violl, which was so excellent that I thinke no man could surpasse it." On the following day he was still more fortunate. "I was for the time euen rapt vp with St. Paul into the third heauen. Sometimes there sung sixteene or twenty men together, hauing their master or moderator to keepe them in order, and when they sung, the instrumentall musitians played also. Sometimes sixteene played together upon their instruments—ten sagbuts, foure cornets, and two violde-gambaes of an extraordinary greatness; sometimes tenne, sixe sagbuts and foure cornets; sometimes two, a cornet and a treble violl. Of those treble viols I heard three seuerall there, whereof each was so good, especially one that I obserued aboue the rest, that I neuer heard the like before." He says the players on the treble viols sung and played together, and that there were two fine players on the theorbo, who also sung. The eccentric writer John Taylor, the Water Poet, seems to have been equally in raptures during his travels abroad in 1616. He describes at a town he calls Buckaburgh, not far from Minden, belonging to the Graff of Shomburgh, "a faire set of organs, with a braue sweete quire of queristers; so that when they sing, the lutes, viols, bandores, organs, recorders, sagbuts, and other musicall instruments all strike vp together, with such a glorious delicious harmony, as if the angelicall musicke of the spheares were descended into that earthly tabernacle."

There were numerous publications in the first half of this century (to those in the second half we shall refer hereafter) adapted for violins and viols, and again the strange fellowship of instruments will amuse. A few examples must suffice, but all that are connected with madrigals and songs of this period will be found in "Bibliotheca Madrigaliana," by Dr. Rimbault, whose accurate research and extensive knowledge of the literature and music of this age are well known.

Among the earliest publications in the century are those by Thomas Weelkes, of "Madrigals of five and six Parts, apt for Viols and Voices;" by Dowland, the celebrated lutenist, of " Songs or Ayres, with Tablature for the Lute or Orpherion, with the Violl de Gamba," and by Morley, " Aires, or Little Short Songes to sing and play to the Lute with the Bass-viol," all in 1600. In 1603 Thomas Robinson published "The School of Musicke; the perfect Method of true fingering the Lute, Pandora, Orpharion, and Viol da Gamba." Tobias Hume, called also Captain Hume, who was himself an excellent performer on the viol da gamba, published in 1605 a work with the following curious title, to attract amateurs; a practice not lost sight of in the present age, when occasionally the best part of a work is contained in a promising advertisement, or an important but fallacious title-page—" The First Part of Ayres, French, Pollish, and others together, some in Tabliture, and some in Pricke-song. With Pavines, Galliards, and Almaines for the Viole de Gambo alone, and other Musicall Conceites for Two Base-viols, expressing Five Partes, with pleasant Reportes one from the

other, and for Two Leero Viols, and also for the Leero
Viole with Two Treble Viols, or Two with One Treble.
Lastly, for the Leero Viole to play alone, and some
Songes to be sung to the Viole, with the Lute, or better,
with the Viole alone. Also an Invention for Two to
play upon One Viole." We have ourselves heard two
performers play a duett on one violin. Captain Hume
in 1607 published " Poeticall Musicke," where the bass-
viol is varied with other instruments in eight different
ways. In 1609 Rosseter published " Lessons for Consort,
for Six severall Instruments—Treble-Lute, Treble-Violl,
Base-Violl, Bandora, Citterne, and the Flute." A short
time before this, John Dowland published, " Lacrimæ,
or Seaven Teares figured in Seaven passionate Pavans,
with divers other Pavans, Galiards, and Almands, set
forth for the Lute, Viols, or Violons, in Five Parts."
Here we observe viols and violins are both mentioned
together. About 1611 the celebrated Orlando Gibbons
brought out " Fantasies of Three Parts for Viols."

The pavans, galliards, almaines, and corantos named
in many of these publications, to which Morley adds the
passamezzo, the jig, the hornpipe, the Scottish jig, and
others, were tunes adapted to dances of the same name.

The pavans, almaines, corantos, and passamezzos,
were slow, solemn dances; the pavans being so called
from pavo, a peacock, the ladies wearing gowns with
long trains, the gentlemen having a cap and sword;
those of the long robe in their gowns, and princes and
peers in their mantles; the movements resembling the
spread of the peacock's tail. A great contrast to the
sliding shuffle or hop of the present day, which by
courtesy is considered to be dancing; though even this
is graceful in the fair sex, especially when two dance
together. Sir Christopher Hatton we know was a great

dancer, and in the " Critic " is made to turn out his toes
by way of identity : as Gray says—

> " Full oft within the spacious walls,
>   When he had fifty winters o'er him,
>   My grave lord-keeper led the brawls ;
>   The seal and maces danc'd before him."

Sir W. Leighton, in "Teares, or Lamentations of a
Sorrowful Soule," 1613, has introduced in one of the
pieces, which may be considered as a paraphrase of the
150th Psalm, the names of numerous musical instruments,
but the description is too long to be inserted here. Two
verses will suffice to show his style—

> " 3. Praise him with simballs, loud simballs,
>   with instruments were vs'd by Iewes :
>   With syrons crowdes and virginalls,
>   to sing his praise do not refuse.
>   4. Praise him upon the claricoales,
>   the lute and sinfonie,
>   With dulsemers and the regalls,
>   sweet sithrons melody."

The gittron, bandore, theorba, and vialls are also
mentioned.

We may conclude this chapter by stating that Edward
Alleyn, the benevolent founder of Dulwich College, was
himself a performer on the lute, and at the time of his
death, Nov. 25, 1626, had a " lute, a pandora, a cythern,
and six vyols."

CHAPTER XI.

IT would seem from some accounts that Cromwell was not insensible to the charms of music, when he could unbend, or was in his own private domestic circle, although publicly he yielded to the Puritan feeling of his age. Theatrical representations were restrained, and music checked, although still practised in private; and in 1656-7 an act was passed against vagrants, forbidding any fiddlers or minstrels to go about to inns, ale-houses, or taverns, &c.

On the restoration of Charles II, music and festive meetings again flourished, and the revels and gaieties of the court spread in different degrees through society in general. The superiority of the violin over the viol was gradually established, as it was found to be more capable of producing power, and better adapted for execution than the latter instrument, of which the tone was frequently sweet, but at the same time of a nasal quality, and deficient in vigour. The violin proper, as we have shown, was known in England at least a century before this time, and we may have received some suggestions tending towards the modification of the viol to the form and details of the violin from the Low Countries in the time of Elizabeth, when the intercourse between the countries was not unfrequent. The first violin-makers, however, of any great repute, established themselves in Italy, where the wood probably was particularly suitable.

Charles II, in imitation of the French court, introduced his celebrated band of twenty-four violins, or, as Durfey says,—

> " Four and twenty fiddlers all of a row,
> And there was fiddle, fiddle,
> And twice fiddle, fiddle,
> 'Cause 'twas my lady's birth-day,
> Therefore we kept holiday,
> And all went to be merry."

This band consisted of six violins, six counter-tenors, six tenors, and six basses, with salaries varying from 40*l.* to 100*l.* per annum. The celebrated Baltzar, the "incomparable Lubicer," who had come over to England a few years before, was at the head of it. The anthems and services in the Chapel Royal were sung to these instruments instead of the ancient wind instruments, and Evelyn complains of their French fantastical light way of playing there. The organ was also in use.

At the commencement of Dryden's " Tempest," about 1667, the front of the stage was opened, and the band of twenty-four violins, with the " harpsicals " and theorbos, which accompanied the voices, were placed between the pit and the stage. The band was therefore placed just as in the present time, and this seems the first notice of their having any regular position. These twenty-four violins were either the celebrated four-and-twenty fiddlers, or a rival company in imitation of them. Burney says that the different expressions of crescendo, diminuendo, and lentando, were first used by Matthew Lock, in the music to the " Tempest." In Lock's own piece of " Psyche," about 1675, no instruments are mentioned for the ritornels but violins.

Music parties were now frequent. Anthony Wood,

who was himself a self-taught performer on the violin, which he tuned in fourths until better instructed by one Charles Griffith, gives an account of these meetings; some being before the Restoration, but in a quiet way. Gentlemen who attended them " play'd three, four, and five parts with viols, as treble-viol, tenor, counter-tenor, and bass, with an organ, virginal, or harpsicon. They esteemed a violin to be an instrument only belonging to a common fidler, and could not endure that it should come among them, for feare of making their meetings to be vaine and fidling. But before the restoration of King Charles II, and especially after, viols began to be out of fashion, and only violins used as treble-violin, tenor, and bass-violin; and the king, according to the French mode, would have twenty-four violins playing before him while he was at meales, as being more airie and brisk than viols."

He mentions among his friends, Ralph Sheldon, admired for his smooth and admirable way in playing on the viol; Thomas Jackson, a bass-violist; William Ellis, counter-tenor viol; Gervace Littleton, a violist; Will Glexney play'd well on the bass-viol; Joh. Haselwood, an apothecary, a conceited player on the bass-viol, sometimes on the counter-tenor, with little skill—being ever ready to take up a viol before his betters, was called Handlewood; Proctor (a pupil of the celebrated John Jenkyns), skilled on the lyra-viol, division-viol, treble-viol, and treble-violin; Nathan Crew, afterwards Bishop of Durham, violinist and violist, but always out of tune; Richard Rhodes, a confident Westmonasterian, a violinist, to hold between his knees; Matthew Hutton, excellent violist; and several other violists. He tells an amusing anecdote of himself and some of his companions. Himself and Will. Bull on the violins, Edm. Gregorie,

B.A. and Gent. Com. of Mert. Coll., who played on the
bass-viol, Joh. Nap, of Trinity, on the citerne; and
George Mason of the said Coll. on another wyer instrument, but could do nothing. They disguised themselves
in poor habits, like country fiddlers, and went about to
the country places, receiving drink and money for their
performances. On one occasion they were met by some
soldiers, who made them play in the open field, and then
left them without giving them a penny. Other players
named were Charles Perot, Christopher Harrison, John
Vincent, Sylvanus Taylor, Henry Langley, Samuel
Woodford, and Francis Parry, violists; and Kenelm
Digby, violinist. Mr. Sherard, an apothecary, was a
fine player on the violin, and Capt[n] Marcellus Laroon
on the violoncello. Lord Keeper North and Sir Roger
L'Estrange were both fine players on the viol. Much
interesting information relating to music will be found
in Dr. Rimbault's edition of "North's Memoirs of
Musick."

The lyra-viol, on which Proctor excelled, and which
is frequently mentioned among the instruments of this
time (the leero-viole in Hume's work lately referred to),
and on which Pepys says his brother played so as to
show that he had "a love to musique and a spirit for it,"
was a viol da gamba tuned differently from the common
six-stringed bass, and the notation for it was written in
tablature, like that of the lute. Playford says, this way
of playing the viol was of recent invention, and an
imitation of the old English lute or bandora. John
Jenkyns, the master of Proctor, was the best performer
on it then known. There would appear, however, to be
some allusion to such an instrument or mode of playing,
quite in the beginning of the century, as in "Lingua,"
by Anthony Brewer, about the end of Elizabeth, Tactus

says, "But, Auditus, when shall we hear a new set of singing-books? or the viols? or the concert of instruments?" and afterwards, "Come, come, Auditus, shall we hear thee play the lyre-way or the lute-way, shall we?" Daniel Farrant, towards the beginning of the century, was one of the first who set lessons for the viol lyra-way.

That amusing writer Pepys was in the habit of frequenting musical parties as well as the theatres, where his flirtations with Mrs. Knipps and others, render it not surprising that he was occasionally obliged to keep his wife in good humour by the present of some piece of finery. He was also himself a practised musician on the lute, violin, viol, and flageolet, besides being able to sing at sight. He seems to have had a tolerable estimate of his own skill (a habit of thinking not yet obsolete). On 21st Nov. 1660, he says, "At night to my vialliu (the first time that I have played on it since come to this house), in my dining roome, and afterwards to my lute there, and I took much pleasure to have the neighbours come forth into the yard to hear me." Dec. 3rd. "Rose by candle, and spent my morning in fiddling till time to go to the office." He occasionally favoured his wife with his music, to solace her domestic labours, which, according to the Diary, frequently consisted of those little artistic re-arrangements of dress so well known to ladies. 12th April, 1669, "Home, and after sitting a while, thrumming upon my viall, and singing, I to bed, and left my wife to do something to a waistcoat and petticoat she is to wear to-morrow."

He was not, however, satisfied with being a mere practical musician, but aspired to improving the theory, for on the 20th of March, 1668, he was "All the evening pricking down some things, and trying some conclusions upon my viall, in order to the inventing a better theory of musick than hath yet been abroad; and I think, verily, I shall do it." However, we do not find that he did do it, but in this he only failed with other great men.

It might be considered presumptuous in us to suggest even, whether the rules of harmony might not be somewhat simplified; but in such case, what would become of the learning of those who know the nomenclature, are acquainted with the tools, but know little of the working, yet still keep you at bay with hard terms, unless you are able to meet them with their own weapons. However, all professions, whether musical, medical, legal, or carpentering, must have their technicalities, though the genius of the age is tending gradually to remove or lessen them. Even, however, with the use of them we cannot fix on the pitch in music. We find a certain natural note has thirty-two vibrations, and *therefore* fix upon a certain number of vibrations, the figures denoting which form no multiple of 32, as the recognised pitch of a note of the same name four octaves higher. We are not agreed upon the division of the minor scale—scarcely, indeed, of the major—and as to the variation in the different keys, involving however, probably, some troublesome calculations, we can give little if any explanation. Harrison, the celebrated chronometer-maker, as mentioned in Smith's "Harmonics," took the interval of a major third to that of the octave, as the diameter of a circle to its circumference, and adjusted the frets on his viol accordingly; so that, as the circumference of a circle is a little more than three diameters (that is, about $3\frac{1}{7}$), so is a perfect octave a little more than three major thirds. However, under all circumstances, it is not surprising that Pepys did not do it.

He refers to different companies of musicians. The Dolphin Tavern had "an excellent company of fiddlers," and on the 27th March, 1661, he goes there "to a dinner of Mr. Harris's, where a great deal of mirth, and there staid till eleven o'clock at night; and in our mirth I sang and sometimes fiddled (there being a noise of fiddlers there), and at last we fell to dancing, the first time that ever I did in my life, which I did wonder to see myself to do." That habit of doing something to be wondered at, towards the conclusion of a tavern dinner, we are told still exists occasionally in this country. He mentions the Duke of Buckingham's musicians, to whom on one occasion he gave 3*l.* for a dance at his own house, as the best in town; they consisted of two violins, a bass-violin, and a theorbo. The witty Killigrew said that no ordinary fiddlers of any country were so well paid as our own. Heylin, in his "Voyage of France," 1679, says it was the custom at Tours for each man at table to pay the fiddlers a sou; they expected no more, and would not take less. Pepys was probably considered as an authority in his own circle for musical arrangements. On 7th May, 1660, Admiral Sir Edward Montagu, afterwards Earl of Sandwich, whom he calls "my Lord," gave him directions "to write for silk flags and scarlet waistcloathes; for a rich barge, for a noise of trumpets, and a set of fiddlers." On 10th April, 1661, he gives an account of a duet, not complimentary to the performers. "Here (Rochester) we had for my sake two fiddles, the one a base-viall, on which he that played, played well some lyra lessons, but both together made the worst musique that ever I heard." On the Coronation Day, 23rd April, 1661, he took a great deal of pleasure "to go up and down, and look upon the ladies, and to hear the musique of all sorts; but above all, the twenty-four violins." On 8th May following he refers to a circumstance which sometimes occurs in the present day, of a country fiddler having been a person who had seen better days. His uncle had written him to beg an old fiddle for Perkin the miller, whose mill the wind had broken down, and he had nothing to live by but fiddling; he wanted it by Whitsuntide to play to the country girls. Pepys adds that he intended to send him one on the morrow. On the 5th Oct. 1664, he describes an instrument called the arched viall, tuned with lute strings, and played on with keys like an organ, a piece of parchment being always kept moving; the strings being pressed down by the keys, were thus scraped as by a bow; and it was intended to represent several viols played on with one bow, "but so basely and harshly that it will never do." After three hours' stay it could not be fixed in tune. Several instruments on this principle have from time to time been invented, but have not been brought into use.

In July, 1666, he heard one of Lord Lauderdale's servants play some Scotch tunes on the violin, which he did not appreciate, or the selection was bad, or our best Scotch tunes are of more recent date, as no doubt many are. The performer played "several and the best of their country, as they seem to esteem them by their praising and admiring them: but, Lord! the strangest ayre that ever I heard in my life, and all of one cast." He mentions 8th October, 1667, the death of Saunders by the plague at Cambridge, " the only viollin in my time."

The greatest performer of the time, however, and one who seems to have been in advance of his age, was Thomas Baltzar, born at Lubeck about 1630. He came over to England in 1655, and is said to have been the first who taught the use of the whole shift, but it had probably been attempted before him. He appears to have caused almost as great a sensation in the musical world as Paganini did, when he came over and astonished us. Anthony Wood says that at a music meeting at Oxford, Professor Wilson stooped down humorously to see if he had not a hoof. The following is Evelyn's account of him, 4th March, 1655-6 :—" This night I was invited by Mr. Roger L'Estrange to hear the incomparable Lubicer on the violin. His variety on a few notes and plaine ground with that wonderful dexterity, was admirable. Tho' a young man, yet so perfect and skilful, that there was nothing, however cross and perplext, brought to him by our artists, which he did not play off at sight with ravishing sweetnesse and improvements, to the astonishment of our best masters. In sum, he plaid on y[t] single instrument a full concert, so as the rest flung down their instruments acknowledging their victory. As to my own particular, I stand to this hour amazed that God should give so greate perfection to so young a person. There were at that time as excellent in their profession as any were thought to be in Europ, Paul Wheeler, Mr. Mell, and others, till this prodigie appear'd." Davis Mell was then the greatest English performer, and in sweetness of tone is even said to have excelled Baltzar. The Lubicer was made the leader of King Charles's band, but died in July, 1663, having been of dissipated habits. He was succeeded by John Bannister, who died in 1679, whose son John was a fine performer on the violin, and one of King William's band, and the first violin at Drury Lane on the introduction of operas there.

About 1672, Nicolas Matteis came over, as great a performer even as Baltzar. North says, every stroke of his bow was a mouthful. Evelyn also heard him, and thus describes him, Nov. 19th, 1674 :—" I heard that stupendous violin, Sig'. Nicholao (with other rare musitians) whom I never heard mortal man exceed on that instrument. He had a stroak so sweete, and made it speak like ye voice of a man, and, when he pleas'd, like a consort of severall instruments. He did wonders upon a note, and was an excellent composer. Here was also that rare lutenist Dr. Wallgrave ; but nothing approach'd the violin in Nicholao's hand. He plaied such ravishing things as astonish'd us all." On the following 2nd of December, he went to his friend Mr. Slingsby's, the Master of the Mint, and heard Signor Francisco, esteemed one of the greatest masters in Europe on the harpsichord ; " then came Nicholas with his violin, and struck all mute." On the 20th November, 1679, he again is at Mr. Slingsby's, " to heare musiq, which was exquisitely perform'd by foure of the most renown'd masters ; Du Prue, a Frenchman, on ye lute ; Sig'. Bartholomeo, an Italian, on the harpsichord ; Nicolao on the violin ; but above all for its sweetnesse and novelty, the viol d'amore of 5 wyre-strings plaid on with a bow, being but an ordinary violin, play'd on lyre way by a German."

By a warrant dated the 24th of October, 1662, we find that Cremona violins brought a high price, as Mr. John Bannister, one of his Majesty's musicians in ordinary, had an order for 40l. for two Cremona violins bought by him, and also 10l. for strings for two years.

Simpson, himself an excellent performer on the viol da gamba, in his " Division Viol " calls the viol in Latin chelys, and gives three figures of the instrument, which are in fact all bass-viols. The first of these, which he says is best for sound, is much like the modern violon-

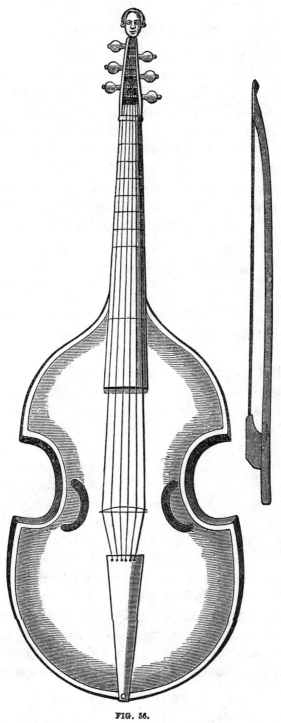

FIG. 56.

cello, but of somewhat longer form, and has six strings
with seven frets, besides a small one in the middle of
the strings for the octave.　The lower string is tuned to
the lowest D in the bass, while the others are successively
G, C, E, A, D, being two octaves ; the bridge is rounded
so that each string may be taken separately.　The strings
are thirty inches in length from the nut to the bridge.
The two other figures have deeper inward curvatures,
and the upper part of the model slopes off towards the
neck, instead of being rounded like the modern instrument ; the strings and frets are as in the first figure
(Fig. 56).　The bow is stiff but not heavy, with the hair
twenty-seven inches long, and used underhanded like the
modern double-bass bow.　From the examples given by
Simpson, the performers in his time must have attained
considerable facility of execution, though probably without much tone or power.

Playford, in the " Introduction to Skill in Music,"
1683, names the treble-viol in the G cliff, the tenor-viol
in the C cliff, and the bass-viol, with six strings and
seven frets, in the F cliff ; usually called the viol de
gambo or consort-viol, because the musick thereon is
played from the notes of the gamut, and not as the lyra-
viol by tablature.　The bass is tuned as described by
Simpson, the treble an octave higher, and the tenor a
fourth higher than the bass ; he also gives a method of
tuning by tablature.　He calls the treble violin a cheerful sprightly instrument, much practised of late, usually
strung with four strings and tuned in fifths ; there should
be six frets, as on the viol, but this was rarely done, and
was contrary to the character of the instrument ; but, he
adds, " This (tho tis not usual yet) is the best & easiest
way for a beginner who has a bad ear ;" the representation he gives has no frets.　The treble violin seems to

have been tuned as at present, and the tenor a fifth
lower, while the bass violin was tuned in fifths; the first
string being the higher G in the bass, and the fourth
therefore B flat below the line, and therefore one tone
lower than the violoncello.

Mace, in his quaint book, "Musick's Monument,"
1675, gives an amusing direction for the care of a lute,
which he would probably extend to the violin race. He
recommends the lute to be put into a bed in the day-
time that is constantly used, between the rug and the
blanket, but never between the sheets, because they may
be moist. It will save the strings from breaking, and
keep the lute in good order. He adds, no person must
be so inconsiderate as to tumble down on the bed whilst
it is there, as he had known several spoilt with such a
trick. We should think this very probable.

"Mantua, væ miserum! nimium vicina Cremonæ."

In that once very popular book by Comenius, "Orbis
Sensualium Pictus," which went through very many
editions, and in several languages, among the musical
instruments are introduced, "Secundo, in quibus *chordæ*
intenduntur & plectuntur, ut *nablium* cum *clavicordio*
utrâque manu." He mentions also, "*Testudo* (chelys)
(in quâ *jugum, magadium,* & *verticelli,* quibus *nervi*
intenduntur super *ponticulam,*) & *cythara,* dexterâ
tantum, *pandura, plectro,* & *lyra,* intus rotâ, quæ versatur.
Dimensiones in singulis tanguntur sinistrâ." Thus
translated: "*Secondly, upon which* strings *are stretched
and struck upon, as the* psaltery, *and the* virginals, *with
both hands; the* lute (*in which is the* neck, *the* belly,
the pegs, *by which the* strings *are stretched upon the*
bridge), *the* cittern, *with the right hand only, the* vial,
with a bow, *and the* harp *with a wheel within, which*

is turned about ; the stops *in every one are touched with the left hand.*" He gives two representa-
tions of the viol; we have represented the largest of them (Fig. 57). The instrument translated harp, is more like the hurdy-gurdy, and the nablium or psaltery like the harp, but the figures are not clear.

FIG. 57.

Hawkins gives a list of instruments bought for the use of the Music School at Oxford, about 1667, which included " 2 violins, with their bowes and cases, bought of Mr. Comer in the Strand ; cost 12*l.* 10*s.* and are at 2^d hand."

There were numerous publications for the varieties of the violin and viol in the last part of this century. Matteis had his compositions engraved on copper plates for the use of his scholars and others, and made much money by them. Baltzar also composed for the violin, viol, and " harpsicon ; " also for lyra-violin, treble-violin, and bass. Playford in 1655 published " Court Ayres; or Pavins, Almaines, Corants, and Sarabands, Treble and Basse, for Viols or Violins ; " and in 1662, something similar ; John Jenkins, Davis Mell, and John Bannister being among the composers. John Jenkins, about 1660, published twelve sonatas for two violins and bass, with thorough bass for the organ, which are said to have been the first of the sort known in England. Matthew Lock and Henry Purcell both composed trios of the same description.

There appears to have been an improvement in the bow in this century. It was originally made of reed or some light and flexible wood, and in the earlier times was much curved, somewhat similar to our double-bass bow, and frequently of awkward make, with a strand of coarse hair rudely stretched between the two extremities. In the sixteenth century some improvement was made, and in the seventeenth it began to assume its present shape, and by means of a sort of metal band with teeth towards the handle of the bow, power was given to alter the tension of the hair. Tourte, of Paris, the first of this well-known family, is said to have introduced the screw and button. His son, who died in 1835, at an advanced age, made further improvements. It is stated that he began to make them with common wood from pipe-staffs and sugar barrels, and sold them for twenty or thirty sous each. Afterwards he discovered that Brazil wood was best adapted for the purpose, and latterly sold his best bows, ornamented with mother-of-pearl and gold, for as much as twelve louis, and those with ebony and silver, for three and a half louis ; whilst his common bows, without ornament, were sold for about thirty-six francs each. He is said to have invented the method of keeping the hair flat by means of a clasp or plate of metal or mother-of-pearl. His violin and tenor bows were about thirty inches long, and that for the violoncello about an inch shorter. Simpson, we may remember, gives twenty-seven inches as the length of the bow, and towards the end of this century the sonata bow, it is said, was only twenty-four inches, while the common bow was shorter still. The usual length now is about twenty-nine inches from the extreme point of the head to the end of the bow, without the screw ; leaving from twenty-five and a half to twenty-five and three quarter inches for the useable portion of the bow. Tartini caused an improvement in this as well as other things connected with the instrument. We need scarcely remind our readers that we have English makers of the bow, as Dodd, Panormo, and Tubbs, with others, who are surpassed by none.

The first of the Dodd family distinguished as a maker of bows was Edward Dodd, who was born at Sheffield, and died in Salisbury Court, Fleet Street, in 1810, at the great age, as it is stated, of 105 years. He left four sons, of whom three, John, James, and Thomas, were makers of bows; the fourth having been brought up to the medical profession. Of these, John, the eldest, is considered one of our best English makers, and his bows are much sought for. Most of them are rather short, but can easily be lengthened. He died at Richmond, where, and at Kew, he had resided for many years.

James Dodd, the eldest son of the above-named James Dodd, is now living, and supports the reputation of the family as a maker of good bows, and is also a musical-string coverer.

Louis Panormo was the son of Vincent Panormo, the instrument maker, and was himself a maker of guitars and violins. His bows were esteemed, but a lighter class is now generally preferred.

Of the family of Tubbs there are two generations still living, all excellent workmen. Thomas Tubbs, the elder of the family, died very recently, and might have vied with any workman living, especially if he could have obtained Brazil wood of fine quality for musical purposes.

CHAPTER XII.

IN 1717, the Corporation of Musicians in France had their privileges renewed under Louis XV. Lutes, violins, viols, and all wind or stringed instruments could only be made or played on by members of the Corporation, under penalty of 300 livres and forfeiture of the instruments. They were poor, however, as a body, and declared to the king that their poverty prevented them from paying the usual tribute at the time of the coronation.

Gerbert, in his valuable work " De Cantu," &c., says that stringed instruments were introduced into churches about the end of the seventeenth century, and that Campra was the first who brought them into use at Notre Dame, Paris; and they then only required two or three bass-viols or bass-violins for the continued basses, and as many violins for the preludes and ritornelles. Before this time the music in the chapel royal was confined to wind instruments. Laborde says the first masses in Italy with violins and basses, were about 1650. Tarquin Merula, master of the chapel at Bergamo, is named as one of the first musicians who introduced viols and violins into the church service in Italy, in aid of choral singing. There was great objection to their use at first, in the fear that it would tend to make the

sacred music too much like the secular; but Cornelius
Agrippa does not give a very flattering account of church
singing previous to their admission: "Non humanis vo-
cibus, sed belluinis strepitibus cantillent; dum hinniunt
discantum pueri, mugiunt alii tenorem, alii latrant con-
trapunctum, alii frendent altum, alii boant bassum, et
faciunt ut sonorum quidem plurimum audiatur, verbo-
rum et orationis intelligatur nihil."

Towards the middle of the eighteenth century, the
order of church music would appear to be somewhat reversed, as about 1749, Benedict XIV. refers to the use
of "violoni, violoncelli, fagotti, viole, et violini," in the
sacred services, whilst "i timpani, i corni da caccia, le
trombe, gli oboe, i flauti, i flautini, i salteri moderni,
i mandolini, & simili stromenti," were excluded. Fey-
joo, the Grand Master of the Benedictines in Spain, objected to violini, but allowed the violone called the basso,
arpa, cembalo, &c. At St. Paul's Cathedral, London,
about the time mentioned by Gerbert, there were only
four or eight voices, without any other musical instruments than the organ and the barbiton, e.g. fidiculare,
violoncello, theorba.

Laborde gives the composition of the orchestra of the
French opera in 1713, and also the salaries in livres, it
was the following:—

Un batteur de mesure . . .	1000
Petit chœur de dix	6000
Douze violons	4800
Huit basses	3200
Deux quintes	800
Deux tailles	800
Trois hautes-contres . . .	1200
Un tymbalier	150

In the year 1778, the proportions were changed, and

wind instruments introduced ; the salaries are not particularised, but the total is 69,482 livres. Un directeur, un adjoint, 24 violons, 7 flutes & hautbois, 2 clarinettes, 2 cors, 2 trompettes, 5 bassons, 6 alto, 10 basses, 4 contrebasses. The tymbales, trombones, tambourins, hautbois de foret, &c., were filled by some of the above.

The eloquent preacher, Bourdelot, was a performer on the violin, and there is an interesting anecdote of him in that capacity related by Spence. He was appointed to preach on Good-Friday, and the proper officer to attend him to church having arrived at his house, was directed to go to the study for him. As he approached he heard the sound of a violin, and the door being open a little way, saw Bourdelot stripped to his cassock playing a brisk tune on the instrument, and dancing about the room. He was much surprised, and knocked at the door, when the distinguished divine laid down his instrument, and putting on his gown, told the officer with his usual composed look that he was ready to attend him. On their way, his companion expressed to Bourdelot his surprise at what he had seen, who replied that he might be, unless made acquainted with his practice on these occasions. On thinking over the intended subject of his discourse, he found he was too depressed to treat it as he ought, and thus had recourse to his usual method—some music, with a little bodily exercise—and thus put himself into a proper frame of mind to enable him to go with pleasure to what would otherwise have been a work of pain and labour to him. It would be presumptuous in us even to hint at the adoption of such a course by any of our own spiritual pastors.

In the beginning of this century, Pere Tardieu de Tarascon is said to have introduced the violoncello as an accompaniment in the place of the viol da gamba, or

perhaps, more correctly confirmed it in the higher position of the two instruments, by means of his superior skill,
as the violoncello appears to have been used as an accompaniment before this time, and the viol da gamba did not
fall into disuse until afterwards.   He used five strings at
first, four of them tuned in fifths, and the first string a
fourth higher than the present; but in 1730 this was
suppressed, the instrument then remaining as the modern
violoncello.   John Sebastian Bach introduced an instrument he called the viola pomposa, in consequence, it is
said, of the heavy style of violoncello performers in his
time; a fifth string, E, was added, with the intention of
giving greater facility for the execution of the higher
passages ; this instrument, however, does not appear to
have been much used.   About the same time, Risch of
Weimar invented a keyed instrument, to imitate the
bass-viol, or viol da gamba ; it had gut strings, played
on by small wheels properly resined, which were put in
motion by a larger wheel.   De Knonow, of Haute-Lu-
sace, also made a kind of harpsichord, to be played on
with a bow; both these instruments followed the usual
fate of these inventions.   A gentleman near Leeds has
invented an instrument played on by keys, the notes
being produced from gut strings by friction.   At a moderate distance the sound is very good and quite orchestral,
but on nearer approach it becomes rather harsh.   It is,
however, capable of being subdued in tone, and the sound
can be increased or lessened by pressure, or management
of the keys.

In the Letters of Baron de Pollnitz, he mentions, in
1739, at Mersebourg, the residence of an enthusiastic
amateur, a Duke of Saxony, a large saloon filled with
bass-viols ; in the middle was one which reached to the
ceiling, and had a set of steps to mount to it; the most

powerful bass ever made. The duke himself executed some airs on a bass he called his favourite. The baron was told by one of the Court that the duke had quite a passion for these instruments, and that any one wanting a favour, made him a present of one. The giant bass was given to him by one who wished to be made a privy-councillor, and succeeded accordingly. It must have surpassed by far the great bass, of which we have formerly given an account, where a page was concealed in the body ; but appears to have been rivalled afterwards by a huge double-bass, mentioned by Gardiner in his gossiping book of Music and Friends : one made for a person called Martin, who kept a public-house. It was so large that it was necessary to cut a hole in the ceiling to let the neck through, so that in fact it was tuned in the room above the player ; the bow was in proportion. Boyce, a fine performer on the instrument, and a tall powerful man, went to see and try it, and with one stroke of his bow made it roar and vibrate so, as to shake the house.

In an unfinished treatise commenced by Louis Carré, who died in 1711, he mentions among the several instruments, the bass-viol, dessus de viole, archiviole, violin, poche, rebec, vielle (probably the hurdy-gurdy), and trumpet marine. Bonanni's curious "Gabinetto Armonico," 1722, abounds with representations of musical instruments, some rather fanciful, but still useful, to show the character of the instruments then in use. What he calls the viola, is like a very large violoncello, resting on the ground, with a very thick clumsy neck ; the performer is sitting down ; it has four strings, and no frets ; the bow much like that of the double-bass. The violone is like a large double-bass, with considerable inward curvatures ; there are but four strings in the representation, although there are six screws, and Bonanni says there are six strings ; it has also numerous frets. He mentions another instrument of the same class, invented by the Earl of Somerset, as referred to by Kircher, which had eight strings. The Latins, he says, called these instruments vitula, or vidula, or violla, whence the performers were called vitularii. The accordo (called by Mersennus lira moderna), to which we have before referred, was a still larger instrument, having twelve or fifteen strings, of which necessarily two or three were struck together ; it also had frets. The lintercolo, or sordino, was a small instrument of the fiddle kind, with four strings and no frets; it is of guitar shape, the neck appearing to be of one piece with the body, and with a detached finger-board. (Fig. 58.) One of his figures is a peasant riding on an ass, playing on a sort of guitar, like a banjoo with two strings ; the performer is evidently singing, and the ass joining with open mouth, forming an admirable trio. The monocordo

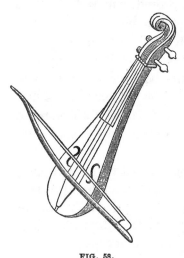

FIG. 58.

is something like a clumsy trumpet marine, having, in addition to the usual single string, one much shorter, extending about half the length of the instrument, but not nearly meeting the bridge. The tromba marina given by him, is contracted for the space of about a third of the length from the nut, so as to form a sort of finger-board, though of one piece with the rest of the front; it has one thick string the whole length, and a small bridge very near the bottom of the instrument; the bow is short and like that of the double-bass. Bonanni says, that by moving the thumb of the left hand in various places, tones are produced like those of a trumpet (probably harmonic notes) and that it was frequently used at sea to prevent the trouble of blowing, and hence was called the tromba marina. The violino represented by him is like a large clumsy tenor; he says the Latins called it cheles, or viola, and the Italians, viola, violino, or violone, &c., according to the size. The viola, or violino d'amore, is much of the same make and style, but larger. The violino Turchesco, used by the Turks, has a very long neck with frets, and only two strings; the body is nearly round and hollowed, and covered with parchment, it has neither bridge or sound-holes, but a long foot to support it on the ground. The Persians had a similar instrument they called Kamaantsich, in the Arab tongue Chemena. The violino Persiano is mentioned by Kempfer; it has four strings but no sound-holes, bridge, finger-board, or tail-piece. The violino de' Cafri has a small round body with a long neck, and only one string; without bridge, finger-board, or sound-holes, and played on with a short curved bow. An instrument of the same sort is found among the negroes and Indians, but not usually confined to one string. The representations of musical instruments in this work bear a very liberal interpretation, as he includes the whistle, the brass pan for bees, the rattle, the comb, and even the postilion's whip, with others equally simple.

Laborde, whose "Essai sur la Musique" was published in 1780, is very fanciful in many of his representations, introducing most poetical illustrations of some of the instruments in the hands of full-dressed ladies and gentlemen; but this is of far less consequence than the play of

imagination he has allowed in the adjuncts of several of
the ancient instruments.   He includes many that are in
Bonanni's work.   The contre-basse, he says, is much
larger than the violoncello, and is of three sorts.   One
with three strings, tuned according to his directions, G,
D, A, beginning from the lower string; one with four
strings, F, G, D, A, or G, D, G, C; and one with five
strings, E flat, A, D, G, C, or F, A, D, F sharp, A.
The quinte, or taille, or haute-contre de violon, was like
our modern tenor, having four strings, and tuned a fifth
below the violin.   The viole d'amour was a viol with
seven strings, larger than the violin, and of a softer tone.
The par-dessus de viole was of the same sort, with five
strings, and had frets, and was played on the knee.
Several other sorts of violes are mentioned, but then out
of use for a hundred years and more; as the viole de
Bordone, with forty-four strings (there was the sambuca
Lyncea, invented by Colonne, a Neapolitan, in the sixteenth century, which, it is said, had five hundred strings),
viole batarde, viole d'amour with metal strings, and viole
di braccio (from whence the German name bratsche, for
the tenor); also five sorts of violes, or violettes, differing
only in size; and the basse de viole, and le par-dessus,
then still in use.   He mentions the violon d'amour, then
obsolete, as he says, which had four metal strings placed
below the regular gut strings, and so tuned as to render
the harmonics, but produced confusion.   Also the viola
alto, or quinte, which seems to have been like the quinte
before named; it was sometimes called the violette, and
Stamitz, the son of the distinguished musician of that
name, was a fine performer on it.   The description and
fingering of the violoncello in his work were written by
Nochet, a fine performer on the instrument at that time,
and a pupil of Cervetto.   Laborde also gives a figure of
the poche, or sourdine, or kit.

There were several fine performers during this century, but with some few remarkable exceptions, this must be taken with reference to the state of practical music at the time ; as probably many members of an accomplished orchestra of the present day could have successfully competed with the greatest names on record of these times. In the present chapter we shall confine ourselves to a few Continental celebrities, and in referring to them we may mention some anecdotes known to many of our readers, but we thought our subject would be made more complete by venturing to introduce them, and we will refer to Mr. Dubourg's interesting work on the violin for many others. With respect to the extent of the usual practical skill of the early part of the century, we may state that John Lenton, in 1702, published an instructor for the violin, wherein there are no directions given for the shift ; though, as he gives the scale up to C on the second leger line, it must have been occasionally in use. He objects to the instrument being held under the chin, or so low as the girdle, in imitation of the Italians ; it is to be presumed, therefore, that he intended it should be placed upon the breast.

We may claim the great Pergolesi as a violin player, that having been his principal instrument, but one of the best known names, probably, is Tartini, who was born in 1692, and was skilled in the theory as well as the practice of music, and his method, as it is called, is still esteemed : the story of the Devil's Sonata is too well known to be repeated here. Amongst his best pupils were Pagin, Lahoussaye, and Nardini, whom Burney, in his " Musical Tour," names as the completest player on the violin in all Italy. Gavinies, who was born in 1726, had great execution, and was particularly skilful in accompanying the voice ; he is considered the founder of the French school of the violin. Ferrari, another pupil of Tartini, is stated to have been the first who introduced the harmonics, and passages in octaves. Locatelli, born in 1693, a pupil of Corelli, had more caprice of hand and fancy than any of his time, and is said to have made use of some of the effects afterwards reproduced by Paganini. Guignon, the last " roi des violons," who taught the Dauphin, the father of Louis XV, was also a distinguished performer in this age. Pugnani, born in 1727, another pupil of Tartini, and who was teacher of Viotti, was an absent and eccentric man : once, when playing a cadence before a large audience, he quite forgot himself, and walked about in the middle of the room till he had finished it, quite unconscious that he was not alone. On another occasion, being somewhat at a loss in a cadence, he said to a friend near him, " Pray that I may get safely back." Olivieri, a pupil of his, born at Turin in 1757, was a fine performer, but obliged to leave the theatre there in consequence of the following sforzando passage. He was in the habit of attending the concerts of a gentleman attached to the Court, but arriving one day rather late, the courtier abused him so that at length Olivieri, who was tuning his violin, lost his temper, and broke his instrument on the head of his astonished patron. Veracini, a Florentine, born about 1685, was a fine player, but excessively vain. A trick was once played on him by Pisendel, the leader of the orchestra at Dresden, for the purpose of mortifying him. He taught an inferior player in the chapel a concerto for the instrument till he became perfect in it ; he then showed it to Veracini, who played it, but was immediately surpassed in it by the subordinate player. He was so vexed that it is said he threw himself out of window three days afterwards, but fortunately escaped with only a broken leg. On his recovery he went to Prague, and afterwards, in 1714, to London. He had two fine Jacob Steiner violins, which he called St. Peter and St. Paul, and affirmed that they surpassed all the best instruments of Italy. He was shipwrecked on his way to France, and thus lost these treasures. Haranc, born at Paris 1738, was a great player; it is said that he began the instrument at the age of three, and at six could play the most difficult music at sight. Benda, born in Bohemia 1709, is considered the founder of a violin school in Germany. A violin player called Bohdanswicz, is mentioned in the latter part of this century, who had eight children all musical, and he seems to have endeavoured to attract audiences by numerous strange contrivances; for instance, at Vienna he advertised for a concert a sonata for one violin, to be performed by three persons with twelve fingers and three bows; and an andantino, to be played by his four daughters on one pianoforte, with eight hands and forty fingers. Scheller, about the same time, first produced the performance on the four strings together, unscrewing the bow for the purpose. Rolla, born at Paris in 1757, and who died at Milan as recently as 1837, was a distinguished player and a fine composer for the instrument; he was also one of the finest tenor players in the world, but it is said that his performance so affected the nerves of females that he was forbidden to play this instrument in public: this seems a strange restriction. A performer called Leprince certainly turned his talents to better account, for on his passage from Holland to Petersburgh, having been taken prisoner by an English privateer, he played so cheerfully to the sailors that they gave him his liberty, and restored all his property. Diana, born at Cremona about 1770, was a great player, and applied to Rolla to give him instructions, which he declined, say-

ing he required none. Diana was angry at this, and
resolved to be revenged, and as Rolla was preparing a
concerto for some approaching ceremony, he watched
him closely when he was practising, and thus learned
his best passages. Three days before the intended performance, Diana gave notice that he was going to play
in the church, as was then the custom in Italy. Professors and amateurs flocked to hear him, and among
them Rolla; when, what was his surprise and annoyance, to hear all the best subjects and passages he had
been so carefully studying, played off by Diana as his
own.

Jarnovick, or Giornovick, born at Palermo in 1745,
was another fine performer, though it is said somewhat
deficient in tone. There was, however, no deficiency in
his self-estimation. "My dear Viotti," says he on one
occasion, "it must be admitted that only we two know
how to play on the violin." He was of dissipated habits,
and irritable temper; on one occasion he quarrelled with
St. George, the celebrated fencer, who was also a fine
violinist, and struck him, when St. George with great
moderation told him he admired his talent too much to
fight with him. He once advertised a concert at Lyons,
with six francs for admission, but nobody came. He
was irritated, and adjourned it till the next day, reducing
the price to three francs, and a crowd of people consequently came. After waiting for some time it was
found he had left the place, no doubt taking the money
with him. Another anecdote is told of his breaking a
pane of glass in the shop of Bailleux, the music-seller,
for which he was required to pay thirty sous; he offered
three francs, but Bailleux having no change, Jarnovick
said, Never mind, and breaking another pane, added, We
are quits now. Kreutzer, born at Versailles 1766, was

distinguished as a performer and composer for the instrument.

Many performers towards the end of this century belonged equally to the former part of our present century, and will be mentioned in a future chapter; but we may name Baillot, who was born near Paris in 1771, and is known not only as one of the finest French players on the violin, but as the author of one of the best set of instructions for the instrument. Bonazzi, a clever player, who died in 1802, may be noticed from his having left a collection of not less than one thousand concertos, quintetts, and quartetts, by different composers, together with forty-two violins, by Stradiuarius, Guarnerius, Amati, and other great masters, of the estimated value of 6500 ducats.

In the early part of the century, Forqueray, born at Paris in 1700, was the most skilful performer on the bass-viol of his time, as his father had been previously. Hawkins mentions Francheville as a fine performer on the viol da gamba at the Castle concerts; while at a later date Charles Franz, born 1738, and Antoine Lidl, are named as distinguished players on the baritone, or violoncelle d'amour. Franceschelli, in the early part of the century, was an excellent performer not only on the bass-viol, but on the violoncello, and was particularly admired for the manner in which he played the violoncello parts of Scarlatti's cantatas, which were so good that none but superior players could do them justice. Marc Antoine Bononcini, about the same time, was a fine performer, and is said to have been one of the first to show the capabilities of the instrument, and to make it sing, if we may use the expression. Giovanni Bononcini, the opponent of Handel, was also a good performer. The fine performance of two brothers called Saint-Sevin, known also by the name of Labbé, about 1730, contributed much to the establishment of the violoncello, and the disuse of the viol da gamba. Bigati was celebrated for his style of accompaniment, and his improvising. Playing once at the church of Avignon, and accompanying Dubrieul, they sought to outdo each other, in consequence of Boccherini being present. One of the assistants in the church was a purblind canon, whose little dog had followed him in, but had twice been turned out by his master. On returning after the second expulsion of the animal, the canon saw something in the shade, moving backwards and forwards, which he took for granted was the tail of his intractable dog, instead of being in any way connected with the tail-piece of a violoncello ; so he gave a heedless but vigorous kick, and struck not the poor beast, but Bigati's instrument, which, with the unlucky canon, Bigati, and Dubrieul, all came down together, to the great dismay of the attentive but now astonished congregation.

Bertaud, who died in 1756, by his skill added much to the reputation of the violoncello, and may be considered the founder of the French school. Amongst other pupils he had the two Duports, both excellent players, with fine tone and execution, of whom the eldest, Jean Pierre, born at Paris in 1741, was one of the most skilful performers of his age ; he died in 1818 ; and his brother, Jean Louis, born in 1749, in 1819 ; he has left a valuable work on the fingering of the instrument. The two Jansons were fine players about the same time. One of the Jansons was in London in 1772, and is mentioned as a pupil of Duport in one of the publications of the day (the "Theatrical Review"), "his taste and execution is very astonishing, we cannot give him the preference of his master." On two nights one of the Duports also played solos, "this gentleman's execution is truly masterly, his tone very brilliant, and his taste pleasingly delicate and chaste." Burney, in his "Tour," mentions the famous old Antonio Vandini,. and observes that the Continental violoncello is still played with the bow underhanded. Louis Boccherini, who was born in 1740, excelled not only as a performer, but also in his numerous compositions, where the instrument takes a leading or prominent part, many of which remained popular until a recent period, although now seldom heard; he died in Spain, 1806, with, it is to be feared, very reduced means of subsistence. Baudiot, a skilful performer, wrote instructions for the instrument; Tricklir, born at Dijon 1750, was a fine performer; and Levasseur is said to have nearly equalled the Duports in tone. Bernard Romberg, born about 1770, was an excellent performer, and composed some good music for the instrument; he also wrote an elementary book for the instrument of considerable size, which scarcely realised the expectations raised by the work of so accomplished a musician. His brother Andrew was a good performer, and well known as a pleasing composer. Max Bohrer was also a distinguished performer, and had a brother a fine player on the violin. Fetis says that Duport and Lindley are the only persons that France and England can oppose to the two German players on the violoncello just named.

We have omitted several names of fine performers of Continental birth, such as Geminiani, Giardini, and others, because so great a part of their lives was spent in England, that it seems more convenient to join them with the English names, but without the least wish to claim for ourselves merit that may in strictness belong to other countries.

CHAPTER XIII.

THE bass-viol was still occasionally practised by ladies in England in the eighteenth century (indeed we have known lady performers on the violoncello at the present time). In Vanbrugh's "Relapse," it is said of one, "the parson of the parish teaches her to play on the bass-viol, the clerk to sing, her nurse to dress, and her father to dance." In "The Levellers," a dialogue between two young ladies concerning matrimony, 1703, Politica, a tradesman's daughter, describing her education at a boarding school, says she "learned to sing, to play on the bass-viol, virginals, spinnet, and guitar."

The first opera on the English stage was " Arsinoe," set to music by Thomas Clayton, and performed at Drury Lane in 1707. William Corbet was the leader, but we do not know of what instruments the orchestra was composed. Corbet, who was a fine player, advertised for sale, " Stainers' Cremona violins and bases, with the four celebrated violins of Corelli, Gobbo, Torelli, and Nic. Cosimi;" he left his best instruments to Gresham College, and 10*l.* a-year for the care of them.

Concerts now became frequent, gradually increasing in merit, until the establishment of the professional concerts in the latter part of the century, the Ancient Concerts, the Philharmonic, now of half a century standing, and so down to the Musical Society of London, which, if it carries out the regulations on which it is founded, promises to advance the science, to the improvement and advantage of the amateur and the professor; and nothing can be more finished than the performance of the accomplished orchestra under its very skilful conductor Mr. Alfred Mellon. At one of the earlier concerts in 1722, the celebrated Carbonelli played no less than two concertos, and one solo; while a concerto on the bass-violin was played by a performer called Pippo.

The component parts of an orchestra, even towards the end of the last century, were very different from those at present; several instruments, indeed, now in use, were then unknown. For instance, in 1789, the orchestra at the Academy of Ancient Music, consisted of 1 organ, 14 violins, Barthelemon being the first; 4 violas, 3 hautboys, 2 trumpets, 2 horns, 1 drum, 4 violoncellos, 2 double-basses, and 3 bassoons. Let us put in contrast the orchestra of the Musical Society of London on 28th January, 1863; for although the numbers are double, the proportions of the instruments can be readily seen. Mr. Alfred Mellon conductor; 16 first violins, Blagrove and Sainton principals; 16 second violins, William Watson principal; 10 violas, R. Blagrove and Webb principals; 10 violoncellos, Paque principal; 9 double-basses, Howell principal; 2 flutes, 1 piccolo, 2 oboes, 2 clarionets, 2 bassoons, 4 horns, 2 trumpets, 3 trombones, 1 ophicleide, 2 cornets, 1 drum, 1 bass-drum and cymbals, 1 side-drum, 1 triangle, 2 harps. The band of the Royal Italian Opera, Covent Garden, for 1862, which is not to be surpassed, consisted of Signor Costa conductor; 16 first violins, Sainton principal; 16 second violins, Willey principal; 10 violas, Doyle principal; 11 violoncellos, Lucas principal; 11 double-basses, Howell principal;

2 harps, 2 flutes, 2 oboes, 2 clarionets, 2 bassoons, 4 horns, 2 trumpets, 3 trombones, 1 ophicleide, 1 drum, 1 triangle, and 1 bass-drum.

In the celebrated Musical Festival in Westminster Abbey, in 1786, there were 1 organ, 106 violins, the elder Cramer being the leader, 32 violas, 28 oboes, 6 flutes, 19 violoncellos, Crosdill and Cervetto being the principals, 34 bassoons, 1 double-bassoon, 13 double-basses, 14 trumpets, 12 horns, 6 trombones, 1 drum, and 2 double drums.

The Handel Festival at the Crystal Palace in 1862, according to the announcement, comprised in the orchestra no less than 194 violins, 75 violas, 75 violoncellos, and 75 double-basses, with 86 wind and other instruments. The chorus consisted of the extraordinary number of 3120 singers, the whole under the control of that distinguished conductor Signor Costa.

The band for Handel's "Water Music," 1715, was composed, according to the valuable life of him by Mr. Schœlcher, of 4 violins, 1 viol, 1 violoncello, 1 counter-bass, 2 hautboys, 2 bassoons, 2 French horns, 2 flageolets, 1 flute, and 1 trumpet. In "Julius Cæsar," 1723, he used in the orchestra, flutes, hautboys, bassoons, trumpets, a harp, a viola da gamba, a theorbo, kettle-drums, and four horns, besides what is called the quatuor of stringed instruments, the first and second violins, the viola or tenor, the violoncello, and double-bass. In his hautbois concertos, opera 3rd, 1734, there are compositions for 2 violins, 2 hautboys, 2 flutes, 2 viols, 2 bassoons, 2 violoncellos, and a thorough-bass. Many of his airs have a simple accompaniment for the violoncello with harpsichord. In some of his accompaniments the violette is mentioned, a name we have already noticed as a variety of the viol, but an air in "Orlando," 1732, is accompanied by " 2 violette marine con violoncelli pizzicati." This violetta marina is said to have been introduced in the same year by Castrucci; Burney calls it a kind of viol d'amour with sympathetic strings, and the air in "Orlando" is the only one written for it, so it is to be presumed there were some objections to its use.

Corbet was succeeded as leader of the opera orchestra by Castrucci, born at Rome about 1690, a pupil of Corelli; who is said to have been the original of Hogarth's enraged musician, though Trusler names another. He was difficult to manage, and was superseded by John Clegg, a very fine player, who became insane from over-study, and it was the fashion to go to Bedlam to hear him play. Clegg was born in 1714, and played concertos in public at the age of nine. Castrucci died in 1769, in reduced circumstances. Many instances have occurred in all professions, of the mind giving way from the effect of over-study or undue excitement, but Passenans, in " La Russie et l'Esclavage," gives a melancholy example of the pressure of arbitrary tyranny on over-wrought and sensitive nerves, inducing a fit of passion and resistance, which may be considered as a case of temporary insanity. A Russian noble, having a serf who showed great musical talent, sent him to Italy to study; he much distinguished himself there, and in due time was ordered home by his master. He was one day summoned to play before a numerous assembly, and when any new person of rank arrived, he had to recommence a brilliant concerto of Viotti. Worn out at length by three hours of this work, he asked to be allowed a little rest, when his brutal proprietor replied, " No, play on, and if you are capricious, mind that you are my slave, and that I can have you bastinadoed." The unfortunate young man ran down to the kitchen in despair, and cut off the first finger of his left hand with a hatchet, saying, " Cursed be the talent that will not place me beyond the treatment of a slave."

The reputation of Geminiani, born at Lucca about 1680, though some give an earlier date, a pupil of Lunati (Il Gobbo), is well established, not only for his skill as a player, but for his arrangement of Corelli's music, and his own concertos; he came over to England in 1714, and died in Dublin in 1762, in the house of his friend and pupil, Matthew Dubourg. Dubourg, who was born in 1703, was a fine player; and when a child played solos at Britton's concerts. It is of him the story is told of playing a cadence once before Handel, when he seemed rather undecided towards the close, but having safely finished, Handel exclaimed, " You are welcome home, Monsieur Dubourg." Mrs. Delaney speaks in high terms of him: after hearing the music in honour of St. Cecilia at the Crown Tavern, she writes in a letter dated the 11th of Nov. 1727, " Dubourg was the first fiddle, and every body says he exceeds all the Italians, even his master Geminiani." Carbonelli, a pupil of Corelli, who came over to England in 1720, was leader of the opera band for a time, but is probably best known as the founder of the celebrated wine establishment bearing his name; he died in 1772.

Felix Giardini, born at Turin, 1716, was a pupil of Somis, a fine player, Corelli's best pupil, and one of the great masters of his time. He came to England about 1749, and remained 35 years, leading at the opera during part of the time. He was celebrated as a solo player, and particularly excelled in an adagio, and was remarkable also for the volume of tone he produced. He had amassed a fortune, but unfortunately lost it, as many others have done, by undertaking the management of the opera, in which he was joined by Mingotti. He afterwards went to Russia, and died at Moscow, in very reduced circumstances, in 1796. Michael Christian Festing, a German, resided in London about the middle of the century; he was a fine performer, but may be more particularly mentioned with honour as one of the founders of the Royal Society of Musicians. Richard Charke, a dissipated fellow, who married Charlotte, the daughter of Colley Cibber, is said to be the first who composed medley overtures. He treated his wife ill, like a beast, or rather worse, for the animal creation does not indulge, generally, in these abominable practices, except, perhaps, the gigantic salamander, and the spider, and a few others; indeed, as to the spider, it is the lady who is in fault, but at the same time she makes her spouse useful, for when any domestic disturbances arise, she occasionally eats him. Poor Mrs. Charke lived at one time in a state of great penury, and there is an account of her life extant. Barthelemon, born at Bordeaux in 1741, was the leader of the opera band for several years, and was employed by Garrick. He is said to have excelled in the performance of Corelli's solos; he died in London in 1808.

The celebrated Viotti will be still remembered by some of our readers, for the vigour of his style and the purity of his tone, and his music is still highly esteemed. He was born in Piedmont about the middle of the century, and was the pupil of Pugnani. He came to London about 1792, and succeeded W. Cramer as leader at the opera. Viotti possessed considerable talent independent of his profession, but was also of a somewhat violent and decided disposition, and in 1798, when republican principles were rife, was sent out of the country for some real or supposed political offence, but was allowed to return in 1801; and died in London in 1824. There were several firstrate performers amongst his pupils, most of whom more

properly belong to the present century, as Rode, who was
also a good writer, Labarre, Libon, Mori, whose brilliant
execution is familiar to many, and Pinto, who was an extraordinary performer, but died from the effects of dissi-
pation in 1808, in his 21st year.   William Cramer, just
mentioned, was born at Manheim in 1745, and besides
having been for some time leader of the opera band, was
the leader, as before mentioned, at the Handel Com-
memoration in 1787.   He was the father of J. B. Cramer,
one of the first pianists of his time, and F. Cramer, the
well known violin player, and leader at the Ancient
Concerts, and others.

As we have before intimated, some names now omitted,
will be mentioned as of the present century, although they
belong in fact to both ; but as the well known Jean Pierre
Salomon was born at Bonn as far back as 1745, we will
introduce him here.   He came to England in 1781, and
in 1791 was first violin at the Academy of Ancient
Music, and played concertos; and at the same time we
find Master Bridgetower, distinguished afterwards as a
good player, playing a concerto on the violin.   Salomon
was not only celebrated as a performer on the violin,
particularly as a quartett player, but also had considerable
general knowledge and ability, and to him we are indebted
for the introduction to the musical world of the celebrated
twelve grand symphonies of Haydn, all of which were
written expressly for his concerts.   He continued for
many years the leader of various concerts at the Hanover
Square Rooms, and was also the leader, with a host of
first-rate talent assisting him, on the opening night of the
Philharmonic Concerts, fifty years since.   His instrument
had been formerly Corelli's.

The finest performer on the viol da gamba in England,
about the middle of the century, was Charles Frederick

Abel, a German, born in 1719, who came over in 1759. He was one of the greatest performers on the instrument ever known, particularly in the performance of slow movements, which seem best to suit the character of the instrument. On the formation of Queen Charlotte's band, he was made chamber-musician, with a salary of 200*l.* per annum. He died in 1787. Dahmen about this time was a fine performer on the same instrument, as well as on the violoncello.

The elder Cervetto, whose Christian name it appears from the registry of his burial was Jacob, was born in Italy in 1682, came to London in 1728, and passed the remainder of his long life in England, his death not taking place until the year 1783. He brought the violoncello into favour by his great skill and taste, but his tone is said to have been hard. He is the musician who roused Garrick's wrath by yawning aloud in the middle of one of that great actor's pathetic speeches, which he had probably heard twenty times before ; but adroitly excused himself, by saying he always yawned when he was pleased. Caporale was a rival of Cervetto, but does not appear to have equalled him. He was permanently attached to Handel's orchestra, as were Clegg and Dubourg ; and he, with the elder Cervetto, Ravenscroft, and Festing, as before mentioned, were among the first subscribers to the Musical Fund, afterwards the Royal Society of Musicians. The younger Cervetto, who was called James, was born about 1747, and excelled his father both in style and tone, which was particularly sweet, and his expression very fine. He, like his father, lived to a great age, and died in February, 1837 ; he had, however, retired from the profession some time previously. John Crosdill, born in London in 1755, went to Paris from 1775 to 1780. He was the first performer on the violon-

cello of his time, his tone especially was remarkably fine
and powerful, and Mr. Parke, in his " Musical Memoirs,"
mentions having heard him play the favourite minuet in
" Ariadne," in three parts, as distinctly and perfectly as if
they had been performed by three of the most distinguished
players.   He retired in 1794, having ample means.
John George Christopher Schetky, born near Frankfort-
on-the-Maine, about the year 1740, of good family, was
originally intended for the law, and was sent to the University of Jena, but did not prosecute the study, and in
the course of the Seven Years' War, under Frederick the
Great, from 1756 to 1763 served as a volunteer, and the
celebrated Blucher was the captain of his company.
Being passionately fond of music, he followed the bent of
his inclination, and studied both theoretically and prac-
tically under Emanuel Bach, and also under Schrœder
for the pianoforte.   The violoncello being his favourite
instrument, he took some lessons from Abel (the celebrated
performer on the viol da gamba), under whom he soon
became a proficient.   After travelling for several years
in Germany and France, he determined to visit England,
wishing to be present at the coronation of George the
Third, but was prevented by illness.   However, he arrived
soon afterwards in London, and not intending to settle
there, was about to return to Germany, when he obtained
an engagement as first violoncellist for the Edinburgh
Saint Cecilia Concerts, which were then of great repute.
They were very aristocratic, many amateurs of rank and
station being members, including several of the nobility,
and men eminent in the learned professions.   The leading professors were also of first-rate talent.   These concerts flourished until the Peace of Amiens, when the fa-
cilities given for travelling on the Continent induced many
people of station to go abroad, and they were thus broken

up. In the mean time Mr. Schetky had married, and remained at Edinburgh following his profession, where his talent, polished manners, and generous character caused him to associate with the best society, and he was on intimate terms with many of the distinguished literary characters of his time, and he died there at an advanced age in the year 1824. He was particularly admired for his fine adagio playing, and the delicate expression of the cantabile ; his own compositions are pleasing, particularly some of his pathetic passages, and one of the last pieces that Lindley played with a friend, after his retirement, was one of Schetky's duetts. John Christian Schetky, Esq., the present well known and accomplished marine painter to the Queen, is his son, and possesses a genuine taste and feeling for music.

In 1783 Joseph Kœmpfer came over here. He was an extraordinary performer on the double-bass, playing difficult violin passages on it, and particularly excelled in the use of the harmonics. He also invented a most useful variety of the instrument, which could be taken to pieces for the convenience of travelling. He was eclipsed, as all others were, by that giant in power and talent, Dragonetti, whom we shall mention in the ensuing chapter.

CHAPTER XIV.

IN the present century, the instruments of the violin class have been perfectly established, the viol class being now obsolete, except as matters of curiosity. But with all our advances in practical skill, we have been unable to improve on the models known three hundred years since, unless it may be in some of the minor details. Some experiments were made in France for the purpose, as was considered, of improving the shape and tone of the violin. Chanot, an officer in the French army, and the son, it is said, of the violin-maker Chagniot, proposed to make the violin of a flatter model, with the sides less curved inwards, the sound-holes straighter, and the bar in the centre of the upper vibrating plate; in fact, something in shape like the old viol, or modern guitar. It was submitted to a committee of the French Academy in 1817, who, after three trials, decided in its favour, considering the tone to be of superior quality, and not inferior, indeed, to the Italian instruments. It was not, however, brought into use, and it was found, after a time, that the tone did not last. Baud, a maker at Versailles, submitted to the Institute in 1810 a violin without bars, which he fancied interfered with the vibrations; however, the report of the Institute was not favourable. In 1819 Felix Savart, M.D., published " Mémoire sur la Construction des Instrumens à Cordes et à Archet," in which he describes a new form of violin, invented by him, on strictly scientific principles, explaining his reasons at length. The shape was a trapezium, not raised or arched, the sound-holes straight, with some other peculiarities in the details. A favourable report of it was made by a select committee, to the Académies des Sciences and des Beaux-Arts, but the instrument did not get into use.

The nineteenth century has produced many performers of first-rate talent and celebrity. In some cases, perhaps, the execution of mere mechanical difficulties has been too much relied on, but in many others, exquisite taste and expression have been joined to the most finished execution; and solo and quartett playing, with orchestral music of the highest class, may now be heard, not only at select concerts, such as the Musical Society of London, the two Philharmonic Societies, and the Musical Union, with its choice chamber-music, but at those more accessible to the general body of society, who by its extensive patronage shows how truly it appreciates the excellent music presented to it. Progress in music has fully kept pace with the progress in society. As we have before observed, several of the performers now about to be named were also known in the last century, but the greater part of their career was in the present. Among them are Yaniewicz, a Pole, distinguished for his pure tone; and Vaccari, born at Modena in 1773, whose tone was particularly sweet, with great expression. Kiesewetter, born in 1777, had great power with taste and expression; he died, unfortunately, soon after attending the Leicester Festival in 1824. He was so ill during the performance as to require to be supported to his chair; and afterwards went on to Norwich, but was too ill to play there, and died soon after his return. The committee

very properly paid him his stipulated sum, and a subscription was made for him at Leicester. Lafont, born
in Paris 1781, had a good tone, and fine taste ; he commenced playing in public at the age of fourteen. Habeneck,
born at Mézières in the same year, led the opera at Paris for
a considerable time. Louis Sphor, born at Saesen in
Brunswick, about 1784, and only recently dead, was celebrated not only as a fine performer, with finished execution and expression, but also as a great composer, with
a perfect knowledge of the theory of music ; his compositions are, of course, well known to and admired by our
readers. At the same time was born at Gênes the
greatest performer on the violin that ever lived, Nicholas
Paganini. So much has been said of him, and so much is
known, that a slight notice here will suffice. Those who
were fortunate enough to see and hear him will never forget
the impression produced by his strange, almost unearthly
figure, when, advancing to the front of the orchestra, he
seized his violin as if it were a cherished living creature,
and then, with his marvellous bow, and wonderful fingers,
produced such an extraordinary effect from his beautiful
tone, double stops, pizzicatos, and harmonics, on which
long and rapid passages were played, that his auditors
became breathless with astonishment. No doubt his extraordinary style of play has tended to advance the character and power of the instrument, and as professors of
talent studied the passages introduced by him, a higher
scale of eminence was established, and the great powers
of execution of some of our accomplished modern performers may originate from the time of Paganini. He
began the instrument at the age of six, and after a time
was placed under the tuition of Giacomo Costa, the director of the opera at Gênes ; he was then placed under
the excellent player Alexander Rolla. In 1805 he was

director of the orchestra of the Princess Eliza, sister of Napoleon, and afterwards Grand Duchess of Tuscany. While with her he played one evening a solo on the third and fourth strings of his fiddle, and in 1810 played variations on the fourth string alone, which he performed in public for the first time at Parma, on the 16th of August, 1811. He is said to have written his first sonata at the age of eight, and many of his compositions contained such difficulties, that for some time they were considered insuperable. He died at Nice in 1840. Mayseder, born at Vienna in 1789, is known as a good writer, as well as a fine performer, and Festa is another good writer for the instrument. Joseph Reicha, born in Prague 1746, was a good player, and Artot, a Belgian, a most finished performer, died at the early age of 30, in 1845. There are so many excellent performers now constantly before the public, that it would be presumptuous in us to give any opinion on their relative merits, which would be out of our province; and therefore we will follow the example of the account given of the brave Gyges, and the brave Cloanthus, and their companions, by Virgil, and name De Beriot, born in 1802, skilled equally as a writer and a performer, and with taste and volume of tone excelled by none; Ole Bull, the distinguished Norwegian, Ernst, Sivori, Vieuxtemps, Lotto, and Wienawski, all of first-rate talent, to whom others are from time to time, by their skill, entitling themselves to be added; but we must particularly name Herr Joachim, whose tone, taste, and execution are unrivalled in every style. We shall name some other foreign players among those of England, as being, in fact, naturalized amongst us.

As finished players on the violoncello on the Continent, Arnold Schoenebeck, Muntzberger, Danzi, and Hus-Desforges, wrote and adapted many pieces of music for

the instrument, but their tone was not equal to their facility of execution.   Kummer was a good writer as well
as player.   Aubert, Breval, and Raoul all published instructions for the instrument.   Lamare is mentioned as a
fine quartett player; Ganz has an excellent tone; and
Servais and Franchomme great execution.   As a double-
bass player, Bottesini probably excels in execution any
previous performer; it is indeed marvellous, and the facility with which he plays passages on double stops and
harmonics must be heard to be fully appreciated.   His
tone is clear and mellow as a trumpet, but has not the
wonderful power and vigour of Dragonetti's; and indeed
his instrument is of a smaller make than that of his great
predecessor.

Amongst the English players of this time, Richard
Cudmore, born at Chichester in 1787, was a fine performer
not only on the violin, but on the violoncello and pianoforte; at one concert he played a concerto on the violin
by Rode, one by Cervetto on the violoncello, and one by
Kalkbrenner on the pianoforte.   Thomas Cooke had
great musical talent, both vocal and instrumental, and
played in concert at the early age of five.   He was occasionally first violin at the Philharmonic Concerts, and
was for a time the principal singer at one of the theatres;
he also composed several popular glees.   At a benefit
about 1823, he played solos on nine different instruments.
One of the writers can speak of him as a kind friend of
many years' standing.   Charles Weichsel, for many years
the distinguished leader at the opera, played in public
also at the age of seven.   Spagnoletti will also be remembered at the opera, and Venua, who for a time led the
ballet, was very skilful as a quartett player.   Many others
of first-rate talent might be mentioned, and Blagrove,
with his finished execution and perfect intonation, stands

unrivalled as an English performer; while Carrodus has
recently established his claim to stand in the first rank in
the profession, and Sainton is now so domesticated with
us, that we have placed him here instead of among the
foreign players, and his skill and taste, not to be excelled
in quartett or solo playing, are fully appreciated and admired by all lovers of music. Molique also may be considered as naturalized, distinguished alike for his theoretical as well as his practical talents. Moralt and Hill
will be remembered as most skilful players on the tenor.
Powell, Charles Ashley, and Crouch, together with
Reinagle of Oxford, were among the leading performers
on the violoncello, in the beginning of this century, and
to the time of their respective deaths; but the unrivalled
performer Robert Lindley stands alone as the master of
this difficult instrument, whether from the grandeur and
power of his tone, or the brilliancy of his execution;
playing on strings of such size that can alone produce
such body of sound, but which now unluckily are generally
discarded in consequence of the greater facility afforded
to the player by those of smaller size. He was born at
Rotherham in Yorkshire, on the 4th of March, 1775, and
showed his genius for music at a very early age, and, indeed, at the age of nine years played the violoncello in
the Brighton and Lewes theatres; his brothers John and
Charles being also in the orchestra. When he was of
the age of twelve, he and his brothers, as violin and tenor,
were frequently sent for when at Brighton, to play before
the Prince of Wales, and at that time he could play all
the usual solos or concertos for the violoncello. At the age
of fifteen he commenced writing music for himself, and was
anxious to get engaged at some of the professional concerts,
but could not succeed until the following year, when on
the morning of the second concert, the professor who was

to have performed a solo on the violoncello was suddenly
taken ill, and the directors in this emergency sent to
Lindley's father, to say that his son might play in the
evening as a favour.   He eagerly embraced the opportunity, and played a concerto in such an admirable style,
that he was rapturously encored.   On the following
morning, two of the directors called, requesting him as a
favour to play at the next concert, when he was again encored ; and he played concertos at the nine subsequent
concerts, and was encored on every occasion, thus reaching the top of his profession at the age of sixteen, and
there remained unrivalled for the next sixty years, universally respected for his talent and integrity.   At the
time of his joining the professional concerts he was a
pupil of the younger Cervetto, with whose approbation,
at the age of eighteen, he took the place of first violoncello
at the King's Theatre on the retirement of Sperate, where,
and at the Italian Opera, which he joined on its opening,
he remained for fifty-eight years, thus exceeding the time of
Theobaldo Gatti, who died in 1727, and was for fifty-two
years principal bass-viol in the French theatre.   Soon
after Lindley joined the opera orchestra, Bernard
Romberg came over to England, and Crosdill invited
him to a music party at Mr. Thompson's, where he lived,
and which was usually given after the rehearsals of the
Ancient Concerts, on Mondays during the season. Lindley
and a large party of professors and amateurs were also
present, and Romberg played many of his difficult compositions for the instrument in fine style, and with much
execution.   When the party broke up, Crosdill said to
Lindley, who he knew was going to play a concerto that
evening at a concert where Salomon, a friend of Romberg,
was to lead, " They have heard Romberg ; now, Lindley,
let them hear what an Englishman can do."   In the

evening Lindley played one of his most difficult concertos, containing passages with double stops, octaves,
and even tenths, which his large and powerful hand
enabled him to play readily; the applause, when he had
finished, was very great.   At the end of the first act,
Salomon asked Romberg, who had been standing opposite to Lindley during his performance, what he thought
of it.   Romberg replied, " He is the devil !"   With reference to his power of reading at first sight, it may be
related that when he was a young man he was at a music
party at Clement's Inn, when copies of Romberg's first
four concertos for the violoncello were produced, which
had only arrived the same morning from the Continent.
Lindley played the whole of these without the slightest
hesitation or difficulty.

The beauty of his tone, and extraordinary power of
execution, his skill in accompanying, especially in the
few but effective notes in a recitative, will be in the
recollection of a great part of our readers. 'A friendship of very many years' standing down to the day of his
death, will, we hope, prove our excuse for dwelling a
little on the subject; indeed, one of the writers was the
last with whom he ever played: stopping then, in the
middle of a duett, like Haydn in his unfinished quartett,
and saying, " I can no more," and he never again played
on the instrument.

He would sometimes in private take the first violin
part of a quartett, not only on the violoncello, but when
with a few friends would do so on the violin, imitating,
good-humouredly, some of the leading performers of the
time.   His son William, born in 1802, at one time gave
promise of equalling his father in tone and execution,
until ill-health unfortunately compelled him to leave
town.   They would play the violin and tenor parts of

Beethoven's trios on two violoncellos, a friend taking the
regular violoncello part.   His brother, Charles Lindley,
was a fine performer, especially on the tenor, though he
usually played the violoncello in public ; and but for his
retiring habits might have taken a high position. Lindley
died on the 13th of June, 1855, after a gradual decay of
some duration.   One of his daughters is married to John
Barnett, the eminent composer.   He had some good
pupils, as may be expected, and among them the accomplished musician, Lucas, the Principal of the Royal
Academy of Music, may be considered the chief.   He
succeeded Lindley as principal violoncello at the Italian
Opera, and has but very recently retired, having been
succeeded by that excellent performer, Mr. Collins.
There are other very good English performers, but
for finished execution, taste, and expression, especially in
solo and quartett playing, Signor Piatti is not surpassed.

Anfossi was known as a good player on the double-
bass some thirty years since; but all former players on
this instrument were surpassed by that extraordinary
performer, Dominique Dragonetti, born at Venice in
1766.   He came over to England in 1795 ; and for the
greater part of their lives he and Lindley were associated
together, and their performance of Corelli's music will
never be forgotten by those who were fortunate enough
to hear it.   When young, Dragonetti practised much
with a fine violin player, Mestrino, whom Dragonetti often
said he considered one of the most accomplished masters
of the instrument he had known.   At the age of thirteen
he was appointed first bass to the Opera Buffa, at Venice.
The richness and power of his tone were marvellous ;
and his execution such that he would play the violoncello
or violin part of a quartett on his unwieldy instrument,
or even join in a violin duett.

We may add Mr. Chorley's truthful remarks as to the long musical union of Lindley and Dragonetti. "Nothing has been since heard to compare with the intimacy of their mutual musical sympathy; nor is a pair of figures so truly characteristic now to be seen in any orchestra. Those two are among the sights of London that have vanished for ever."*

At present Howell may be considered our principal orchestral player, with whom there are other excellent performers.

We will now proceed to give some account of the various makers to the best of our power; but the difficulties of arranging these have been great in some cases from the deficiency of genuine information—from the vagueness and contradictory nature of the results of our inquiries and researches in others, so that a degree of uncertainty pervades the history even of some of the best known names. There seems, for instance, to be a difference of opinion as to the number of makers of the name of Amati. We hope, however, to be able to supply the names of all the makers of any note, and rather than be deficient in this respect shall include many that will be but little known to the generality of our readers; we have used every means in our power to make our account as correct as possible, but we must claim indulgence for the deficiencies which we fear may be found, in consequence of the scanty, imperfect, and conflicting materials with which in numerous cases we have had to deal.

* "Thirty Years' Musical Recollections," i. 80.

CHAPTER XV.

WE have already referred to the old makers, Ott, Frey, and Kerlin, and shall commence our account with the sixteenth century, wherein several foreign names occur, including the Amatis, but very few English. And the same remark will necessarily apply to makers as to performers, that in many cases they must belong to parts of two centuries. We may observe also, that we shall reserve a more detailed account of the English makers for an after part of the work.

In that curious collection of persons, occupying about ninety lines, who resort to "Cocke Lorelles Boke," printed by Wynkyn de Worde in the early part of the reign of Henry VIII., there appear "orgyn makers," and "harpe makers," but no viol makers. Are we to assume that this omission arose from the paucity of their numbers, or from their being more select in the choice of their companions.

There are many continental names handed down from this period; but, as we have before observed, the difficulty in some cases of ascertaining the dates, and even, though more rarely, the identity of the individual, is great; and we suspect that occasionally one maker may appear under two different names. The late Dr. Forster, in his "Epistolarium" and "Travels," gives the names of many makers; but his books are very inaccurately printed, and his dates, and even frequently his names, are very confused and not to be depended on.

Pietro Dardelli, of Mantua, about 1500, made good rebecs, violas, and viols da gamba, some of which, Fetis states, still to exist in the cabinets of the curious; and Morglato Morella, perhaps his pupil, of the same place, about 1550, made the same class of instruments. There were also Venturi Linelli or Linarolli, at Venice, 1520; and Peregrino Zanetto, at Brescia, 1540; with Lauxmin Possen, about the same time in Bavaria, who was maker for the chapel at Munich. Jean Kohl was "luthier" to the Court at Munich in the latter half of the century; and Fetis states that, from some old accounts, he was paid two florins for a lute. Jean Meusiedler and Jean Gerle are mentioned as celebrated makers at Nuremberg, about 1540. These makers were probably more particularly confined to the manufacture of violas and lutes, &c., than of violins; but the term "luthier," as is well known, applies to makers of violins and violas, as well as lutes.

There was, however, a celebrated maker of violins as well as of viols, Gaspard Duiffoprugcar, born in the Italian Tyrol in the latter end of the fifteenth century, who flourished in the former part of the sixteenth. He was established at Bologna in 1510, but went to Paris in 1515, by invitation from Francis I.; the climate, however, not agreeing with him he moved to Lyons, where he is said to have died about 1530. He made several instruments for the Chapel and Chamber of Francis, some of which are still to be found in the possession of amateurs. They are said to have had a powerful and penetrating tone. Choron states (1817) that Mons. Roquefort, at Paris, well known as a literary man, (and, who had himself written a work on the Poetry, Music and Instruments of the French, as mentioned in his Glossary (2—33), but which was never published,) possessed three basses of this maker, having necks curiously carved.   The first had seven strings tuned thus :—

On the back was a representation of Paris in the sixteenth century, executed in different coloured wood, and on the front was St. Luke, after Raphael.   The second had this inscription within, "Gaspard Duiffoprugcar a la Coste Sainct Sebastien, à Lyons."   On the back was a representation of the Moses of Michael Angelo; a salamander, the device of Francis I. was carved on the neck.   The third had the figure of St. John, after Raphael, on the back, and on the finger-board the following lines, which were frequently used by this maker :—

> " Viva fui in sylvis, sum durâ occisa securi,
>   Dum vixi, tacui: mortua dulcè cano,"

This couplet is said to have been on the violin of Palestrina, which was probably therefore one by this maker. The late celebrated tenor player, Hill, left some manuscript collections towards the history of the violin; he does not in general give any authorities, and his dates and names are in several cases doubtful; but his anecdotes and particular descriptions may probably be depended on.   He says that Mons. Cartier had a beautiful bass-viol and an alto-viol of this maker; but the most interesting instrument made by him was a violin of large pattern, the only one known, having his name and the date 1539; this date, however, must be wrong.   The tone was powerful and penetrating; the head of a fool

with cap and frill was carved on the scroll. It belonged
to Mons. Merts, first violin solo of the Grand Theatre at
Brussels. Mons. Raoul had a bass-viol of this maker,
distinguished for its beauty and tone, which Fetis states
to be then in the possession of Mons. Vuillaume, and
that the back had a representation of Paris in the fifteenth
century; it was probably therefore the same as the instrument of Mons. Roquefort before mentioned, notwithstanding the difference of date stated in the picture of
Paris. There is a portrait of him in medallion, quarto
size, dated 1562. He is represented with a long beard
and surrounded with instruments, having a pair of com-
passes in one hand and the neck of an instrument in the
other.

In "Luthomonographie," it is stated, but we know
not on what authority, that Testator (il Vecchio), a
maker at Milan, in the early part of this century, appears
to have been the first who diminished the size of the
viol, and gave the name of violino to the new-fashioned
instrument. His instruments were like those of Gaspar
di Salo, but the model rather more raised, and are now
very rarely met with.

The earliest violins of any considerable repute, except
of course the early ones of the Amatis, are those by
Gaspar di Salo, who worked at Brescia from about 1560
to 1610, or a little later, if we could rely on Dr. Forster,
who states he had one with this ticket, "Gaspar di Salo,
Brescia, 1613." He describes it as rather long, and
high built, with a beautiful varnish, and perhaps the
prettiest sides ever seen, but it had a new head and
neck; the tone of the first and second strings was lively,
bright, and piercing, a dry golden sound, as Dr. Forster
calls it; the third string sweetly soft and musical, and
the fourth round and very fine. Other writers have

stated that the workmanship of Di Salo's instruments is not highly finished, but the tone full of vigour ; the S S holes straight, large, and well cut, and parallel, forming one distinctive mark of the school of Brescia, which was the cradle of the Italian school. He employed strong wood, and used a deep brown varnish ; his instruments are scarce, and produce a good price. Dragonetti's instrument was by this maker, and after his death was returned to the convent from which it originally came. In "Luthomonographie" there is a copy of a ticket with the date 1652, which we conclude should be 1562. At the Conversazione of the Musical Society of London on the 29th January, 1862, at St. James's Hall, the celebrated performer, Ole Bull, exhibited a violin of this maker with the following description :—

"The celebrated '*Treasury Violin*' of Inspruck, by Gaspar di Salo, with Caryatides by Benvenuto Cellini, sculptured by special command of Cardinal Aldobrandini, and by him presented to the Museum of Inspruck, in the Tyrol. After the assault upon the said city by the French in 1809, the museum was plundered, and the violin carried to Vienna, where the Councillor Rhehazek placed this unique gem in his celebrated collection of ancient musical instruments, refusing to sell it at any price. He left it by will to Ole Bull, in 1842. Up to that period it had never been played upon ; had no bar, only a bridge of boxwood, sculptured and painted, and a very short and inlaid finger-board."

As the instrument was exhibited under glass no accurate opinion can be given of it ; it is smaller than any other instrument which has been seen of this maker, and the varnish less brown in hue than usual, being of a dull yellow colour, and meagre. Only the upper vibrating plate or belly could be viewed, with the carved head, which appeared wanting in the usual energy and expression of the great master whose work it is stated to be. This maker was particularly famous for his instruments of the viol class, and is stated by some writers to have been the master of the elder Amati, with whom, however, he was contemporary; and Giovanni Marc, del Bussetto, who flourished at Cremona from 1540 to 1580, is said with more probability to have had that honour. The violins of the latter are of long shape, the vaulting distinct, and the varnish brown; the openings of the S S holes large. One with the date of 1570 is mentioned having the back in two parts, the varnish a deep yellow, the corners elongated, and the model high vaulted.

Jean Paul Magini, with others of his family, will be mentioned in the following century. There were two other makers at Brescia towards the end of this century, 1580, Javietta Budiani and Matteo Bente, also Antonio Marini or Mariani, at Pisaro, from 1570 to 1620. Bente's instruments are said to be sought for by collectors. In the Fureteriana a maker of and performer on organs, spinetts, viols, violins, &c. is named about the end of this century, called Martin Chastelain of Warwick in Flanders, who was born blind.

We have now arrived at the time of the celebrated Amati family, of whom we will treat together in this chapter, whether belonging to this century or the following. There is great difficulty notwithstanding, or perhaps in consequence of the various accounts of the several families of distinguished violin makers, in making out an authentic history of them; some uncertainty will remain as to dates, though we have paid every attention and used every means to insure as much accuracy as possible. We have had inquiries made by a friend at Cremona, and have been able to procure but little addi-

tional information beyond what has already appeared in
print; and Mons. Fetis appears to have made similar
inquiries with like want of success.   The following is
the most accurate account we can give of the Amati
family, which we believe to be substantially correct.   It
may be observed here, that the genuineness of tickets
cannot always be depended on, as sometimes these are
imitated, and a genuine ticket may also be found on a
spurious instrument.   It would be a good speculation to
buy some of these instruments for what they are really
worth, and sell them for what their owners profess them
to be worth, like Laharpe—

" Si vous voudrez faire bientôt,
Une fortune immense autant que légitime,
Il vous faut acheter Laharpe ce qu'il vaut,
Et le vendre ce qu'il s'estime."

The first maker of this name was Andreas, born at
Cremona about 1520; he made as early as 1546, Fetis
mentioning a rebec, or violin with three strings, bearing
his name with this date.   The Baron de Bagge had a
viola with his name and the date 1551.   He made twenty-
four violins, twelve of large, and twelve of small pattern;
six violas, and eight basses for Charles IX. of France.
These, it is said, were kept in the Chapel Royal at Versailles, until October, 1790, when they disappeared; but
M. Cartier recovered two of them many years afterwards.
Nothing, it is said, could surpass the beauty of the workmanship, the varnish being of golden amber colour,
reflecting a reddish brown.   On the backs were painted
the arms of France, and other devices, with the motto
" Pietate et Justitia," not very appropriate for Charles IX.
The heads were decorated with a sort of arabesque of
much taste.   In the sale of the instruments of the late
Sir Wm. Curtis, on 3rd of May, 1827, Lot 9 was a violon-

cello by Andreas Amati, Cremonensis, faciebat 1572.
The auctioneer (Mr. Musgrave) stated in the catalogue,
" A document was given to the proprietor when he purchased this instrument, stating that it was presented by
Pope Pius V. to Charles IX., King of France, for his
chapel.   It has been richly painted, the arms of France
being on the back, and the motto ' Pietate et Justitia' on
the sides.   The tone of this violoncello is of extraordinary power and richness."   This was evidently one of
the instruments made for Charles IX.   Mr. Hollander
sold it to Sir William Curtis; it was put up at 500
guineas, and bought in at 280.   Andreas Amati made
numerous instruments; his violins were generally of
small and middle pattern, the model raised towards the
centre, and of proper thickness, the varnish being a clear
brown; the tone sweet, but not powerful.   The greater
number of violoncellos of this maker that we have seen
have a dark reddish brown coloured varnish, with a little
tinge of yellow, the wood of the lower plate and sides
plain, and the work not so highly finished as those of
some of the later members of the family; but it must not
be forgotten he was the first of the name, and had not
arrived at the same perfection.   The colour of the varnish may have been influenced by that of the old lutes,
as Mace states that was " dark-black-reddish colour,
though I believe it contributes nothing at all to the
sound; only the best authors did use to lay on that
colour, especially Laux Maller."   As he progressed in
his art, Andreas improved his varnish, and made it more
transparent, and of a reddish yellow colour, with more
body, and much more grateful to the eye. He was joined
about 1568 by his brother Nicolas, who worked till 1586,
Andreas, it is supposed, having died about 1580.   They
soon become distinguished by the skill of their workman-

ship and sweetness of tone. Nicolas was celebrated for his basses, for which he used oil varnish, and the sounding-boards had a very inconsiderable swelling. The upper vibrating plate was thickest in the centre near the bridge, and diminished about one-third to the S S holes, and then gradually diminished towards the sides, where the thickness did not exceed half of that in the centre. The lower vibrating plate also diminished from the centre to the sides in the same proportion, but was generally rather thicker than the upper plate. The first and second strings were brilliant and pure in tone, the third round and mellow, with power, but the fourth frequently dry and feeble, arising from the instrument being too narrow and short in proportion to the thickness. It may in general be considered as a distinction that the instruments of the Amati family have a pure and sweet tone, but not much power; those of the Stradiuarius, a rich and powerful tone; those of the Guarnerius family, still more volume of tone; and those of the Steiner, a sharp piercing tone, particularly on the first string.

The next of the Amati family were Antonius and Hieronymus (or Jerome), both sons of Andreas, of whom Antonius, the elder, was born about 1565. They made at first together from 1589, but afterwards separated. Antonius was superior to his brother, and made after his father's pattern; his instruments were sweet, but the fourth string defective. The upper plate was rather thick in the centre, gradually diminishing towards the sides. The small violins of Antonius have not been surpassed for sweetness and mellowness, but the sound is deficient in intensity, and he endeavoured to counterbalance the smallness of his model and the lowness of the ribs by the height and extension of the arches. He is said to have worked up to 1627, and to have died

about 1635. There were some instruments made for
Henry IV. with the names of the brothers, and Mons
Cartier had one of these, which are of the greatest rarity
and value, it was dated 1595. The model was of the
largest size, and the purfling of tortoise-shell, the oil
varnish of rich golden amber colour, which is one of the
characteristics of the Amatis. The back was decorated
with the arms of France and Navarre, surrounded by
the insignia of the orders of Saint Michel and the Saint
Esprit above the crown of France, with many other
devices.

The instruments made when the brothers worked together were of handsome form, and richly varnished,
but generally small. The lower plate usually made of
finely figured maple, of a deep brownish red colour, the
alternate stripes being of a rich orange buff, the variation
of colour arising from the medullary rays crossing the
fibres of the wood. The upper plate made of fine
grained deal, and the scroll rich and elegant. The
quality of tone is much like that of the other instruments
of the family; and it may be observed in respect to
these, that they often do not appear strong when the
hearer is near to them, yet are heard with great distinct-
ness and effect at some distance. Dr. Forster says he
had a beautiful instrument with a ticket, which he gives
thus, but the letter h in Anthonius seems to be an error:
" Anthonius et Hieronymus Amati, Cremonen, Andreæ,
fil. A. 1624." Tickets are found of many makers, with
a blank space for the last figure or two to be added when
attached to an instrument; like the following, for instance, from " Luthomonographie," " Antonius Hieronimus Amati Cremonen, Andræ filii, 16 . ." Hill mentions
the following ticket in an instrument formerly belonging
to Dragonetti: " Antonius & Hieronymus Amati, Cre-

monen, Andreas fil: F. 1592." At the sale of the instruments of Sir Wm. Curtis there were two violoncellos
and a tenor by these makers.   One of the violoncellos,
Lot 10, was stated by the auctioneer, in the catalogue,
to be " undoubtedly one of the most beautiful and finely
toned instruments ever manufactured by these distinguished artists, and is, moreover, in the highest state of
brilliant preservation."   We have never seen any instrument with such brilliant and *golden* varnish.   It can
only be compared with a new gold coin in which an alloy
of copper has been used, and which imparts a depth of
colouring so different from the undefined colour of this
coin in which silver has been used as the alloy.   It was
put up at 150 guineas, and bought in for 135.   The
Rev. Sir Frederick Gore Ouseley had in his possession,
in 1859, a viola made by these makers for the noble
family of Radetti at Venice, with their arms emblazoned
on the back; it was purchased from them by General
Kyd, in 1793, and given by him subsequently to Sir
Frederick's father, so that the pedigree is undoubted.   It
was altered and reduced in size for General Kyd, in 1811,
by Dodd, of St. Martin's Lane.   The printed ticket is,
" Antonius et Hieronymus Fr. Amati Cremonen Andreæ
fil. F. 1620."   This instrument has been reduced in size,
both at the fore and hind ends; it has also been made
narrower by cutting pieces out from the joint lines the
whole length of the upper and lower plates.   The wood
of the lower plate is not cut the usual way with the
figure and grain prominent, but at right angles with the
medullary rays of the wood, which, crossing the direction
of the fibres of the wood, form what is known as the
silver grain.   It is made of a species of maple (*Acer
pseudo-platanus*), and the sides are of the same wood,
and the grain is the right or usual way; the head and

neck are also made of maple wood. The varnish is of
a brownish yellow tint, with a fine yellow ground; the
vehicle must have been very thin, as there is little body
of colour, although it is rich, but age may have assisted
in this particular. It is now the property of Mr. Richard
Blagrove. Hieronymus Amati had two patterns, of
which the largest is considered the best. The sides are
strong and well finished, and then tapering from the
hind-bout to the fore-bout, where the neck is attached,
thus giving a graceful appearance. The edges are ob-
tuse, and do not overlap much; the upper plate is of fine
deal, of regular grain, and is raised gradually about an
inch from the sides to the centre ; the S S holes well cut,
but somewhat narrow, with their higher points approaching. The lower plates made generally of one piece,
and, together with the sides and neck, of beautiful maple,
the figure running from right to left somewhat sloping.
The volute, or scroll, is handsome, and rounded with the
greatest care. The varnish is of yellow amber, with a
mixture of light brownish tinge. The purfling broad, as
is the case with most of the Italian instruments, giving
an appearance of the finest construction; while the
school of Cremona is known by having a particular bend
in the purfling, and that of Brescia by having a double
purfling. The tone of these instruments is fine, the
second string brilliant, the third full and round, the
fourth powerful, but the first sometimes a little thin.
This Hieronymus Amati is said to have died about 1638.
Hill states that our Queen has a fine viola of his make.
There is a Joseph Amati mentioned at Bologna in the
beginning of the seventeenth century as one of the
family, who made basses and violins possessing a silvery
tone, which are now very scarce; he used the Amati
varnish.

The most celebrated maker of this family was Nicolas Amati, the son of Hieronymus, who was born in 1596, and died in 1684; he was a pupil of his father, and followed the models of his family, but was more finished and paid greater attention to the proportions. He had two patterns; his instruments of the earlier form being small, but handsome, with a sweet tone, and well calculated for quartetts and other chamber music. His instruments most sought after, however, are those of the large or grand pattern, which are powerful as well as sweet in tone, and the violins equal to most of those of Stradiuarius. The upper plate, which is generally made of handsome deal, is flat towards the sides, but then rises about an inch towards the centre. The lower plate, which, with the sides and neck, is made of beautifully figured maple, also rises towards the centre; the sides are well hollowed out, and the edges rounded. The S S holes are not far apart, but are not so straight as those of the other Amatis. The varnish is usually of a golden hue, sometimes approaching to brown; the tone brilliant, with considerable power on the first string, and round and full on the third and fourth strings, but sometimes a little nasal on the second string, arising, it is supposed, from the elevation in the centre, and the diminution of the thickness of the wood from the centre to the sides being too great. His instruments are much sought after, and valued at from 80*l.* to 200*l.* each. Fetis mentions a remarkably fine instrument of his make, with the date 1668, in the collection of Count de Salabue at Milan, and another in the possession of Allard, the violin player, which was said to be one of his best. Dr. Forster, writing in 1849, states that Mr. Betts had one of the finest Amatis, which was worth 250*l.*, and another of Andrew and Jerome, meaning probably Antonius and Hieronymus, valued at nearly half that sum; they had rich reddish yellow varnish. He gives tickets dated 1655, and 1661, and also the following, "Nicolaus Amati, Cremonæ, Hieronymus et Antonius Nepos, fecit Anno 1664." Whether the eccentricity of the syntax is due to the inaccuracies in Dr. Forster's book, or is a specimen of Nicolas's Latinity we cannot say. "Lutho-monographie" describes shortly several Amati instruments, and gives the following ticket, "Nicolaus Amati Cremonen. Hieronomi filii Antonii Nepos fecit: Anno 16..;" some little inaccuracy apparently here.

In the "Day Book" of the second William Forster, and the first who gave celebrity to the name, commencing 1st January, 1790, and ending on 20th April, 1799, there is the following entry on the first fly-leaf:— "No. 1. A Violoncello by Nichlaus Amatius, 1669, with Case and Bow, 17*l*. 17*s*.," meaning the price at which it was to be sold; a very insignificant one indeed compared to the present value. On the 5th July, 1804, William Forster, the third of the name, appears to have sold an Amati violin to the Rev. Mr. Vinicombe for 31*l*. 10*s*.

At the sale of Sir William Curtis's collection, lot 3 was a violoncello by Nicolaus Amati fil. Hieronymi; it was described in the catalogue as made by Antoine and Jerome, but the mistake was corrected by the auctioneer at the time of the sale. The instrument was put up at 100 guineas, and was bought by Mr. Kramer for George IV. for 70 guineas. Lot 8, was a violin by the same maker, dated 1647; it was stated in the catalogue, "This is justly considered as one of the most beautiful and finest instruments in THE WHOLE WORLD. It was put up at 150 guineas, and bought in at 185. Nicolas had two sons, of whom the elder, Hieronymus, born in 1649, followed his father's art, but was inferior and made but few instruments. "Luthomonographie" gives a ticket which appears to be of this maker—"Hieronimus Amati fecit Cremonæ, 167 .;" he may be considered the last of the Amatis. The "Biografia Cremonese," as we are informed, speaks of a Nicolas Amati, and an Antoine Jerome Amati, sons of Andreas Amati, who flourished from 1640 to 1670; but we do not know the authority of this work, and there is apparently some confusion of names and dates. Fetis also mentions a descendant of the family who, as recently as 1786, engaged as a workman with Messrs. Lupot at Orleans, and his violins were much admired; but he would not disclose the nature of his varnish, saying it was a secret of the family, and left Orleans rather than divulge it. It was not known what became of him afterwards.

CHAPTER XVI.

IN the seventeenth century we have a crowd of names of makers requiring more or less notice, including Guarnerius and Stradiuarius. Some will demand nothing more than a passing notice, and of others we know scarcely anything but the name—he lived, worked, and died.

In the early part of the century Claud Pierret, Jacques Bocquay, Veron, Antoine Despons, and Guersan were good makers at Paris, and we shall shortly refer to some other French makers. The instruments of Despons were said to be held in esteem, and to be rare ; and in Britton's sale there is a violin by " Claud Pieray of Paris as good as a Cremona." Guersan was a pupil and the successor of Bocquay ; his violins were of small pattern, and finely made, but are scarce. They had fine oil varnish, and some were said even to equal those of Andreas and Antonius Amati. "Luthomonographie" describes one instrument having the lower plate in two parts, and the varnish a deep yellow ; also another, a viola of middle size, with the lower plate in two parts, and the varnish brownish red. We have a ticket of a maker called Valler, at Marseilles, in 1683. Giovanni Paolo Maggini, born at Brescia, was a celebrated maker from 1590 to about 1640, and is said to have been the best pupil of Gaspar di Salo. His instruments are rare, and much esteemed.

His pattern is generally large, though he made some of a smaller form. The model is somewhat elevated, while the lower plate is flattened towards the extremities, but swelling towards the sides, which are large, with the curves lessened towards the corners. There is a double purfling, terminating sometimes at the top and bottom like a trefoil. They have generally spirit varnish of a fine golden colour, but sometimes of a deep brown. The tone is less mellow than the instruments of the Stradiuarius family, and less powerful than those of the Guarnerius, having more analogy with the tone of the viol. His ticket was thus, " Gio : Paolo Maggini in Brescia." De Beriot, celebrated for his fine and powerful tone, of which the younger Cervetto told one of the writers of this work he had not heard the like since the days of Giardini, brought the instruments of this maker into notice in England by playing on a very fine one. Mr. George A. Osborne, the eminent pianist and composer, and, from his finished musical taste and skill, a most competent judge, who has written, also, many pieces in conjunction with De Beriot, says that the tone of this particular instrument was equal to any he had ever heard. Maggini left a son called Pietro Santo Maggini, who worked from 1630 to 1680, imitating his father's models, and was particularly noted for his double-basses. There were several makers of the family of Ruggeri, but it is difficult to state their order of succession, or even their numbers accurately. The eldest appears to have been Francesco, who worked at Cremona from 1640 to 1684, or later ; there being tickets mentioned of the latter date. He was a pupil of Antonius Amati, and followed his principles of construction. He made some good instruments ; his model was large, the wood thick, the purfling broad, with deep brown varnish. He was known by the name of Il per, as in the following ticket, for instance, from " Luthomonographie," " Francesco Ruger, detto il per in Cremona dell anno 1645." This " detto il per," probably only means " commonly known as the father." He had a son called Giacinto Giovanni Batista Ruggeri, who apparently worked in the latter part of this century at Brescia, but there is difficulty in ascertaining his dates ; he was called Il buono. His ticket is " Giacinto filio di Francesco Ruggero detto il Per 1696." There was a Pietro Giacomo Ruggeri, who worked at Brescia from 1700 to 1720, and might have been his son. The accomplished performer Piatti has a fine violoncello of his make, with the following label, " Petrus Jacobus Ruggerius de Nicolaij Amati Cremonensis fecit Brixiæ 1717." A Vincent Ruggeri at Cremona from 1700 to 1730 is mentioned, but little is known of him.

Of the Grancino family, the first were Giovanni and Paolo, who worked at Milan during great part of the seventeenth century ; Paolo, it is said, had two sons, Giovanni and Giovanni Baptista, who worked till the early part of the eighteenth century at the same place ; the former made good instruments after the plan of Gaspar di Salo, but the shape was not very good, and the wood not handsome ; he left a son named Francesco, who worked up to the middle of the eighteenth century. A very fine instrument of one of the Giovannis was brought over from Italy, about eighty years since, by Mr. Waterhouse, page to the Duke of Cumberland, brother to George III ; it afterwards became the property of Mr. Lindley, who played on it at the Italian Opera, and its fine telling tone induced Mr. Farsyde to purchase it. In 1837 he sold it to Mr. Thomas Masterman, of Essex. The tone was very fine and powerful ; the varnish of a light yellow colour, mellowed by time to a slight reddish brown. The wood of the lower vibrating plate, sides, and head, remarkably plain; but the wood of the upper vibrating plate exceedingly fine.

The only Albani of much reputation is Mathias, who was born at Botzen, or Bulsani in the Tyrol, about 1621; Fetis calls him a pupil of Steiner, while in "Lutho-monographie" it is stated that he was a pupil of Nicolas Amati, and the first instructor of Steiner; but from the precocious talent of Steiner the probability is that he was the teacher, if either, or they may both have worked together under the Amatis, though their violins do not partake of the outline or model of that family. Mathias made some fine instruments of rather high model, the varnish being of reddish brown; the first string gene-rally rather brilliant but dry, the second powerful, and the third and fourth nasal. "Luthomonographie" de-scribes one, having the lower plate in two parts, made of fine wood, with reddish varnish, and ornamented with ivory and ebony; the date given is 1712, but this may have been one of his son's, of the same name, who was a good maker, and may have been the maker also of two violins that belonged to Francesco Albinoni, of Milan, with the respective dates of 1702 and 1709. Gerbert mentions an instrument of Mathias with the date of 1654; Hill gives a ticket with the same date, which appears to be the same as that given by Hawkins; we have the following ticket—"Mathias Albani Fecit Bulsani Tyrol 1651." Dr. Forster mentions a violin of Signor Albani at Palermo, 1659; this may be the same as Paul Albani, named by "Luthomonographie," of Cremona, in 1650, a pupil and imitator of the Amatis, but inferior. We have before referred to a son of Mathias, and a Michel Albani is mentioned at Greece of a later date, whose instruments are of no repute.

In "Luthomonographie" a ticket is given of Carlo Giuseppe Testore, showing that he worked at Cremona, "Carlo Testore me fecit Cremona del Anno 16 . ." He made good violins, after the Amati pattern, and the small double-bass played on by Bottesini, with such extraordinary execution, is of his make; Dr. Forster mentions three makers of the name, calling them the founders of the Milanese school.

Giaochino, or Giofreda Cappa, a pupil of the Amatis, was born at Cremona 1590, established himself in Piedmont 1640, and founded the school at Saluzzo. His violoncellos were his best instruments; he had two pupils, Acevo and Sapino, whose instruments were formerly esteemed. There was also a Giuseppe Cappa at Saluzzo, at the end of the century. Jean Paul Castagnery was a maker at Paris from about 1639 to 1662; his violins were esteemed for their silvery tone, but had not much power. About the same time St. Paul and Salomon, a pupil of Bocquay, were good makers at Paris; the latter made his instruments after the pattern of Guersan, and his bass-viols are said to have been good. Medard, who is supposed to have been a pupil of the Amatis, was afterwards, it is said, at Paris, and subsequently at Nancy, became the founder of the school of Lorraine in the early part of this century; he took the small pattern of the Amatis for his model, and his instruments, which were silvery and mellow, though not powerful, were sometimes mistaken for theirs. A ticket that we have seen in a violoncello belonging to Lord Stafford, is "Henry Medart a Nancy 1627." Lagetto was another Parisian maker, a little later; his instruments were also after the Amati pattern, with spirit varnish. Sympertus Niggel is another name mentioned. Joachim Tielke was a celebrated maker at Hamburg, in the latter part of this century, and the beginning of the next, and his instruments are still esteemed in Germany; he was the maker of the barytone of the date of 1687, exhibited to the Society of Antiquaries, as before mentioned, and as a viol d'amour at one of the Conversaziones of the Musical Society of London. Martin Hoffman was a good German maker about the same time, and his instruments are still in request; but from their size, the form of the sound holes, the sharp corners, and weak edges, have an ungraceful appearance. He died at Leipsic in 1725, leaving two sons, of whom the eldest, Jean Chretién, was more distinguished for his lutes, and the younger for his violins and bass viols. Other good German makers of this century were Hans Fichtold, about 1612, whose instruments are praised by Baron, in his " Treatise on the Lute." Philip Mohr, at Hamburg, about 1650; Johan Schorn, at Inspruck, about 1688; Cornelis Weynman, Amsterdam, about 1682; Johan Andreas Kambl, about 1635; Christian Roth, Augsburg, 1675; Nicolaus Diehl, at Darmstadt; Wolfgang Vogel, at Nuremberg, and Martin Schott, at Prague, whose best instruments were his lutes and theorbas. Dr. Forster mentions a violin in his possession that came from Gotha, of which, in the present pogonoferous age, it might be useful to get the model; it had an appendage that could be attached to it for the purpose of receiving the beard of the performer.

Antonio Maria Lausa was an imitator of the school of Brescia, in the latter part of the century; his instruments were not easily distinguished from the models he followed, but the tone was inferior. Other makers at Cremona were Paul Gerans, about 1614; Trunco, 1660; and Giuliani, 1660, a pupil of Nicolas Amati, and distinguished principally for his good copies. At Milan,

Antonio Maria Lacasso, and Sanza Santino; but there is some doubt whether this Lacasso is not the same as Lausa just mentioned. At Verona were Jean Baptiste Sanoni, and Bartolomeo Obue. At Trevisa, Pietro Antonio della Caesto, said to have been a clever imitator of Stradiuarius, and Alexandre Mezzadi, and Dominiscelli at Ferrara, in the latter part of the century. There were at Rome Francesco Juliano, Jerome Teoditi, and David Techler, a German, a pupil of Steiner, and a maker of considerable merit. He was first established at Salzburg, and went afterwards to Venice, where he caused so much jealousy among the other makers that at length they threatened him with assassination unless he left the place immediately. He very prudently took this strong hint, and went to Rome, where, whether because the skill of his fellow-workmen was greater, and therefore not so much injured by him, or their jealousy less, he was allowed to remain in peace, and ended his days there. The following is given as a ticket: "David Techler Liutaro Fecit Romæ Anno 1706." His violoncellos were very large, and of powerful tone. A fine one was purchased by Capt. Robins, R.N., after the peace of 1815, for 5l., which he afterwards sold to Mr. Lindley, who was much pleased with it, and used to play on it after it had been somewhat reduced for modern play. It is now in the possession of Henry Mann, Esq., of Cleckheaton, Yorkshire. At Modena, Antonio Cassino was a maker. At Bologna, Florinus Florentus, and Michael Angelo Garana, whose instruments had a sweet tone, but were uncertain. François Gobetti, Pietro Vimercati, and Paul Farinato, were at Venice, and it may be presumed, therefore, among the principal persecutors of Techler; Vimercati is said to have made instruments after the style of the school of Brescia, but without the tone of

Gaspar di Salo, or Maggini. Laux Maller is mentioned
by Mace as the most esteemed maker of lutes, and is
supposed to have been of Venice. Mace says he has
seen two of his lutes ("pittifull old, Batter'd, crack'd
Things") valued at 100*l.* a piece. He probably, also,
made violins, and other instruments of that class. At
Marseilles there was Valler, 1683, and at Mantua Racceris,
1670, said to have been in partnership with one of the
Gaglianos. Egidius seems to have been the best maker
of the Klotz family, working in the latter part of the
century, from 1675, and generally putting his own name
to his instruments; he was particular in using good wood,
and his instruments are well made, and have a finer and
fuller tone than any other of the Tyrolese make; they
have amber varnish. He was a pupil of Jacob Steiner,
and imitated him. After Steiner's reason became affected,
Egidius Klotz, or his sons (for this seems a little doubtful)
and Techler, worked in his shop, and placed Steiner's
tickets in the instruments then made. George, Sebastian, and Joseph, are named as his sons, and Joseph's
instruments are considered superior to his father's. We
have the following ticket of George: " Georg Klotz in
Mittenwald an der Iser 1761 ;" also one of Joseph, but,
from the date, he would seem to be more probably a
grandson than a son of the original Klotz, " Joseph Klotz
in Mittenwald an der Iser. An. 1774." There was also a
Michael Klotz, whose ticket we have, dated 1771. Parke,
in his " Musical Memoirs," says that Mr. Hay, formerly
an excellent leader of the King's band, had a celebrated
Klotz instrument, with a sweet and powerful tone, for which
a noble lord offered him 300*l.* and an annuity of 100*l.*
(the price seems incredible). Hay, having an independence, declined the offer, and on the sale of his effects
after his death the instrument was sold for 40*l.* only.

A manufactory of spurious instruments seems to have been established in the Black Forest, where instruments of all the great masters were provided, just as choice pictures of the most renowned ancient painters can now, it is said, be provided to order; and, as it is whispered also, that instruments of any of the old makers may yet be found by the curious in these matters, who have sufficient confidence, and believe somewhat in the lines of Hudibras—

"Doubtless the pleasure is as great,
Of being cheated as to cheat."

In the eighteenth century these imitations were numerous, and were generally called Midwalders. They were sometimes oddly shaped, and had a dark brown and ugly varnish, occasionally it was too red and bright to be taken for old varnish. The genuine violins of the great masters may be readily distinguished by any person of tolerable experience, by their superior workmanship and form, and by their mellow and sweet tones. Some instruments have been improved in consequence of an accidental fracture, when after the repair, if skilfully done, the tone of a dull or stiff instrument has been benefitted. Dr. Forster mentions one that was trod upon and crushed by Signora Columba, and was so improved after the accident that it bore the motto, "a vulnere pulchrior." We cannot, however, recommend the experiment, for in one instance certainly of decided fracture that has come before our notice, the improvement was very problematical.

The celebrated Jacob Steiner was born at Absom, a village of the Tyrol near Inspruck, about 1620. He was intended for the church, but would not apply to the necessary studies, his mind being set on the manufacture of violins; and while yet almost a child he made some of a rude form, after the model of an old instrument of Kerlin he found in the house. His parents at last yielded to his wishes, and he ultimately went to study under the Amatis at Cremona, where, after some years practice, he acquired skill nearly equal to his distinguished masters, or in beautiful finish perhaps excelled them, and began to work on his own account. The instruments made at this period of his life are some of his best, and also the rarest to be met with. They have a written ticket, dated from Cremona, and signed by himself. The model is higher than that of the Amatis, the sound holes rather smaller, and the scroll less prolonged, and wider in the forepart: the wood broad veined, and the varnish like that of his teachers. The finest instruments of this period are about 1644. He now married the daughter of Antonius Amati, and established himself at Absom; when, being compelled to work to maintain his family, he attended more to expeditious workmanship in order to provide for their immediate wants, than to working for fame, and his instruments of this period are inferior to those of his first period; he rarely got more than six florins for his violins, and had to carry them out himself. His varnish of this time was of a dark reddish colour and opaque. After a time the merits of his instruments became known, and as he could then get better prices, he again made them with care, and engaged pupils and assistants, and among them his brother Marcus, the brothers Klotz and Albani, and founded a school. Some of his instruments of this period, made for persons of rank, have the scrolls ornamented with heads of lions and tigers, and other animals, adopted frequently from the arms or crests of his patrons. The instruments of this second period are generally dated from 1650 to 1667 at Absom, but Hawkins gives a ticket of three years' earlier date, "Jacobus Steiner in Absom, prope Œnipontum 1647." The wood used by him at this time is generally of a fine grain; he took the best deal of Switzerland for the upper, and the finest maple for the lower plate, sides, and neck; his varnish was of mahogany colour now embrowned by time. Mons. Alard, at Paris, is said to have had a violin of this period of the greatest beauty; and the excellent player Sivori also had a very fine instrument. Mozart used to play on an instrument of his make; and at the Salzburg Mozart Festival, in September 1856, this with the name and date, Jacobus Steiner, Absom, 1659, and another small one by Andrea Ferdinand Maier, Salzburg, 1746, on which Mozart first learned to play, were produced for sale, having at his death come into the possession of his sister. In "Luthomonographie" there is the following ticket of this period, "Jacobus Steiner in Absom prope Œnipontum, 1663." After the death of his wife, he retired to a convent of Benedictines, where, according to Fetis, he passed the remainder of his life; but "Lutho-monographie" states that towards the end of it he lost his reason, either from a violent attachment formed for Clara Vimercati, (he being then approaching the age of threescore years and ten,) or from mortification in consequence of having sold his instruments at too low a price—two very different reasons; but at that age we might match Plutus against Cupid. There is no doubt, however, that he did retire to a convent, and then wishing to distinguish himself, obtained, through the influence of the superior, some wood of rare quality, of a close and regular figure, from which he made sixteen violins of a perfect model. He sent one to each of the twelve Electors, and the remaining four to the Emperor; and these are known as Steiner Electors. The tone is pure and silvery, the form elegant, and the details most highly finished; the purfling a little removed from the edge and finely inlaid; the varnish of a transparent golden amber colour. Fetis says that only three instruments of this third period of Steiner are known to exist; namely, one given by the Empress Maria Theresa to the violinist Kennis, at Liege; another bought in 1771, for 3500 florins, by the Duke of Orleans, the grandfather of King Louis-Philippe, who, when he gave up playing himself, presented it to Navoigille the younger; and, in 1817, the instrument passed into the hands of Mons. Cartier; the third was in the cabinet of Frederic William II. of Prussia. A curious history has been told us of a Steiner violin, for which many years ago the father of General Morgan Neville, of Cincinnati, (the General himself having told our informant, Mr. James Forster, and the father having been aide-de-camp to General Lafayette in the revolutionary war,) gave 1500 acres of land, worth at that time a dollar per acre—a pretty large price even at that rate, though a much higher one than this has been given for a Stradiuarius violin. But what as to the value of these "dirty acres" now, when we understand that a large part of the city of Pittsburgh has been built on them! No marvellous reward given to a Roman professor on the flute, or to a marvel on the tight-rope, or flying trapeze will equal this. Sir F. M'Clintock, in his "Voyage of the Fox," relates an anecdote of an Esquimaux who gave a large quantity of whalebone for a fiddle to which he had taken a fancy; the fortunate seller afterwards disposed of this whalebone for upwards of a hundred pounds. Otto, in his work "On the Construction of the Violin," makes observations to the following effect, respecting the Steiner instruments. The upper plate is modelled higher than the lower one; the highest part of the model under the bridge extends exactly one-half of the instrument towards the lower broad part, and then diminishes towards the end edge, and it decreases in like manner at the upper broad part towards the neck. The breadth of this model is uniformly the same as that of the bridge, from which it diminishes towards the side edge. The edges are very strong and round; the purfling somewhat nearer to the edges than in the Cremonese instruments, and also narrower. The S S holes are beautifully cut, and somewhat shorter than the Cremonese, with the upper and under turns perfectly circular. The neck is particularly handsome, and the scroll as round and smooth as if it had been turned. In some the screw-box is varnished dark brown, and the upper plate deep yellow. These instruments are rarely to be found with any labels inside, and they are simply written. In the Tyrolese imitations of Steiner they are printed, and in the genuine Cremonese instruments they are also printed. The general character of the Steiner instruments is free, somewhat piercing, and sparkling, especially on the first string, having a flute-like quality. Some instruments of Klotz have occasionally been confounded with those of Steiner; but the varnish of Klotz is of a dark basis, with a tinge of yellow, while that of Steiner is of a red mahogany colour embrowned by time, besides the superiority of tone. The date of Steiner's death is unknown.

Marcus Steiner, who worked at Inspruck, is called by "Luthomonographie" the son of Jacob; but we have seen that he had a brother of that name who worked with him. His instruments were good, but inferior to those of his namesake.

CHAPTER XVII.

E now arrive at the time of Antonius Stradiuarius, who is generally considered the
greatest maker that ever lived; and wish
we could introduce him to the sweet music
of one of his own quartett of instruments, such as we at
no distant period heard when in the charge of one of the
writers of this work.

Antoine Stradiuarius was descended from an old
family at Cremona, and was born there about the year
1644, as there is an instrument of his in existence having
a ticket written by him with the date 1736, stating his
age, ninety-two. He was a pupil of Nicolas Amati, and
made after his model, until about the year 1690; from
the year 1670, however, he placed his own name in his
instruments, having for the three previous years placed
that of his master. "Luthomonographie" describes an
instrument of the date of 1681, of a long form, with the
back in two parts, made of fine wood, and the varnish
brown, bordering on red. In the year 1690 he altered
his style, and the proportions of his instruments; his
model was larger, and the form of his arching somewhat
flatter, the gradation of the thickness of the vibrating
plates more strictly regulated, and the choice of wood
carefully attended to; but he still retained some similarity to the workmanship of his master. His best

instruments were made from about 1700 to 1725, and then approached nearest to perfection. The wood united beauty with great capability for conducting sound, and his model was designed with taste and skill that have never been exceeded. The thickness was greatest towards the centre, in order more fully to support the pressure of the bridge under the tension of the strings, and gradually decreased towards the sides, to give all the necessary vibration. The S S holes were formed with great taste, and the scroll finely carved ; the varnish of a beautiful warm reddish or yellowish colour, of which the secret appears to be lost. The lower plate, sides, and neck, were made of beautifully figured maple, the corners not too salient, and the purfling well inlaid. The four strings are generally of equal beauty of tone which cannot be surpassed. The details of the interior of the instrument are equally attended to with those of the exterior, all being the result of study and scientific calculation, and in harmonious proportion.

After 1725 his instruments are said to have rather fallen off in workmanship, he was now an aged man ; the arching became a little more raised, and the varnish of a browner hue, the tone also less brilliant. Probably he worked less himself, but gave directions to his assistants, among whom were his sons Homobono and Francesco, who were inferior to him, and Charles Bergonzo is also said to have worked with him. Several unfinished instruments were left at the time of his death which were completed by his sons, who placed his ticket in them, thus causing some doubt as to the entire authenticity of the instruments towards the close of his life. He died at Cremona in December 1737, having attained the great age of ninety-three. He had three sons and one daughter, Catherine, who died at the age of seventy, in 1748. Two of the sons, as before-mentioned, worked with their father, of whom Homobono died in June 1742, and Francesco in May 1743. The unusual duration of his life will account for the great number of instruments reported to have been made by him; but though there are many that bear his tickets, genuine specimens are scarce, and it is to be feared that instruments are sometimes put forward with great pretence, of which the authenticity may well be doubted, the proprietors not having the prudence of La Monnoye, in his epitaph on " Louis Barbier Abbé de la Riviere," who, in 1670, left 100 crowns for one—

> " Ci-git un tres-grand personnage,
> Qui fut d'un illustre lignage,
> Qui posseda mille vertus,
> Qui ne trompa jamais, qui fut toujours fort sage,
> Je n'en dirai pas davantage;
> C'est trop mentir pour cent escus."

Antoine Stradiuarius is described as having been tall and thin, and he was in easy circumstances, his usual price for a violin having been four louis d'or, for which now probably from 100*l.* to 200*l.* would be given, while violoncellos would much exceed this price; we shall refer to some particular instruments directly. The following ticket is given in " Luthomonographie "—" Antonius Straduarius Cremona faciebat anno 16.. ." In the same work there is an account of a violin dated 1702, purchased of the family of Stradiuarius in 1790 by Giov. Gagliano; it had never been varnished, but was acknowledged by Paganini in 1820 as a genuine instrument. Prince Youssoupow bought it in 1854, and added it to the celebrated collection of instruments in his palace at St. Petersburgh. It is probably this instrument that is described in the same work as of grand pattern, with the back in two parts, the body, sides, and neck, of wood much veined, with reddish varnish approaching to yellow. A violoncello is also mentioned of middling size, with the back in two parts, the wood fine, and the varnish red, verging on brown; the violoncello of Count Wieliehorsky is said to be known to all the musical world. Mons. Servais, the celebrated performer at Brussels, had a violoncello of large pattern of extraordinary power, with a silvery mellowness of tone. We may here observe, that in stating certain celebrated instruments to be in the possession of particular persons, changes may occasionally have taken place since our notes respecting the ownership were originally made, so that our remarks may be considered to apply to the present or comparatively recent ownership. Mons. Franchomme, the skilful violoncellist, had an instrument of the smaller pattern that formerly belonged to Duport, and of the greatest value, 500*l*., it is said, having been asked for it. A very fine violoncello was brought over by the Earl of Pembroke in the last century, and by him given to Sperati, then one of the principal performers of the day; it became afterwards the property of Mr. Morse, and at the sale of his musical property, in June 1816, was purchased by the third William Forster for Mr. Cervetto, jun., at the price of 105*l*. After his death it was purchased by the distinguished musician, Mr. Lucas for 200*l*. and ultimately became the property of Mr. Charles Finch of Staines. A curious circumstance may here be mentioned, which was related by the younger Cervetto himself to one of the writers of this work. The elder Cervetto, before he entered the musical profession, had been an Italian merchant, and had dealt with Stradiuarius himself in musical instruments, and brought some of his make over to England; but as he could not obtain as much as *five* pounds for a violoncello, they were taken back as a bad speculation. At the sale of Sir Wm. Curtis's instruments, lot 7, was a violoncello of the date 1684, said to have been made by Stradiuarius for a Corfiote nobleman, and deposited by him in a chest with cotton, and there left for at least a century; it was put up at 200 guineas and bought in for 235. Mara, the husband of the gifted Madame Mara, was a good player, but a drunken fellow, and behaved ill to his wife. He brought over a fine instrument of this maker, the tone of which was everything that could be desired, especially that of the first string, it was musical and rich, with much power; the figure or mottle of the wood was extremely beautiful. It is believed that Mr. Crossdill purchased this instrument from Mara, and that he sold it in the beginning of the present century to General Bosville, afterwards Lord Macdonald. His son disposed of it to Mr. Lucas, who played on it for some time at the Italian Opera, where he succeeded Lindley as principal violoncellist, and subsequently parted with it to Mr. John Whitmore Isaac, of Worcester. Before parting with Mara we will relate a couple of anecdotes of the effects of his temper and pride, for though he frequently ill-used his wife, yet he was proud of her talent, and would at times become enthusiastic in this respect. We will begin with the result of a drunken bout. When the Maras were at Berlin, Frederic the Great heard that Madame Mara had been unable to sing before him, in consequence of a severe beating her husband had given her, amongst other effects of which was a discoloured, or what schoolboys would call a black eye. The enraged monarch sent for the culprit, and after giving him a severe reprimand, told him as he was so fond of beating he should be indulged in his propensity, and accordingly sent him away to act as drummer in one of his regiments for a month; a different version, however, says that this punishment was for attempting to leave Prussia without permission. The other story refers to one of his fits of enthusiasm; being once on a visit to the Earl of Exeter, at Burleigh, the capricious lady complained to her husband, that she did not like his lordship's claret, on which Mara sent to Stamford for a chaise and four, and proceeded to London, returning the following day with a case of claret from their own cellar. It is not stated how long their visit was afterwards allowed to continue. To return to the instruments, the late Mr. Frederick Perkins had a fine instrument of this maker, possessing a pure tone of first-rate quality; it had formerly belonged to Boccherini, and is now the property of Mr. Robert Garnett, of Sutton Coldfield.

A tenor of Stradiuarius was in the sale of Sir Wm. Curtis, lot 6, which the auctioneer stated to be one of the most valuable specimens of the maker, and not to be surpassed; it was put up at 150 guineas, but no offer was made for it. Gardiner says that Mr. Wm. Champion gave 300 guineas for a violin and tenor of this make in one case, of a beautiful yellow colour, inclining to orange. The violins of Stradiuarius have been valued and sold for most extravagant prices, from 200 guineas upwards; the late Mr. Betts had one for which it is stated the sum of 500*l.* was refused. Fetis mentions one in the possession of Mons. Vuillaume possessing united power and sweetness, a model of exterior beauty and perfection of tone, made in 1716, but rarely played on. A remarkably fine one is said to be in the collection of the Grand Duke of Tuscany, and two magnificent specimens in the possession of Count San Grado, at Venice. The highest price ever given for a violin, was for one by this maker, unless we choose to take the present value of the land given as before mentioned for a Steiner instrument. The violin to which we refer was sold in 1856, for literally more than its weight in gold, as on weighing the violin it appeared that the price given was at the rate of nearly 40*l.* an ounce. At the sale of Mr. Goding's instruments, in February 1857, Mons. Vuillaume gave 212*l.* for a tenor by this maker, for which it is said Mr. Goding had given 400*l.* to Mr. Hart; it was one of a quartett of Stradiuarius instruments, formerly belonging to Lord Macdonald. Dragonetti had a celebrated Stradiuarius double-bass, for which it is said that a well-known amateur offered 800 guineas, but 1000 were required. Stradiuarius also made viols and quintons, guitars, lutes, and mandoras.

It really would almost appear that the possession of one of these splendid instruments would make a person, in spite of nature and of the stars, to fiddle and discourse sweet music. Let it be remembered, however, that great mechanical skill is not the only requisite for fine playing; indeed, such skill may exist with scarcely any real musical feeling. Hear some of our most distinguished performers, observe the delicacy of taste and expression, joined to the most finished execution, where the sense of difficulty is overcome by the impression of the beauty of the performance. Not so with mere digital dexterity, where a considerable degree of facility has been obtained by hard practice, perhaps, and so far praiseworthy, but where no feeling of the poetry of music exists. This sort of performance reminds one of a story of a young priest, in one of the numerous French gossiping memoirs, who was a popular preacher, but one day, when in the pulpit, suddenly lost the thread of his discourse; he did not, however, lose his presence of mind, but proceeded with much gesticulation, considerable inflection of voice, and great emphasis, but, in fact, without pronouncing any sentences intelligibly; the only words striking the ear being such as, car—enfin—mais—si—donc—Messieurs, &c. When he had finished, the congregation was delighted: such energy, such learning, such eloquence. To be sure they all agreed that they could not hear very well, or connect the parts of the discourse, but attri- buted this to having been badly placed: either too near, or too far off, or in an awkward corner, and determined to choose better places next time, in order not to lose the advantage of such a talented preacher.

We have now arrived at another great name—Guar- nerius—of which family there were several; the first being Pietro Andreas, or, as he is generally called, Andreas. He was born at Cremona in 1630, and is considered to have been a pupil of Hieronymus Amati, after whose model, with some little distinction, his instru- ments were made, and principally of large pattern. The tone is good, but, in general, not strong; and they fre- quently have a fine shape and good varnish. In Sir William Curtis's sale there were a violoncello and a tenor by this maker, each put up at 100 guineas, and bought in for seventy-nine. Andreas worked from about 1650 to 1680, or, perhaps, later. The following is a copy of a ticket in our possession, or, more correctly, in the possession of one of us, which is the case with all the tickets or labels so referred to :—" Andreas Guarnerius Fecit Cremonæ sub titulo Sanctæ Teresiæ 1675." He had two sons, Giuseppe and Pietro, of whom Giuseppe was the best, and rather followed the model and imitated the varnish of Stradiuarius, and afterwards that of his cele- brated cousin and namesake. His instruments are esteemed, though the fourth string is sometimes dry and hard, and are generally of small pattern, with a brilliant reddish varnish. The instruments of Pietro have a full tone, but want brilliancy, and the form is not elegant; the varnish of a brownish hue. The two brothers worked from about 1690 to 1720; and in the latter part of his life Pietro removed to Mantua. There was a very fine violoncello by this maker in Sir William Curtis's sale, bought in for 125 guineas. A son of Giuseppe's is mentioned, called Pietro, who worked at Cremona from 1725 to 1740, and followed his father's models, but with less finish.

The great artist of this family was Giuseppe, or Giuseppe Antonius Guarnerius, commonly known as Joseph, the nephew of Andreas, often called del Jesu, in consequence of many of his tickets having I. H. S. marked on them, and frequently a cross. His father, Giovanni Baptista Guarnerius, the brother of Andreas, was not a maker himself. Joseph was born at Cremona on the 8th of June, 1683, and became a pupil of Stradiuarius; but he was not a mere imitator, and was guided by positive principles. He worked at Cremona until the year of his death, 1745; but, unfortunately, in his latter years, he became careless and dissipated, and addicted to drink; his instruments became inferior in make, and the wood and varnish also deteriorated.

It is stated that he was confined in prison for a considerable time; and Fetis relates that while he was there the gaoler's daughter procured some inferior tools and wood, and assisted him in his work, and then took the instruments out for sale in order to obtain some comforts for him in his reduced circumstances. She bought the varnish, as required, from different makers, which accounts for the variety of tints on his later instruments. At the commencement of his career his instruments showed no particular marks of skill, and there was even an appearance of negligence in his work ; but after a few years he paid great attention to it, and was very particular in the choice of his wood. The model was carefully worked out, generally of the smaller pattern, and the arching not much raised, gradually decreasing towards the sides in a gentle curve, and the S S holes finely cut: the thickness, perhaps, towards the centre of the lower plate sometimes too strong, so as to interfere with the vibration and power. His varnish remarkably fine, and of a brownish red, or sometimes of a deep yellowish tint. He occasionally made some admirable instruments of a larger pattern. " Luthomonographie " describes one of these, dated 1723, having the lower plate in two parts, the wood veined, and the varnish brownish red. The tone of his instruments is brilliant, and some of them are scarcely inferior to those of Stradiuarius, bearing a high price. The extraordinary performer, Paganini, played on one. At the sale of Mr. Crossdill's instruments, in May 1826, a very fine violoncello, by this maker, was bought by Mr. Kramer for George IV. for 125 guineas, Mr. Cervetto, jun., having offered as much as 110l. for it. Hill mentions a tenor of his make, of beautiful workmanship, formerly the property of Dragonetti, and afterwards in the possession of the lamented Prince Consort. Mr. Willett L. Adye, of Merly House, Dorsetshire, a well-known amateur, has a remarkably fine violin by this maker, of which the history is somewhat interesting :—It belonged to Mr. Mawkes, formerly distinguished as an excellent performer, who left the profession to enter the Church, and was ordained many years since. He bought it in 1831, at Spohr's recommendation, from Professor Hoffmann, of Frankfort, when he was studying under the

former celebrated musician at Hesse Cassel. Hoffmann
bought it at the time Rode was at Frankfort, it having
been a *facsimile* of an instrument by the same maker,
played on by him. Spohr told Mr. Mawkes, if he could
purchase it, he would have one of the finest instruments
in the world; and he would have given his famous Stradiuarius in exchange for it. Mr. Mawkes refused several
offers for it, and, having been the possessor of it for
about thirty years, disposed of it to Mr. Adye. The late
Mr. Mori had a fine instrument by this maker. The
following are some of our tickets of this maker:—

> " Joseph Guarnerius
> Cremonensis Faciebat 1724."

> " Joseph Guarnerius fecit
> Cremone anno 1738.   IHS "

Dr. Forster gives copies of two tickets by Antonius
Guarnerius, 1722; but his book cannot be depended
on. It may be observed that Joseph does not appear
to have made use of his name Antonius. A Catherine
Guarnerius is named, who was probably the daughter of
Andreas, and worked with her brothers.

CHAPTER XVIII.

HERE are numerous makers in the eighteenth century, many of whom will be known to most of our readers, while of others perhaps even the names will not have reached them. The same difficulties occasionally exist as to the identity of some of the least known persons named, and in some instances the makers will equally belong to the preceding or succeeding century.

Among the Italian makers, the family of Gagliano, at Naples, is well-known. The founder of this, as makers of instruments, is said to have been Alessandro, the son of a Marquis of the name, who was obliged to leave Naples about the beginning of the century, in consequence of some crime committed in a fit of jealousy. He retired to reside in a deep wood, and there amused himself with making violins, and finding that he succeeded, returned in a few years to his native place, where, his offence having been forgotten, he founded a manufactory for instruments. He took Stradiuarius for his model, and made good violins with a lively quality of tone, but not very powerful. He left two sons, Januarius and Nicolaus, of whom we have the following tickets: " Januarius Gagliano Filius Alexandri fecit Neap. 1741," and " Nicolaus Gagliano Filius Alexandri fecit Neap. 1785"; they followed their father's model. There are four other makers of the name mentioned, Ferdinando and Giuseppe, the sons of Nicolaus, who made as late as from 1780 to 1790, or later, there being a ticket of Giuseppe dated 1789, and Giovanni and Antonio, of whom Giovanni is reputed the best. Giovanni, it is said, had two sons, Rafael and Antonio, but it is by no means improbable that this and the former Antonio are the same person ; these sons after a few years abandoned the manufacture of instruments, and established a factory for strings, which became one of the best in Italy, and they are stated in "Luthomonographie" to be still, living. The essential importance of good strings is recognized by every performer. Angelo Angelucci, of Naples, who died in 1665, had more than one hundred workmen in his employ, and discovered that the best strings were made from mountain bred sheep of seven or eight months old.

The Bergonzis were good makers at Cremona; a Francisco Bergonzi is named as early as 1687, who might have been the father of Carlo. Carlo Bergonzi, or Baganzi worked from about 1712 to 1750, and made some excellent instruments, which are held in considerable estimation ; they generally possess beauty and brilliancy with a fine tone. He worked at one time with Stradiuarius, but according to some of his tickets calls himself a pupil of Nicolas Amati, as for instance, " Carlo Baganzi allieue di Nicola Amati fecit Cremonæ anno 1723." He had a son called Nicolas living at Cremona in 1739, whose instruments are sometimes sold for his father's, but are inferior. A Michelo Angelo Bergonzi is mentioned of about the same date as Carlo. Lorenzo Guadagnini, was born at Placentia towards the end of the seventeenth century, and was living in 1742. He was a pupil of Antonius Stradiuarius, whose models he followed, generally of the small pattern. He finished with care, using good oil varnish, his S S holes are elegant, and his purfling neat; the first and second strings brilliant, but the third occasionally dull. After working for some time at Placentia he removed to Milan. Giovanni Baptista Guadagnini is generally called his son, but if a ticket we have seen with this name and the date 1731, is genuine, it would appear probable that he was his brother, as stated in " Luthomonographie ;" he worked at the same places, and made instruments very similar to those of Lorenzo, and of about the same value; he calls himself in some of his tickets a pupil of Antonius Stradiuarius. A Giuseppe Guadagnini is mentioned at Turin in 1751, and another of the same name at Parma in 1793; and some of the family were at Naples a very few years since.

Francesco Milani, of Milan, worked on the model of Guadagnini about the middle of the century; and Guiseppe Carlo, of the same place, 1769; and Thomas Palestieri, a pupil of Stradiuarius; and Spiritus Sursano, at Coni, about the same time, if there be not some mistake in the name; Alessandro Zanti, at Mantua, about 1770; Camilus de Camile, of the same place, a good pupil of Stradiuarius; and Tommasso Circapa, and Giovanni Santi at Naples, about 1730. At Cremona, Gregorio Montade, a pupil of Stradiuarius, whose instruments were in repute in the early part of the century; Pietro Palestieri, Alberto Giordane, 1735; Davido Camillio, 1755; Nicolao Guletto, 1790; Johann Christian Ficker, 1722; Johann Gottlob Ficker, 1788, and Johann Gottlob Pfretzschner, of whom there is a ticket dated at Cremona 1794; but the three last names are evidently of German origin; and there was a musical firm of the last name at Neukirch, of which we have seen several tickets; a Carl Frederick Pfretzschner is also mentioned at Cremona. Lorenzo Storioni, who was living there in 1782, was the last maker of any great repute of that celebrated place. His violoncellos especially are esteemed for their powerful tone. His violins resemble those of Joseph Guarnerius, and Dr. Forster speaks in high terms of them, particularly of one then in his possession of a singular shape, and of a dark reddish or nut brown colour, with a metallic or golden sound as he terms it. The celebrated performer Vieuxtemps, we are informed, used one in 1861 for his solo instrument, which was much admired. There were several makers called Tonini, at Bologna, in the early part of the century; Felice, Antonio, Carlo, and Guido; the instruments of the latter are said to have been esteemed, and sometimes to have been taken for those of Nicolas Amati. At Brescia, about the same time were Gaetano Pasta, and Domenico Pasta, and Nella Raphael of the same school, whose instruments have good volume of tone, but are not equal, and may be known by having the scroll sculptured, with inscriptions on the sides. Rome was deficient in good makers, the first who commenced making there on the principles of the school of Cremona, was Gaspard Assalone; we have already mentioned Techler, who was the best. Antonio Pollusha, 1751, and Antonio Pansani, 1785, were also two of the principal makers there. Florence did not abound in good makers, only three are mentioned of any repute, Giovanni Baptista Gabrielli, Bartolomeo Christofori, and Carlo Ferdinand Landolfi, who is also stated to have been of Milan, and there are tickets with his name as of this place, one called Quidantus, is also named, but is probably the same as Giovanni Florenus Guidantus, whose ticket is of Bologna. There were several makers at Venice of different degrees of merit; they generally attended to the elegance of form, and excellence of the varnish, but their instruments were inferior in tone to those of Cremona. One of their most distinguished makers was Dominico Montagnana. His instruments, especially his violoncellos, are of large size, and his varnish exceedingly brilliant. The work altogether is excellent, and the figure or mottle of the wood large and beautiful. The late Mr. Frederick Perkins had a fine violoncello by this maker, which was originally sold as a Joseph Guarnerius; it had been reduced in size, but not judiciously. It was purchased by Mr. Alfred Guest, the professor, a pupil of Lindley, who fully appreciates and does justice to its excellent qualities. Montagnana worked at Venice in 1725, and there are tickets of that date; but in later years he appears to have moved to the Tyrol, as we have the following ticket, " Dominicus Montagnana sub signo in Ab prope Oenipontum, fecit, Anno 1730." Santo Seraphino, of the same period, was an excellent workman; his instruments are generally good and prized, the wood beautiful, and of small mottle or figure, and the varnish a good yellow with a brown tinge; which may have been caused by age. Two brothers, Matteo and Francisco Gofriller, in the early part of the century, made strong and good instruments after the Cremona model, but were inferior to the two last-named makers. Pietro Valentino Novello, and Marco Antonio Novello, have acquired a well merited reputation, the violins of the latter especially are good and rare. Other Venetian makers are the brothers Carlo and Giovanni Tononi, Pietro Anselmo, Bellosio, and Bodio. At Padua was Pietro Bagatella, about 1766, of no great merit; but Antonio Bagatella, a few years later, was not only a good maker, but published, in 1782, a valuable work on the construction of instru-

ments from which Maugin, in his " Manuel du Luthier,"
took his method of tracing a fine model of a violin with only
a rule and compass, which may also be seen, somewhat
shortened at the end of Bishop's translation of Otto on
the violin.

Other Italian makers of this period are Paulo Aletsie,
at Monaco, about 1726, skilful in making bass instruments; Antonio Gragnarius, Tomasso Eberti, Giacomo
Horil, Rovelli, Gattanani, Speiler, and Guiseppe Odo-
ardi, who, although a peasant, and self-taught, made
several excellent instruments, but died at the early
age of 28; Carlo Broschi, of Parma, 1744; and J.
Andreas Borelli, 1741. Joseph Contreras is mentioned
as a good maker at Madrid about 1746, making fine
copies of Stradiuarius, which were often sold for genuine
instruments. Galerzena, a Piedmontese, is named, 1790;
Nicholas of Geneva, 1790; and Joseph Wagner of
Constance, 1773.

There are several good and well-known makers at
Paris during this century. One of the earliest was
Augustine Chappuy, about 1711, whose instruments
were much esteemed in France; another of the same
name is mentioned in 1794; Pichol, Amelingue, who,
however, principally made clarionets; Pique and Andrea
Castagneri are other names. Saunier, who was born in
Lorraine about 1740, and established in Paris about 1770,
was a favourite maker, and was the master of Noel Piete,
born about 1760, who was esteemed as a maker of violins
and basses. Saunier was the pupil of Lambert of Nancy,
nicknamed the Lute carpenter, who made a vast number
of instruments, but not of high merit. Finth, or
Fendt, a German maker, lived in Paris from 1765 to
1780, and took Stradiuarius for his model; his instruments were good and well finished, and said to have been

sometimes taken for those he imitated; he used oil varnish; his nephew came over to England, and established himself there. François Nicolas Fourrier, generally called Nicolas, was born at Mirecourt, in 1758, but went to Paris, where he died in 1816. His instruments are frequently good; he imitated the Cremona school, was correct in his proportions, and particular in his choice of wood. Koliker also was a maker of repute at Paris towards the end of the century; and other names there are—Chevrier, Bernadel, Benoist Fleury, Gavinies, Leclerc, Simon, and Remy; also Nicolas Viard of Versailles, and Cherotte at Mirecourt. In naming this last place, we must mention Jean Vuillaume, who made good instruments there from 1700 to 1740, and had worked with Stradiuarius; Chanot was also a maker of merit there. Nicholas Lupot was born at Stuttgard, in 1758, and was the son of Francois Lupot, a maker at that place. Nicholas became a celebrated maker, following the models of Stradiuarius. He first worked at Orleans, where a firm of Lupot and Son existed in 1786. In 1794 he established himself in Paris, where he died in 1824. He published a work, to which we have referred occasionally, called "La Chelonomie, ou le parfait Luthier;" but it was written by the Abbé Sibire, from materials supplied by Lupot. His instruments sometimes reach a high price; and he was very skilful in repairing and restoring old instruments. Namy, also about the same time, was noted as a skilful restorer and repairer of old instruments. Ambroise Decombre, of Tournay, made some good instruments, particularly basses, from 1700 to 1735, and had worked with Antoine Stradiuarius; Jean Raut, of Bretagne, who worked at Rennes down to 1790, made good instruments on the model of the Guarnerius school.

There were several makers in Germany in this century, of whom some have obtained high repute. Many of them imitated the Steiner and the Cremona schools with great success. One of the best was Charles Louis Bachmann, who was born at Berlin, in 1716, and was himself a skilful performer on the viola, and chamber musician to the King of Prussia. His violins and violas were much esteemed in Germany, and rank next to those of Cremona; they were made after the model of Stradiuarius, with amber varnish, but under his own name; he lived till the year 1800. Schmidt, of Cassel, who more correctly may be called of the present century, being mentioned by Otto, in 1817, as then working, made some fine violins after the model of Stradiuarius; but the edges are larger, and the purfling inclines more towards the centre. There were several makers of the name of Rauch, towards the middle of the century, who made good instruments; as Jacques Rauch, at Manheim, from 1730 to 1740, whose violins approached those of Steiner in tone; Sebastian Rauch, in Bohemia, from 1742 to 1763; Rauch of Breslau, who made some good instruments; and Rauch of Wurtzburg. Johann Gottfried Reichel, of Absam, is named, who made after the model of Steiner; and Johann Conrad Reichel, of Neukirch, in 1779. At Prague, there were two, named Edlinger, father and son, who were more particularly in repute for their lutes; those of the father, Thomas, who was a pupil of Steiner, being equal to those of Gaspar di Salo; he was living at Prague in 1715. His son, Joseph Joachim, lived for many years in Italy, visiting Cremona, Rome, Naples, Bologna, Ferrara, and Venice; he died at Prague in 1748, and his instruments, especially his lutes, were much esteemed. The lutes of Jacobi, at Meissen, about the same time, were also in repute. Zacharie Fischer, born at Wurtzburg in 1730, and who was living there in 1808, announced, in 1786, that he had a plan by which his instruments should equal those of Steiner and Stradiuarius. This was by drying the wood in an oven. Other makers also have tried this plan ; but it did not succeed, as it dried the wood too rapidly, and weakened it, thus injuring the effect of the vibrations. Johann George Vogler was also of Wurtzburg, about 1749. " Luthomonographie" mentions Bauch, of Breslau, as one of the best makers of his time, giving a peculiar form to his instruments; but he may be the same as Rauch. Leopold Widhalm, at Nurenburg, from 1765 to 1788, was a skilful maker, his instruments closely resembling those of Steiner, and scarcely to be distinguished from them; his harps were also in repute at one time. Leonhard Mansiell was of the same place, about 1724. Jaug, or Jauch, of Dresden, made some good instruments on the Cremona model, with amber varnish, and made of fine wood, but the tone is occasionally weak and shrill; he was living in 1774. He was the master of Christophe Frederic Hunger, born at Dresden in 1718, who established himself in Leipsic, where he died in 1787, and was esteemed for his violas and violoncellos, which were made after the Italian model, with amber varnish. Samuel Fritzche, of Leipsic, his pupil, also imitated the Cremona models ; and a Barthold Fritz of the same place, in 1757, is named.

Jean Ulric Eberle, living at Prague in 1749, was an excellent maker, and one of the best of the German school, some of his instruments being scarcely inferior to those of Cremona, for which they have been mistaken; but the tone is not so round and full. Charles Helmer, born in Prague, 1740, was a good pupil of his ; but his fourth string frequently of an inferior quality.

Gaspard Strnad, born in 1750, was settled at Prague from 1781 to 1793; he made some good violins and violoncellos, and his guitars were much esteemed. There appear to have been two Stadelmanns, or Stadlmanns, of Vienna, as we have a ticket of Daniel, 1744, and of Johann Joseph, 1764; these instruments successfully imitated those of Steiner, with deep yellow-coloured amber varnish. There was an Andreas Nicolas Parth of the same place; and about 1700, an Antoine Lidl, who made improvements in the barytone; Buchstadter, of Ratisbon, was another imitator of the Cremona model, though his make was rather flat, and he used inferior wood, with dark brown varnish; his instruments are rather harsh, and not much esteemed. Hassert, of Rudolstadt, made his instruments with much care, of high model, and the upper plate formed of excellent wood, but the tone rather harsh or hollow. His brother, of Eisenach, surpassed him, and carefully imitated the Italian models, with amber varnish, and used beautiful wood for the upper plate. Reiss, of Bamberg, also successfully imitated Steiner. Durfel, of Altenburg, particularly excelled in his double basses. Artmann and Binternagel, of Gotha, were imitators of the Cremona school. A. Grobtiz, established at Warsaw about 1750, made some good violins on the Steiner model. At Erfurth, Francis Ruppert adopted rather a flat pattern; his instruments had a powerful tone, and were well proportioned, but were slightly constructed, the sides not being lined, and the corner blocks omitted; they were not purfled, and had a dark brown amber varnish. Francis Schonger, of the same place, made some handsome looking instruments, but the tone dull, and they are considered inferior to those of Ruppert. His son, George, made some good instruments in the Italian style, and had much skill as a repairer of old ones. At Munich were Joseph Paul Christa, about 1730, and Mathias Johann Kolditz, or Koldjz, 1750. A Jacques Kolditz is mentioned at Ruhmbourg, in Bohemia, who made some good violins and violas, and died there in 1796. At Salzbourg, were Simon in 1722; Andrew Ferdinand Mayrhof, 1740; Jacob Weiss and Gregor Ferdinand Wenger about 1761; and Johann Schorn. "Luthomonographie" names seven makers at Fissen, in Bavaria, from 1756 to 1798, including Thomas Edlinger beforementioned at Prague. The others are Gugemmos, though there would appear to be some mistake about this name, Johann Antony Gedler, Johann Benedict Gedler, Franz Stoss, Ruf, and Maldonner. Philip Knitting worked at Mittenwald, as did Joseph Kriner and Joseph Knitl, 1791, of whom we have a ticket, marked 2090; probably he thought a cypher meant nothing. Straube, at Berlin, about 1770, made some good violins after the Cremona model, with amber varnish, and was skilful in repairing old instruments; and Johann Henry Lambert was there about 1760; Theodore Lotz, at Presburg, and François Plack, at Schœnback, in Bohemia, about 1738, made good violins; and there was Augustine Huller, at Schœneck, 1776. At Amsterdam were Gysbert Vibrecht, 1707; Jan Bremeister, Peter Rimbouts, and Jacobs, of whom the latter made some good instruments after the Amati school, but could not attain their tone. François Antoine Ernst, born in Bohemia, 1745, was an excellent violin player, and became Concert Director at Gotha. He was a good maker also, many of his instruments being scarcely inferior to the Cremona model that he followed. Spohr used to play on one of them, which is a proof of their merit. He wrote a short memoir on the construction of the violin, which was published in the "Musical Gazette" of Leipzic. Jacob Augustus Otto was born at Gotha in 1762, and died in 1830; he was established at Halle, in Saxony, and was a good and careful maker, though for many years of his life he seems to have been employed almost exclusively in the manufacture of guitars; he was also very skilful in the repair of old instruments. He had no less than five sons who were makers; some at Halle and some at Jena. His work on the violin is well known, and we beg to acknowledge our obligations to it for many particulars of the German makers. Simon Joseph Truska, born in Bohemia, in 1734, made pianofortes as well as violins, altos, viols d'amour, and bass-viols; he was also a performer on the violin and violoncello; his death took place in the Convent of Strahow, in 1809. Matthias Frederic Scheinlein, born in 1710, lived at Langenfeld, in Franconia, where he died in 1771; he began as a violinist and a harpist. His son, Jean Michael Scheinlein, born in the same place, in 1751, was a better maker than his father, and the tone of his instruments was full and agreeable; but both those of his father and himself were weak in construction, and apt to give way in repairing. They were much used in the chapels. Michel Christophe Hildebrant, of Hamburg, towards the end of the century, was a good maker, and a skilful repairer. J. G. G. Heubsch wrote a work on the manufacture of musical instruments about 1764, and Charles Greiner, born at Wetzlar, 1753, invented an instrument to be played on with keys, which, by moving small cylindrical bows, put gut-strings into vibration; another of many experiments of this sort which never seem to have produced any permanent result. A Sweno Beckman is named at Stockholm in 1706, and Sawes Kiaposse at Petersburg, 1748.

We have several other German names in our list, which it does not seem necessary to mention, nor do we propose to give a list of the Continental makers in the present century, it would be long and moreover imperfect, from the difficulty of obtaining accurate details, although we have compiled a tolerably extensive list; but our work would decidedly be defective did we not name Mons. Jean Baptiste Vuillaume of Paris, but of Continental celebrity, well known for his enterprise and intelligence, and not surpassed by any living maker. He is also equally skilled as a successful repairer and imitator of the old instruments. We have seen it stated that Paganini once broke his favourite Guarnerius violin, which Vuillaume not only thoroughly repaired, but at the same time made another so like it in every respect, that even that great master himself was puzzled to distinguish which was the real Guarnerius. Vuillaume has always some instruments of the finest make and quality in his collection; the following is one of his labels :—

"J. B. VUILLAUME,
A Paris,
3, Rue Demours aux Ternes,
Ci-devant rue Croix des Petits Champs 42."

Gand is also a maker of first-rate skill, and is the son-in-law of Lupot, to whose business he succeeded.

CHAPTER XIX.

THE supporters of the theory of the eastern origin of the bow, may perhaps suggest that there is still some uncertainty in our history of its introduction; but we submit that we have given sufficient evidence to claim it for our country. In what way the violin, as known at the present time, was first perfected in England cannot now be authenticated; but the model and outline of the violins of the earliest English makers are different from the Cremona instruments. They partake more of the high swollen model of the earlier violins, made at Brescia and in the Tyrol, but more of the former pattern than the latter, particularly in the outline of the body and the volute or scroll of the head. We have before mentioned as the oldest makers, Joann Kerlin, 1449, of Brescia or Brittany, and Gaspard Duiffoprugcar, born in the Tyrol: neither of these names are Italian, and some may ask whether the violin-proper might have come from Brescia or the Tyrol, and passed through Germany to the Netherlands? The intercourse of the English people with the Low Countries being greater in the reign of Elizabeth than with the Italian nation, it may be suggested as the probable route by which we obtained the Continental instrument of this class, and may have somewhat modified ours accordingly. Indeed there were makers at Brescia and in Germany prior to and contemporary with those in Cremona. It must be observed, however, that the lute and viol makers of England, in olden times, were considered of high repute, and were competent themselves to introduce improvements in their instruments, and fiddles, as before-mentioned, were in use in our country in the time of Queen Elizabeth. The English makers are alluded to by Vincentio Galilei, the father of the great Galileo, in his work "Dialogo della Musica," where, according to Sir J. Hawkins' "History of Music," (Novello's edition, p. 404), he remarks, that in his time (1583) the best lutes were made in England. Yet it does not appear that they have kept to "Schools" connected with the chief makers in the art to the same extent as in Italy; consequently there is some difficulty in tracing the style from Jacob Rayman (1641), Thomas Urquhart (1650), and Edward Pamphilon (1685), the earliest makers of violins-proper known in England, to the time of Norris (1818), and Barnes and old John Betts (1823), which may be considered to terminate the chain; however, an endeavour will be made to accomplish this desired end, by comparing the style and character of the work of each maker, assisted by the dates at which they lived. In the perusal of the following pages it will be seen that many of the persons who are there taken notice of, have been prompted to try their skill as violin makers by the love of, or from being connected with music, and have been thus induced both to repair and make instruments.

The earliest authenticated name that comes down to us as a maker of viols in our country is Richard Hume, or Home, 1535; and it is stated in "Dauney's Ancient Scotch Melodies" that he was the great viol maker in Edinburgh, although an Englishman, and then had a grant of 20*l*. to buy stuff for the same.   There can be but little doubt that many other makers of lutes and viols were in existence at the same time and previously, but no record of their names has been preserved.   The maker's name of the instrument of the violin kind formerly mentioned, and considered to have been made by command of Queen Elizabeth, and given to Robert Dudley, Earl of Leicester, is not known ; but an engraving on the tail-pin, $J_{78}^{15}P$, is supposed to signify the year it was made in, and the initials of his name.   Whoever he was, whether English or foreign, he must have seen the true violin, as the improved form of sound-hole is used, and only four strings are applied.   Between the years 1562 and 1598 there would be living several instrument makers held in much esteem; and Thomas Mace, in his curious and eccentric book, " Musick's Monument," published in 1676, mentions some of them ; however, it had better be told in his own style :—" Your best provision, (and most compleat) will be a Good Chest of Viols; Six, in number ; viz. 2 Basses, 2 Tenors, and 2 Trebles : All truly, and Proportionally suited.—Of such, there are no better in the world, than those of Aldred, Jay, Smith, (yet the Highest in Esteem are) Bolles, and Ross, (one Bass of Bolles's, I have known valued at 100*l*.)   These were Old ; but we have now, very excellent good Workmen, who (no doubt) can work as well as those, if they be so well paid for their work, as they were ; yet we chiefly value Old Instruments, before new ; for by experience, they are found to be far the best."

We do not learn of any line of succession from Aldred or Bolles ; they seem to be the last of their race as musical instrument makers.   With regard to the other names, a little more detail can be given ; and those of

Jay and Smith will be met with in the seventeenth and eighteenth centuries.

John Ross, or Rose, the elder, who was dwelling at Bridewell in the 4th of Elizabeth (1562), and was the inventor of the bandora, an instrument of the guitar sort, with wire strings ; also made. viols and instruments of that class ; but Stow says he was excelled by his son in making bandoras, " voyal de gamboes," and other instruments.

In a collection of airs, called " Tripla Concordia," published in 1667, a chest of viols is advertised, containing two trebles, three tenors, and one bass, made by Mr. John Ross, the son, in 1598.

Henry Smith lived over against Hatton House, in Holborn, about 1629, and in the work just alluded to there is also an advertisement of a chest of viols, consisting of two trebles, two tenors, and two basses, made by him in 1633.

The other name (Jay), which Thomas Mace mentions, is supposed to be Thomas Jay, who, no doubt, was dead at the time he wrote the " Musick's Monument," as he alludes to the instruments of the several makers being old. There were other viol makers, whose labels have been seen (Hill's MSS.), which will continue the link :—" John Shaw att the Goulden harp and Hoboy nere the May pole in the Strand 1656. ' Also " Christopher Wise, in Half Moon Alley, without Bishops-gate, London, 1656 ;" and " William Addison in Long Alley over against Moorfields 1670." This brings us to Barak Norman, 1690, whom Sir J. Hawkins states (p. 793, Novello's edit.) " was one of the last of the celebrated makers of viols in England; he lived in Bishopsgate, and afterwards in St. Paul's Church Yard."

This maker will again be alluded to in connection with his partner, Nathaniel Cross.

The violin-proper was known in England some years before it became the favourite in " *good society ;* " and although we find it in the band of Queen Elizabeth, yet it was generally associated with wakes, revels, and other noisy merry-makings; but on Charles II. introducing his band of twenty-four violins, the instrument rose in estimation, much to the annoyance and great grief of the author of " Musick's Monument," that the noble and brave lute, also the majestic theorbo, should be " over top'd with squaling-scoulding fiddles " (p. 204). Again, in alluding to " those choice consorts " of his period (p. 236), and the great pleasure those performances gave both to the listeners and performers, which he states made " the musick lovely and contentive," he then makes further remarks : " But now the modes and fashions have cry'd these things down, and set up a great idol in their room ; observe with what a wonderful swiftness they now run over their brave new ayres ; and with what high priz'd noise, viz. 10, or 20 violins, &c. as I said before, to some single soul'd ayre ; it may be of 2 or 3 parts, or some coronto, seraband, or brawle, (as the new fashion'd word is) and such like stuff, seldom any other ; which is rather fit to make a man's ears glow, and fill his brains full of frisks, &c. than to season, and sober his mind, or elevate his affections to goodness. Now I say, let these new fashion'd musicks, and performances, be compar'd with those old ones, which I have before made mention of ; and then let it be judg'd, whether they have not left a better fashion, for a worse. But who shall be the judges ? If themselves ; then all's right."

Yet he cannot withstand recommending the intruder,

with certain qualifications, to complete the collection
of instruments requisite for the various performances
(p. 246): "After all this, you may add to your press, a
pair of violins, to be in readiness for any extraordinary
jolly, or jocund consort occasion; but never use them,
but with this proviso, viz. Be sure you make an equal
provision for them, by the addition, and strength of
basses; so that they may not out-cry the rest of the
musick (the basses especially), to which end, it will be
requisite, you store your press with a pair of lusty full-
sized theorboes, always to strike in with your consorts,
or vocal musick; to which that instrument is most natu-
rally proper."

The first maker of violins in England to whom we
have any guide, is Jacob Rayman, about 1641; but no
record is known to indicate of whom he learned the art.
It has been asserted by some persons that he made violins
of a large size, but those which have been seen are small,
and not of an elegant outline or model; the fore-bout
being wide, the short-bout long, and out of all proportion
with the lower part of the instrument. However, he was
a maker of talent and ability: the tone was clear, penetrating and silvery; not possessing the reedy quality of
the Cremona violins, but partaking more of the Brescia
character; and his instruments were highly prized. In
the extracts from the catalogue of musical instruments
for sale, the property of Thomas Britton, "the small-coal
man," who died in 1714, lot 8, a violin is stated as "an
extraordinary Rayman;" and in a note Sir J. Hawkins
remarks, "The tenor violins made by him" (Rayman)
" are greatly valued." Notwithstanding the purfling is
done indifferently, yet the work, generally, was neat and
good, the fluting at the edge where the purfle is inlaid is
deep and acute. The sound hole is rather small, like that

used at times by Steiner; the varnish very good, and of
a yellowish brown colour with a little tinge of red, and
the vehicle used appears to be oil.   Labels in genuine
violins as used by the maker are,

> " Jacob Rayman dwelling in Blackman
> Street Long—Southwark
> 1641."

> " JACOB RAYMAN at yᵉ Bell
> Yard in SOVTHWARKE
> LONDON 1648,"

and Hawkins states he dwelt in Bell Yard, Southwark,
about the year 1650.

The three makers whose names follow, two of whom
still retain a character for excellence, are Thomas Urquhart, 1650; Edward Pamphilon, 1685; and —— Pemberton, supposed to be about 16—, 1680, but these dates
are doubtful.   Tradition has brought down to us, that
these three persons were partners, and their place of
business was on London Bridge; but there is no evidence
such was the case, although it may be very probable, as
that locality at the date would be the best for trade.
Urquhart, it is believed, came from Scotland, and was a
maker of unusual merit for the period in which he lived;
the violins are of the full size, with an oil varnish of a
dark amber colour inclining to brown, yet it is bright
and grateful to the eye, and much resembles the Italian
varnish.   The tone is clear, pure, and silvery; and appreciated even at this period.   The violins and violas
are very scarce, and no violoncello has been seen of this
maker.

It has been stated that Urquhart came to England at
the time the two countries happily became united, but

this is doubtful when the dates are compared. James the Sixth of Scotland ascended England's throne 24 March, 1603, and entered London 7 May, 1603; yet nothing is known of this maker's instruments until about the date previously given.

Who instructed Edward Pamphilon in the art of violin making, or from whence he came, cannot now be ascertained. It is generally considered that Thomas Urquhart was his master, and the style of work, the colour and description of varnish favour this opinion; however he was not so successful with his violins as the elder maker. The outline is not graceful, the short-bouts are too long and out of proportion with the upper and lower parts of the instrument, the model high and swollen, and the sound-holes rather small. The varnish is either oil or turpentine of a red colour and brown tinge with a yellow ground, and now looks rich and beautiful, which age no doubt has greatly assisted. The violins—and no other instruments have been seen—are strong in wood, the tone clear, pure, and penetrating. The professors of this period greatly approve of them for orchestral uses. The following is a copy of a genuine written ticket or label, and the maker seems rather precise, as the day of the month is also added :—

" Edward Pamphilon
April the 3rd 1685."

Little can be related of —— Pemberton, the Christian name is not known, and some doubt exists whether he was the younger or the elder of the firm; if the latter, the supposed date of 1680 may be wrong, and he may be the J—— P——, 1578, the maker of the violin, presented to the Earl of Leicester by Queen Elizabeth; should this be so, he would be the first of the English makers that manufactured the violin as known at the present day : not that the gift above noticed is such an instrument ; nevertheless, whoever made it must have seen one of more graceful form and of greater elegance ; without all the elaborate and useless ornamental carving, most detrimental to tone and practical utility.

A maker named Thomas Cole was living about the same time as the three just noticed ; but no instrument has been preserved to this time to support his title as a workman. The label was as follows :—

" Thomas Cole, near Fetter Lane
in Holborn. 1672."

Daniel Parker, of London, 1714-15. This maker evidently was a pupil of one of the previous persons who lived in the latter half of the seventeenth century, and by the scroll or volute of the head it would probably be Urquhart or Pamphilon ; however he has shown himself a person not inclined to adhere to old instructions, but to progress in the art, and he made a first step towards improvement both in the outline and model.

Violins are the only instruments known of this maker, neither viola or violoncello has been seen, and the general character of the body of the instrument approached to the shape and form of the Amati school, however not quite so elegant. The varnish may be alcoholic, of an unpleasant brick-dust red colour, thickly laid on the instrument and not agreeable to the eye. The figure of the wood is generally handsome, the tone very good, clear, and powerful. About 1793 the violins of this maker were valued at five guineas, and in the beginning of the first half of the present century they have realized twelve and fifteen guineas, but now are again reduced in amount, from the desire of performers to possess none but Italian instruments, and other causes which depress the manufacture of such articles. Daniel Parker may be considered to terminate the first school of English violin makers. A new era now opens with the violin makers of England, in which the style of work is greatly improved; the model, with most of them, partaking of that used by Jacob Stainer, or Steiner, for it is spelt both ways, the beautiful and exquisite finish of this once favourite maker is closely imitated, and it has influenced all the workmen in the commencement of the eighteenth century; indeed all through this century the Steiner claimed preeminence; some of the violins having realized 100*l.*, and on one occasion a much larger sum; whilst the instruments of the Amati family, and other Cremonese makers, would scarcely reach an amount remunerative to the vendor, which, compared with the amounts since realized for the instruments of these deservedly great makers, seems perfectly absurd and ridiculous; however, in the latter part of the century the instruments of Cremona began to be sought for and appreciated.

The catalogue of musical instruments of Thomas Britton, previously alluded to, contains some names of violin makers which may form the link between the seventeenth and eighteenth centuries; but it is not known by whom they were instructed. "Lot 5, a good violin by Ditton;" this name only lives by the notice which Sir J. Hawkins has given him. It is different with that of " Baker of Oxford," for he deserves much commendation as a violin maker; two or three instruments of this class have been seen, and it is a pleasing recollection to allude to them: " Lot 20, a fine viol by Mr. Baker of Oxford." The work, in every respect, of the modern instruments was very good, indeed of excellent finish, the varnish of a light yellow colour, and probably oil or turpentine was the vehicle used. The tone was very pure and clear in quality, but not great in quantity.

Thomas Jay, supposed to be a descendant of the celebrated viol maker named in "Musicks Monument," who also made similar instruments, is stated to be living about 1690 to 17—, and the style of work in the few violins which have been seen, may be considered as an advancement towards superior workmanship. The instruments of Baker of Oxford and the maker under present notice are about equal in excellence. "Lot 22, another (viol) said to be the neatest that Jay ever made." This may be the maker just mentioned, or the elder one of the same name. It will be seen, about fifty years after that the work of another of this family name commanded a good price even for an inferior description of instrument. Edward Lewis was a maker of London, and stands preeminent for his good workmanship; his style was excellent, and the few violins which have been seen were varnished of a light yellow colour, however others assert that he also used a red colour with a golden ground. Be this as it may, there can be but one opinion that his violins, which are scarce, have much beauty, and are remarkable for their fine varnish. "Lot 19, another ditto (tenor) by Mr. Lewis; also Lot 24, another (bass violin) rare good one by Mr. Lewis." Some persons say that Jay and Lewis were partners, but there is no evidence known to decide this point.

Barak Norman has been mentioned as a maker of viols, and it is believed he was in business from 1690 to 1740. There is evidence of violoncellos being made in 1718, but no violin has been seen of his work. The violas and violoncellos of this maker are generally of full size, although one of the latter is known unusually small, of which mention will be made directly.

It will be seen by the varnish that he adheres to early recollections of colour, similar to the lutes and viols of old, by using a dark brown with a blackish hue, as if produced by nitric acid and accelerated in drying by heat, which heightens the colour, after which a coat or two of oil varnish to enrich the whole and help to preserve the instrument. This tint or colour may be considered the one generally used by him. The monogram will be seen inlaid either in the centre of the back, or in the upper vibrating plate just under the wide part of the fingerboard of his violoncellos; however the same device was used in the similar instruments made by Cross when they were partners. The tone, both of the violas and violoncellos, is very good and deservedly held in esteem. A tenor by this maker has been associated with the principal performers on this instrument for sixty or seventy years. Frederick Ware, celebrated for the great quantity of tone he produced, possessed it either before or at the commencement of the present century; and some time after his decease, it became the property of another professor of eminence, who delighted the frequenters of the Royal Italian Opera House in the romance or recitativo " Quale Spettacol," and aria, "Ah! Piu Bianco," in Meyerbeer's opera, "Les Huguenots," which was exquisitely sung by Mario, and the viola obligato was played by Henry Hill, which drew forth merited applause. Soon after his death the instrument passed into the ownership of Mr. Doyle, another principal viola performer of the same opera establishment. The small-sized violoncello, previously named, was seen by William Shield, the composer, at a humble shop or general dealer in the Borough; it was suspended by the head outside the house, and blowing about in the wind; although very dirty, the appearance of the instrument attracted his notice, and an arrangement was made not to sell the same until a friend of his had seen it. On his return home the circumstance was mentioned to James Crossdill, who ultimately bought the violoncello at a very small cost; and on its being cleaned and put in order, it was acknowledged a genuine Barak Norman, of superior quality of tone, having much power, although so small in size; the varnish was of a brown colour, but not so dark as that in general use. This instrument became a special favourite with the owner, who frequently used the same in his professional duties, and being the instructor to the Prince of Wales, afterwards George IV. it was taken to Carlton House on some occasion, when the tone much pleased the Prince, who expressed a desire to possess it; however the professor withstood several liberal offers. At a subsequent period a page was sent for this instrument, as the Prince wished to use the same that evening. The result was that the violoncello was never returned; and His Royal Highness stated that Crossdill might keep an Amati violoncello which had cost seventy guineas in lieu of it. About this time also a sinecure place of one hundred pounds per annum became vacant, which was given to Crossdill as the *amende honorable* to sooth the disappointment and loss, which sinecure he retained until his decease.

A violoncello made by Barak Norman in 1718 was, in the year 1790, considered of the value of fifteen guineas, since that time they have realized much larger sums. Nathaniel Crosse, or Cross: it is not known by whom this maker was instructed; his style greatly resembles that of Steiner, the fluting round the edge where the purfle is inlaid is very acute, and his instruments are beautifully worked in all particulars. The printed label used by him previous to becoming a partner with Barak

Norman, may be supposed to infer that he was a pupil of Steiner (but this borders on the impossible), or that he adopted the characteristic style of that excellent foreign workman; however it bears a fabulous number, as if the instruments he had made reached to so large a figure, the last figure being added in ink:—

" Nathanaeli Crosso Stainero
fecit. No. 2417."

He lived in Aldermanbury, London, and the instruments which have been seen, chiefly violoncellos, were very similar to those he made during his partnership with the previous maker; they are small in size and squat, and are varnished of a light yellow colour, the vehicle or body varnish is considered to be made of one of the soft gums, mastic or sandarac dissolved in alcohol, which renders them of easy blemish and disfigurement by any slight scratch, similar to the defect observed in the ornamental wood-work of Tonbridge Wells. The tone is clear and rather penetrating in quality. His violoncellos are generally sold as Barak Norman's, but the style of work of the two makers, in every particular, is very different. Cross is supposed to have been living in 1751. It has been previously noticed that the monogram of the elder partner is generally, if not always, inlaid either in the upper or lower vibrating plates of the younger workman.

It cannot be stated when these two makers became partners, but there is evidence that they were so about 1720, as the following copy of a printed label used by them will prove; the Maltese cross is at the top, and only three figures are in print, leaving the pen to complete the date:—

✠

" Barak Norman
and
Nathaniel Cross
at the Bass viol in St.
Paul's Church Yard.
London.   Fecit 172—."

John Barrett certainly is of the same school as Nathaniel Cross, whoever may claim to be the originator;
but he could not have been a pupil, as some persons suppose, for it will be seen they were contemporaries; he in
1722 carrying on business in Piccadilly, and the other in
St. Paul's Church Yard in 172—.   The genuine violins
that have been seen are of a long and high model,
approximating to the Amati pattern, with the Steiner
blended in the same.   There is a characteristic mark in
this maker's violins (for no other description of instruments have been seen), they all have ink lines instead of
purfle, and the fluting where the ink lines are and purfle
should be is very acute, similar to the work of N. Cross,
forming almost the inner half of a circle.   A perfect instrument of this maker is in the possession of Mr. C. Ward,
of Chapel Street, West, May Fair; the tone of which
is very pure and of superior quality, but not powerful.
The varnish on this violin when first used must have
been a pale yellow colour, but age has mellowed and
produced a brown tint.   The same defect exists with the
body varnish as that used by the maker previously noticed.
Copies of printed labels or tickets used by him in the
violins are as under :—

" John Barrett, at the Harp and Crown
in Pickadilly, 1722."

In 1731 the following was in use; a lyre with the crown on the top of it, printed on the left corner before the name, and in the date only two figures were printed, leaving space for the other two, to be added by a pen :—

> " Made by John Barrett, at ye Harp
> & Crown in Pickadilly, London, 1731."

The value of this maker's violins, in 1802, was considered to be six guineas; since then they have produced eight and ten guineas; but now a cloud o'er-shadows them as well as all other English makers.

The name of Joseph Hare is little known as a violin maker, nor can it be stated of whom he learned the art; however, he deserves especial notice as being, it is considered, the first person in England who used the flat model in his instruments. The varnish was a rich red colour, very good, and transparent. From the improvement in the principles or mode of work, and a varnish of different colour and brilliancy than previously used by the makers, it may be inferred that he was self-taught, and the first of a new school, but having no imitators until more modern times, when the Stradiuarius pattern became paramount. The following is a copy of the printed label used :—

> " Joseph Hare at ye Viol & Flute
> near the Royal Exchange
> in Cornhill London
> 1726 "

Peter Wamsley was a maker that once stood high in repute, his violoncellos more especially realizing great prices; the work was good and neat, with a bias towards the outline and model of John Barrett, but modified. Most of his violins, violas, and violoncellos, have only ink lines instead of purfle, although there are exceptions, and but few instruments are known that have this ornamental and useful inlaying. The varnish is generally of a red colour, with a brown tinge; but there are some instruments that have a brownish yellow colour, rather opaque. This maker fell into a great error by endeavouring to anticipate age, and worked the instruments so thin, the violoncellos in particular, that many years since they were liable to compress for want of sufficient thicknesses to withstand the tension of the strings; and in hot rooms they gave way in tone for want of greater stamina. Professors said "they played them out," and were far from satisfying either in quality or endurance. From this defect the tone is mostly hollow in sound, and wolfy, if the musical term may be allowed, which may be expressed by stating that many faulty or hard notes are created by this imperfect mode of gauging the instruments. However, there are a few violoncellos known of this maker in which more wood has been left, and the tone of them is good. The external appliances to remedy the defect alluded to will be a low bridge of rather hard wood, and strings of small size, with a sound-post full long and tight. Peter Wamsley made but few double basses, which are now very scarce. Those which have been seen were very good in tone, and stronger gauging; the varnish was of the red colour similar to that used in his other instruments. The following are copies of printed labels used by this maker :—

" Made by Peter Wamsley
at yᵉ Golden Harp in Pickadilly
London
1727."

The two last figures added with a pen. The two labels

following are printed on a narrow slip, and the last
figures on each are also added with a pen :—

"made by Peter Wamsley at the
Harp and Hautboy in Pickadilly 1735."

Also—

" made by Peter Wamsley at the Harp and
Hautboy in Pickadilly London. 1737."

The next printed label is very small, with plain black
lines as a border to it :—

" Peter Wamsley
Maker at the Harp
& Hautboy in Picaddilly
17 London 51."

There can be but little doubt that Henry Jay was a
descendant of the one previously named in the latter
part of the seventeenth and beginning of the eighteenth
centuries, but there is no proof that it be so, although
the style of work almost justifies the assertion. He was
a good and neat workman, and was celebrated for the
kits he made for the use of dancing-masters, each one
realizing five or six pounds. The varnish was of red
colour, with a brownish hue. The labels he used were
chiefly written, but some are printed :—

" Made by Henry Jay
in Long Acre. London. 1746."

Where it appears he resided for twenty-two years; then
the following printed label was adopted, the two last
figures put in with a pen :—

" Made by Henry Jay in
Wind-Mill Street, near
Piccadilly. London. 1768."

If the surmises regarding this family of Jay be correct,
they will have held a prominent place as makers of lutes,

viols, and violins, for more than one hundred years
and passed through the transition state from the more
antiquated instrument to that of more perfect character,
Henry Jay being the last of the family as a maker.

There were several violin and violoncello makers
residing in the City, in the latter half of this century,
who appear to have adopted small-sized violoncellos, not
exactly of the squat pattern used by Nathaniel Cross,
but something of that character, and still adhering to
the high model. It is not known who instructed them ;
but neither their work or goodness of tone has added any
lustre to their names, although the instruments have
been made more than one hundred years. Unless the
various thicknesses are properly blended, age will not do
much to improve them. The instrument must be good
from its first manufacture to derive the essential qualities
which age certainly imparts, although it cannot be denied
that age and much use may improve these instruments.
These makers form a portion of the links in the chain
we are endeavouring to elucidate. The first of this
class is,

> " Robert Thompson att the Bass Violin
> In pauls Ally St. pauls church yard
> London　1749,"

who appears to have taught his sons, or some other relatives, as there are others of the same surname.

> " Made by
> Thompson & Son
> at the Violin &c
> the West end of
> St. Pauls Church Yard
> London
> 1764."

Probably this is the firm mentioned in the Musical Directory of 1794 :—

"Samuel and Peter Thompson
Instrument Makers and Music Sellers
No. 75. St. Pauls Church Yard."

In 1775 and 1785 printed labels from instruments exist as—

"Made and Sold by
Chas. and Saml. Thompson
in St. Paul's Church Yard;"

but it is not known if they were relatives of those previously mentioned ; the dates and locality create a probability that they were so.

There was also another maker of this class who used a written label without date :—

"Sold by John Johnson
Cheap Side. London."

And others printed were used in 1753 and 1759, the last figure put in with a pen :—

"Made & Sold by John Johnson
at the Harp & Crown in Cheapside
17   London   53."

And the same for the later year.

Thomas Smith was a pupil of Peter Wamsley; the model and outline of his instruments were similar to his master's, but fortunately thicker in wood. As a maker, he held a good position in his day ; but at the present time the violoncellos are considered deficient in quality of tone. The first concerto that the late eminent Professor Robert Lindley played in public was upon a violoncello of this maker, and the instrument is still in possession of his second son, Mr. John H. Lindley. The varnish on the instruments is meagre and poor, of a brownish yellow colour, and not even approaching that used by his instructor. From 1756 to 1766 the following narrow printed labels were in use, so much like that formerly adopted by his master, that the conclusion may be drawn he had succeeded Wamsley in the business, and merely altered the name in the plate:—

"made by Tho*. Smith at the Harp and
Hautboy in Pickadilly. London. 1756."

The violoncellos of this maker, in 1799, were sold for a price varying from five guineas to eight pounds, and it is questionable if he made either violins or tenors.

John Norris and —— Barnes were instructed in violin making by the foregoing Thomas Smith, and they were fellow-apprentices. On the completion of the allotted time they had to serve, they became partners; and as there is evidence of their dwelling in Windmill Street on the 10th February, 1785, it may approximate to the time at which they commenced business on their own account. The Musical Directory previously alluded to, for 1794, shows at that time they had removed to No. 34, Coventry Street, Haymarket. No instrument of any description has been seen as made by either of these persons, and it is generally considered they became dealers in and repairers of violins, &c. A violoncello is known stamped with their names on the back, at the top, near the neck, but it is certainly the work of Edmund Aireton. The partnership was not one of congenial nature, and as soon as the expiration of the deed of partnership would allow it they separated. It is stated that Barnes retired from business and kept a farm at Hayes, near Uxbridge, and that he died there; however, the church books have been examined, and there is no evidence of his death. It is more probable that he opened a house of business in the old locality, as the Directory for 1794 has "Robert Barnes, violin maker, Windmill Street, Haymarket"; therefore, as the firm is also mentioned in the same book as existing, perhaps 1794 was the year of separation. The following is a copy of the label used by them :—

> " Made by Norris and Barnes
> Violin Violincello and Bow Makers
> To Their Majesties
> Coventry Street. London."

John Norris continued to carry on business at the usual residence; but statements differ regarding his retiring in favour of his shopman, Richard Davis. Some assert he died at Coventry Street, others say it was at a relative's house in Walham Green; but it is certain he is interred in the burial-ground of Fulham Church. The spot is marked by a stone, on which is engraved—

> " John Norris
> Died 10 March 1818,
> Aged 79 years."

Richard Duke attained to great celebrity as a maker, and was quite the fashion at the period in which he lived; but there is no positive evidence of whom he learned the art of making violins, tenors, and violoncellos, all of which instruments have more of the Steiner pattern in them "than is consistent with a fine reedy tone," which in the violins is clear and silvery. The pattern rather long, and a yellow varnish. Some of the tenors are small in size, about the length of a violin, and the endeavour has been made to obtain a larger and deeper tone by making them very broad; the tone is good, but more power is wished for on the two lower strings. The varnish of some of these instruments is very poor; the colour seems to have been obtained by a weak solution of walnut-stain, and a thin coat of varnish put on afterwards. The few violoncellos which have been seen are of a long pattern, with high model, and a yellow varnish; the tone very good. At one period he lived in Red Lion Street, Holborn. The following are copies of some of the labels used in the various instruments, and they mostly were written with pen and ink:

" Richd Duke
Londini fecit   1767."

Also, a similar one in 1769; but eight years afterwards he had changed his abode, and the label used was

"Richard Duke
Maker
Holborn. London. Anno 1777."

Probably about this time a printed one was adopted ; but there is no date upon it :—

" Richard Duke maker
near opposite
Great Turn-Stile
Holbourn. London."

There was a son of the foregoing, whose name is also believed to be Richard Duke ; and by the style of work he evidently was instructed by his father. However, the world did not smile on him, and in the early part of the present century he solicited purchasers of his violins and tenors, from house to house, of those in the trade. Both father and son generally stamped their names on the back of the instruments, at the top, near the button. At times the surname only, and at others with London underneath the name.

John Edward, or better known as old John Betts, and his nephew, Edward, commonly named Ned Betts, were both pupils of the elder Richard Duke ; they came from

Stamford, Lincolnshire, or its vicinity. John Betts was born in the year 1755, and in due time was sent to London to learn violin-making, but whether he proved a first-rate workman cannot be certified; report speaks to the contrary. As a dealer, great knowledge of the Italian makers is assigned to him. The instruments which bear his name often show an altered style, occasioned by the various workmen employed by him at different periods; namely, John Carter, Ned Betts, Panormo, Bernhard Fendt, and his sons, and others could also be mentioned. Much of their work, particularly of the nephew and the Fendts, being imitations of the Italian and old English makers, some of which are excellent copies. Dr. Forster, in his " Epistolarium," vol. ii., page 140, states : " Some of the best modern imitations of the Cremona violins are those of John Betts, of London, who for many years sold them, together with others of his own excellent form, in his house, under the Royal Exchange, in London." John Betts died March, 1823, and is buried at Cripplegate Church. Copy of a label used in 1782 :—

" J°. Betts N°. 2

Near Northgate the

Royal Exchange

London 1782."

The nephew had ability as a maker of violins, and was employed by his uncle ; his own style is admired, the tone being good, bold, and masculine ; but he became more proficient as an imitator of the old makers, both of Italy and England. It paid better, as H^y. Hill observes, than adhering to modern workmanship. The time of his death is not accurately known ; probably between 1815 and 1820. It is certain he died before his uncle.

Here may be considered to terminate the succession and second portion of violin-makers, from Jacob Rayman to John Betts, notwithstanding the last name, as a house of business, still exists. However, as the successors have not studied the art of violin-making, they can only be considered as dealers. Mr. Arthur Betts, who succeeded to the business of his brother, old John Betts, was a teacher and professor of the violin, and held an honourable position as a performer. At his death, the business became the property, or perhaps was under the guidance of the elder son, the present Arthur Betts, who had been a clerk in a large banking establishment in Lombard Street, consequently not a person using the various tools to develop a violin or violoncello. There was another nephew, named —— Vernon, who acted as shopman in the latter years of his uncle, old John Betts, and soon after the death of the latter, in 1823, opened a house of business in Cornhill, or near that locality; but in a very few years death terminated his career. He could not make a violin, and was only the dealer. Although but few allusions have been made to the Cremona instruments in this portion of the book, yet they were gradually arriving in England during the period just noticed, and their superiority of tone created a want which the supply, unfortunately, could not satisfy; it therefore led to the debasement of genuine instruments to gratify the love of gain. Two instruments were made out of one, by taking portions—say the head and upper vibrating plate or belly—then adding the sides and lower vibrating plate or back, also *vice versâ*, or any other mode of separation; then perfecting the whole as a violin, or whatever instrument it might be. Of late years these instruments have been brought before the public for sale, and it is greatly to be deplored that a truly genuine one is rarely to be seen. A new handle or neck is of no importance; but to divide a perfect article creates a disgust for the perpetrators, whoever they may have been.

It is a triumph of skill to be able to make a violin that shall be considered by the connoisseur and all others as a genuine Cremona; but then comes the test of true honesty: will you stoop and degrade yourself by selling it as a genuine article?

There are still several names in the eighteenth century to be noticed, which occasionally causes an encroachment on the present century, many of whom were indifferent workmen, and employed by the music publishers; they may be called fiddle-makers, not artists in making a violin; however, when a more favourable statement can be made of their skill it shall be mentioned. The names are arranged alphabetically.

CHAPTER XX.

ASTLEY, No. 9, Fleet Lane, 1785.

BAINES, pupil of Matthew Furber.

BARTON, GEORGE, Elliot Court, Old Bailey. Died about 1810.

CARTER, JOHN, worked for John Betts, and respected by him. It is said his employer paid the expense of his funeral. Label used:—

"J. Carter. Violin—Tennor
& Bass Maker, Wych Street, Drury Lane
London. 1787."

CLARK, Turnmill Street, Clerkenwell, pupil of Matthew Furber.

COLLIER, SAMUEL, musical instrument-maker, at Corelli's Head, on London Bridge, 1755.

COLLINGWOOD, JOSEPH, at the Golden Spectacles, on London Bridge, 17—.

CONWAY, WILLIAM, 1745.

CROWTHER, JOHN, Haughton Street, Clare Market, about 1755. Worked occasionally for John Kennedy, as well as the music-houses. Died about 1810.

DICKSON, JOHN, Cambridge, 1779.

DICKINSON, EDWARD, 1754 and 1790. Printed label used:—

" Edward Dickinson
maker at the Harp &
Crown in the Strand
near Exeter Change
London 1754 "

EVANS, RICHARD. This name was in the Crwth
mentioned in the former part of this work, which looked
much older than the date in the following label, with its
peculiar spelling :—

" Maid in the Paris of
Lanïrhengel by Richard
Evans Instrument maker
in the year 1742."

FRANKLAND, Robin Hood Court, Shoe Lane, 1785,
occasionally employed as an outdoor workman by William Forster, numbers two and three.

FURBER, DAVID, was the first of this name that made
instruments. The times of his birth and death are not
known; but the grandson, John Furber, said he was
buried at Clerkenwell Church. He no doubt showed
ability, as John Johnson, a violin-maker, living in Cheapside, in 1759, gave him further instruction.

FURBER, MATTHEW, was the son of the previous
named David Furber, and was taught by his father.
Died about 1790, and buried at Clerkenwell Church.

The second and third sons of the foregoing Matthew,
named Matthew and John, were taught by their father;
but whether the eldest son James was a fiddle-maker is
not known. Matthew, the second son, died about 1830-1,
and was buried at Clerkenwell Church. John Furber,
in 1841, was living in Cow Cross, Smithfield, and has
instructed his son, Henry John; both father and son, it

is believed, are living at this time. Copy of a written label used by the elder John :—

> "John Furber maker
> 13 John's Row top of Brick Lane
> Old S^t. Saint Luke.   1813."

HARBUR, or HARBOUR, ——, in 1785, lived in Duke Street, Lincoln's-inn Fields, and moved to Southampton Buildings, Holborn, in 1786.

HARRISS, CHARLES, lived at Cannon Street Road, Ratcliffe Highway, and was a Custom House officer, tide-waiter, as well as a fiddle-maker, and was chiefly employed in making instruments for shipping orders and the trade, but it is not known of whom he learned to work. Samuel Gilkes, who will be noticed elsewhere, was an apprentice of this person (*vide* the third William Forster).

HARRISS, CHARLES, was the eldest son of the above, and fellow-apprentice with Gilkes. However, little is known regarding him; he became possessed of some property in Northamptonshire from a branch of the family, and was called Squire Harriss; but some adverse circumstances compelled him to seek employment amongst the trade about the middle of the present century.

HEESOM, EDWARD, Londoni. Fecit 1749.

HOLLOWAY, J., 31, Gerard Street, Soho, 1794.

MARSHALL, JOHN, was a tolerably good workman, and the violins which have been seen are made of the Steiner pattern. Some of the labels used by him were as follows :—

> "Johannes Marshall
> Londini. Fecit 1750."

The above was printed on a narrow slip of paper, with

plain line border. The label which follows is taken from Hill's MSS. :—

> " Johannes Marshall (in vico novo juxta
> Covensam hortum) Londini. fecit 1757."

And this is a written label in our own collection :—

> " Marshall. London 1759."

On this last he makes known—

> " Good Beef 1^d A pound
> But trades all very Bad."

MARTIN, ——, was living at Hermitage Bridge, Wapping, in the years 1790 and 1794.

MERLIN, JOSEPH, appears to have possessed a mental development for invention, with mechanical skill, which powers were exerted to produce many articles, both musical and otherwise, and were exhibited at his museum in Princes Street, Hanover Square. In Madame D'Arblay's "Diary and Letters," vol. ii., p. 432, she states— "He invented many ingenious objects, some of which were of real utility, but most were mere playthings, or objects of curiosity. He was at one period of his career quite ' the rage' in London, where everything *à la Merlin*—Merlin chairs, Merlin pianos, Merlin swings, &c.; " also, it may be added, Merlin fiddles, and Merlin's mechanical pegs for violins and violoncellos. Frequent mention is made of him in the second volume of this Diary, with statements of sayings and actions, which shows she considered him a vain, conceited person. The violins he made were of the high model, similar to Steiner; the work was good, but the tone was of the usual quality of high-built instruments. The printed label he used was an oval to enclose the name and his ambition, with the direction written underneath. Here is another instance of the uncertainty of the number of instruments made by the figures on the labels. A copy of a label, with the date 1778, has the number of 106 upon it; and an original one, in 1779, has No. 104; therefore we must leave our readers to guess where he begun. The word "Improved" has been written with a pen on both labels :—

" Josephus Merlin

Cremonæ Emulus

Nº 104   Londini   1779

Improved

Queen Ann   Nº 66   Street East

Portland   Chapel"

Dubourg, in his work on the violin, p. 244, gives an amusing tale of a " Skating Fiddler," and alludes to a circumstance of which Merlin was the cause, and which occurred at Carlisle House, Carlisle Street, Soho Square; but no doubt much deplored by the lady who gave the entertainment.

MIER, of London, in 1786; but nothing is known of his instruments at this period.

MILLER. The original printed announcement of this person is much injured and mutilated, and it is questionable whether it be not that of the widow, as the last three letters appear to be " lez "; or it may be the termination of Eliza. Some interest may be created in the statement made, therefore a copy of the label is given :—

" Sold by . . . . lez Miller at the Signe of the

Citern London Bridge all Sorts of Musical

Instruments and Strings fitt for them

& old Instruments mended & also there

you may have all Sorts of New Tunes &c

Musick Books & Songs ruled Books

and ruled Paper at Reasonable rate."

The houses on London Bridge were all cleared away between the years 1757-1759 ("Chronicles of London Bridge," second edition, p. 378, *et seq.*); but this label seems much older.

MORRISON, JOHN, it is believed, was born about 1760, and it is not known who taught him the fiddle trade. He had a small shop in Princes Street, Soho, the beginning of this century, but quitted it in 1819, and, after residing in Shadwell for a time, ultimately located in Little Turnstile, Holborn, where he died between the years 1820-30. His work was very common, and he was mostly employed in making instruments for the music houses.

NAYLOR, ISAAC, was a pupil of Richard Duke, and lived at Headingley, near Leeds, Yorkshire, 1778-1792.

NEWTON, ISAAC, was a maker of average goodness, and occasionally employed to repair and make violins and violoncellos for Betts; the new instruments being varnished at the house of the latter, as the varnish of his own was a dingy yellow, somewhat like that used by Smith. He died about 1825, and his age is supposed to be between seventy and eighty years.

PEARCE, JAMES AND THOMAS, were brothers, and very common workmen, living in Peter Street, Saffron Hill, one of the Rookeries of London, the latter part of the last century or the beginning of the present one.

PRESTON, JOHN. It is not known if this person be related to John Preston the music publisher, who formerly resided at 97, Strand, London, and also called himself a musical instrument maker; but the latter only dealt in them as a music house. Labels used by the former of this name—

"Preston Pavement York 1789;
and

" John Preston, York.
1791.   Fecit."

POWELL, ROYAL AND THOMAS, were brothers, and both
neat workmen of average goodness; and were employed
about 1785-6 or 1787, as outdoor workmen by William
Forster, numbers two and three.   The label used by one
of them—

" Made by thomas
Powell Nº 18 Clemens
Lane Clare Market
1793."

There were two sons of the above Thomas, also named
Royal and Thomas.   In 1800 they were living in St.
John's Square, St. Lukes, and it is said they were between
twenty and thirty years of age at that time, but nothing
is known of their work; however one of them went to
sea, and being able to repair violins, met with favour
from his lieutenant, who was an amateur on the instrument.

SATCHELL AND FORSCHLE.   In the Musical Directory
for 1794, p. 57, we find the name of this firm as, " Instrument Makers, No. 21, Mark Lane;" but whether or no
they made violins we are unable to assert.   None have
been seen.   It may be probable they were military instrument makers.   The first name is also met with in
the " Memoirs of Harriot Duchess of St. Albans," by
Mrs. Cornwall Baron Wilson, vol. i. p. 208 :—" The
latter apartments Mrs. Entwistle considered might be let
for a shop, so as nearly to pay the whole rent; but Miss
Mellon received an application from a tenant, connected
with her own loved profession, which she favoured beyond any other more advantageous one; and she let the
ground-floor at a rate which was quite a matter of charity.

Her tenant was Mrs. Benson, the sister of Mrs. Stephen Kemble, both daughters of Satchell, the musical instrument maker to the Prince of Wales."

SIMPSON, JOHN. Although instruments have been seen possessing printed labels similar to that given at the conclusion of this article, yet it is doubtful if he was a maker of the violin class. Those fiddles which have been seen were not of good workmanship or tone, and looked like the style of those usually sold at the music houses. There can be little doubt but this John Simpson was the father of the following James Simpson, therefore prior to the date ascertained of the latter, the label being so much alike and in the same locality :—

" John Simpson,
Musical Instrument Maker,
At the Bass Viol and Flute,
in Sweeting's Alley,
Opposite the East door of ye Royal Exchange
London."

The Musical Directory for 1794, p. 60, gives the name of a firm : "James Simpson and Son, Instrument Makers, No. 15, Sweeting's Alley, Cornhill." The label used was—

" J. & J. Simpson,
Musical Instrument Makers,
At the Bass Viol & Flute,
in Sweeting's Alley,
Opposite the East Door of the Royal Exchange,
London."

SMITH, WILLIAM. There were two makers of this name, or it may be the same person moved to another place, and it is believed he or they were not related to the Thomas Smith of former years.   One of the labels used was " Wm. Smith, Real Maker, London, 1771." The other—

> " William Smith,
> Violin Maker,
> Hedon, 1786."

TAYLOR.   About 1820 this person was living in Princes Street, Drury Lane ; but at that time an elderly man, perhaps near seventy years of age. It is said he was regularly initiated into the business of fiddle-making, but it cannot be learned from whom he gained the knowledge. In the latter period of his life, double-bass-making and repairing became the favourite instruments to work upon ; and he must have arrived at some excellence, as Signor Dragonetti occasionally employed him.

THOROWGOOD, HENRY.   The work of this maker is not known, but the following is a copy of the printed label used by him ; the two first figures only of the date were upon it :—

> " Made and Sold by
> Henry Thorowgood
> at the Violin & Guitar under the
> North Piazza of the Royal Exchange
> 17   London."

TORING, OR TORRING, kept a shop in Shug Lane, Haymarket, now better known as Tichborne Street, about the spot at which the opening is made, and the County Fire Office is the corner.   He was a player on the fiddle as well as a maker and repairer of it, and attended balls ; however report says he did not reach much excellence in any department.   The late Mr. Hendric, the perfumer, of Tichborne Street, who died in April 1862, at the age of eighty-four years, had a lively recollection of dancing to Torring's fiddling, and the inquiries of him regarding this person seemed to recall all the pleasures of youth. It may be interesting to state that Shug Lane is an abbreviation of Sugar House Lane, taking its name from a sugar baker's establishment having been built there in Charles the Second's reign. It was then the high road from the village of Charing to Tyburn.

WEAVER, SAMUEL. No instruments have been seen of this person's make; but the copy of a printed label is as follows :—

" All Sorts of
Musical Instruments
made & Sold by
Saml. Weaver
on London Bridge."

WIGHTMAN, GEORGE. Nothing is known of this workman or his instruments, but he used a written label thus :—

" George Wightman
Wood Street London 1761."

WRIGHT, DANIEL. The same remarks as the preceding may be applied to this maker; the date being about 1745 :—

" Made by Daniel Wright
in Holborn, London."

WORNUM. The Musical Directory for 1794, p. 71, gives this name as a violin and violoncello maker, No. 42, Wigmore Street. No instruments have been seen.

YOUNG, JOHN, lived at the west corner of London-house Yard, in St. Paul's Church-yard, at the sign of the Dolphin and Crown, about the year 1724, and is styled a maker of violins and other instruments by Sir John Hawkins (Novello's edition, p. 807): "He lives not by his works!" Nevertheless concerts of instrumental music were advanced by him and his son, Talbot Young.

CHAPTER XXI.

ALTHOUGH many of the persons in the list just ended were very common workmen, yet there were others, during the same period, who by their talent and industry were gaining a position and becoming some of England's best artists in violin, viola, and violoncello making; not only creating a style of finish in their work by which they are known, but also producing a quality and character of tone to which professors will allude and draw comparison. With these names of violin-makers it is intended to commence with the oldest date and carry each school through to the present time, enumerating, as far as our knowledge will enable us, all those persons who have been pupils, and others who have followed a similar style, that the character and style of each artist may be kept separate.

Dr. Thomas Forster, in the preface to his " Epistolarium," vol. ii. p. 4, states the Forster family to be very ancient, and believed to have come from Normandy with William the Conqueror; also, that distinguished services were rendered at the battle of Crecy and also at Agincourt by one of this name, for which the king conferred the coat-of-arms and created General Sir Ferdinand Forster, knight banneret.

It is not known from what branch of the family Dr.

Forster reckons; however, it is in Scotland and the northern counties of England we must search for the Forster family, to which our inquiries are directed. In the "Border History of England and Scotland," by the Rev. George Ridpath, there is frequent mention of the name, and a statement that one Adam Forster, or Forrester, was sometimes serving as a royal commissioner, and at other times as an ambassador from Robert III. of Scotland to Richard II. and Henry IV. of England; also acting as conservator, with others, to various truces and peace arrangements regarding the Border district, from 1397 to 1402, and that about the last date he had been made Sir Adam, and was taken prisoner at the battle of Homeldon, and with other captives was " committed to the care of the steward of the household, to wait the king's pleasure." Whether he died a natural death, is not known; but to trust to the clemency of the Bolingbroke, who had been opposed, makes the result very doubtful. In 1424 we find John Forster acting as conservator to a truce between England and Scotland, and in 1429 he appears to become Sir John Forrester, Baron of Liberton, serving as a Scotch commissioner, with other persons named, for "mutual redress of injuries, and the speedy and effectual execution of justice in all matters under debate between the subjects of the two kingdoms;" and in the same year he is named John Forster of Corstorsyn. From the last date above stated until 1553, there is no mention of this name; we then find Sir John Forster, knight, was acting as the arbitrator for England; and in 1557, "about Martinmas, the Earl of Northumberland sent his brother, Sir Henry Percy, accompanied with Sir John Forster and others, chiefly those of the Middle March, to make an inroad into Scotland; they were met by Sir Andrew Ker and

a great body of the men of Tiviotdale, in the neighbourhood of Cheviot, almost on the boundary between the
kingdoms. A sharp engagement ensued, in the beginning
of which the English were beaten back; but recovering
themselves, they gained a considerable advantage over
the Scots, taking prisoner their leader, with several of
his followers. Sir John Forster fought bravery (bravely)
in this skirmish, wherein he was sore wounded, and had
his horse killed under him; and to his·prowess was
chiefly ascribed the victory gained by his countrymen."

In 1561 Sir John Forster was warden of the Middle
Marches, and retained that appointment for many years.
When James VI. of Scotland passed through Northumberland, in 1603, to ascend the English throne, he was
met by Sir Nicholas Forrester, the sheriff of that county,
by order of the Council of England. There is frequent
mention of the name in the " Border Minstrelsy," and Sir
Walter Scott, in the edition of 1848, has occasionally
added notes which enter into particulars of much interest
connected with our subject of inquiry. The song of
" Jamie Telfer of the Fair Dodhead," the second stanza,
vol. ii. p. 13, has—

> " There was a wild gallant among us a',
> His name was Watty wi' the Wudspurs;
> Cried—' On for his house in Stanegerthside,[3]
> If one man will ride with us!' "

Note 3, a house belonging to the Foresters, situated
on the English side of the Liddel.

Again, at p. 21, in the song, " The Raid of the Reids-
wire," second stanza—

> " We looked down the other side
> And saw come breasting ower the brae,
> Wi' Sir John Forster for their guyde,[4]
> Full fifteen hundred men and mae."

Note 4, " Sir John Forster, or, more properly, Forrester, of Balmborough Abbey, warden of the Middle
Marches in 1561, was deputy-governor of Berwick, and
governor of Balmborough Castle. He made a great
figure on the Borders, and is said, on his monument at
Balmborough Church, to have possessed the office of
Warden of the Middle Marches for thirty-seven years.
This family ended in the unfortunate Thomas Forster,
one of the generals of the Northumbrian insurgents in
1715; and the estate, being forfeited, was purchased by
his uncle, Lord Crewe, and devised for the support of
his magnificent charity."

There is also a note to the song, "Dick o' the Cow,"
p. 72. "A challenge had been given by an Englishman, named Forster, to any Scottish Borderer, to fight
him at a place called Kershopefoot, exactly upon the
Borders. The Laird's Jock's only son accepted the
defiance, and was armed by his father with his own two-
handed sword. The old champion himself, though bed-
ridden, insisted upon being present at the battle. He
was borne to the place appointed, wrapped, it is said, in
blankets, and placed upon a very high stone to witness
the conflict. In the duel his son fell—treacherously
slain, as the Scottish tradition affirms. The old man
gave a loud yell of terror and despair when he saw his
son slain, and his noble weapon won by an Englishman,
and died as they bore him home. . . . The stone on
which the Laird's Jock sat to behold the duel, was in
existence till wantonly destroyed a year or two since.
It was always called the Laird's Jock's Stone. 1802.
[The reader will find Sir Walter Scott recurring to the
fate of the Laird's Jock in 1828. See Waverley Novels,
vol. xli. p. 377.]" There is also an official tract in the
British Museum worthy of notice regarding this name,

and the portion connected with our subject is now ex-
tracted from the "Archæologia," vol. xxii. p. 161. It is
thus headed: "Copy of a Manuscript Tract addressed
to Lord Burghley, illustrative of the Border Topography
of Scotland, A. D. 1590; with a Platt or Map of the
Borders, taken in the same year, both Preserved in one
of the Royal MSS. in the British Museum. Communi-
cated by Henry Ellis, Esq. F.R.S., Secretary, in a Letter
addressed to the Right Honourable the Earl of Aberdeen,
K.T, President.

"Read, 31st May, 1827.

"My Lord,   British Museum, May 29, 1827.

"Among the Royal Manuscripts in the British Museum
is a volume of Saxton's Maps (Bibl. Reg. 18, D 111),
published in 1579, upon the margins of which the names
of the justices of the peace in England at that time, or
soon after, are written, with occasional miscellaneous
remarks. Several manuscript maps and draughts of
sea-ports, towns, &c. are added in different places of the
volume, likewise accompanied by memoranda in the
handwriting of Lord Burghley, to whom the volume at
one time belonged.

"Among these latter articles is a manuscript map with
the date of December, 1590, entitled, 'A Platt of the
Opposite Borders of Scotland to the West Marches of
England.' Upon this the different castles and houses of
strength, with the names of many of the owners, are
minutely specified, and I cannot but think that a copy
of it would be valuable for the 'Archæologia' of the
Society of Antiquaries. At the bottom of this map or
platt is written, 'The moste of these places on the
Scottish syde are tower and stone houses, with some

fewe plenashed Townes, as Dumfreis, Annand, Lough-
maben, and such like; for the rest not put downe, they
are but onsetts or stragling houses, th' inhabitants
followers of some of these above described. For those
on the English Coaste, they are referred to the tract
lately sent to your L. of the Description of them in
particular.' The tract here alluded to, follows a page or
two after, and if my judgment does not deceive me, is a
curious abstract of the state of Border topography towards the close of the reign of Queen Elizabeth. I
have had it transcribed, and here present it to your
Lordship and the Society.

" I am, my Lord,

" Your Lordship's faithful Servant,

" HENRY ELLIS.

" To the Right Hon. The Earl of
    Aberdeen, K.T., President of
    the Society of Antiquaries."

Then follows " The Division of the severall Charge
of the West Borders of England and Scotland." At
p. 166, " LEVEN or KIRKLYNTON. Next it towardes the
Borders runneth the river Leven. Upon which river
dwelleth Grames, Etheringtons, and Forsters, and others;
under the governance of a bayliffe for a gentleman, one
Mr. Musgrave of Haton, lord of that mannor called Kirklynton. But the castle where he should lye is Scaleby.
Now in these tenauntes, who are able border men, if they
were well governed, is a great quietnes for staunching of
theft, for they are the onely men that ride both into
England and Scotland, who cannot be letted without
their masters residence, or careful watch of the country
within them."

Page 168. " The severall surnames of the English

Borderers and their dwellings.   Eske. Upon both sides
of the river dwell the Grames, which is the greatest
surname at this daie upon the West Border.   For the
Grames of Eske and Leven are able to make V C ser-
viceable men.

" Leven. Upon this river also dwelleth many Grames,
and above Kirklynton in Sompert dwelleth a great surname of Fosters, and about Hethersgill is a surname of
Hetheringtons.   Bewcastle. There dwelleth Fosters,
Crosers, and Nixsons, but sore decayed."

By reference to the platt or map in the work from
which the foregoing has been copied, it will be seen that
the strong houses of the Forsters's were opposite to that
portion of the country held by the Armstrongs on the
Liddle, therefore hard knocks no doubt had been inter-
changed. Stanegirthside has been previously mentioned ;
more to the eastward, on the banks of the same river,
was another castle held by Robert Forster ; and more
easterly still is Kirksopfoote, where the duel took place
between the Laird's Jock and a Forster, before alluded
to, therefore we may infer this castle also to have belonged to the latter name.

We have thus endeavoured to trace the name of Forster
to the locality in which those connected with our inquiries
were known to have resided, but we are not prepared,
at present, to prove they were related to the statesmen
and warriors previously named, although there are some
circumstances which makes this more than probable ;
but as the Scotch say, " it is not proven," therefore no
further comment will be made on the subject.   The first
of this family who made violins was John, but whether
the name was spelled Forester, Forster, or Foster, is now
difficult to determine ; the general belief is, that the first
mode was the original, and the probable cause of the

variations may be the careless manner, in early times, of writing names which may be seen in the church register, also in the engraving upon the tombstones of this family.   At this distant period of time there is much difficulty in obtaining correct information of the town or village in which he was born, but in the researches made ten or twelve years since amongst the aged inhabitants of Brampton, in Cumberland, they named several places in that part of the country from whence he probably came ; but none could assert what pursuit or vocation he followed in early years ; almost the whole of them said he came from " Ayont the Wood," but others named Kirklington, Bewcastle, Longtown in the Netherby quarter ; but the town which had more advocates than any other was Kirkandrews, on the Esk, which, from the many kind inquiries made on this matter by Mr. Samuel Irving, of Stanwix, Carlisle, may be considered to be proved almost to a certainty ; but it should be "Ayont the Wood, in Nichol Forest, in the parish of Kirkandrews, on the Esk." From this place the aged people said, he moved to little Easby, two or three miles from Brampton, in the parish of this last name, and left there for the town of Brampton, at which place they all agreed he died about 1790, at the great age of one hundred and two or three years, and was buried at the old parish church, a mile, or little more, from the " Town Foot."

The family, however, state that he left Longtown for Brampton.   On searching the church book of burials we find a John Foster buried 7 Oct. 1781, aged ninety-three years ; but there is no statement to identify that it is the desired one ; however, as this date so nearly coincides with the information gained, and will agree with the birth of his son William, supposing that he married at twenty-four or twenty-five years of age, it is assumed

that this must be the record of his death; consequently
he would have been born in or about 1688.

Only vague accounts could be learned of the vocation
he followed, but it was generally asserted that, latterly,
he made spinning-wheels, or was a wheelwright, and at
one period of his life he was a gun-maker, and considered
by all of them to be " a very ingenious man, and occasionally made fiddles." A violin was seen in 1850, said
to be his make, and with some degree of truth could be
traced back. The work was rude and unfinished, the
model very high, resembling the Steiner, but the outline
approached nearer to the pattern of the Amati. It was
much decayed and worm-eaten, and if strings had been
to the instrument, it is doubtful if it would have borne
tuning to try the tone. This violin was possessed by
Joseph Rook, a violin maker and performer, who lived
in Rickergate, Carlisle. He had been intimate with
Joseph Forster, grandson (if we are correct with the
identity) of this said John, from the first year of the
present century.

Not only were many of the facts just enumerated
known to the family, but it can be added that John
Forster was of stature more than six feet, also of athletic
frame of body, with great muscular development.

Presuming the identity of John Foster or Forster is
established, then William Forster was the son of the
previous named John; but as there are four in this
family of the same Christian name connected with violin
making, a number will be attached to each for the
advantage of any required reference. It cannot be
positively asserted whether William Forster (1) was born
in Brampton; it is believed to be so, but there is no
proof; however he must soon have located there. He
was born about 1713-14, and by the books of the old

church of that town he married in 1736; his first wife, who died in the prime of life, being only forty-four years of age; but she had borne him a son who added lustre to the name in after years. This William Forster (1) was a spinning-wheel maker by trade; also repaired and made violins. In the former vocation he gained some celebrity, as the following extract from a letter of Joseph Rook, written in Nov. 1850, when he was in his seventy-seventh year, shows:—" I can give no more of the history of your ancestors at Brampton than I have already given you, only your great grandfather William was a noted maker of spinning-wheels as well as violin maker, and his son Joseph, my old acquaintance, practised making wheels so long as they were in use in the country, but it is many years since they were put out of use by the invention of machinery."

Whether in or about 1775-7 he was pressed in pecuniary circumstances, or whether the love of the drama tempted him to accept, as inmates or lodgers, a family connected with the theatrical company then performing at Brampton, yet it was in his house that Miss Harriot Mellon was born! This information is obtained, or rather, it should be stated, corroborated by one that became employed in the sequel of events (the fact being known to the family); therefore it had better be given in his own language, written December 1850, although there are some trifling inaccuracies which, at his age, may be overlooked:—" * * * * I must endeavour to exert myself and will give an account of a remarkable circumstance that happened in your G. Grandfather's House at Brampton. Upon a time a Company of Itinerant Comedians were at Brampton, and one of them of the name of Melon and his Wife had an apartment in your G. Grandfather's House during their stay at Brampton.

Mrs. Melon was brought to bed of a Daughter, the Child
was Baptized at Brampton; they left and nothing was
heard of them afterwards. About Octr. 19, 1824, a Lady
with a Splendid Equipage containing a number of Car-
riages and Servants of every description arrived at the
Howard Arms in search of her Register, and the Lady
in question was M^{rs}. Coutts; that some time after that
became Dutchess of S^{nt}. Albans. She inquired if your
G. Grandfather was living, [and] she gave such a
description as the people soon knew it was Willm.
Forster; a certain proof that her Father and Mother
had talked about your G. Grandfather repeatedly; she
went to see the place where she first drew breath in, and
saw Jo; and had some conversation with him. She no
doubt would ask him many things and understanding
that he played the Violin she desired him to raise her a
Band of a few Violins and Violoncells and go to Carlisle
where she gave a splendid Breakfast to all the Genteel
people in Carlisle and the neighbourhood. We were
verry handsomley rewarded for our trouble: a Guinea a
piece for us in Carlisle and something handsom for
Joseph for coming from Brampton. The Splendid doo,
was on the 21 of Octr. 1824, at the Bush Inn, Carlisle.
About mid-day she set off for London with all her
retinue. I consider this something marvelous but an
absolute truth as good a subject for a Novel as ever Sir
W. Scott had.

"Your &c

"S. A. Forster."   "JOSEPH ROOK.

A violin of this maker is possessed by one of the
writers of this book, and it has a label inside thus:—

"William Forster
Violin Maker
in Brampton."

The work is not of a high class; the tone deserves commendation, although more quality could be desired. The varnish is alcoholic, and not very transparent, nor is the instrument purfled; but on the whole it is an evident improvement on the fiddle seen of his father's make. The following is a copy of the inscription engraved on the tomb-stone, in the burial-ground of the old parish church of Brampton, about a mile, or little more, from the Town Foot :—

> "In memory of W^m. Forster
> Violin Maker of Brampton
> who died March 4th. 1801
> aged 87 years."

Being recorded on this grave-stone as a violin-maker, and the spinning-wheel trade not being mentioned, may probably have arisen from the celebrity his son, William, had achieved in London as a maker of musical instruments of the violin genus.

CHAPTER XXII.

ILLIAM FORSTER, the second of this name, but the first who gave renown to it as a maker of violins, violas, violoncellos, and double basses, became one of England's greatest artists, and received the patronage of royalty and many of the nobility. He was also greatly appreciated by the professors of these instruments; and is better known in the musical world, and amongst the trade, as " Old Forster."

From a memorandum written by his son, William Forster (3), in one of his old account-books, stating that " my father died on the 14 Decr. 1808, aged 68, on the 4th of May last," it is considered, in the absence of more positive information, that this date may be correct, but no corroborative proof could be found in the book of the register of births belonging to the old church of Brampton, Cumberland. However, there is a baptismal register at the Presbyterian Chapel of that town, " 1739, May 5th, William, lawful Son to William Foster, Brampton," which no doubt relates to this person; therefore he would be rather older than stated by the son.

William Forster (2) was instructed by his father in making spinning-wheels and violins, both of which trades he followed during the earlier years of his life, and further obtained employment by playing the violin at the various merry-makings and other festivities of the locality. Report says he excelled in the performance of reels; and the elder branches of the surviving family know that in after years, when trying violins which had either been made or repaired, the owners would frequently request to have one of them played. He also composed several Scotch reels, some of which were published by himself, when it was the custom of each music establishment at Christmas time to bring out a book of dance-tunes for the new year.

Whether it was ambition that first occasioned him to come to London in the hope of bettering his fortunes, or whether, as some persons say, it was an aversion of his parent to the female whom he loved, and who ultimately became his wife, that induced him to leave his native place, we are unable to say; the most probable cause may be the disrespect shown to the memory of his mother by the other parent marrying a second wife only four months after the death of the first. The time of his leaving Brampton is not known; but if the above suppositions be correct, then it would be about 1759, he being between twenty and twenty-one years of age; whatever the irritating cause may have been, it must have been felt most acutely, as he left with little or no pecuniary resources, and engaged himself to a drover to assist in bringing cattle to the south.

The neighbourhood of the Commercial Road and Prescott Street, Goodman's Fields, is said to be the first locality he resided in; and, not being able to get employment in either business which he had learned, he at length obtained work as a gun-stock maker, occasionally making violins and selling them to the music shops. The privations and sufferings endured during this period of his life he was always of opinion caused the aggravated dyspepsia and other constitutional evils which were never eradicated ; indeed, it is questionable if some of the present generation are not sufferers from the internal debility then created, which has descended to them, although their own struggles in life have been sufficient to cause it.   Ultimately he gained permanent employment at a music-shop on Tower Hill, kept by a person named Beck; and the violins made by him being much approved of, with a quick sale of them, he solicited for greater remuneration ; the employer refusing to accede, he left him and came westward to a house on the right-hand side, and about the middle of Duke's Court, St. Martin's Lane, Charing Cross.   The houses are all now pulled down, and the National Picture Gallery erected partly on the site ; he pitched his tent here for a time, and afterwards resided in St. Martin's Lane, near to and on the same side as May's Buildings.   The following is a copy of the label used at that period :—

> " William Forster,
> Violin Maker
> in S^t. Martin's Lane.   London
> 1762."

While residing here, a Colonel West, of the Grenadier Guards, who was the father of the late Temple West, of Malvern Lodge, Worcestershire, Esquire, gave him an order for a new violin, to be made similar to a pattern then shown, which he completed so successfully that the colonel became a kind, generous, and sincere patron. He also, being an amateur desirous of improving the violin, had numerous experiments tried in the manufacture of such instruments, which this artisan executed for him.   The advantages thus gained were always gratefully acknowledged by William Forster (2) as being of essential assistance and advancement to him in the art. He always felt pleasure in stating that his first real success in life was through Colonel West.

Between the years 1762 and 1782 his skill and exertions had been rewarded, and he had become a musicseller and publisher; he had also changed his residence. Sometime during the above period a different label had been used in the instruments, particularly the violoncellos, and it bears evidence of being part of a title-page of some work published by him, which probably had not been successful; he therefore used the name as a label, which is in a written character, with some ornamental engraving cut through, that is neither useful, nor, in this particular, any embellishment. In those instruments where this label is used, it will generally be found that the name William Forster, in the Roman letter, is placed also on the inside of the short bouts, just above the lining which is attached to the sides and the back. It is the same printing taken off the label used in 1762, as will be readily seen by the ornamental flourishes corresponding and now cut through. At what time he first was honoured by working for royalty we are unable to state, as the account-books before the 14th November, 1773, have either been destroyed or lost; and those books which still exist were kept imperfectly. However, there is proof of his living in St. Martin's Lane in 1781, and he may have moved to 348, Strand, in 1784-5. The following copy of a label or card will show he had this high patronage before changing his residence to the more public thoroughfare; and it also shows that the varnish he used had become celebrated and specially referred to :

" William Forster
Violin, Voloncello, Tenor & Bow-maker

Also Music Seller,
To their Royal Highnesses the
Prince of Wales and Duke of Cumberland
Opposite the Church S^t. Martin's Lane.   London.

N.B.
The above Instruments are made in the best manner
and finished with the original varnish
and a Copy of every Capital Instrument in England
may be had."

The house was the corner of Duke's Court, and believed
to be that one nearest to Charing Cross.   The Duke
of Cumberland here mentioned was the brother of
George III., who died in September 1790.   He was a
great patron of musical art, and performed on the violin.
An incident occurred at the house above stated with this
Prince, who had called to try a violin that had been
repaired.   Whilst amusing himself in playing various
pieces to test the quality of tone, a noisy peel struck up
from " the bells of Saint Martin's," which sadly interfered with his power of resolving any improvement or
not ; he therefore said, hastily, " confound those bells ; I
cannot hear a note for them ; " and immediately opened
the door at the end of the shop, leading to the sitting-
room, on the table of which had been placed the family
dinner, which was one of humble quality, but yet gave
forth savoury exhalations.   With all promptness and
courtly ease he exclaimed, " Forster, what a nice dinner
you have, I'll have some with you," and drew a chair to
the table, and, perhaps for the first time in his life, par-
took of—shall it be named ?   Yes ; black puddings !

In 1781 negotiations were commenced, through the
kind assistance of General Jerningham, with that genius
and improver of modern instrumental music, Guiseppe,

or, as he has always signed his letters, Joseph Haydn. Agreements and other documents were drawn up and signed for the supply of certain pieces of music, as sonatas, trios, quartets, and sinfonias. These transactions, no doubt, will be of interest to the lovers of music, therefore they are now made public, together with some original letters connected with the works of this intelligent composer. The opening of commercial transactions between Guiseppe Haydn and William Forster (2) is copied from the account of the solicitor, named James Mainstone; the first entry bears date 17th August, 1781.

" Attending Mr. Forster in conference on a contract, intended to be entered into by Mr. Forster with Mr. Haydn, for Mr. Forster's purchasing of him and printing his compositions, and advising thereon."

" Taking Instructions for drawing Agreem[ts] between Mr. Haydn and him, for the sale and purchase of Mr. Haydn's Musical Compositions by Mr. Forster."

" Drawing same, fo. 15."

" Attending to read over and settle same."

" Engrossing same for Execution."

" Attending and advising Mr. Forster as to the mode of execution of same by Mr. Haydn, and which he was to communicate to Gen[l] Jerningham, who had undertaken to get it signed by Mr. Haydn at Vienna."

The document alluded to in the above, no doubt, was sent to General Jerningham, as the following answer is elicited by it :—

" Sir,—I received your favour 21 ins[t], & send you here enclosed a letter for Mr. Guiseppe Hayden, to whom I have wrote very circomstantially, and inclosed to him a procuration which he is to get drawn up either in French, German, or Lattin, and authenticated by two witnesses,

and a publick notary, which gives it full force in all Countries; you may depend on it that what I have sent to
Mr. Hayden is to the full as strong as the letter of Attorney you sent me in which there's nothing but a repe-
tition of words.

"If you receive from Hayden a letter for me, send it
to Lady Jerningham's in Grovener square, she will take
care I gett it; when Hayden has sent you his procuration
to print his musick, lett me know it, and am,

" Sir,

" Your most obed.^{t.} humble Servt.

" CHARLES JERNINGHAM.

" Cawsey, *August 24th*, 1781."

This letter is addressed to Mr. William Forster, Musical Instrument Maker, Duke's Court, St. Martin's Lane,
London; and has also written upon it—

" A Monsieur.

" Monsieur Juiseppe Hayden
de Chappelle de S: A^s Le Prince
Esterhazy de Galantha
en Autriche.   A Vienne."

THE AGREEMENT.

" Je reconnois d'avoir reçu de Monsieur Guillaume
Forster, Marchand et Imprimeur de Musique; demeurant
dans le Strand à Londres la Somme de Soixante et dix
livres Sterlins, pour les Simphonies, Sonates, et autre
pieces de ma composition ci-dessous mentionées, et qui
comencent de cette façon Savoir. No. 1 une Simphonie
à plaisieurs Instruments qui comence ainsi :—

" Trios à 2 Flutes traversieres et Violoncello qui comencent de cette manier :—

" Premier Recueil de trois Sonates, pour le Clavecin,
avec l'accompag d'un Violon :—

" Second Recueil de 3 autres Sonates, pour le Clavecin, avec l'accompag d'un Violon.

" Et je certifie, et déclare à tout le monde qui j'ai
vendu au dit Monsieur Guillaum Forster les dites Simphonies, Sonatas et autres pièces, et que je lui ai envoie
les manuscripts aux dates suivantes, savoir :—

" Les six Sonates pour deux flûtes traversières et
violoncello, le 31 de May 1784.

" Le Simphonies marquées ci-dessus No. 1 et 2 par
Monsieur le General de Jerningham, le 19 de Juin
1784.

" Les Simphonies No. 4, 5, et 6, avec le dit premier
Recueil de 3 Sonatas, pour le clavecin, le 25 d'Octobre
1784.

" Les Simphonies marquées ci-dessus No. 7, 8, et 9,
le 8 de Novembre 1784.

" Et le dit Second Recueil de 3 Sonatas pour le clavecin le 28 d'Octobre 1785.

" Je certifie aussi, et déclare, qu'il m'en paya le prix
convenu, entre lui moi ; et qui montoit en tout à la ditte
some de soixante et dix livres Sterlins, par des lettres
d'Echange sur Vienne ; qu'il m'a remis pour cet effet
(a l'ecception du prix de deux Simphonies No. 1 et 2,

le prix des quelles il paya pour mon compte à Monsieur le General de Jerningham, alors à Londres). Et je certifie et déclare de plus, que le dit Guillaum Forster est le seul Propriétaire des dites pièces; que je lui ai ainsi vendu, et que je lui ai cedé et transporté tous mes droits et toutes mes pretensions là-dessus. En fois de quoi j'ai souscrit mon nom à cet Ecrit a Esterhaz ce. 1786.   " Guiseppe Haydn,

" Maestro di Capella di S. Alt. S.
il principe Esterhazy." L.S.

The following exhibit is also written on the same document:—

          " D.   Forster agt. Longman & anr.
" This paper writing was shewn to Jos. Haydn at the time of his examn. in this Court before   Ja. Eyre."

There is next a letter from Haydn in German relating to the sale of some symphonies, and pianoforte sonatas, together with the composition, known as " The Last Words." The following is a translation of it:—

" Sir,   " Estoraz, the 8th April, 1787.
    " After a long silence I must at length inquire after your health, and at the same time inform you of the following new musical works which are to be had of me: namely, six grand symphonies, a grand concerto for pianoforte, three short divertimentos for pianoforte for beginners, with violin and bass; one sonata for piano-forte alone.
    " An entire new work, consisting of purely instrumental music, divided into seven sonatas, of which each sonata lasts from seven to eight minutes, together with an introduction, and at the end a terremoto or earthquake. These sonatas are composed in accordance with the

words which our Saviour Christ spoke upon the cross; these seven words are—

1st words, Pater, dimitte illis, quia nesciunt quid faciunt.

2nd words, Hodie mecum eris in Paradiso.

3rd words, Mulier, ecce filius tuus.

4th words, Deus meus, Deus meus, ut dereliquisti me ?

5th words, Sitio.

6th words, Consummatum est.

7th words, In manus tuas commendo spiritum meum.

" Immediately after follows the conclusion; namely, the Earthquake.

" Each sonata, or each subject, is produced simply by instrumental music, in such a manner as to leave the deepest impression on the mind of the most unmusical. The whole work lasts somewhat more than an hour, but there is after each sonata some pause, that one may be able to think on the next following subject. All the sonatas together contain somewhat more than four of my symphonies. The whole will be contained in thirty-seven pages.

" Also, I have three more pretty notturnos, quite new, with violin obligato, not at all difficult, with a flute, violoncello, two violins ripieno, two French horns, viola, and contre-bass.

" If you should wish to have some of these musical pieces, you will have the kindness to let me know, and at the same time also the price which you are willing to give me for them, as soon as possible. The seven sonatas are already nearly copied out fair upon soft paper, and waiting an early answer. I am, with much esteem,

" Your most obedient Servant,

" JOSEPH HAYDN.

" I beg you will answer me in the French language.

" I hope to visit you at the end of this year, but as I have not yet received an answer from Mr. Bremner, I shall go for this winter to Wegel Argagiers; meanwhile I thank you for the accommodation you have offered me."

Then are the three following letters in French :—

" MONSIEUR,

" Je vous envoie la musique composée d'après les sept dernières paroles que Jesus Crist prononces sur la croi pour les quelles je laisse à votre disposition de m'envoyer ce que vous jugerez que j'ai mérite.

" J'espére que j'aurai peut-être le satisfaction de vous voir cet hiver en attendant. Je suis très parfaitement,

" Monsieur,

" Votre très-humble et
obeiss'. Serviteur,

" JOSEPH HAYDN.

" Estorz, le 28 Junii, $\overline{787}$."

" MONSIEUR,

" J'espére que vous avez reçu ma lettre, & la musique de sept paroles; je vous fair à savoir, que je composé Six quartets et six sinfonie, qui ne sont pas encore sorti de ma main. Si vuos vuole les achté vous même, aye la bonté de me le faire savoir par la premier occasion, je vous donne toutes les douze pièces pour vint-cinq guinēs. Je suis avec tout l'estime possible

" Votre très-humble Servit.

" JOSEPH HADYN.

" Estorz, le 8th Août, $\overline{787}$."

This is addressed

" To Mr. Forster, Musical Instrument Macker To the Prince of Wales, No. 346 in the Strand, London."

" Monsieur,

" J'ai reçu votre lettre avec un grand plaisir. Je vous fais savoir, que j'ai reçu de Mons. le Général Jerningham cinq guiné ; mais vous verrez vous même, que pour une tel musique comme les Septs Paroles j'ai plus mérite ; vous pourrez bien encore me donner au moins cinq guiné. Je vous envoies en attendant six quattuors pour lesquels vous aurez la bonté en égard au contrat de m'envoier vingt guiné sitôt qu'il sera possible. Je ne manquerai pas de vous envoier les Six Sinfonies par la primièr occasione. J'attend bientôt une réponse de vous, et je suis avec toute l'estime possible,

" Monsieur,

" Votre très-humble obéiss'.

" Serviteur,

" Joseph Haydn.

" Estoraz, le 20 7bre. $\overline{787}$."

The next is a letter in German, dated the 28th of February, 1788, of which the following is a translation :

" Estoraz, Jan. 28th, $\overline{788}$.

" My dear Mr. Forster,

" Are you not annoyed with me, that on my account you have had trouble with Mr. Longman. I will satisfy you another time on that point. It is not my fault, but that usurer, Mr. Artaria. So much I promise you, that as long as I live neither Artaria nor Longman shall receive anything from or through me. I am too honourable and upright to annoy or injure you. So much, however, you will of yourself plainly perceive, that whoever will have six new pieces from me must give more than 20 guineas. I have, in fact, some time ago concluded a contract with somebody who pays me for every 6 pieces

100 and more guineas. Another time I will write you more. Meanwhile I am with all respect,

"Your obedient servant,

"JOSEPH HAYDN.

"To Mr. Forster, Musical Instrument Macker
to the Prince of Wales, No. 348, in the
Strand, London."

On the fly-leaf of one of the old account-books for 1786 is written, "The dates of the years when Haydn's works came," which are as follows:—

Aug^t.	22,	1781	. . . .	Haydns Ov^t.	N° 1
June	20,	1782	. . . .	D° D°	„ 2
Feb^y.	14,	1784	. . . .	D° D°	„ 4
„	24,	1784	. . . .	D° D°	„ 5
May	6,	1784	. . . .	D° D°	„ 6
July	6,	1784	. . . .	D° Trios, op. 38	
Nov^r.	22,	1784	. . . .	D° Ov^t.	N° 7
„	26,	1784	. . . .	D° D°	„ 8
Dec^r.	6,	1784	. . . .	D° D°	„ 9
Jan^y.	3,	1785	. . . .	D° Sonatas, op. 40	
Dec^r.	26,	1785	. . . .	D° „	op. 42

The above are alluded to in the agreement, and the terms for which they were composed there specified.

The following compositions arrived as under:—

"July 16, 1787. Recd. of Haydn M.S.S. of the Crucifixion published with the title of 'Passione.' Ten guineas was paid for this instrumental piece; and the Postage cost fifteen shillings.

"5 Octr. 1787. Received the M.S.S of Haydn's quartets, op. 44. Twenty guineas was paid for these; and the Postage cost twenty shillings."

On the 3rd December, 1787, there is an entry of

"Paid Postage of six Overtures from Haydn £2. 5. 0."
It is supposed these are the sinfonias Nos. 10 to 15.

Perhaps some extenuating reasons should be offered
why the classical composition of the "Passione" should
have received so small a remuneration as ten guineas;
small, indeed, does this amount appear, compared with
the sums given for trifling songs, when we hear of as
much as fifty pounds being paid to a fashionable and
favoured composer for a mere ballad. However, let it
be remembered that the name of Haydn was little known
at that period except by those who cultivated the science;
also, that instrumental music was not much appreciated.
Perhaps it is not yet sufficiently admired by the British
public, although greatly advanced—first, through the
exertions of a Committee of English Musical Professors
who gave promenade concerts, *à la Musard*, at the
Lyceum Theatre, about the year 1836-7, and introduced
a sinfonia and overtures during the evening's performance, interspersed with waltzes, quadrilles, and other
light pieces. The first season or two was remunerative
to the common wealth; but soon after they ceased to be
so, or were given up from other causes. Soon after, a
professor, named Eliason, a violin-player, made a similar
venture, but success did not attend his rule, he bringing
Julien to this country to conduct them. At length concerts of this class were carried on under the management
of Julien, who ultimately introduced vocal music, omitting some of the classical instrumental pieces, which
gave a new and greater delight to the audience; consequently they were very successful. But now the rising
taste is fully shown by "the rush" for a place at the
"Monday Night Popular Concerts," where the music that
is performed consists only of the most classical compositions, performed by a few professors of the highest

standing in the art. But to return from this digression; the "Passione" is a large, or, as the trade would say, "heavy work," from the number of plates required, and all other expenses attendant on bringing it before the public; the probable cost in 1786-7 would be as here enumerated:—

	£	s.	d.
65 Pewter plates, at 1s. 6d. per plate .	4	17	6
Engraving the same, at 4s. 6d. do. .	14	12	6
Copper title and engraving	1	11	6
66 quires of perfect paper for 75 copies, at 1s.	3	6	0
Printing 75 copies, at 1s. 2d. . . .	4	7	6
	28	15	0
Cost of the manuscript	10	10	0
Making in the aggregate £39	5	0

Fifty copies was the first number which was printed; and about the year 1817-18 another twenty-five were struck off, making a total of seventy-five copies; the full price of each copy was fifteen shillings; but many of those first printed were sold to subscribers for 10s. 6d. each, and it is questionable if any of the remaining copies realized more than the trade price of twelve shillings, therefore averaging them at the last sum a total of forty-five pounds would be the result. However it is known that several copies of those last printed were disposed of as waste paper, therefore no very profitable trade specu-lation. Publishing orchestral and other instrumental music in England was not, nor is it at this time, a suc-cessful adventure; but William Forster (2) appreciated the merit of Haydn's music and hazarded the result; being the first in this country to introduce the works of this talented composer to public notice. It may be interesting to give a condensed list of the numerous works of Joseph Haydn, published by him and his son William Forster (3), the plates being all destroyed.

Sinfonias known by letters from A to W	. .	23
Do.	numbered 1 to 15	15
Do.	„ 1 to 12, with a star . .	12
Do.	Op. 10, Three; Op. 12, Four; Op. 15, Six; Op. 29, Three; Op. 31, Six; and Op. 35, Six	28
Do.	The London, or the celebrated in the key of D	1
Do.	La Chasse, the Concertante and the Toy	3
Do.	The Passione	1

Some of which sinfonias were also known by other designations, as " The Candle one," letter B, in which each performer extinguishes the light at his desk and retires from the orchestra. In letter F, the fourth string is lowered in one of the movements. Letter L, the minuet and trio for the second parts of each have the same notes reversed or played backwards. Letter Q, it is said, was the exercise given in to the College at Oxford when the Doctor's degree was presented. No. 14, La Reine de France. No. 4 with star, The Roxalana. The Toy, in which children's toys are used with the other instruments.

Quartets—Op. 33, Six; Op. 44, Six; Op. 65, Six; Op. 72, Three; Op. 74, Three . .	24
Violin Solos, Six; Duet—Violin and Violoncello, One; Trios—Flute, Violin and Violoncello, Six; Sonatas, with accompaniments for Violin and Violoncello—Op. 40, Three; Op. 42, Three; Op. 43, Three	22

Being one hundred and twenty-nine pieces besides a few others of lesser importance.

The Steiner pattern was the one adopted by William Forster (2) to work by, in 1762; and for several years later it was more or less used; however, about ten years afterwards the Amati outline was employed, but the model was high and swollen, and very deficient in the elegant *ensemble* of those instruments constructed through the remaining years of his life.

The violins of the first period were coloured of a brown tint, as if produced with dilute walnut stain and then varnished. The violoncellos are of a dark red with a blackish tinge, and much stronger of gum than that used for the treble instruments. The exact period is not known when such fine varnish was used by this maker; but a violoncello was made in 1772 for the chemist who had assisted him in the knowledge of the method to dissolve the gum amber; therefore the improvement, probably may date from that year; although the varnish on this particular instrument is not to be compared for beauty or richness of colour with those of later times. A further notice will be taken of this violoncello when relating its history.

The violas and violoncellos of this maker were the most esteemed, he was not as successful with the violins, although many of them are very good; and the reasons may be that sufficient attention was not paid to the various thicknesses of the gauging connected with the height of the model used; however it is certain the violins had not such fine tone as the other instruments. Many violas could be enumerated of known excellence, as the one made for Dr. Walcot, *alias* Peter Pindar; also, for Bartolozzi, the celebrated engraver; and another made for Mr. Henry Leffler, a professor, formerly of the Italian

Opera, and husband to the celebrated singer of that name. This viola is now possessed by Gordon Gairdner, Esq. of Hamilton Terrace, St. John's Wood; and others could also be named. Many violoncellos could have attention drawn to them for their special excellencies, but a few only will be noticed; and a reference to the list of the instruments made, which will soon be specified, will more fully develope the names of eminent persons and professors of high repute that had them. Robert Lindley used one at the Italian Opera for nearly forty years; he named it "The Eclipse." This violoncello is now in the possession of Mr. Charles Lucas, the principal of the Royal Academy of Music. James Crossdill had a famous one. Cervetto the younger had one that was burned when the Italian Opera House, Haymarket, was destroyed by fire on the 17th June, 1789. The regret felt at the loss of this instrument was so acute, that he retired from the profession, being sure he never could have another violoncello that would suit his purposes so well. The fact may be explained thus:—When a young man he procured the instrument, and with the professional practise it ripened in tone as he ripened in years, therefore was greatly admired and appreciated. But it would tire to fill up space with the many fine violoncellos that could be brought to notice. There were only four double basses made by William Forster (2), three of which were made by the command of his Majesty George III.; and some interest was excited regarding one of them, which will be seen by the two following letters from professors in the king's private band. Mr. H. Niebour was the person who had to play upon it when completed.

" SIR,—You will probably receive a letter from Mr. Niebour concerning a double-bass upon a much larger

scale than the one we already have. I hope you will
have no objection to attempt the making it. His Majesty, from the specimen you have given, has a very high
opinion of what you could produce on an enlarged scale.

" I am, Sir,

" Your sincere friend,

" And humble servant,

" H. COMPTON.

" Gariboldi has, I understand, one coming from Italy;
do not let us be outdone. I shall not be in town till
Tuesday next, I wish to see you on the above subject,
and will call on you on Wednesday. Get my tenor
finished and sent home by that time. Don't forget Nico-
lay's tenor."

No date was to the above letter, but it may have been
received about the time the following one was written.

" Windsor, *July 4th*, 87 (1787).

" SIR,—By his *Majesty's* order you are to form a
plan for a new double-bass; it is to be at least four
inches wider, if not more, than that which you made, and
the depth according. You are to make it as well as
possible—so as not to let aney exceed it in England—
as Garriboldie has sent to Itally for an uncommon large
one, so you are desired to exert your utmost skill, and
exceed both in goodness and size by the performance at
the Abby next year. I shall be glad of my violincello
as soon as possible.

" Am with respect,

" Sir, your hum^{le}. ser^t.

" H. NIEBOUR."

The body of a fifth double-bass was made, but from
some cause was laid aside; however it was completed in

October, 1822, for Mr. Samuel Deacon, of Leicester, who, it is believed, still retains it. All the double-basses were made of the same shape as the violoncello; not tapered off and bevelled at the fore end of the sides, and the back for greater convenience to the performer, but at the same time a probable injury to the tone.

Previous to giving the list of instruments made by William Forster (2), assisted by his son and workmen, it will be proper to mention that it can only approximate to correctness from the deficiency in the account-books before referred to. It is with some difficulty that the list in its present state has been accomplished; but, as far as enumerated, it may be relied on. The numbers on the instruments do not assist to arrive at satisfactory conclusions, as they are occasionally marked for those made in each year, at other times altogether omitted, and sometimes marked in succession from year to year.

Three distinct classes of work were adopted; but the style, to a certain extent, was retained through all of them; therefore known as from this maker. The commonest instruments were not purfled, and they had oil varnish of an inferior quality; and in later times, when the name became famous, few of this class were made in consequence of the deceit and fraud practised by persons getting them purfled, and selling them as "genuine Forster's," for a larger sum than they were really worth.

The next class was much better finished; they were all purfled, and a superior varnish used; therefore formed an intermediate instrument to the next or highest style of workmanship, in which everything was embodied to conduce to excellence, to beautiful appearance, and to the finest tone.

The earliest or first entry that is met with in the old

account-books now in existence is on the 14th November, 1773 :—

1773. *Violin*—Mr. Cole. *Tenor*—Mr. Mainstone.

1774. *Violins*—Mr. Crosdill; Mr. Hay; Mr. Stone. *Tenor*—Mr. Stone, of Okehampton. *Violoncellos*—Mr. Ritchards; Col[l]. Hamilton.

1775. *Violins*—Mr. Minehouse, Clare Hall, Cambridge; Mr. Hawkes, Steiner copy. *Tenor*—The Rev. Mr. Waller.

1776. *Violin* — Mr. Hackwood. *Violoncello* — Mr. Skardon.

1777. *Tenor*—The Rev[d]. Mr. North.

1778. *Double Bass*—The Rev[d]. Mr. Hodgson.

1779. *The account-books are lost or destroyed.*

1780. *Tenor*—G. M. Molineux, Esq[re]. *Violoncello*—The Rev[d]. Mr. Hodgson.

1781. *Tenor*—Mr. Hawkes.

1782. *Kits*—Mr. Bishop (three). *Violins*—Mr. G. Burchell, Musician, Manchester; Mr. Mainstone, Attorney, Essex S[t]. Strand; Mr. Edmund Lee, Dublin (three); Mr. A. Foster, Whitehaven, Cumberland (four); *Tenor*—Mr. Edmund Lee, Dublin. *Violoncellos*—His Royal Highness the Prince of Wales (two).

1783. *Violins*—Mr. Jones (two); Colonel Edgerton; Mr. Sykes; D[r]. Pollock; Mr. Wilson, Kensington. *Tenors*—Mr. Cheere; Mr. Borghi. *Violoncellos*—Mr. Ashley; Mr. Gray, Marsham Street, Westminster; Rev[d]. J. G. Honnington, Eaton; Mr. Hole, Jesus College, Cambridge; Mr. Cervetto; Mr. G. Lewis, Moss Hills, Leominster, Herefordshire.

1784. *Kits*—Mr. Bishop. *Violins*—Mr. Ware; Mr. Cousins (two); Mr. Johnston; Mrs. Gibbs; Mr. Emly, at Mr. Gilbert's, Bodmin, Cornwall. *Tenors*—Captain Armstrong; Rev[d]. Mr. Rokeby; Mr. Ayres, Woolwich.

Violoncellos—Mr. Webb, Temple ; Mr. Dixon, Felstead, Essex ; Rev^d. Mr. Savery ; Mr. Yatman ; Shaw, Esqre., North Street, opposite Whitfield's Tabernacle ; Mr. Johnston.

1785. *Violins*—Mr. Warler ; Mr. Compton (two) ; Mr. Cole ; Sir John Palmer ; Rev^d. Mr. North ; Mr. Ware (three) ; Mr. Smith, Grange Court ; one sold in the shop ; Mr. Marsh, Attorney at Law, Canterbury ; Mr. Dale. *Tenors*—Mr. Compton (two) ; Longman ; Mr. Abbot ; Sir John Palmer ; Lord Rivers ; Mr. Holcroft, 46, Upper Mary-le-bone Street, near Tichfield S^s., Oxford Road ; Mr. Jeremiah Clark, Organist, Birmingham ; Mr. Panton. *Violoncellos*—Mr. Dorrien ; Mr. Broadwood ; one sold in the shop ; Mr. Compton ; Mr. Tucker ; Sir John Palmer ; Rev^d. Mr. Savery, Plymouth ; Mr. Bradstreet, S^{nt}. John's College, Cambridge ; Robert Williams, Esqr., Trinity College, Cambridge, by order of D^r. Bostock ; Mr. Griesbach.

1786. *Violins*—Rev^d. Mr. Savery (two) ; Mr. Barrett, Organist, Northampton (two) ; Mr. W. Dale ; Mr. E^d. Clay, King Street, Covent Garden ; Honble. Mr. Champion Dymocke, N°. 120, New Bond Street ; Mr. Holcroft, Upper Mary-le-bone S^t., Tichfield Street, Oxford Road, (two) ; Lord Malden ; Mr. Wood, Devonshire Street ; Brimner ; Mr. Smith, Grange Court. *Tenors* —Captain Lucas ; Mr. Nathaniel Dance ; Mr. Dymoke ; Mr. Clarke, Organist, Birmingham ; Lord Malden ; General Jerningham ; Mr. Jackson, Clerkenwell Close ; Mr. Mitchell ; Mr. Compton. *Violoncellos*—Mr. Smith, Grange Court ; Mr. Claget ; Mr. Bartolozzi ; Mr. Compton ; Colonel Edgerton, G^t. George Street, Hanover Square ; Mr. Vinicombe ; Mr. Borghi ; Rev^d. Mr. Townley ; Mr. Dance ; Mr. Tucker ; Mr. Roper, Hertford S^t., May Fair.

1787. *Violins*—Mr. Smith, Grange Court; Mr. Eley, for Lady Nudegate; Rev^d. Mr. Savery (two); Mr. Blake. *Tenors*—Mr. Stephenson (two); Mr. Baumgarten, sent to the Ox Inn, for him at Liverpool. This Viola was paid for by the M.S.S. of his five celebrated Fugues for the Organ; Mr. S^t. Ledger. *Violoncellos*—Mr. Hare; Mr. Gordon, N°. 3 Bass; Mr. Cervetto for Mr. Randel, Southampton Street, Bloomsbury; D^r. Chas. Bostock, Weverley Abbey, near Farnham, Surrey; Mr. Johnstone; Mr. Oliphant, Sloane Square; Mr. Corfe, Salisbury; His Grace the Duke of Richmond; Mr. Holcroft; Mr. Hunter, Kings Arm Yard, N°. 4 Bass; Mr. Morse. *Double Bass*—His Majesty King George the third.

1788. *Violins*—Mr. Kellner for Mr. Grandler; Rich^d. Dupuis, Esqre. Queen's Dragoon Guards; The Rev^d. D^r. Chas. Bostock; Mr. Emley. *Tenors*—George Dorrien, Esqre. N°. 19, Somerset Street, Portman Square; Capt. Cooper, 75, Lambs Conduit Street; Mr. Lanzoni; D^r. Chas. Bostock; Mr. Pennington; Captain Lucas; Mr. John Skynner, Birmingham. *Violoncellos*—Mr. Benson, sent to Salisbury; Rev^d. Mr. Savery; Mr. John Skynner, Birmingham; Mr. Pickering; Mr. Clark, Birmingham; Mr. Buckley, Manchester, N°. 5 Bass; Sheldon, Esqre., Sunning, near Reading, Berks; Mr. Shaw; Mr. Iscard.

1789. *Violins*—Mr. Fuller, 5, Dover Street; Captain Cooper, Lamb's Conduit Street; Mr. Blake for Mr. Rogers, Stamford; Mr. W^m. Griesbach; Mr. Webb; Mr. Stephenson; Rev^d. Dean Palmer, Great Torrington, Devon; Prado, Esqr., Twickenham. *Tenors*—Rev^d. Mr. Savery; Mr. Fuller, 5, Dover Street. *Violoncellos*—Mr. Thos. Smith, Emanuel College; Mr. Stewart, Hill Street, Berkeley Square; Mr. H. A. Hole, Exeter;

Lord Delewar; the Rev^d. Mr. Lewin, Bushey Mill, Watford; Mr. Corfe, Salisbury; Mr. Cervetto, a new Steiner copied Bass, N°. 1; Miss Abrams; Rev^d. Dean Palmer, Great Torrington, Devon; Major Price, Tiverton, Devon; Rev^d. Mr. Morres, Windsor. *Double Bass*—His Majesty King George the third, a large Double Bass.

1790. *Violins*—Mr. Smith for Mr. Cater; Mr. Smith; Rev^d. Mr. Wright; Miss Abrams; Mr. Newbery, Surgeon of His Majesty's Ship *Assistance*, Portsmouth; Mr. J. B. Pierson. *Tenors*—Mr. Hunter, Kings Arm Yard, Coleman Street; Mr. Smith for Mr. Cater; Mr. Thos. Shaw, Drury Lane Theatre; Miss Abrams; Mr. Papendick. *Violoncellos*—Earl of Uxbridge; Mr. Aldersey; Mr. Cervetto (two), N°s. 2 and 3 made in 1789, Steiner copies; Peter Shaw, Esq^e.; Mr. Hole, N°. 2, 1790; Mr. J. B. Pierson; R. Sheldon, Esq^e., Skitty Hall, near Swansea.

1791. *Violins*—Mr. Scheener, 11, Upper John Street, Tottenham Court Road; Charles Shaw Lefevere, Esq. Bedford Square; Captain Henry, Tenterden, Kent (two); Mr. Blake for Mr. Rogers, Lincoln (two); Mr. Holcroft, Steiner copy; Mr. Yatman.

1791. *Tenor*—Lord Balgonie. *Violoncellos*—Mr. Twining, Junr. Strand; Mr. Otley; Mr. Fuller; Peter Shaw, Esq^e.; Lord Archibald Hamilton; Mr. Yatman.

1792. *Violins*—Mr. Barrett, Organist, Northampton; Lord Archibald Hamilton; Mr. French.

1792. *Tenors*—Captain Henry, Tenterden, Kent; Mr. Yatman, Percy Street. *Violoncellos*—Mr. Eley (two); Captain Henry, Tenterden, Kent; Dr. Eden, Red Lion Street, Clerkenwell; Mr. Cervetto.

1793. *Violins*—Mr. Yatman; Rev^d. Mr. Lewin; Mr. H. Potter, 39, Margaret Street, Cavendish Square; also another for Mr. G. Nicholls. *Tenor*—Mr. Morse.

1793. *Violoncellos*—Mr. Armstrong, Apothecary, Portman Square; Mr. Scola; Mr. Eley; Mr. Cervetto.

1794. *Violins*—Mr. Cole, Carlton House; Rev^d. Mr. Clark, Bedale, Yorkshire; Mr. French; Mr. Smith, Bromley.

1794. *Tenors*—Although no tenors appear to have been sold in this year, yet there is an entry worthy of remark. " *Dr. Haydn. Putting in order and stringing a tenor.*" *Violoncellos*—Mr. Lindley; Mr. Attwood.

1795. *Violins*—Mr. Blake for —— Dare, Esq^e. Nottingham Place; Captain Boden; Captain Chalmers; Mr. Nicks.

1795. *Tenor*—Captain Chalmers. *Violoncellos*—His Majesty George the Third; William Franks, Esq^e. Beech Hill; Mr. Ware, Senr.; Dr. Brown, Artillery Lane; Mr. Attwood; W^m. Sheldon, Esq^e.; Mr. Eley; Captain Chalmers.

1796. *Violins*—Mr. French; Colonel St. Clare, 25, Reg^t.

1796. *Violoncellos*—Mr. Brant, Highbury Terrace, Islington; Rev^d. H. A. Hole, Exeter.

1797. *Tenors*—Mr. Bright, Stradiuarius copy, large; Dr. Walcot.

1797. *Violoncellos*—Mr. Yatman (two); W^m. Sheldon, Esq.

1798. *Violins*—Rev^d. Mr, Vinicombe, a mute violin; Mr. Osbaldiston, Twickenham; Mr. G. Ashley, Stradiuarius copy; Mr. Bauch.

1798. *Tenor*—Mr. Corson. *Violoncello*—Mr. Linley.

1799. *Violins*—Rev^d. Mr. Chudleigh; Mr. Blake, 7, Nottingham Street, Marylebone, for Mrs. Farhill, 43, Mortimer Street, Cavendish Sq^e.; Mr. Blake, for Mr. Deane, 21, Nottingham Place, Marylebone; Mr. Yatman, a mute violin. *Violoncellos*—Rev^d. Mr. Poole, at

Mr. Ruscombi Poole's, attorney at law, Bridgewater, Somersetshire.

1800. *Violins*—Mr. T. Blake, 55, Hans Place, Sloane Street (two).

1800. *Tenor*—Mr. Yatman.

1801. *Violins*—Mr. French, for the Grotto Concert; Mr. Yatman.

1801. *Tenor*—Mr. French, for the Grotto Concert.

1802. *Violin*—Mr. B. Blake, 55, Hans Place, Knightsbridge.

1803. *Tenor*—Mr. Corson, Brentford. *Violoncello*—Rev^d. H. A. Hole.

1804. *Tenor*—Rev^d. D^r. Nicholas.

1805. *Violoncello*—Mr. Yatman; *Double Bass*—His Majesty George the Third.

1806. *Violoncello*—Rev^d. H. A. Hole.

A statement has been made public and believed to be correct, although no entry appears in the account books to prove it, that the last violoncello, and probably the last instrument made by William Forster (2), was manufactured by express wish for Mr. Crossdill; and it was one of the violoncellos offered at the sale of his musical property, on the 9th May, 1826. " Lot 6. A violoncello— of the long Stradiuarius pattern—by Forster, Sen., the very last instrument manufactured by that justly celebrated maker, and most highly valued by Mr. Crossdill, with bow, in a most excellent dove-tail case, covered with leather, brass nails, lock and key."

It was bought for forty-six guineas by Thos. Dodd, the dealer in musical instruments, for Edward Prior, Esq. late of York Terrace, Regent's Park. Henry Hill, in his manuscripts alluding to this William Forster, writes that he was " a highly and justly esteemed maker of violoncellos, &c. &c.; it is said he was not originally bred to the occupation, but came to it by chance or accidental preference; if so, he must have possessed a rare talent, for his instruments are second in merit to none, but the best Europe has ever known; especially his *amber coloured violoncellos*, they are renowned for mellowness, a volume and power of tone, equalled by few, surpassed by none. His dark red coloured are not so much admired, though the difference in merit is scarcely discernible. He was not so successful with his violins and altos; he does not appear to have given the same care and judgment to their production; he followed the grand Amati in his forms and model without being a mere copyist, and had a rare excellence in the facture of the violoncello peculiarly his own. The expression—*a true Forster tone*—is not a *jeux d'esprit*."

William Forster (2) died at the residence of his son, No. 22, York Street, Westminster, on the 14th Dec. 1808, and was buried, on the 21st of the same month, in the family grave at the Church of St. Martin's in the Fields, Charing Cross, on the north side, near to the steps, and opposite to his former residence, the corner of Duke's Court. A black marble slab once marked the spot, but it has been taken away, and probably the ashes of the dead were desecrated and blown hither and thither at the time the alterations of that locality took place, and the neighbourhood altered to its present appearance.

HISTORY OF A VIOLONCELLO MADE BY WILLIAM FOSTER (2).

This violoncello was made in or about the year 1772, and is well known in the musical circle under two names or designations—" The Rev^d. Mr. Hole's or Crossdill's violoncello." It is of the Amati outline, with a very

high and unusual model, and was originally manufactured for Mr. Charles Alexander, a chemist, who had
greatly assisted the maker in the method of dissolving
the gums amber and copal for varnishes. At the time
the order was given, it was promised that if a better
instrument could be supplied than any hitherto made, it
should now be produced for the essential services rendered. How or when this violoncello became the property of Mr. Hugh Reinagle, of Oxford, is not known,
but we arrive at positive information regarding it by an
article in an old newspaper—" *The General Advertiser*
for Tuesday, 6 November, 1787"—which has been preserved by the family as being identified with this instrument, and as the paragraph is amusing, it is given ver-
batim. " The rage for music was never more conspicuous
than now. A few days ago, a violoncello, made by
Forster, was sold for the sum of one hundred guineas
and an Amati bass, worth at least fifty guineas, in exchange. The purchaser was Mr. Kole (Hole), an amateur, in whose praise much has been, though too much
cannot be said. This valuable instrument was formerly
the property of Mr. Hugh Reinagle, the celebrated bass
player, whose death has been universally lamented by
the *musical cognoscenti*. At his demise it was bought
by Mr. Gunn, who has now sold it. To such a nicety
is the manufacture and sale of musical instruments now
brought, that a fiddle, like a race-horse, must have a
pedigree, and his whole *get* announced, before any attention will be given to it." The Rev. H. A. Hole was
one of the best amateur performers on the violoncello of
the day, and it is remarkable he should have been so, as
the two first joints of the forefinger on the left hand had
been amputated, in consequence of mortification having
set in; therefore he was compelled to use the thumb from

the first position; he must also have possessed great courage, for after the operation of taking off the first joint by the surgeons in attendance, he, from symptoms experienced, wished them to operate on the second joint, which they deemed useless; when on their retiring to partake of some refreshment, he excused himself, and went to his dressing-room and cut off the injured part, with his penknife, at the second joint, and then returned to the surgeons to have the wound properly dressed. On medical examination of the joint he had operated on, they acknowledged that disease had taken place, and that at some future time it must have been amputated. So choice was he of this violoncello that, when he travelled with it, he endeavoured, if possible, to secure an inside place in the mail or stage coach; but there were times when it was otherwise conveyed, and on one of these the instrument received the fracture in the back, with other injuries not of such serious nature; however when it was repaired, William Forster (2), and other persons did not consider the tone at all affected, although detrimental to its appearance. The following letter will explain Mr. Hole's feelings regarding the injuries:—

"By this time you have received my old and *once famous* violoncello. It is a melancholy accident, and as you did not as usual enter it at 500*l.* value, I cannot recover any compensation from the carrier. He has made this proposition, that he will pay all expenses of repairing; and you will please to state to me the real damage done to the value of the instrument, if it were to be sold, that I may attempt to recover it, or have some allowance. You will please to repair it as soon as possible, & not send to me, as I shall be in London in March.

" Yours very truly,

"*January* 13, 1798.   " H. A. HOLE.

" P.S.—Lest it should come to a law suit, you should also take Lindley's evidence, adding the loss sustained by the accident, or any other person else you think right."

From the date of the above letter, the link of interest in this violoncello is now lost, until 1814, when Mrs. Hole sends a letter to William Forster (3), dated from the " Vicarage House, Okehampton, Devon, May 29th, 1814," a portion of which is as follows:—

" I wish to ask your advice in regard to my late husband's violoncello—I mean the *fine instrument* made by your father which Mr. Hole bought of Mr. Reinagle, and which he so highly valued. Mr. Hole was offered for it, some years ago, 500*l.* If I could get a very large sum for it, I might be induced to sell it; but, as I am perfectly aware of the very great value of it, I will not part with it otherwise. * * * * *

" I remain, Mr. Forster,
" Y^r ob^t hu^l Ser^t
" S. HOLE."

It will be observed, that the widow states the violoncello was " bought of Mr. Reinagle." The previous extract from the old newspaper says Mr. Gunn. It is not in our power to prove which Professor it really was that sold the instrument to the Rev. H. A. Hole; indeed, it little matters, as both were eminent men of the period. Perhaps the newspaper claims the greatest reliance, being printed at or about the time when the violoncello changed ownership; and Mrs. Hole's remark is made in 1814.

We now arrive at the commencement of a correspondence between Mrs. Hole and Mr. James Crossdill relative to the disposal of the violoncello; there is also a letter to William Forster (3) which corroborates the sale. The three letters are as follows :—

> " Mrs. Hole,
> > " Mrs. Horne's,
> > > " Uxbridge Common.

" Sir,

" I take the liberty of troubling you with a letter in consequence of a conversation which I had with Mr. James before you left Denham, when Mrs. J—— informed me of your most kind and friendly offer of taking Mr. Hole's violoncello under your care, and of disposing of it to the best advantage. I beg to assure you that I feel the kindness of this offer, which I shall be happy to accept. Mr. Robert Hole (Mr. Hole's brother) has made several inquiries amongst his professional friends as to the value of the violoncello. They all agree in saying, that for so *very* fine an instrument we should scarcely be justified in parting with it for less than two hundred guineas. Mr. Hole, I know, refused a much larger sum for it some years ago. As I am afraid of sending the violoncello to London by a public carriage, and my daughter goes to London in my mother's carriage on Monday next, the 23rd, will you permit me to send it on that day in the carriage, and it shall be deposited safely at Mr. Thompson's between twelve and one o'clock? I shall esteem it a favour if you will have the goodness to inform me, before the 23rd, if I may take this liberty.

> " I remain, sir,
> > " Y^r ob^t hu^l ser^t
> > > " S. Hole.

" Jan. 16, 1815."

The above letter is addressed to

" — Crosdale, Esq.
" at — Thompson's, Esq.
" Grosvenor Square,
" London."

The next letter is dated,

" May 22nd, 1815,
" Uxbridge Common.

" SIR,

" I beg to return you my most sincere thanks for your *very* kind and friendly exertions, and for the great trouble which you have taken about the violoncello. Believe me, it affords me great pleasure that the instrument is in *your* hands. It was highly valued by my dear and much lamented Mr. Hole, and I am certain that there is no person he would so much have wished to have it as yourself. I called this morning at Messrs. Hall and Co. Uxbridge, that I might be able to acknowledge to you the receipt of the 70*l.* for the violoncello, but the clerks informed me that no intimation had been received from Messrs. Masterman and Co. of the 70*l.* lodged in their hands, the reason of which is, that they receive communications from them *only* on a Thursday, and on that day, therefore, I shall receive the money. Wishing you a long continuance of health to use the violoncello, which will, I dare say, sometimes remind you of your departed friend,

" I remain, sir,
" Y^r much obliged and
" Faithful hu^l ser^t

" May 22."   " S. HOLE.

Addressed to
" James Crosdill, Esq.
" — Thompson's, Esq.
" Grosvenor Square,
" London."

The following letter written to William Forster (3) and dated 21 May, 1815 :—

> " Mrs. Hole,
>> " Mrs. Horne's,
>>> " Near Uxbridge,
>>>> " Middlesex.

" Mr. Forster,

" I have a very beautiful violoncello here of the late Rev. H. A. Hole's of your father's making. As I keep two for my son, I wish to dispose of this. I have sold the *fine* instrument, about which I wrote to you, to Mr. Crosdale. Will you take this, or dispose of it for me? I will not part with it under 25*l.* Mr. Monzani has offered to dispose of it for me, but as you are an old acquaintance of the late Mr. Hole's, and it is your father's instrument, I prefer making you the first offer of it. Let me know immediately whether you will take it, or dispose of it for me, and I will send it up to you safely by the coach. I am not certain, but I think Mr. Hole called the instrument a Steiner.

> " I am, Mr. Forster,
>> " Yours, &c.
>>> " S. Hole."

Mr. James Crossdill had retired from the musical profession several years before the purchase of this famous instrument, and after his death all his remaining violoncellos, seven in number, were sold by auction on the 9th May, 1826, at which time Robert Lindley, the celebrated violoncellist of the day, bought it for fifty guineas. Two or three gentlemen had attended the auction with the intention of buying this well-known violoncello; but on Lindley naming the first price for it, fifty guineas, no person then present would compete; and, on the auctioneer announcing the purchaser's name, great approbation was shown, and the room resounded with plaudits. Fortunately for Mr. Robert Lindley the person sent, by command of George IV., to buy this and two other violoncellos, was absent in the ante-room, talking with some acquaintance, when Lot 2 was put up; therefore the opportunity of buying was lost. He (Mr. Kramer, Master of the King's Private Wind Instrument Band), learning that his chance was gone, offered Mr. Lindley 100*l.* for his bargain, but it was not accepted. After delighting the musical public with his performances and extraordinary quality of tone on this instrument for nine or ten years, with the fine and glorious sweeping chords when accompanying the Recitatives, of which style he claims to be the original, and with the leading notes for the singer, which notes sung with the vocalist, always merited a portion of the applause. No doubt many persons remember, with feelings of exquisite pleasure, his accompaniments to Handel's air, " O Liberty ! " also Haydn's " In native worth;" and Mozart's " Batti, Batti; " but above all that unrivalled performance of the violoncello obligato to Dr. Pepush's cantata " Alexis," which, in the original composition, is only a simple semiquaver movement; but, with his new reading, it became a performance of wonder and excellence. Many other parts, in orchestral pieces in which the violoncello was made prominent could also be enumerated, which caused Bernard Romberg, a contemporary and rival, to acknowledge " he was great in the orchestra, great as an accompanyist, and great as a soloist." About 1835-6, Mr. Lindley sold this violoncello to Captain West, of the 1st Regiment of Royal Life Guards, for 200*l.* in money, a violoncello valued at 30*l.*, and a picture considered worth 100*l.* During this ownership, Monsieur Servais played on the violoncello at Paris, and delighted

—indeed, if report speaks true, astonished—the Parisians with the fulness of tone produced, being so different from that thin and hard quality of tone which they had been accustomed to hear. Captain West stated that Onslow and other celebrated musical composers had endeavoured to persuade him to sell the instrument to Servais. Be this as it may, the violoncello again came into the English market, and was purchased by the late Frederick Perkins, Esq., of Chipstead Place, Seven Oaks, Kent, about the year 1839; but this date cannot be positively asserted, although believed not to be much in error. This fine violoncello is now the property of Lieutenant-General Sir Hope Grant, G.C.B.

CHAPTER XXIII.

WILLIAM FORSTER, the third of this name as a violin-maker, was the son of the previous William Forster (2), and was born on the 7th January, 1764, in Prescott Street, Goodman's Fields; it is believed the house was No. 12. He must have evinced an early talent as a workman, for the first violin in the list of the best instruments he made is entered in the year 1779; but precocious talent, in general, seldom advances; at first it bursts forth like the bright rays of the sun from behind a dense cloud; the praises then bestowed, and the flattery given, make it conclude it is perfection, and produce a self-confidence and sufficiency that often lead to idleness, and consequently it ceases to exert mental energies, and the probability is its possessor becomes of lymphatic temperament, and moves not onwards to keep pace with the world's advancement. However, there may be a cause in this instance why he became averse to the confinement and toil of the work-room. He was fond of the drama, and associated with private theatricals. It has been told to one of the family, by the late Mr. Charles Wodarch, a cousin of the Kembles, and formerly the leader of the orchestra of Covent Garden Theatre, that he had talent for acting, and that he had seen him perform the characters of Scrub, in "The Beaux's Stratagem;" and Fribble, in the farce of "Miss in her Teens;" and that in the former character he considered him better than the public's great favourite, Mr. Keeley.

It would appear, by a statement in Mr. James Mainstone's bill of costs, that the father and son had been partners at one period; but the nature of the compact is so strange that it can scarcely be believed; and the only thing which entitles it to credence is an old catalogue which is supposed to have been printed before 1787, as Haydn's quartets, op. 44, are not inserted. There is no proof of this partnership by books of accounts, or by knowledge of the elder branches of the present family; but there is full evidence of the son having all the music portion of the business, with liberty to obtain work in his own behalf, by the books which commence 17th July, 1786, being the day after his marriage, the father having his own account-books and customers through all the years that had previously passed, and continued until his death.

The following extract made from the account of the lawyer:—

"1783. Octr. 1st. Attending and taking Instructions for drawing agreement between Mr. Forster Senr. and Mr. Forster Junr. for the former serving the latter during three years under a special Contract."

"Drawing Articles of Agreement accordingly fo 18."

"7th. Attending the Party to read over and settle same."

"Novr. 1. Engrossing same two parts. Stamps. Attending Execution."

Should this contract have been acted on, which is very doubtful, it shows how much a parent will yield to the wishes of a son, who was the only surviving offspring.

The work of William Forster (3) was of high finish and neatness, but he did not take an interest in his vocation, though there are some of the instruments made by him exceedingly good in tone. He was generally denominated "Young Forster," and the labels put into the instruments were signed William Forster, Junr., the Junr. being added with a pen, as also the year in which the instrument was made, and the number of it. These particulars were also written inside the instrument, on both vibrating plates, and at the tail-pin, under the varnish. Some persons have often obliterated the Junr. at this place, no doubt for dishonest purposes, as the instruments of this maker do not command so large a price as those of his father.

The following is a copy of an original label, the Royal Arms at one corner, and the Prince of Wales's Feathers on the opposite corner:—

" William Forster Junr.
Violin, Violoncello, Tenor & Bow-maker
1810   Also Music Seller   N°. 43
To their Royal Highnesses the
Prince of Wales and the Duke of Cumberland."

The label used in later years had the Feathers of the Prince of Wales on one corner, and the Lion upon the Crown, surrounded by the Garter, on the other side, the paper of the label being much narrower than the former label; the number of instrument, the year, and the Junr. to be added with a pen:—

" William Forster
Violin, Violoncello, Tenor & Bow-maker
to their Royal Highnesses the Prince of Wales
& Duke of Cumberland.   London."

After pioneering through the account-books of this violin-maker from 1786 to 1816 it is found that a list of the instruments manufactured cannot be produced even approaching tolerable accuracy, therefore it is abandoned. Four different classes of instruments were made by William Forster (3), assisted by his son and workmen; and about the year 1786-7 the German fiddles, of cheap and common workmanship, were introduced into England, it is believed, by Astor, of Wych Street, Strand, of whom tales could be told connected with German clocks and German musical wind instruments; and entries are seen in the books for fiddles as low as nine shillings, which were mostly sold to dealers; but others have participated in the low prices. Moreover, there are many exchanges and re-purchases of instruments, so that it is very probable the same instrument may have been disposed of more than once.

All these circumstances baffle the endeavour to produce a similar list to that previously given of the instruments made by his father. There is a book, however, in the writing of William Forster (3), still preserved, which has some account of the instruments made by him. It is imperfect as regards the numbers, particularly of the second-class violins and tenors, and there is no mention of the violoncellos of inferior workmanship. The following are the entries, with slight alteration in the arrangement:—

" Number of best Violins made by W^m. Forster Junr.

Put down to the year

Forster, Junr. N°s. 1, 2, 3, and 4	1779
,,	,, 5, 6, 7, and 8	1780
,,	,, 9 and 10	1782
,,	,, 11, 12, 13, and 14	1783

Put down to the year

Forster, Junr. N°s. 15, 16, 17, 18, and 19 . . . 1784

„   „ 20, 21, and 22, this last of small

size 1785

„   „ 23 1789

„   „ 24, 25, and 26 1793

„   „ 27, 28, 29, 30, 31, 32, 33, 34,

35, 36, 37, 38, 39, and 40 . . 1813

„   „ 41, 42, and 43, all three of

small size 1814

In another part of the book is inserted, "Violins at £3 3s. 0d."

Put down to the year

Forster, Junr. N°. 1 1782

„   „ 2 and 3 1783

„   „ 4 1789

Many more of this class violin have been seen entered in the account-books as disposed of, so far as they were examined.

The best tenors were made as follows :—

Put down to the year

Forster, Junr. N°s. 1, 2, and 3 1783

„   „ 4, 5, 6, 7, 8, 9, and 10 . . 1784

„   „ 11 and 12 1785

„   „ 13 and 14 1786

„   „ 15 1787

„   „ 16, 17, 18, 19, and 20 . . . 1789

„   „ 21 1793

„   „ 22 1794

„   „ 23 1795

„   „ 24 and 25 1798

Then follow " Tenors at £3 3s. 0d."

Forster, jun. Nos. 1 and 2, made in the year 1783,

and No. 3 in the year 1789. The same remark as made on the violins of this class, can be applied to the tenors.

With the list of violoncellos made of the first class there has been taken a little more care; but it is far from perfect; and no account whatever of instruments of five guineas value and less has been kept, although numerous entries in the account-books prove that such were made and sold.

"Best violoncellos made by Wm. Forster, jun."

No.		Put down to the year
1, for Mr. Clay		1787
2, Sold to Mr. Hook—3, for Mr. Tillard		1788
4, Sold to Mr. Cartwright		1789
5,		1791
6, Mr. Crouch—7 and 8,		1792
9, 10, 11, and 12		1795
13, Crouch—14, Col¹. Hawker		1797
15, Lindley—16, Yatman		1797
17, Day		1798
18, Major Bothwell—19, James Leffler		1801
20, Rev. Mr. Landon—and 21, Lieut. Heaviside		1801
22, Crosdill—23, Henry Bedford, Esq.		1804
24, Sold to Oxford—and 25, Lord Aylesford		1804
26, Col¹. Bothwell—27, Crosdill		1805
28, Lord Aylesford		1806
29,		1807

About this time the eldest son, William Forster (4), was becoming perfected in the art; and there is a remark written on the margin, "The first violoncello made by my son was made for Charles Ashley." This instrument, it is believed, was the violoncello known in the musical circle as the "Blood Red Knight."

The following No. 30 shows that the son either assisted

in or made the whole, as it has " Bill No. 2 " attached, to it, and a similar remark continues to several other instruments :—

No.	Put down to the year
30, Bill No. 2—31, Bill No. 3, Lord Lewisham	1807
32, Bill No. 4, Gladstanes—33, Bill No. 5, Hole	1807
34, Bill No. 6—35, Bill No. 7, Blake, Bath .	1807
36, Bill No. 8—37, Bill No. 9, Cervetto . .	1809
38, B and G No. 10—39, B and G No. 11, Captain Deacon	1810
40, B and G No. 12—41, B and G No. 13 —42, B and G No. 14	1810
43, G, and 44, Bill No. 15	1810
45, 46, 47, Lindley—48, 49, 50, 51, 52, Mr. Bedford, Steiner pattern—53, Lindley, Steiner pattern, and 54	1811
55, 56, 57, the two last had by Mr. Lindley, and of the Steiner pattern—58, Lord Aylesford—59, Steiner pattern — 60, 61, 62, and 63, these four last were of the Stradiuarius pattern	1812
64, 65, 66, and 67, the two last had by Lindley, and of the Steiner pattern . . .	1813
68, 69, 70, 71, these four were the Stradiuarius pattern	1814
72, Bill (No. 16) for Iscard—73, Bill (17?) Stradiuarius pattern	1815
74, Bill and Andrew, Steiner pattern . . .	1823

Five or six double-basses, of second-class workmanship, were made chiefly for letting out on hire; and there was one of the best work finished for a person named M'Calla, which instrument was destroyed either when the Royalty Theatre, at the east part of London, was burned down in 1826, or crushed to pieces when the roof of the Brunswick Theatre unfortunately fell in, killing several of the performers whilst at rehearsal, on the 28th Feb. 1828. The latter is believed to be the cause of its destruction. These double-basses were all made of the same shape as violoncellos. Some interest may be attached to the violoncello marked No. 26, 1805. It was made of the long Stradiuarius pattern, similar to Mara's celebrated violoncello of that Italian maker, and was first sold to Colonel Bothwell. Ultimately Robert Lindley bought it of Messrs. Withers and Co., and the tone is so grand and fine that it became the favourite violoncello. It is the instrument on which he performed when he made his last public appearance, and played the celebrated trio of Corelli with Charles Lucas and James Howell, at the Philharmonic Concert in the season of 1850. From the commanding tone of this violoncello, and its being made in the year 1805, Lindley named this instrument " Nelson," being the year in which this great Admiral fell at the battle of Trafalgar.

This violoncello is now the property of A. Allan Webbe, Esq. of Hereford Street, Park Lane, who purchased it of the younger son of Robert Lindley, soon after the decease of his talented parent.

William Forster (3) was a person fond of speculating in houses, for which he had not judgment or ability, and much too amiable and kind, although of hasty temper, to be the landlord of such small houses as were purchased. Better property was occasionally bought, but something unlucky was always attached to it; so that the whole of these transactions may be considered a complete failure. But the climax which brought ruin upon him was entering into a grocery business, about 1815-16, with another person of whom he had little knowledge. The consequences may be arrived at very easily. These misfortunes compelled the sacrifice of the freehold and leasehold property, also what money remained in the funds, all of which descended to him from the father, and were absorbed to liquidate large debts, greatly to the detriment of a family of thirteen children then living, consisting of nine daughters and four sons; one son had died in the early part of this century by an accident through the carelessness of the nurse. A broken spirit and the despondency which existed in the latter years of the life of W. Forster (3), were very painful to witness; and at length death relieved him of mental and bodily sufferings on the 24th July, 1824, and he was buried a few days afterwards in the family grave, in the churchyard of Saint Martin's in the Fields.

We have now arrived at the fourth and last of the name of William Forster that have been makers of violins, tenors, and violoncellos. He was the eldest son of the previous W. Forster (3), and was born the 14th of December, 1788, at No. 348, Strand; he possessed good mechanical abilities, with mental endowment for invention; but this last qualification was chiefly employed upon articles of pleasure and enjoyment, although many branches of the business were improved and facilitated by him. He little cared whether it was wood or metal he was working, all were made obedient to his manipulation. He was an excellent workman, and the instruments he made were beautifully finished. But the workroom had little inducements for him; athletic and rural sports absorbed his thoughts, and having a hasty temper little could be accomplished with him at home. He was instructed in violin-making partly by his grandfather and father; but his wild career could not be subdued, and at length it was deemed advisable to place him from home, and Thomas Kennedy undertook the task, and by humouring his foibles, gained more control over him than perhaps any other person, except his mother. He returned home again, but soon left it and joined the theatrical company of the late — Trotter, Esq. of Worthing, who had the Kent and Sussex circuit; sometimes acting on the stage, and at others playing the violoncello in the orchestra.   At Worthing, he indulged with other persons in athletic pastimes; and in one of these trials of strength received some internal injury, from which, perhaps, he never thoroughly recovered. He made very few instruments on his own account, probably twelve or fifteen.   Two or three of these were violins, and one violoncello of the best class; the latter instrument was made for the late Mr. James Brooks, a professor on the violoncello, the remainder being of inferior workmanship for wholesale orders.   He, however, would occasionally repair instruments; but having, generally, an engagement as a violoncello player either at the Sans Pareil, Sadlers' Wells, or the Surrey Theatre, then called the Circus, he little sought for that kind of employment.   During this period of his life fishing was the absorbing desire, and he would take every opportunity to walk to some favoured spot at Woodford in Essex, or to places on the river Wandle celebrated for the sport.

It is said that he performed clown at the Sans Pareil Theatre during the whole of one Christmas holiday-time, under the name of Signor Paulo, who was too ill and unable to fulfill his engagement.   His wild career weakened his constitution; and being recommended to go out of town for change, he accepted an engagement as violoncellist at Cheltenham.   On a leisure evening, whilst playing a game of chess or drafts, a fit of apoplexy deprived him of life, almost instantly, on the 8th October, 1824, in the prime of manhood, being only thirty-six years of age.

The particulars regarding Gilkes perhaps should be inserted here; but it is deemed advisable to carry the family name to a close, as the one next mentioned, who yet struggles with the "battle of life," is the last of the race that is likely to be violin, viola, and violoncello maker.

Simon Andrew Forster is the fourth son of William Forster (3), and was born on the 13th May, 1801, at No. 348, Strand, the house which was known as the *Courier* Newspaper Office, and pulled down for the approaches to Waterloo Bridge from Catherine Street. He is indebted to his father and brother William Forster (4), particularly the latter, for the knowledge acquired in making violins, tenors, and violoncellos, &c. Gilkes also has a small claim, but very small, of imparting instruction. It was not to his interest to do so, therefore the progress in early years was not very rapid. However, at that period, perhaps the work-room may have been neglected, as music was studied as a profession in the choir of Westminster Abbey, which gave the right of education in Westminster School. Notwithstanding Gilkes did not do his duty, when it is taken into consideration how much his position in life was advanced by the improved knowledge imparted to him in the style of work of the family, and the receipt of wages at the time from the parent. This deficiency was fully rectified by the attentions of the father and brother, after Gilkes had ceased to work for the house.

A list will now follow of the best instruments, and the year in which they were made, also the name of the person who first purchased them. The label used in them was as follows, and the initials signed on the opposite corner to the number—

> " S. A. Forster
> Violin, Tenor & Violoncello Maker
> N°.   London."

The name and London are engraved in the old English letter, and the other part in the written character. It is also written with a pen, " S. A. Forster, London," and the number of the instrument by the tailpin, under the varnish, and on both vibrating plates inside the instrument. In most instances the dates take place from the time the body of the instrument was put together, and not always finished in sequence.

Violins of the First Class.

No.		
1,	Mr. George Key	1828
2,	Charles Rowland, Esqʳᵉ.	1830
3,	Stowel Chudleigh, Esqʳᵉ.—4, R. H. W. Ingram, Esqʳᵉ.	1835
5,	Mr. Henry Thorn—6, Mr. William Cramer	1839
7,	J. W. Cochrane, Esqʳᵉ.—(*this violin had the prize medal awarded at the Great Exhibition of* 1851)	1839
8,	Unsold—9, Mr. Thomas Key—10, Sir James Emerson Tennant—11, Unsold—and 12, Mr. Thomas Key	1839
13,	Mr. Richard Stannard—14, Revᵈ. R. G. Buckston	1844
15,	James Uglow, Esqʳᵉ.—and 16 to 26 are still unfinished	1844

Violas or Tenors of the First Class.

No.		
1,	James Reynolds, Esqʳᵉ.—2, doubtful	1839
3,	Frederick James Rawlins, Esqʳᵉ.	1840

No.

4, William Davis, Esqre.—5, John Beardmore, Esqre.—6 and 7, Unsold—8, 9, and 10, still unfinished—and 11, Captain Edward J. Ottley—(*this viola had the prize medal awarded at the Great Exhibition of* 1851) 1843

From No. 3 to 11 are instruments all of very large size.

Violoncellos of the First Class.

From No. 1 to 12 were marked when the instrument was varnished, therefore shows some irregularity in the completion of them; but from No. 13 they were numbered when the body of the instrument was put together.

No.

1, Mr. John Smith	1825
2, Robert Lindley, Esq.—and 3, Mr. John Smith	1826
4, Dr. Boisragon	1827
5, Mr. Acraman	1828
10, Colonel John Montague	1830
8, James Forster—and 9, Mr. William Glanvill	1831
6, Colonel Whitby—7, Rev^d. Dr. Barrett—and 11, Mr. Thomas Binfield, for W. Cull, Esqre.	1832
12, Christopher Rawlins, Esqre.	1835

13, Mr. T. J. Noble—14, Honble. Major Legge, for the Bishop of Oxford—15, Stowel Chudleigh, Esq^e.—16 and 17, E. Woollett, Esqre.—18, Sir Richard Bulkely Phillipps, Bart.—19, Henry Knight, Esqre.—20, Honble. Major Legge (this was a very small violoncello for the son;

No.   it has since been cut down and converted into a tenor) 1836

21, Frederick Perkins, Esqre.—22, Charles
Lucas, Esqre. 1836

23, Mr. Henry Thorn 1836

24, —— Gribble, Esq. 1837

25, R. H. W. Ingram, Esqre. 1838

26, James Lintott, jun^r. Esq^e.—27, George J.
Eyre, Esqre. 1839

28, William Davis, Esqre.—29, Walter Pettit,
Esqre. 1839

30, Honble. Arthur Lascelles—31, Captain Edward J. Ottley—and 32, Captain Hunter Blair 1839

33, James Howell, Esqre.—34, 35, 36 and 37
are still unfinished—and 38, Joseph
Laing Oldham, Esq.—(*this violoncello
had the prize medal awarded at the
Great Exhibition of* 1851) 1841

No.   Double Basses of the First Class.

1, Mr. Boulcott 1833

2, Mr. S. J. Noble—and 3, Frederick Perkins, Esq^e. 1835

4, Samuel Brook, Esqre. 1836

5, Unsold 18

From these large instruments being heavy and cum-
bersome to handle in the working of them, it became
imperative to have assistance, even in some essential
parts, through debility of constitution.

The second class instruments had only this writing at
the tailpin, "Forster, No.——;" and alcoholic varnishes
have been used with all of them. The memory will not
assist to state exactly how many instruments of this class

have been made; perhaps not more than twenty-four violins, four or five tenors, and about ten violoncellos. A correct account of these has not been kept, as the interest in them experienced a check by the cheap and very common instruments from Germany, France, and other countries, which sadly interfered with the welfare of the English artizan, who could not compete in price, as this class of foreign goods could be purchased for a less sum than the materials cost for making them.

The foregoing facts have taken a long time to collect and arrange, and the details from their length may be deemed to require some apology. It was considered, however, that they might be useful to the rising generation, and to a future age. At the present time we should be much gratified to know how many instruments had been made by the Amati, the Stradiuarius, and the Guarnerius families, and especially by Joseph Guarnerius, as his instruments are in great request. Many boast of possessing one, yet when examined and compared how different the style of work, and quality of the varnish, so that even the tales told about the prison and the keeper's daughter scarcely justify the dissimilarity.

George Pearce was born in Warminster, on the 16th November, 1820, and came to London with his parents in the fourth year of his age. He entered into the service of Simon Andrew Forster, as an errand boy, in July 1834, and soon evinced a mechanical talent, and showed expertness in the use of the tools; he was, therefore, instructed in the art of violin-making, and became a very neat and first-rate workman. As years advanced, however, he selected companions of vitiated minds and debased habits, and he was consequently discharged in July, 1844, for neglect of his duties. He ultimately gained employment as a fret-cutter at Messrs. Broad-

wood's pianoforte manufactory, where he continued until
the 3rd July, 1856, on which day he died through his
own act and deed by swallowing poison, and was buried
at the Victoria Cemetry, Bethnal Green, on the 9th of
the same month. It is not known whether any instruments were made by him on his own account, but he for-
warded many of those of his employer, and in one instance only did he make a first-class instrument all
through, which was a violin; but he was fully capable
to execute work of the highest finish. He was not
related to James and Thomas Pearce before noticed.

It will now be requisite to retrace a few years to give
the particulars of Samuel Gilkes, who was born in 1787,
at a village named Morton Pinkney, near to Blisworth,
Northamptonshire, and was sent to London to learn
fiddle-making of the elder Charles Harriss alluded to in
a former part of this work, and completed his term of
apprenticeship about 1809-10. In the course of the
latter year he became journeyman to William Forster
(3), and at length, being initiated into the style of
work of his employer, we find, by the remark B and G
in his list of instruments made, that Gilkes assisted in
making the violoncello No. 38, which appears to be the
first instrument he had joined with others in making, and
continued to do so during the whole of his engagement,
which lasted for nine or ten years, sometimes alone, at
others assisting, but always under the surveillance of his
superior, who minutely examined the gauging before the
instruments were put together. It will be well to take
special notice of the year 1810, for, after he had commenced business on his own behalf, at 34, James Street,
Buckingham Gate, Westminster, a report was freely
propagated by some one that Gilkes was the pupil of
Old Forster (2), and, strange to relate, it went so far as

to state that he had imparted to him, in preference to the family, the method of making the fine varnish. The date of 1810 is sufficient to falsify these statements, as William Forster (2) died in 1808, and it is most probable that Gilkes had never seen him. Samuel Gilkes became an excellent workman, and received much patronage during his own career, both as a maker and dealer, which, however, was of short duration, for he died in November 1827, at his residence, previously given, and was buried in his native village. He made instruments of three or four different classes, and supplied many to music sellers and dealers in the country; but we are unable to state the number or quality of those manufactured. The label used was as follows:—

> " Gilkes
> From Forster's
> Violin, and Violoncello Maker
> 34 James Street, Buckingham Gate
> Westminster."

His son, William Gilkes, who was born in Grey Coat Street, Tothill Fields, Westminster, about 1811, was taught violin-making by the father, and succeeded him at his residence, but subsequently was in Dartmouth Street; however, he did not long continue as a maker of musical instruments, giving a preference to per. forming on the violin in quadrille bands, and occasion. ally at theatres. At length the business was given up altogether, and he accepted some appointment on board one of the ships of the Peninsular and Oriental Steam Navigation Company. No instrument has been seen made by William Gilkes, therefore an opinion cannot be offered as to his capabilities of workmanship.

John Hart was born 17th December, 1805, in Westminster, near to the Green Coat School, and was apprenticed to Samuel Gilkes, in May 1820, and his term of servitude had not long expired when his master died. From that time he could not obtain much employment in the vocation he had learned, consequently he accepted an engagement at Lang's Shooting Gallery, next door to the Haymarket Theatre, and in time the house he now resides in was opened as a depôt for guns and pistols, with a few violins interspersed. At length the Joe Manton's, the Purday's, and the guns of other makers, had to give place to violins, violas, and violoncellos, with Italian names, he having become a dealer in them, and no person in a similar business—if report can be relied on—has had greater success in their journey through life. He has sons, but whether they have been taught to make violins is not known. Dealing in this class of property being far more remunerative than making it, we may infer the former claims the preference. The label used by him :—

" John Hart
Maker
14 Princess Street, Leicester Square
London. Anno 18— "

Before concluding with the Forster school it will be requisite to give one other name, although he was not a pupil, but at first only an amateur maker, and ultimately partly obtained a living by working at the business, and adopted the style of the Forster family, probably from the half-brother of William Forster (2) being his acquaintance. His name was Joseph Rook, late of Rickergate, Carlisle, who was born 7th June, 1777, at Calbeck, Cumberland. As a youth, he sorted copper ore, and in 1795 worked as a farm-servant to a Mr. Scott, of Haltcliff, near Hesket New Market, who was also an amateur fiddle-maker, and from whom some knowledge was gained. In 1800 he went to Carlisle to reside, and was engaged at the theatre to play the violin, and became acquainted with Joseph Forster in consequence of being made one of the musicians to the corporation; both also belonged to the band at the winter assemblies. In June 1807, Joseph Rook was appointed vicar-choral at the cathedral, and held that office until 25th December, 1840, when a retiring pension was given to him, which, in November 1850, he still enjoyed, and it is believed it was continued until his death, which took place in September 1852, and his body was interred at St. Mary's Church, Carlisle.

In a letter, dated 7th December, 1850, alluding to violins, he writes—" I never made many ; I have made Twelve Tennors, and Five Violoncellos; no Double Basses. I marked my name with a small stamp,

" ' J. Rook
Carlisle.'

I generally wrote my name in the inside of the Bellys with a black lead pencil."

He could not supply a label, having mislaid or lost them. Only violins of this maker have been seen, the work of which was very neat, and the tone pure, but weak; the varnish of a brownish yellow colour, and transparent.

CHAPTER XXIV.

NOTHER northern name now claims attention. Alexander Kennedy was born in Scotland, but neither the date nor the locality is precisely known. However, a surviving relative states that he died about 1785-6, and was considered to be ninety years of age. His work was very good, both inside and outside, and the purfling excellent. The Steiner model was followed minutely, and spirit varnish of a brownish yellow colour was used. He only made violins. The following was written inside a violin of this maker, but portions of it had been effaced by some repairs :—

> " Alexander Kennedy, Musical
> In   made this Jany 3rd. 1742/3
> This Violin   A. Kennedy Living in Oxford
>   Market.   1742/3."

And a written label was used in a violin of rather later date, thus :–

> " Alexander Kennedy, Musical Instrument
> Maker, Living in Market Street in Oxford
>   Road, London.   1749."

The foregoing maker instructed a nephew, John Kennedy, who, in the earlier part of his life, resided in Cooper's Gardens, near Shoreditch Church; afterwards in Houghton Street and Clement's Lane, Clare Market;

and lastly, in Long Alley, Sun Street, Moorfields, where he died in adverse circumstances about 1816, aged eighty-six years, and was buried at Shoreditch Church. The age is doubtful, as he was considered an older person by those who had been intimate with him. Violins and tenors were the only instruments he made, and all were of the high model or Steiner pattern.

At one period he was in full employ, having two or three assistants, and chiefly made instruments for the music publishers, and written labels were used. The present Thomas Kennedy (the son) states that no violoncellos were made by his father, and it is very doubtful if any were made by his workmen.

Thomas Kennedy was born in Houghton Street, Clare Market, on the 21st January, 1784, and was the eldest son of the previous John Kennedy by the third wife. He was apprenticed to Thomas Powell, the violin-maker, 17th June, 1795; but he is more indebted to his father for the knowledge of the business, and became a neat and good workman. In making the common class instruments he was exceedingly quick and rapid in every department. At the commencement of the present century he occasionally worked for William Forster (3), but soon entered business on his own account in Princes Street, Westminster, and at length located at 364, Oxford Street, at which place he lived for thirty-three years.

In June 1849 he was enabled to give up business, and retired to Cummin's Place, Pentonville, where his active mind and good health still enable him to reap amusement from his previous vocation. He was much employed by Messrs. Goulding, D'Almaine, and Co., and other music-houses. The exact number of instruments that were made by him is not known, but he says "he must have made at least 300 violoncellos, and the other instruments in proportion; perhaps not quite so many." Although he married very early, yet he has had no family; consequently he will be the last of this race as violin-makers.

Associated with the name of Kennedy, as fiddle-makers, are James Brown, the elder and younger, both of whom, in early life, were silk-weavers, particularly the father, and lived in the locality of Shoreditch. About 1804 an intimacy arose with the Kennedy family, whereby James Brown the elder acquired some knowledge of fiddle-making; and, being made more perfect in the use of the tools by Thomas Kennedy, he at length became a repairer and maker of instruments for future support. About 1830 he slipped down the stairs of his dwelling-house, in Wheeler Street, Spitalfields, and broke one of the ancles; the fracture being most severe, the relatives were advised to take him to the hospital. Within a week of the accident, mortification set in, and he died at the age of seventy-five years, in September 1830 or 1834; the son does not remember the date accurately, but he thinks the former year; and he says they (father and son) resided in Wheeler Street for forty-six years, but not always in the same house. James Brown, the younger, was born November 1786, and learned to make fiddles of his father; but, to assist in other branches of the trade, he was mostly employed in making the various bows for the instruments. Since the death of his father, the greater attention has been given to the manufacture of violins, violoncellos, and double basses. This person died in 1860 at his residence in White Lion Street, Norton Folgate, in his seventy-fourth year. The father and son were good average workmen, but no marked style of finish. A son of this last person learned to make instruments of his father; but, when about twenty years of age, he quitted the business to play the contra-basso at theatres; and it is believed he now has some professional engagement in Australia, as success did not attend his exertions at " the Diggins."

In the early part of the eighteenth century there were three persons of the following names: Edmund Airton, or Aireton, Henry Hill, and Joseph Hill, who became violin-makers, but it is not known for certainty which of them claims the seniority, nor can it be told who instructed them; but the style of work is remarkably similar, also the colour and quality of the varnish the same on most of the instruments which have been seen; therefore it is probable all three learned of the same master. From a circumstance which occurred in re-moving a label, dated 1735, out of a genuine violoncello made by Peter Wamsley, on the underneath side of which was written Edmund Airton, it is probable that the father of the first of the above three names was a workman in the employ of Wamsley, although nothing is known of him, who surreptitiously wrote his name on the master's label previous to attaching it to the violon-cello. The date will not allow of its being the person first named, therefore it will be considered that Edmund Aireton claims the priority from family connections. Little is known of this maker, although he was an excel-lent workman, and produced instruments of a high order, both for tone and neat finishing. About 1805, he was residing in Hog Lane, now better known as Crown Street, Soho; and Thomas Kennedy says, " he was about eighty years of age, and that the shop had more the appearance of a general dealer than a maker of violins, tenors, and violoncellos; " also, he further positively stated the name was spelled " Aireton."

The few instruments which have been seen show that he made inferior as well as highly-finished ones; the violins and tenors were of the Stradiuarius pattern, and of the lower class work, with a glossy varnish, evidently alcoholic, made more ductile by admixture of a soft gum, or, what is more probable, with Venice turpentine. The most perfect specimen that we know of this maker is a violoncello, formerly the property of the late Robert Lindley, who sold it to George J. Farsyde, Esq., of Fylingdales, near Whitby, Yorkshire, in whose possession it still remains, and is fully appreciated. This instrument has an oil varnish of yellow colour, with a slight tinge of red, the pattern rather long, and the model high. The head has a peculiarity which deteriorates from its gracefulness by the volute or scroll having nearly a whole turn more than is usual; they are not, however, all made in that form. It would appear that he occasionally worked for the trade, as a violoncello of this maker has been seen stamped on the back, under the button, with letters exceedingly small, and one name above the other, thus:—

" Norris
and
Barnes."

Also, a spurious label of "Banks" was placed inside.

If conclusions may be drawn from the dates which are known, then William Hill will be the elder of two brothers who settled in London, and in the year 1741 was residing in Poland Street. Henry Hill, a relative, in his MSS., gives copies of two labels that were used, thus :—

" William Hill, Maker, in Poland Street,
near Broad Street.   1741."

And   "William Hill, Maker, in Poland Street,
        near Broad Street, Carnaby Market.   177—."

The work of this maker so much resembles that of
Edmund Aireton almost in every particular, except the
volute of the head, that many persons would be deceived.
The varnish is a beautiful transparent yellow colour; no
doubt of oil.   The tone is not rich in quality, although
good; and if both vibrating-plates, particularly the
upper one, were thickened in the centre, advantageous
results would be obtained ; or, first, for external appliances, may be tried a Parisian bridge of the present form
of Aubert's make, which, there is little doubt, would
prove beneficial, and make the tone more rich in quality.   These suggestions may be applied to all the violoncellos of this family-name ; but an exception has to
be made with the present William E. Hill, whose work
is not sufficiently known to offer an opinion.   Joseph
Hill was brother to the former William Hill, and the
grandson, in his MSS., states that Joseph Hill lived in
Dover Street, Piccadilly, and afterwards in the Haymarket, which dwelling was destroyed by fire, with the
loss of all the stock in trade.   After that calamity,
he resided in the locality of Lock's Fields, Newington,
Surrey, about 1792-3, and his death is believed to be in
1794.   The printed label used was as follows :—

                  " Joseph Hill, Maker,
                    At the Harp and Flute,
                      in the Hay Market,
                      17   London   69."

The last figure put in with a pen.   There are also copies
of written labels, at the same place, in 1772. The grandson further states that this maker " enjoyed a high reputation in his day for his instruments, which have consi-

derable merit, tho' not of the highest order ; his violoncellos and contra-bassi are deservedly held in much
esteem.   There were many of the same family violin-
makers, but none who enjoyed (or) so highly reputed as
William and Joseph ; " both of whom, on the authority
of the present William Ebsworth Hill, came from
Bromsgrove, Worcestershire.   There were two sons of
the former Joseph Hill, named Joseph and Lockey
Hill, who perhaps should have been placed in the list
of fiddle-makers for the trade and music publishers, for
such were their general employments ; but, for reasons previously stated, it has been preferred to keep each
school separate.   Joseph Hill died about 1840, and
Lockey Hill about 1845.   Mr. Henry Hill, an excellent
performer on the viola, who, for several years previous
to his death, held the highest place in the profession,
was a son of the above Lockey Hill.   The present
William Ebsworth Hill is another son of Lockey Hill,
and may be considered to be self-taught in making
violins, although related to a maker, he having been too
young to have reaped any advantage from the knowledge
of his father.

CHAPTER XXV.

BENJAMIN BANKS was born in the early part and died in the latter part of the eighteenth century. His parents' names were George and Barbary; but there is no evidence to show that his father was a musical instrument maker. As a portion of the information obtained regarding this clever workman is from a grandson, Mr. B. T. Banks, we will quote his own letter :—

"June 23rd, 1841. Though I have made many inquiries both before and since my return from London, I have not been able to gain any information respecting my late grandfather and uncle, until this week, or I should certainly have written to you sooner. The enclosed I have copied from a leaf which I suppose belonged to the old family Bible about a hundred years ago. You will perceive that the first is my grandfather and the other my uncle. Should I be able to learn the exact time when the latter died I will immediately let you know."

A copy of the paper enclosed in the above letter :

" Benjamin Banks, the son of George and Barbary Banks, born July 14th, 1727. Died Feby. 18th, 1795."

" Benjamin Banks, one of the sons of the above Benjn. Banks. Born Sepr. 13th, 1754. Died about 1818."

It is generally believed that the first-named Benjamin Banks was born in Salisbury ; that he resided in Catherine Street of that city is evident from the various labels

put into the instruments made by him.   His burial-place
is supposed to be the parish church of Saint Thomas,
Sarum.   Although no trace can be obtained from whom
he learned the trade, it may, as in many other instances
with violin makers, be an innate love of the art which
urged him onwards, so that he ultimately became one
of England's best manufacturers.   Too much cannot be
said in praise of this justly celebrated maker of violins,
violas, and violoncellos.   The work of all the better class
of instruments, both inside and out, is excellent; the
tone good of all, but that of the violoncellos in particular
is full, sonorous, and much esteemed by the professors.
He mostly worked from the pattern of the Amati, both
in model and outline; the style of finishing is very
marked and decided, so that persons at all conversant
with musical instruments of this class can easily tell the
maker.   Much anxiety seemed to be shown that he, as
the maker, should be known; for many of his instruments have labels in various parts of them; also they
are stamped upon in several places either with the name,
or B. B., but no fixed plan of marking them seemed
adhered to.   One label used was—

> " Benjamin Banks,
> Fecit,
> Salisbury."

Other printed labels have been used at various dates
thus—

> " Made by Benjⁿ. Banks,
> Catherine Street, Salisbury, 1773."

Another—

> " Benjamin Banks Musical Instrument
> Maker.   In Catherine Street, Salisbury, 1780."

And frequently they are stamped on the back or lower

vibrating plate, under the button, " B. Banks, Sarum." This maker was not successful with the varnish put on the various instruments; there is a want of brilliancy in the colouring, and a sad defect in the method of application, which destroyed the grain of the upper vibrating plate and gave it a white appearance, or, as the trade would pronounce, "the grain was killed." The colours of his varnish were a deep red with a blackish tinge, and a yellow brownish red; the latter seemed preferred for those instruments of special make or order. One of the writers of this book has a violoncello of this maker, having the latter coloured varnish, and the quality of tone is very fine : it is of the Steiner model, but rather long, and the Steiner sound hole is used. It was a present to him from his valued friend, that eminent performer, the late Robert Lindley. A violin by the same maker is in possession of Mr. Charles Lucas, the varnish on which has rather more red in it. No contra-basso or double-bass has been seen of this maker, and it is doubtful if he or any of the family ever made one.

There is a class of instruments, more particularly violoncellos, which were made for Longman and Broderip, the music publishers, by this Benjamin Banks, and probably assisted by his sons or other workmen; the pattern of which is long and more of the Steiner model; the work much inferior, and a red varnish used having all the appearance of the tint being produced by an aqueous extract. The names of Longman and Broderip are stamped on the back, under the button, but no writing or label to indicate by whom the instruments were made; the style, however, even in these instruments is easily recognized. The average price of this maker's best violoncellos, between 1790 and 1794, was from ten to twelve guineas; and in the first half of the present century some of them have realized as much as fifty pounds.   Fashion, however, has now declared against these excellent instruments of the Banks family, and all English manufacture must give place to those with foreign names.

About the year 1826 a violoncello of this maker was in possession of the Pembroke family, which was made entirely from the wood of a cedar of Lebanon which formerly grew in Wilton Park, but had been blown down, and a portion of it was used for the purpose above stated. The tone was not good, from the wood being too dense for the upper vibrating plate; but it may be considered a curiosity, and as such no doubt the earl who ordered it to be made considered it.   His lordship having had a silver plate let into the under vibrating plate, or back, on which was engraved the particulars regarding the tree, also the name of the instrument maker.   Although this violoncello was seen at the town residence of the Dowager Countess of Pembroke in Privy Gardens, Whitehall, there is every probability that it may be now at Wilton House, near Salisbury; and if it could not be seen with facility at the family mansion, there is much to admire and elevate the mind by viewing the fine collection of choice paintings of the old masters, and a quadrangle containing sculpture of a high order.

Benjamin Banks, the younger.   There was some doubt, at one time, whether or no this Benjamin Banks, the second son of the former of that name, was a maker of musical instruments; for we learn that about the latter part of the last century he was connected with a person named Cahusac, in a boot and shoe shop, on Fish Street Hill.   There appear to have been intermarriages between the families of Banks and Cahusac, and Cahusac and Banks.   Ultimately he became associated either with his father-in-law, or a son of the same, in the musical establishment of Astor, in Cornhill, and one of the Cahu sacs succeeded to that business. From the circumstance of his being connected with a musical business, and the violin makers generally considering there was an old and young Benjamin Banks who were manufacturers, it was inferred that he could work at the business, and these suppositions have proved correct. In September, 1857, a violoncello was seen, the property of Mr. John Harding, surveyor, living in Salisbury, which had written on the inside of the upper vibrating plate at the hind bout of the first string side, the following—

" Made by Benjn. Banks,
No. 30, Sherrard Street,
Golden Square. London.
From Salisbury."

A written label also was inside the instrument, the same as the above, but omitting " From Salisbury." It can be asserted, almost with certainty, that the elder Benjamin Banks never resided in London; therefore we conclude the above label alludes to the younger of that name, who having tried musical instrument-making in London, and not succeeding, became connected with the shoe shop. He was born on the 13th September, 1754, as previously stated. After his residence in Salisbury and London, he retired to Liverpool, where his two brothers, James and Henry, were living, probably about 1814, for in the month of March in that year he bought a grave at Saint Mary's Church, Edge Hill. He died on the 22nd January, 1820, and at the time of his death was residing in Hawk Street, Liverpool. Upon the grave-stone it is engraved that his age was sixty-eight years; in the Book of Burials it is stated as sixty-five; the latter corresponds with the time of his birth given by the nephew.

As the two brothers, James and Henry Banks, appear to have been associated together, or partners in the musical business soon, if not immediately, after the death of the father, they will not be separated in this account. James Banks was the fourth son, and Henry Banks the sixth son of the first-named Benjamin Banks, both of whom were born in Salisbury. James seemed to inherit, as an artisan, all the excellencies of his parent. He worked from the same patterns, the style of finishing being similar and the tint of varnish the same; but occasionally the red-coloured varnish had more black in it than was used by the father. Henry Banks did not work at the violin trade, but was a pianoforte tuner and repairer. There are numerous labels in instruments showing they were in trade together; and in 1802 they had also become music-sellers. The following is a copy of a label at that period:—

" James and Henry Banks,
Musical Instrument Makers,
and Music Sellers,
18　Salisbury,　02."

The caprice of the parent, regarding the marking of instruments, descended to the sons, as we find a different label used two years afterwards:—

" James and Henry Banks,
Salisbury.　1804."

And, " J. & H. Banks " stamped on the blocks and other parts of the various instruments. They carried on their various departments of business in Catherine Street, Salisbury, until 1811, when they sold the same to Mr. Alexander Lucas, the father of the present Mr. Charles Lucas, the Principal of the Royal Academy of Music, and went to reside in Liverpool. They first located in

Church Street, opposite Saint Peter's Church; the site, or rather a portion of that on which Compton House now stands; afterwards they moved to Bold Street in the same town. A Welshman named William Davis, or Davies, who was living in Liverpool in the year 1849, had been in the employ of these two brothers as a porter in or about 1818, and he spoke in high commendation of their kindness, and stated, "they had a good business, were the best masters he ever had either before or since. Henry was a capital tuner of pianos, and was frequently from home for a fortnight travelling about the country, and went as far as Wales to tune instruments. He did not work at the violin making, but was connected with the pianoforte department. The hands of James, when he knew him, were much contracted, yet he was an excellent repairer of violins, &c. *O it was beautiful to see how he repaired them.* All three are buried at Saint Mary's Church, Edge Hill, and I helped to put them into the grave." A son of the above Henry Banks, whose name is also Henry, and had an office at No. 2, Mersey Chambers, Liverpool, about 1849-50, corroborates much of that asserted by Davis, and also said, "his father did not work at the violin trade, and that his uncle was the maker of violins, tenors, and violoncellos; that the contraction in the hands was caused by gout, and that his uncle was never married." He also said that " very few, if any instruments were made at Liverpool; but some may have been finished there that were previously begun." James and Henry Banks sold the goodwill of their business to two brothers named Palmer, who found in a cellar a number of unfinished instruments of the violin class, which were sold by them in that state; but it was not known to whom they were disposed. On the tombstone at the church before-named it is engraved that James Banks died 15th June, 1831, aged seventy-five years. Some error exists here, unless a period of nearly three years occurred between his birth and christening, as that ceremony took place on the 7th Sept. 1758, at St. Thomas' Church, Sarum. Henry Banks died on the 16th Oct. 1830, aged sixty years. The church Book of Burials of the date 23 Oct. 1830, states the age to be fifty-six, but the former age is nearer correctness, he being christened 2nd Jan. 1771. At the time of his decease he was residing in George Street. He was found drowned in the Princes Dock, and it is said he could not have been very long in the water, as his watch was still in action when the body was discovered. The various extracts from the books of St. Thomas' Church, Salisbury, were kindly made by the late Mr. J. T. Biddlecombe, the clerk to the church, who further stated there were no memoranda or notices taken at what period the birth of either James or Henry Banks took place. He was an intimate acquaintance of the Banks family when they lived in Salisbury.

It has been said by an elderly gentleman, now deceased, who well knew the Banks family before they went to reside at Liverpool, that the elder Benjamin Banks (the father) had an apprentice named Wheeler, who he believed came to London to obtain employment or commence business himself as a maker of violins, &c. Nothing whatever is known of him, nor has any instrument been seen to establish a name worthy of his instructor. There are many violoncellos with the label of James and Henry Banks which may be considered generally very good; and two in particular are in the possession of Mr. Charles Lucas, which have a full and powerful tone, of excellent quality, and were used by him when principal violoncellist at the Royal Italian Opera, Covent Garden.

CHAPTER XXVI.

THERE are many violins, tenors, violoncellos, and double-basses, having labels in them, as made by T. Dodd. This, however, is not correct, as he was not the maker of them; but he was the head of this musical business, therefore all the instruments had his name attached. Several of this family have been associated with violin-bow-making and covering of musical strings. The father of the above Thomas Dodd, named Edward, was born at Sheffield, but his occupation is not known. He died in 1810, at a house in Salisbury Court, Fleet Street, and was buried at St. Bride's Church, in that locality, being of the great age of 105 years. Thomas Dodd was the third son of this Edward, and appears to have been either unsettled or unsuccessful in the various businesses he adopted for support. At first he was a brewer, and from 1786 to 1789 there is evidence he was a violin bow-maker, residing in Blue Bell Alley, Mint Street, Southwark. In or about 1798, he commenced as a dealer in and maker of violins in New Street, Covent Garden, the corner of Bedford Bury, and then employed a young man named Bernhard Fendt to make the various instruments; and in March of the same year John Frederick Lott was engaged to assist, although not educated in the art of making violins. More will be stated of these two persons presently. In 1809, T. Dodd left this abode and moved to 92, St. Martin's Lane, Charing Cross, the corner of Cecil Court; and about

1823-4 he left this house and went to No. 3, Berner's Street, Oxford Street, where he ventured on making harps, which had a mechanical improvement of an index in the metal-plate, at the head of the instrument, showing what pedals were down. These harps were patronized and used by Dizi, the celebrated performer of that day. After this, pianoforte-making engaged his attention; but it is said, with all these numerous adventures, success did not attend his efforts. The time of his death is not accurately known. A nephew states he was buried at St. Giles's-in-the-Fields. An oval label was used at first, as follows:—

" T. Dodd,

Violin, Violoncello,

& Bow Maker,

New Street,

Covent Garden."

And when residing in St. Martin's Lane the label had the representation of a violin or violoncello, with the bow placed obliquely under two of the strings, occupying the centre, and the other particulars engraved parallel with the instrument:—

" Dodd   Maker

92 Saint Martin's   Lane.

Note.—The only Possessor of the Recipe for preparing the Original Cremona Oil Varnish. Instruments Improved & Repaired."

Perfect copies of Stradiuarius, Amati, Stainer, &c. &c.

From this establishment emanated numerous imitations, both of English and foreign violin-makers, as well as those with his own name.

Two sons of Thomas Dodd, named Thomas and Edward, were instructed in violin-making by Bernhard Fendt. Thomas had ability as a workman, and died in the early part of this century, whilst his father was residing in St. Martin's Lane. Edward appears to have given more attention to the manufacture of the harp and pianoforte, and was accidentally drowned on the 29th of April, 1843, in presence of one of his sons, "a youth whom he had just apprenticed to the sea, and who was going away that evening."

Perhaps, before quitting this family-name, some notice is due, and should be taken, of John Dodd, the celebrated violin-bow-maker, *the Tourte of England*. He was the eldest-son of the first-named Edward, and in early years was a gun-lock fitter, afterwards a money-scale maker, but ended in being England's best bow-maker. It is considered that at one period, 1786-9, ꞁe lived in Southwark ; afterwards he went to Kew, in Surrey, and resided there several years ; at length he moved to Richmond, in the same county, where he died, and was buried at the Old Church of that place.

Bernhard Fendt was born at Inspruck, in the Tyrol, about 1775-6, which place he left at the age of seven years, and went to reside in Paris with his uncle Fendt, or Fent, as the name is spelled in France, of whom he learned to make violins and violoncellos, &c. Very few facts of his early years are known by the surviving relatives, nor can they state when he first came to England ; we, however, learn from other sources that he was engaged by Thomas Dodd, and entered into his employ in January 1798, and remained there for eleven years ;

after that period he went to old John Betts, and continued there until the death of his master, in 1823. He then became the workman to the nephew, John Vernon, with whom he stayed until this person's decease. Bernhard Fendt was a workman of high merit, and at the commencement of his career in England the style of work was that known as of Tyrol. A quartett of instruments of this maker was purchased by Mr. Henry N. Turner, of Upper Belgrave Place, Pimlico, at Dodd's house, about 1800-1, which shows the character of the work in a decided manner. However, of late years, his great excellence consisted in the fine imitations of the Italian and other violin-makers. He may be considered to have formed a school, as there were four sons and one grandson instructed in the art, as well as the elder Lott and two of his sons; also John N. Lentz. All these persons may be considered as indebted to him, as the first cause, for their knowledge of violin-making, and, with the exception of the latter person, they were all excellent workmen. A daughter of Bernhard Fendt states that her father died in Aylesbury Street, Clerkenwell, about 1832-3, and was buried in Clerkenwell Church-yard; also that his age was considered to be fifty-seven years.

Bernhard Simon, or Simmon Fendt, was the eldest son of the foregoing Bernhard Fendt, and was born in 1800. He was taught violin-making by his father, probably in the workshop of Old John Betts, with whom he remained until the death of the latter in 1823. Soon after this he was either engaged as workman, or became a partner with —— Farn, who commenced as a dealer in violins in Lombard Street, City; but, this person dying a few years afterwards, he then joined with George Purdy, a professor of dancing and fencing, and commenced business in Finch Lane, City, in September

1832, the firm being known as Purdy and Fendt. In June 1843 they also opened a house of business in Oxendon Street, Haymarket; and about 1850 both these places were closed, and the business concentrated in 74, Dean Street, Soho. Bernhard Simmon Fendt died 6th March, 1852, at 7, Smith Street, Brompton, and it is said he was interred in the burial-ground of Pentonville Chapel on the 12th of the same month, aged fifty-two years. A doubt arises if the burial-place be correct, although stated by a relative, as the son, who died in the same year as the parent, was buried at the Brompton Cemetry.

Martin Fendt was the second son of the elder Bernhard Fendt, and was born in July 1812. He learned to make violins under the guidance of his father, and during the whole of his short life was employed by Arthur Betts, the brother of Old John Betts. Martin Fendt died in Bell Alley, Coleman Street, City, in July 1845, aged thirty-three, and is buried in a churchyard near to that locality, the name of which is not known. Jacob Fendt was the third son of the former Bernhard Fendt, and was born about 1815. He was instructed in violin-making by his eldest brother, and occasionally worked for W. Davis, of Coventry Street, having succeeded G. F. Lott at that establishment. He was also employed, at some other period, by Turner, the dealer in violins, whilst residing in the Poultry. Jacob Fendt died about October 1849, in Blue Anchor Court, Whitecross Street, Finsbury, and his age considered to be thirty-four or thirty-five years.

The fourth son, Francis Fendt, was also instructed in violin-making by his eldest brother, and for some time continued to work for the firm (Purdy and Fendt). In 1856, he was residing in Liverpool, obtaining a very precarious subsistence. Whether he be alive now is not known, neither can the time of his birth be ascertained.

William Fendt was the second son of Bernhard Simmon Fendt, and was born in 1833, in Finch Lane, City. He learned violin-making of his father, and became an expert workman. He died in his twentieth year, at 7, Smith Street, Brompton, in 1852, and was buried in the Brompton Cemetry.

As the youngest son of John Frederick Lott states that his father died on the 13th April, 1853, aged seventy-eight, he would have been born in 1775. Previous to entering the employ of Thomas Dodd, in March, 1798, he had been a chair maker, therefore his knowledge of violin-making was acquired of Bernhard Fendt. For several years previous to his death, he carried on the musical business in King Street, Seven Dials, at which place he died, and was buried in the church-yard of Saint Giles-in-the-Fields. He was celebrated for making double-basses.

There are two sons of this person, the oldest named George Frederick Lott, born about 1800-1, and the younger of the same name as the father. Both of them, at different periods, were in the employ of W. Davis of Coventry Street; and much of the adventurous life of the younger, in after years may be read in the novel, " Cream," and " Jack of all Trades," by Charles Reade. The two sons are still living.

Johann Nicolaus Lentz was a German, from the Tyrol, and in the latter part of the last century had been servant to a gentleman in Duke Street, St. James's. Being an acquaintance of Bernhard Fendt, he had picked up some knowledge of violin and violoncello-making, and in consequence he began as a maker in the early part of this century. The varnish used by him was similar to that upon the instruments known as Dodd's and the elder Lott. The printed label, which has been seen, was as follows, the date being put in with a pen :—

" Johann Nicolaus Lentz, Fecit
near the Church, Chelsea. 1803."

The names of the two violin makers which follow, Matthew Hardie and his son Thomas Hardie, perhaps, in a strict sense, should not be placed in this section ; they were, however, clever workmen, especially the elder, and endeavoured by attention to the gauging to accomplish great power of tone in the violins, tenors, and violoncellos which they made. Although the work was not at all times as neat as could be desired to rank them as first-rate workmen, yet they frequently gained the object they tried for, and could execute first-class work if the mind was not under the baneful influence of whiskey. Matthew Hardie was held in much esteem as a violin maker in his locality, and was living in " The Calton," Edinburgh, in the latter half of the last and the beginning of the present century, about the point where the Waterloo Bridge now crosses that street. He died in the workhouse of St. Cuthberd's, or West Church parish, about 1825-6, and it is believed that he was interred in the burial ground of the Grey Friars Church of Edinburgh.

Thomas Hardie, the son of the former Matthew, was born in 1804, and it is believed learned violin-making of his father ; he was a clever workman, but his dissolute and intemperate habits lost him the employ he could have commanded, and of late years the utmost penury was the penalty. He died on the 19th January, 1856, aged fifty-two, and his death was caused by falling " down a stair in the lawn market ;" and through the kind exertions of a person who knew him, a small subscription was raised, and he was buried in the ground of the Grey Friars Church of Edinburgh, where the father is supposed to be interred.

The place at which the fatal accident occurred was such "that the most sober person might have fallen there, the door of the house from which he emerged opening at once upon a stair without any landing-place." Charles Reade appears to have drawn the picture of this person in his novel of "Christie Johnstone," at p. 122, under the name of Thomas Harvey, but too much intellect has been assigned to him.

There was a violin maker connected with Matthew Hardie, named John Blair, but nothing is known of his ability as a workman.

Whether or no the chamber double-bass can be called an invention, or an enlarged violoncello strung differently, or whichever way it may be considered, the merit of the adaptation is due to an amateur on the violoncello, named Barraud, who held an appointment in the Treasury, and the instrument is generally known as the Barraud bass. These instruments were first made about 1820, and became rather popular, but soon lost their favouritism, partly arising from the excessive pressure required on the strings, to produce anything like a musical sound. It was tuned an octave below the violoncello, therefore the strings were necessarily large and heavy. When first introduced to the public only three covered strings were applied, but latterly all four were covered with wire, the fourth being double covered. These instruments were first made for the inventor by John Morrison, then by Thomas Kennedy, and lastly by Samuel Gilkes, who increased the dimensions of them.

A further modification of this instrument was introduced in November, 1844, by Mr. Thomas William Hancock, one of the violoncello performers at the Royal Italian Opera, under the name of the "basso di camera," at a special meeting convened for that and other purposes, of the Queen Square Select Society, in the presence of many amateurs and professors of music, who gave a unanimous vote of approval. These instruments were made at W. Davis's, in Coventry Street, Haymarket.

It was tuned two octaves below the violin, which method gave the G one note lower than the present mode of tuning the double-basses of three strings; but this also had its difficulties to the amateur by causing transposition, and still requiring additional physical energies, although not so great as the one first invented.

Mr. Hancock has recently adopted another mode of stringing which renders the instrument less difficult to the amateur, the description of which he has kindly supplied for our guidance :—

"The mode of tuning was originally two octaves below the violin, and the same number of strings were used, the two lowest, however, being covered ones; but Mr. Hancock, finding the highest string gave a compass unnecessary for the performance of music written for the contra basso (for which the basso di camera was introduced as a substitute for chamber music), has reduced the number of strings to three, consequently the higher string is now A, the second D, and the third G, one note lower than the double-bass; this alteration leaves a compass sufficiently extensive, as the octave to the first string is reached with the same facility as on the violoncello, and with the same smoothness. By the removal also of the first string E, amateurs on the violoncello are at once enabled to apply their knowledge of that instrument to the basso di camera, which was not quite so easy in the arrangement first adopted.

Size and character of the strings now used.

First. A very large violoncello, second or small double-bass first.

Second. The usual violoncello fourth covered with wire of the smaller size.

Third. A violoncello second, or double-bass first, covered with wire of the largest size used for violoncello fourths, and the string altogether to be about $\frac{1}{8}$ of an inch thick.

Dimensions of the basso di camera.

	Inches.
Length of the body	36
Breadth of do. fore end	$16\frac{1}{2}$
Do. hind end	21
Do. across the sound holes . . .	11
Depth of the sides	7
Length of the neck	$12\frac{1}{2}$
Length of the string from the nut to the bridge	31

Machine pegs are desirable for instruments of this class."

CHAPTER XXVII.

NAMES of violin and fiddle makers, also dealers of the nineteenth century, not previously noticed. The style or character of the work of the greater number of them is not known :—

ABSAM, THOMAS, originally a joiner by trade, then made cases for violins, and at length made fiddles for Pickard, of Leeds, 1810-1849. Label used :—

> " Made by
> Thomas Absam,
> Wakefield, Feby. 14,
> 1833."

ASKEY, SAMUEL, of London, at first was a tinman, and John Morrison taught him to make fiddles; about 1825, he worked for George Corsby; died in or near 1840 by falling down a cellar.

BALLANTINE, of Edinburgh; but, in 1856, he was living in Glasgow.

BOOTH, WILLIAM, Sen., born 1779, and at first was a hairdresser. In 1809, he commenced as a maker and repairer of fiddles, and then lived in Leeds. It is believed he died in 1857 or 1858 :—

> " W^m. Booth maker
> Leeds.   1828."

BOOTH, WILLIAM, Jun., son of the former, born at

Leeds in 1816.   After being engaged by Henri Gugel from 1834 to 1838, he returned to Leeds, and commenced business as an instrument maker in the latter year.   He was a clever workman, but greatly afflicted in health.   Died 1st June, 1856, aged thirty-nine years, and buried at the Burmantofts Cemetery.

BROWN, ANTHONY, it is said, learned violin-making of Joseph Panormo, others state of John Morrison, and became celebrated for his guitars.   In 1855, he was living in Rosomond Street, Clerkenwell; but since that period he has been to "the diggings," and has returned with a little of the mineral riches of that land.   He is not related to the other family of similar name.

COLE, JAMES, of Manchester, learned a portion of the business with — Tarr, afterwards with George Crask, all of the same locality.   A label was used until the year 1858, but now discontinued; and at this period the various instruments are stamped inside " J. Cole."

CORSBY, —, of Northampton, may be living, but very doubtful.

CORSBY, GEORGE, of Princes Street, Soho, London. It is believed he is a brother of the first named, and both were instructed in the musical business by the father. Nothing is known of the parent.

CRASK, GEORGE, of Salford, Manchester.

DAVIS, RICHARD.   This person has been alluded to under the name of the firm, Norris and Barnes.   He entered their employ in a humble capacity, the latter part of the eighteenth century, and was shopman when Norris died, in 1818, he then succeeded to the business more as a dealer than a manufacturer, having little knowledge of the use of the tools. He retired from business in favour of his cousin William Davis, and went to Bussage, near Stroud, Gloucestershire, his native place, and died there in April, 1836, and was interred at the parish church of Bisley.

The cousin continued the business until December, 1846, more as a dealer and repairer of violins, for he cannot be considered a maker, and brought Charles Maucotel from France to this country to work for him. At the above period he sold the business to Edward Withers, and retired to Bussage, where he still resides.

DEARLOVE, MARK, of Leeds, from 1812 to 1820, or perhaps longer; however, he was not originally taught the business. There is a son of this person named Mark William Dearlove that may still be living, who occasionally employed T. Abson, John Gough, and Charles Fryer—the latter became a partner with him, and died about 1840. Copy of label:—

> " Dearlove and Fryer,
> Musical Instrument
> Manufacturers,
> Boar Lane, Leeds,
> 1828."

DELANY, JOHN, of Dublin, used two kinds of labels, one of them very small, thus:—

> " Made by John Delany,
> No. 17, Britain Street,
> Dublin. 1808."

In the other, which is much larger, he is overflowing with good-will to the human family and self-love to his own abilities, which were most doubtful if realized:—

> " Made by John Delany
> In order to perpetuate his memory
> in future ages.   Dublin,
> 1808.

Liberty to all the world,
   black and white."

DENNIS, JESSE, was apprenticed to John Crowther about 1805, and afterwards turned over to Matthew Furber to complete his instruction. He was living in Eweherst Street, Walworth Common, in Feb. 1855, and was then sixty years of age.

DORANT, WILLIAM, of 63, Winfield Street, Brick Lane, Spitalfields, in the year 1814.

EGLINGTON. The copy of a label that has been seen in a fiddle of inferior workmanship, and had chequered purfle. The tone was very good :—

> " Eglington. Fecit,
> Drury Lane,
> London. 1802."

FARN, was merely the dealer, and is mentioned under the name of Bernhard Simmon Fendt.

FERGUSON AND SON, living in Edinburgh at the beginning of this century.

FIRTH, G., of Leeds, pupil of Wm. Booth, Sen. Copy of the label used :—

> " G. Firth,
> No. 110, Briggate,
> Leeds. 1836."

GIBBS, JAMES, was a maker employed by J. Morrison, G. Corsby, and S. Gilkes. Died about 1845, at No. 2, New Street, New Cut, Lambeth, and buried in the Churchyard in Waterloo Bridge Road, Lambeth.

GOUGH, WALTER, brother to — Gough, the leader of some of the minor theatres. Died about 1830.

HIGGINS, P. H., of Montreal, was an exhibitor in the Great Exhibition of 1851.

J'ANSON, EDWARD POPPLEWELL, of Manchester, pupil of William Booth, Jun.

MACGEORGE, of Edinburgh, about the period of Matthew Hardie.

MACINTOSH, of Dublin.   See Perry and Wilkinson.

PERRY, THOMAS, and WILKINSON, WILLIAM, of Dublin. The violins bearing the name of this firm are very neat and well made; but it is not known if they were workmen themselves.   The elder Tobin, who was an excellent workman, is said to be a pupil of the first name, and did much work for Old John Betts.   Latterly he kept a shop in West Street, Soho.   He died in great poverty in the poor-house of Shoreditch.

There was another pupil named Macintosh, and said to be the successor of Perry, who died between 1830 and 1840.   Copy of label, the date of which is doubtful, either 1817 or 1827, used by the firm, in which the long bow appears drawn to the fullest extent, as regards the number of instruments manufactured :—

" Made by

Thos. Perry and W^m. Wilkinson,

Musical Instrument Makers,

No. 4, Anglesea Street,

No. 4361.   Dublin.   1817 or 1827."

And in a label dated 1821 the number is put in as reaching 4534.

STIRBAT, D., of Edinburgh, considered by some persons to be a good workman.   Copy of label :—

" D. Stirbat.   Fecit,

Edinburgh.   181 ."

Space left to put in the last figure of the year.

STURGE, H., has resided in several places.   In 1811 he lived in Stephen Avenue, Clare Street, Bristol; and in 1853 his labels show he was living in Huddersfield, stating on one of them he was from London, and on the other from Bristol.   He is considered to be only a repairer of instruments.

TARR, —, of Manchester, was formerly a cabinet maker, then a fiddle maker; and in 1855 took to photography. It is said he excelled with his double-basses.

TOBIN, RICHARD. See Perry and Wilkinson.

TURNER, JOHN ALVEY, of 19, Poultry, City, and latterly of Cornhill. He was only a dealer, and died in February, 1862.

WITHERS, EDWARD, can only be considered as the dealer, and purchased the business of William Davis in December, 1846, first employing Charles Maucotel as a workman, then Boullangier, both of whom have left him and commenced on their own account. The business is still carried on by Edward Withers, in Coventry Street, Haymarket, where in 1851-2 was introduced an American alteration in the mode of making violins, violoncellos, &c., known as Wm. B. Tilton's Patent, which consisted of bevelling the blocks at each end of the instrument that both vibrating plates should be more free, and the required support was given by letting in a bar of wood into the blocks the whole length of the instrument. Although in some few instances an improvement was perceptible, yet it may be considered a failure, and is now laid aside.

WILKINSON, WILLIAM. See Perry and Wilkinson.

NAMES OF FOREIGNERS THAT HAVE LOCATED IN ENGLAND AS VIOLIN MAKERS.

PANORMO, VINCENT, who is generally alluded to as Old Panormo, was born on the 30th November, 1734, in a village named Monreale, a few miles from Palermo, in Sicily. He was endowed with much mechanical ability, and, unassisted, from sixteen years of age took delight in making various descriptions of musical instruments. The eldest son of the above-named, Francis Panormo, who attained his seventy-fourth year in 1842, has stated that his father made many descriptions of instruments; but most excelled in violins, violoncellos, double-basses, and hautboys. Vincent Panormo became a resident in several parts of Italy, France, England, and Ireland. The first time he came to England was in 1772, the second in 1789, being driven from France by the Revolution, where it is said " he was doing well." The violins, violoncellos, and double-basses of this maker are deservedly much esteemed, and valued for their pure and Italian quality of tone and appreciated by the professors on these instruments. He died in London about 1813.

In the MSS. of Hill is given the copy of the following labels:—

" Vincenzo Panormo me fece Marsiglia, 1760, Sicily ;" and " Vincenzo Panormo, Londra. 1791."

There was another son of the above Vincent, named JOSEPH PANORMO, who was a good workman and thoroughly knew the theory of violin-making. At one period he resided in New Compton Street, afterwards in King Street, Soho. He died about twenty-five years since in the greatest destitution.

PANORMO, GEORGE LEWIS, was another son of the former Vincent, and became celebrated for his guitars, and was in the highest esteem as a bow maker; he was then living in Oxford Street, and latterly in High Street, Saint Giles-in-the-Fields. The time of his death cannot be stated with accuracy, probably ten or twelve years since.

Some persons assert there was another son of Vincent, named Edward Panormo, who, at times, resided in Ireland and London. We do not know him, and it may probably allude to a grandson of Vincent, who of late years has been living in the latter city; the precise locality, however, is not known, as he has changed his abode many times within the last few years.

MAUCOTEL, CHARLES, was born at Mirecourt, 1st Nov. 1807, and learned violin-making of a relative, by marriage, of his mother, whose name was Bloise Mast. In 1834 he located in Paris, and was employed by Gand; ultimately he was engaged by W. Davis, of 34, Coventry Street, and came to London in Dec. 1844, and worked at that house for two years. On the disposal of the business to Edward Withers he remained in the employ about eighteen months, and then left and commenced on his own account at No. 8, Rupert Street, Haymarket. He retired from business about August, 1860, partly through impaired health; but it is generally believed the real cause was that a relative had left him property. He was a good workman, and knew well the vocation he followed.

Copy of the label used, with space left to add the last figure of the year :—

" Carolus Maucotelus
fecit Londini, 185   C†M."

CHARLES, THERESS, came from Mirecourt, and on his card is printed " from Maucotel;" for several years past he has been established on his own behalf as a violin maker, and now resides in King Street, Soho.

CHANOT, whose business is now in Wardour Street, Soho, was engaged as workman to Maucotel, and on the latter retiring he commenced on his own account.

BOULLANGIER, at one time was in the employ of Edward Withers, but now has an establishment of his own in Dean Street, Soho.

INDEX.

BEL, performer, 183.
Abrinces, king's versifier, 73.
Adenez le Roi, 81.
Adye, W. L. Esq., his violin, 233.
Agricola, Martin, 47-8, 93-4.
Aireton, maker, 355.
Albani, makers, 214.
Albinus, or Alcuin, 41.
Aldred, maker, 250.
Alexandre Roman d', 40.
Alleyn, instruments of, 144.
Amati, makers, 201-8.
Amphicordium, 95.
Anacreon, 12.
Anthony Now Now, 109.
Arabian and African instruments, 11-12.
Armin, " Nest of Ninnies," 108.
Arched viall, 152.
Arnold le Vielleux, 65.
Arnold, St. performer, 56.
Artusi, 45.

Baker, maker, 257.
Baltazar, 100.
Baltzar, 146, 152-3.
Banks, makers, 359.
Bannister, warrant to buy Cremona violins, 154.
Barbiton, 12, 119, 121-3.
Barnes, maker, 268.
Barraud, chamber bass, 374.
Barrett, maker, 262.
Bartoloccius, Hebrew instruments, 7.
Bass-viol, large, 93.
Baud, experiments by, 186.

Bede, or Pseudo-Bede, 52.
Bergonzi, makers, 236.
Betts, makers, 270.
Beverley, minstrels, 84.
Bibliothéque de l'Ecole des Chartes, 79.
Bigati, anecdote of, 174.
Blanchinus, 16.
Blegabres, Blæthgabreat, 25, 36, 40.
Bolles, maker, 250.
Bonanni, Gabinetto, 165.
Bourdelot, anecdote of, 163.
Bow, introduction of, 20, 49, 158.
Ditto, length of, 159.
Ditto, makers, 158-60, 369.
Britton, instruments, 253, 257-8.
Brossard, instruments named by, 130.
Brown, makers, 354.
Brut, Roman de, 25, 36.
Bull, Ole, his violin, 200.
Burney's History, 18, 115-16, 146.

Carré, account of instruments, 165.
Carter, ancient sculpture, 29, 67-8, 84, 91-2.
Castrucci, performer, 179.
Cat and fiddle, 135.
Cerone, instruments named by, 117.
Cerreto, the like, 116.
Cervetto, performers, 183.
Chanot, experiments by, 186.
Chappell, Wm., F.S.A., his valuable work, &c. 21, 36.
Charles I., performer, 137.
Ditto, band, 138.
Charles II., four and twenty fiddlers, 146.
Charles IX. of France, 98, 202.

Charles IX. of France, purchase of Cremona violins, 99.
Chaucer, 28, 37, 44.
Chelys, 95-6, 154, 167.
Colin Muset, 44, 58.
Conductor, 16, 68-9, 177-8.
Constantinus Africanus, 24.
Contre-Basse, 168.
Contre-Bass-geig, 117.
Corbet, his instruments, 176.
Cornish Drama, ancient, 29.
Cortusio, curious will, 85.
Coryat, T., account of music, 141.
Coussemaker, Mons. de, 22, 28-9, 41-2, 45, 47-8, 62-3, 66, 83-4.
Crosse, maker, 260.
Crowd, crwth, 20, 28-9, 30-4, 109, 132, 144.
Curtis, Sir Wm., instruments of, 202, 206, 209, 228-9, 231-2.
Cythara, cithara, 12, 22-3, 36.

D'Agincourt, 67, 84.
Dauney, Scottish melodies, 30, 103, 249.
Daverouns, Robt., violist, 65.
Degrevant, Sir, Romance of, 27.
De Muris, Joh., 39.
Details, omission of, 66, 83, 141.
Diana, performer, anecdote, 172.
Dicord, 13, 58.
Di Salo Gaspar, maker, 199.
Dodd, bow-makers, 160, 369.
Dodd, makers, 367.
Doni, instrument, 95.
Doran, Dr., Court fools, 108.
Double-bass, large, 165.
Dragonetti, 194.
Drama, first musical, 114-15.
Dramatic and poetic early pieces, instruments named in, 25, 105-7, 114, 132, 134-136.
Drayton, Polyolbion, 133.
Dubourg, performer, 180.
Dubourg, the violin, 169, 278.
Duiffoprugcar, maker, 197.
Duke, maker, 269.

Earle, Microcosmography, 133.

Edward II., musicians, 65-6, 73.
Edward III., ditto, 66, 74-5.
Edward IV., ditto, 76.
Edward VI., ditto, 102.
Egyptian instruments, 18, 20.
Elizabeth, musicians, 103.
Ditto, her dancing, 126.
Ely Cathedral, 67.
Epigonium, 13.
Eric King, anecdote, 10.
Esquimaux, violin, 11.
Evelyn Memoirs, 153-4.
Exeter Cathedral, minstrel gallery, &c., 68.

Fendt, makers, 369.
Fetis, Mons., referred to, 21, 197, 199, 208, 210, 222, 229, 232.
Fiddle, fidula, fythele, 28-31, 36, 53, 106-7, 110, 119, 132-3, 151.
Fiddlers, 31, 106-9, 133.
Ditto, four and twenty, 125, 146.
Forster, Dr., 196, 199, 205, 208, 214, 216, 219, 234, 238, 271, 284.
Forster family, makers, 284.
Forster, John, 290.
Forster, Wm. (1), 292.
Forster, Wm. (2), 296.
Forster, Wm. (3), 209, 333.
Forster, Wm. (4), 341.
Forster, S. A., 343.
Forster School, 347.
Francis I. band, 97.
Frets, 91.
Frey Hans, maker, 87.
Froschouer, 93.

Gafurius, 91.
Gægliano, makers, 235.
Galilei, V., account of instruments, 97, 248.
Gand, maker, 247.
Garlande, John de, 38.
Geminiani, 180.
Gerasenus, 16.
Gerbert, "De Cantu," &c. 22-4, 51, 69, 161.
Gerson, 24, 44.
Gigue, 25-7, 46-8, 57, 119.

Gilkes, maker, 348.
Gori, Thesaurus, 152.
Grammont, Duc de, anecdote, 125.
Grancino, makers, 213.
Greeks, no bowed instruments, 12.
Gros-Guillaume, &c., 47.
Guadagnini, makers, 236.
Guarnerius family, 231-4.

HALLIWELL, J. O., F.S.A., fairy mythology, 38.
Handel, 178.
Hardie, maker, 373.
Hare, maker, 263.
Harp, Egyptian, 18.
Hart, maker, 349.
Hawes, Pastime of Pleasure, 30.
Hawkin's History, 16, 158, 173, 221, 249, 251, 253.
Haydn, dealings with Wm. Forster (2), 300.
　　Ditto, anecdote, 125.
　　Ditto, letters, 306-10.
Head, carved on instruments, 46.
Henri aus vièles, maker, 65.
Henry IV., musicians, &c., 75.
Henry V., the like, 75.
Henry VI., the like, 76.
Henry VII., the like, 77.
Henry VIII., the like, 45, 78, 101.
　　Ditto, his instruments, 102.
Henry III. of France, 99.
Henry IV. of France, his band, 98.
Hill, Henry, performer, his MSS., 198, 205, 233, 251, 323.
Hill family, makers, 356.
Hole, Rev., his violoncello, 324.
Howell's Letters, 5, 60.
Hume, R., maker, 249.

ICELAND, violin, 11.
Indian Ragas mentioned, 9.
Instructions du Comité, &c., 42, 57, 64.

JARNOVICK, performer, anecdotes of, 172.
Jay, makers, 250-1, 258, 265.
Jehan le Tonneleur, 81.

Jehan le Vidaulx, 80.
Jenkyns, J., performer, 147-8.
John, King of France, payments to musicians, 75.
John, St., Cirencester, 91.
John of Salisbury, 24.
Johnson, maker, 267.
Jones, Relics of Bards, 30.
Jouglet, performer, 65.
Jubal, father of music, 6.

KENNEDY family, makers, 352.
Kepler, music of spheres, 10.
Kerlin, J., maker, 87.
Keyed instruments to imitate stringed, 152, 164, 246.
Kinnor, 6, 7.
Kircher, instruments named by, 6, 124.
Kit, the, 105, 119, 132-3, 168.
Klotz, makers, 218.

LABORDE, Histoire de Musique, 11, 17, 43, 58, 95, 161-2, 167.
Layard, his researches, 19.
Lentz, maker, 372.
Leprince performer, anecdote, 171.
Lewis, maker, 258.
Lidel, Mons., his barytone, 131.
Lindley, R., account of, 191.
Lintercolo, 166.
Lott family, makers, 372.
Louis XI., anecdote of, 88.
Louis XIII., anecdote of, 124.
Louis XIV., anecdote of, 115.
Lupot La Chelonomie, 241.
Luscinius, 95.
Lute, Eastern, 8.
Lyra, Viol, 148.
Lyra Teutonica, 23.

MACE, "Musick's Monument," 157, 203, 218, 250-3.
Magadis, 13.
Maggini, makers, 211.
Makers, ancient corporation of, 98.
Makers, English, 248, *et seq.*
　　Ditto, Foreign, resident, 384.

Makers, French, 65, 211, 215, 240-1, 247.
    Ditto, German, 197, 201, 215-16, 242.
    Ditto, Italian, 197, 201, 215-16, 242.
    Ditto, Midwalders, 219.
Mara, performer, anecdotes of, 228-9.
Marais, performer, anecdote of, 124.
Marguerite, Queen, 96.
Mathurine, anecdote of, 97.
Matteis, performer, 153-4.
Maugard, performer, anecdote of, 129.
Mell Davis, performer, 153.
Melross Church, crwth, 30.
Mersennus, 93, 119-23.
Millin, Galerie, &c., 14.
Minstrel's Galleries, 68.
    Ditto, Corporation, 44, 78.
    Ditto, kings of, 81.
    Ditto, some account of, 72.
Monochord, 25, 27-8, 30, 58, 166.
Montagnana, maker, 239.
Monteverde, 97.
Montfaucon, 13, 14.
Moravia, Jerome de, 45, 63.
Morgan, Bishop, 30.
Morley, Practical Music, 113.
Music, Academy of, in France, 82.
    Ditto, effect of on animals, 3.
Musical Publications, 110, 130, 142, 158.
Musical Society of London, 177.
Musicians, Corporation of, 76, 140, 161.
    Ditto, exempt from subsidies, 103, 138.
Musonii Philosophi Opus, instruments named, 13.

Neumes, 59.
Neghinoth, 7.
Nineveh, instruments, 19.
Norman, B., maker, 258.
Norris, maker, 268.
Northumberland Household Book, 45, 78.
Notation, 16, 59, 87, 112.

Notker, 21, 24.

Oates, Jack, anecdote of, 108.
Olivieri, anecdote of, 170.
Opera, first English, 176.
    Ditto, in France, 115.
Oporinus, 92.
Orchestras, 146, 162-3, 177-8.
Ott Jean, maker, 87.
Otto's work referred to, 222, 246.

Paganini, 188.
Pamphilon, maker, 255.
Panormo, bow maker, 160.
Parker, maker, 256.
Passenans, anecdote from, 179.
Pavan dance, 143.
Pectis, 13.
Pemberton, maker, 255.
Pepys's Diary, 149-152.
Performers, 56, 65, 73-7, 79, 80-1, 96, 99, 100, 102-3, 125, 127-8, 137-8, 153-4, 169, 170-5, 187, 189, 190.
    Ditto, payments to, 65, 73-80, 86, 101-3, 134, 137-8, 151.
Peterborough Cathedral, Mr. Strickland's ceiling of, 55-6.
Piers Ploughman's Vision, 37.
Playford, 156.
Plectrum, 14, 15.
Poche, 118-20, 165, 168.
Poisot, Histoire, 98.
Pollnitz, Baron de, 164.
Potier, Monumens, 42-3, 61-2, 66-7, 83, 92.
Prætorius, M., 117.
Price of Instruments, 103-4, 139, 154, 158, 222, 229, 230, 233, 250, 256-7, 260, 263, 265, 268, 323, 325, 329-31, 361-2.
Promptorium Parvulorum, 40.
Psalterion Sautry, 21, 25-7, 29, 30.
Pugnani, anecdote of, 170.

Rabelais, 46.
Rahere, king's minstrel, 54.
Rayman, maker, 253.

Rebec, rubebe, 12, 27-8, 30, 43-6, 101, 165.
Rheims, musician's house, 63.
Richard II., payments to musicians, 75.
Richelieu, Cardinal, anecdote of, 126.
Rimbault, Dr., 142, 148.
Rolla, performer, anecdote of, 171.
Romans, no genuine representation of bow, 12, 14.
Roquefort, 43, 198.
Ross, makers, 251.
Rote, 21-2, 24-9, 30, 41-3.
Rousseau Traité, 6, 15, 18.
Ruggeri family, makers, 212.
Russian instruments, 12.

Savart, experiments, 186.
Schetky, account of, 184.
Shalme-player, death of Wolsey's, 78.
Shaw's Dresses, &c., 43, 54.
Shift used, 122, 169.
Simpson, division viol, 154.
Smith's harmonics, 1, 150.
Smith, maker, 251, 267.
Soisson, enamelled basin, 64.
Sordino, 166, 168.
Spence, as to spurious antiquities, 14.
Steiner family, 219.
Storioni, maker, 238.
Stradiuarius family, 224-6.
Strings, 64, 111, 124, 154, 236.
   Ditto, experiments with, 111.
Strutt's Manners, &c., 53, 63, 84-5, 140.
Symbola Divina, 124.
Symphonie, chyfonie, 25-7, 29, 30, 40.

Tardieu de Terascon, improved violoncello, 108.
Taylor, Water Poet, 141.
Tempest, orchestra for, 146.
Tems, Pastour Le, 26.
Thompson, makers, 266.

Thoms, W. J., F.S.A., Notes on Fiddle, 38.
Todini, instrument, 130.
Toulmon, Bottée de, 22, 114.
Tourte, bow maker, 159.
Troubadours referred to, 70.
Troveors, Les Deux Ribauz, 40.
Trumpet, marine, 124, 166.
Tubbs, bow makers, 160.

Urquhart, maker, 254.

Venantius Fortunatus, 20.
Veracini, anecdote of, 170.
Vidaulx, Jehan le, performer, 80.
Vielle, 25-7, 40.
Vinesauf, Geoffrey de, 38.
Viol, 30, 40, 43, 50-7, 61-8, 74, 80, 83-5, 91-5, 98, 101-4, 109, 114-19, 123, 125, 130, 133, 138-9, 140-1, 144, 147, 154-8, 161, 165-8, 176, 250-1.
   Ditto, chests of, 116, 250-1.
   Ditto, tuning of, 94-5, 116.
Viol da gamba, 97, 105, 114, 141.
Viol d'amour, 168.
Viola pomposa, 164.
Violetta marina, 179.
Violette, 168.
Violin, 11, 31, 81, 90, 95, 99, 100-1, 103-4, 106-7, 114-15, 117-19, 122, 130, 132, 137-8, 140, 145, 147, 154, 156-8, 161-3, 165, 167, 189, 222, 229-30.
   Ditto, kings of, 81.
Violoncello, 117, 119, 121, 130, 162-4, 168.
Violono, 97, 165.
Viotti, performer, anecdotes of, 128, 181.
Volker, musical warrior, 38.
Vows of the Heron, 74.
Vuillaume, maker, 247.

Walmsley, maker, 263.
Whistlecraft's History, 53.
Wilkinson, Sir G., Ancient Egyptians, 18.

Wood, A., account of music, 147-8.
Worcester Cathedral, crwth, 29.
Wright, T., F.S.A., History of Domestic Manners, 72.
Wynne, W. G., Esq., his crwth, 34.

YORK Cathedral, screen, 68.

Youssoupow, Prince, his Luthomonographie, 11, 199, 200, 205, 210-11, 214-15, 221, 224, 226, 233, 236-7.

ZACCONI Pratica di Musica, 90.
Zwinglius, a performer, 97.

THE END.

A CATALOG OF SELECTED
DOVER BOOKS
IN ALL FIELDS OF INTEREST

A CATALOG OF SELECTED DOVER
BOOKS IN ALL FIELDS OF INTEREST

CONCERNING THE SPIRITUAL IN ART, Wassily Kandinsky. Pioneering work by father of abstract art. Thoughts on color theory, nature of art. Analysis of earlier masters. 12 illustrations. 80pp. of text. 5⅜ x 8½. 0-486-23411-8

CELTIC ART: The Methods of Construction, George Bain. Simple geometric techniques for making Celtic interlacements, spirals, Kells-type initials, animals, humans, etc. Over 500 illustrations. 160pp. 9 x 12. (Available in U.S. only.) 0-486-22923-8

AN ATLAS OF ANATOMY FOR ARTISTS, Fritz Schider. Most thorough reference work on art anatomy in the world. Hundreds of illustrations, including selections from works by Vesalius, Leonardo, Goya, Ingres, Michelangelo, others. 593 illustrations. 192pp. 7⅛ x 10¼. 0-486-20241-0

CELTIC HAND STROKE-BY-STROKE (Irish Half-Uncial from "The Book of Kells"): An Arthur Baker Calligraphy Manual, Arthur Baker. Complete guide to creating each letter of the alphabet in distinctive Celtic manner. Covers hand position, strokes, pens, inks, paper, more. Illustrated. 48pp. 8¼ x 11. 0-486-24336-2

EASY ORIGAMI, John Montroll. Charming collection of 32 projects (hat, cup, pelican, piano, swan, many more) specially designed for the novice origami hobbyist. Clearly illustrated easy-to-follow instructions insure that even beginning papercrafters will achieve successful results. 48pp. 8¼ x 11. 0-486-27298-2

BLOOMINGDALE'S ILLUSTRATED 1886 CATALOG: Fashions, Dry Goods and Housewares, Bloomingdale Brothers. Famed merchants' extremely rare catalog depicting about 1,700 products: clothing, housewares, firearms, dry goods, jewelry, more. Invaluable for dating, identifying vintage items. Also, copyright-free graphics for artists, designers. Co-published with Henry Ford Museum & Greenfield Village. 160pp. 8¼ x 11. 0-486-25780-0

THE ART OF WORLDLY WISDOM, Baltasar Gracian. "Think with the few and speak with the many," "Friends are a second existence," and "Be able to forget" are among this 1637 volume's 300 pithy maxims. A perfect source of mental and spiritual refreshment, it can be opened at random and appreciated either in brief or at length. 128pp. 5⅜ x 8½. 0-486-44034-6

JOHNSON'S DICTIONARY: A Modern Selection, Samuel Johnson (E. L. McAdam and George Milne, eds.). This modern version reduces the original 1755 edition's 2,300 pages of definitions and literary examples to a more manageable length, retaining the verbal pleasure and historical curiosity of the original. 480pp. 5³⁄₁₆ x 8¼. 0-486-44089-3

ADVENTURES OF HUCKLEBERRY FINN, Mark Twain, Illustrated by E. W. Kemble. A work of eternal richness and complexity, a source of ongoing critical debate, and a literary landmark, Twain's 1885 masterpiece about a barefoot boy's journey of self-discovery has enthralled readers around the world. This handsome clothbound reproduction of the first edition features all 174 of the original black-and-white illustrations. 368pp. 5⅜ x 8½. 0-486-44322-1

STICKLEY CRAFTSMAN FURNITURE CATALOGS, Gustav Stickley and L. & J. G. Stickley. Beautiful, functional furniture in two authentic catalogs from 1910. 594 illustrations, including 277 photos, show settles, rockers, armchairs, reclining chairs, bookcases, desks, tables. 183pp. 6½ x 9¼. 0-486-23838-5

AMERICAN LOCOMOTIVES IN HISTORIC PHOTOGRAPHS: 1858 to 1949, Ron Ziel (ed.). A rare collection of 126 meticulously detailed official photographs, called "builder portraits," of American locomotives that majestically chronicle the rise of steam locomotive power in America. Introduction. Detailed captions. xi+ 129pp. 9 x 12. 0-486-27393-8

AMERICA'S LIGHTHOUSES: An Illustrated History, Francis Ross Holland, Jr. Delightfully written, profusely illustrated fact-filled survey of over 200 American lighthouses since 1716. History, anecdotes, technological advances, more. 240pp. 8 x 10¾. 0-486-25576-X

TOWARDS A NEW ARCHITECTURE, Le Corbusier. Pioneering manifesto by founder of "International School." Technical and aesthetic theories, views of industry, economics, relation of form to function, "mass-production split" and much more. Profusely illustrated. 320pp. 6⅛ x 9¼. (Available in U.S. only.) 0-486-25023-7

HOW THE OTHER HALF LIVES, Jacob Riis. Famous journalistic record, exposing poverty and degradation of New York slums around 1900, by major social reformer. 100 striking and influential photographs. 233pp. 10 x 7⅞. 0-486-22012-5

FRUIT KEY AND TWIG KEY TO TREES AND SHRUBS, William M. Harlow. One of the handiest and most widely used identification aids. Fruit key covers 120 deciduous and evergreen species; twig key 160 deciduous species. Easily used. Over 300 photographs. 126pp. 5⅜ x 8½. 0-486-20511-8

COMMON BIRD SONGS, Dr. Donald J. Borror. Songs of 60 most common U.S. birds: robins, sparrows, cardinals, bluejays, finches, more—arranged in order of increasing complexity. Up to 9 variations of songs of each species. Cassette and manual 0-486-99911-4

ORCHIDS AS HOUSE PLANTS, Rebecca Tyson Northen. Grow cattleyas and many other kinds of orchids—in a window, in a case, or under artificial light. 63 illustrations. 148pp. 5⅜ x 8½. 0-486-23261-1

MONSTER MAZES, Dave Phillips. Masterful mazes at four levels of difficulty. Avoid deadly perils and evil creatures to find magical treasures. Solutions for all 32 exciting illustrated puzzles. 48pp. 8¼ x 11. 0-486-26005-4

MOZART'S DON GIOVANNI (DOVER OPERA LIBRETTO SERIES), Wolfgang Amadeus Mozart. Introduced and translated by Ellen H. Bleiler. Standard Italian libretto, with complete English translation. Convenient and thoroughly portable—an ideal companion for reading along with a recording or the performance itself. Introduction. List of characters. Plot summary. 121pp. 5¼ x 8½. 0-486-24944-1

FRANK LLOYD WRIGHT'S DANA HOUSE, Donald Hoffmann. Pictorial essay of residential masterpiece with over 160 interior and exterior photos, plans, elevations, sketches and studies. 128pp. 9¼ x 10¾. 0-486-29120-0

THE CLARINET AND CLARINET PLAYING, David Pino. Lively, comprehensive work features suggestions about technique, musicianship, and musical interpretation, as well as guidelines for teaching, making your own reeds, and preparing for public performance. Includes an intriguing look at clarinet history. "A godsend," *The Clarinet,* Journal of the International Clarinet Society. Appendixes. 7 illus. 320pp. 5⅜ x 8½. 0-486-40270-3

HOLLYWOOD GLAMOR PORTRAITS, John Kobal (ed.). 145 photos from 1926-49. Harlow, Gable, Bogart, Bacall; 94 stars in all. Full background on photographers, technical aspects. 160pp. 8⅜ x 11¼. 0-486-23352-9

THE RAVEN AND OTHER FAVORITE POEMS, Edgar Allan Poe. Over 40 of the author's most memorable poems: "The Bells," "Ulalume," "Israfel," "To Helen," "The Conqueror Worm," "Eldorado," "Annabel Lee," many more. Alphabetic lists of titles and first lines. 64pp. 5$\frac{3}{16}$ x 8¼. 0-486-26685-0

PERSONAL MEMOIRS OF U. S. GRANT, Ulysses Simpson Grant. Intelligent, deeply moving firsthand account of Civil War campaigns, considered by many the finest military memoirs ever written. Includes letters, historic photographs, maps and more. 528pp. 6⅛ x 9¼. 0-486-28587-1

ANCIENT EGYPTIAN MATERIALS AND INDUSTRIES, A. Lucas and J. Harris. Fascinating, comprehensive, thoroughly documented text describes this ancient civilization's vast resources and the processes that incorporated them in daily life, including the use of animal products, building materials, cosmetics, perfumes and incense, fibers, glazed ware, glass and its manufacture, materials used in the mummification process, and much more. 544pp. 6⅛ x 9¼. (Available in U.S. only.) 0-486-40446-3

RUSSIAN STORIES/RUSSKIE RASSKAZY: A Dual-Language Book, edited by Gleb Struve. Twelve tales by such masters as Chekhov, Tolstoy, Dostoevsky, Pushkin, others. Excellent word-for-word English translations on facing pages, plus teaching and study aids, Russian/English vocabulary, biographical/critical introductions, more. 416pp. 5⅜ x 8½. 0-486-26244-8

PHILADELPHIA THEN AND NOW: 60 Sites Photographed in the Past and Present, Kenneth Finkel and Susan Oyama. Rare photographs of City Hall, Logan Square, Independence Hall, Betsy Ross House, other landmarks juxtaposed with contemporary views. Captures changing face of historic city. Introduction. Captions. 128pp. 8¼ x 11. 0-486-25790-8

NORTH AMERICAN INDIAN LIFE: Customs and Traditions of 23 Tribes, Elsie Clews Parsons (ed.). 27 fictionalized essays by noted anthropologists examine religion, customs, government, additional facets of life among the Winnebago, Crow, Zuni, Eskimo, other tribes. 480pp. 6⅛ x 9¼. 0-486-27377-6

TECHNICAL MANUAL AND DICTIONARY OF CLASSICAL BALLET, Gail Grant. Defines, explains, comments on steps, movements, poses and concepts. 15-page pictorial section. Basic book for student, viewer. 127pp. 5⅜ x 8½. 0-486-21843-0

THE MALE AND FEMALE FIGURE IN MOTION: 60 Classic Photographic Sequences, Eadweard Muybridge. 60 true-action photographs of men and women walking, running, climbing, bending, turning, etc., reproduced from rare 19th-century masterpiece. vi + 121pp. 9 x 12. 0-486-24745-7

ANIMALS: 1,419 Copyright-Free Illustrations of Mammals, Birds, Fish, Insects, etc., Jim Harter (ed.). Clear wood engravings present, in extremely lifelike poses, over 1,000 species of animals. One of the most extensive pictorial sourcebooks of its kind. Captions. Index. 284pp. 9 x 12. 0-486-23766-4

1001 QUESTIONS ANSWERED ABOUT THE SEASHORE, N. J. Berrill and Jacquelyn Berrill. Queries answered about dolphins, sea snails, sponges, starfish, fishes, shore birds, many others. Covers appearance, breeding, growth, feeding, much more. 305pp. 5¼ x 8¼. 0-486-23366-9

ATTRACTING BIRDS TO YOUR YARD, William J. Weber. Easy-to-follow guide offers advice on how to attract the greatest diversity of birds: birdhouses, feeders, water and waterers, much more. 96pp. 5³⁄₁₆ x 8¼. 0-486-28927-3

MEDICINAL AND OTHER USES OF NORTH AMERICAN PLANTS: A Historical Survey with Special Reference to the Eastern Indian Tribes, Charlotte Erichsen-Brown. Chronological historical citations document 500 years of usage of plants, trees, shrubs native to eastern Canada, northeastern U.S. Also complete identifying information. 343 illustrations. 544pp. 6½ x 9¼. 0-486-25951-X

STORYBOOK MAZES, Dave Phillips. 23 stories and mazes on two-page spreads: Wizard of Oz, Treasure Island, Robin Hood, etc. Solutions. 64pp. 8¼ x 11. 0-486-23628-5

AMERICAN NEGRO SONGS: 230 Folk Songs and Spirituals, Religious and Secular, John W. Work. This authoritative study traces the African influences of songs sung and played by black Americans at work, in church, and as entertainment. The author discusses the lyric significance of such songs as "Swing Low, Sweet Chariot," "John Henry," and others and offers the words and music for 230 songs. Bibliography. Index of Song Titles. 272pp. 6½ x 9¼. 0-486-40271-1

MOVIE-STAR PORTRAITS OF THE FORTIES, John Kobal (ed.). 163 glamor, studio photos of 106 stars of the 1940s: Rita Hayworth, Ava Gardner, Marlon Brando, Clark Gable, many more. 176pp. 8⅜ x 11¼. 0-486-23546-7

YEKL and THE IMPORTED BRIDEGROOM AND OTHER STORIES OF YIDDISH NEW YORK, Abraham Cahan. Film Hester Street based on *Yekl* (1896). Novel, other stories among first about Jewish immigrants on N.Y.'s East Side. 240pp. 5⅜ x 8½. 0-486-22427-9

SELECTED POEMS, Walt Whitman. Generous sampling from *Leaves of Grass*. Twenty-four poems include "I Hear America Singing," "Song of the Open Road," "I Sing the Body Electric," "When Lilacs Last in the Dooryard Bloom'd," "O Captain! My Captain!"–all reprinted from an authoritative edition. Lists of titles and first lines. 128pp. 5³⁄₁₆ x 8¼. 0-486-26878-0

SONGS OF EXPERIENCE: Facsimile Reproduction with 26 Plates in Full Color, William Blake. 26 full-color plates from a rare 1826 edition. Includes "The Tyger," "London," "Holy Thursday," and other poems. Printed text of poems. 48pp. 5¼ x 7. 0-486-24636-1

THE BEST TALES OF HOFFMANN, E. T. A. Hoffmann. 10 of Hoffmann's most important stories: "Nutcracker and the King of Mice," "The Golden Flowerpot," etc. 458pp. 5⅜ x 8½. 0-486-21793-0

THE BOOK OF TEA, Kakuzo Okakura. Minor classic of the Orient: entertaining, charming explanation, interpretation of traditional Japanese culture in terms of tea ceremony. 94pp. 5⅜ x 8½. 0-486-20070-1

FRENCH STORIES/CONTES FRANÇAIS: A Dual-Language Book, Wallace Fowlie. Ten stories by French masters, Voltaire to Camus: "Micromegas" by Voltaire; "The Atheist's Mass" by Balzac; "Minuet" by de Maupassant; "The Guest" by Camus, six more. Excellent English translations on facing pages. Also French-English vocabulary list, exercises, more. 352pp. 5⅜ x 8½. 0-486-26443-2

CHICAGO AT THE TURN OF THE CENTURY IN PHOTOGRAPHS: 122 Historic Views from the Collections of the Chicago Historical Society, Larry A. Viskochil. Rare large-format prints offer detailed views of City Hall, State Street, the Loop, Hull House, Union Station, many other landmarks, circa 1904-1913. Introduction. Captions. Maps. 144pp. 9⅜ x 12¼. 0-486-24656-6

OLD BROOKLYN IN EARLY PHOTOGRAPHS, 1865-1929, William Lee Younger. Luna Park, Gravesend race track, construction of Grand Army Plaza, moving of Hotel Brighton, etc. 157 previously unpublished photographs. 165pp. 8⅞ x 11¾. 0-486-23587-4

THE MYTHS OF THE NORTH AMERICAN INDIANS, Lewis Spence. Rich anthology of the myths and legends of the Algonquins, Iroquois, Pawnees and Sioux, prefaced by an extensive historical and ethnological commentary. 36 illustrations. 480pp. 5⅜ x 8½. 0-486-25967-6

AN ENCYCLOPEDIA OF BATTLES: Accounts of Over 1,560 Battles from 1479 B.C. to the Present, David Eggenberger. Essential details of every major battle in recorded history from the first battle of Megiddo in 1479 B.C. to Grenada in 1984. List of Battle Maps. New Appendix covering the years 1967-1984. Index. 99 illustrations. 544pp. 6½ x 9¼. 0-486-24913-1

SAILING ALONE AROUND THE WORLD, Captain Joshua Slocum. First man to sail around the world, alone, in small boat. One of great feats of seamanship told in delightful manner. 67 illustrations. 294pp. 5⅜ x 8½. 0-486-20326-3

ANARCHISM AND OTHER ESSAYS, Emma Goldman. Powerful, penetrating, prophetic essays on direct action, role of minorities, prison reform, puritan hypocrisy, violence, etc. 271pp. 5⅜ x 8½. 0-486-22484-8

MYTHS OF THE HINDUS AND BUDDHISTS, Ananda K. Coomaraswamy and Sister Nivedita. Great stories of the epics; deeds of Krishna, Shiva, taken from puranas, Vedas, folk tales; etc. 32 illustrations. 400pp. 5⅜ x 8½. 0-486-21759-0

MY BONDAGE AND MY FREEDOM, Frederick Douglass. Born a slave, Douglass became outspoken force in antislavery movement. The best of Douglass' autobiographies. Graphic description of slave life. 464pp. 5⅜ x 8½. 0-486-22457-0

FOLLOWING THE EQUATOR: A Journey Around the World, Mark Twain. Fascinating humorous account of 1897 voyage to Hawaii, Australia, India, New Zealand, etc. Ironic, bemused reports on peoples, customs, climate, flora and fauna, politics, much more. 197 illustrations. 720pp. 5⅜ x 8½. 0-486-26113-1

THE PEOPLE CALLED SHAKERS, Edward D. Andrews. Definitive study of Shakers: origins, beliefs, practices, dances, social organization, furniture and crafts, etc. 33 illustrations. 351pp. 5⅜ x 8½. 0-486-21081-2

THE MYTHS OF GREECE AND ROME, H. A. Guerber. A classic of mythology, generously illustrated, long prized for its simple, graphic, accurate retelling of the principal myths of Greece and Rome, and for its commentary on their origins and significance. With 64 illustrations by Michelangelo, Raphael, Titian, Rubens, Canova, Bernini and others. 480pp. 5⅜ x 8½. 0-486-27584-1

PSYCHOLOGY OF MUSIC, Carl E. Seashore. Classic work discusses music as a medium from psychological viewpoint. Clear treatment of physical acoustics, auditory apparatus, sound perception, development of musical skills, nature of musical feeling, host of other topics. 88 figures. 408pp. 5⅜ x 8½. 0-486-21851-1

LIFE IN ANCIENT EGYPT, Adolf Erman. Fullest, most thorough, detailed older account with much not in more recent books, domestic life, religion, magic, medicine, commerce, much more. Many illustrations reproduce tomb paintings, carvings, hieroglyphs, etc. 597pp. 5⅜ x 8½. 0-486-22632-8

SUNDIALS, Their Theory and Construction, Albert Waugh. Far and away the best, most thorough coverage of ideas, mathematics concerned, types, construction, adjusting anywhere. Simple, nontechnical treatment allows even children to build several of these dials. Over 100 illustrations. 230pp. 5⅜ x 8½. 0-486-22947-5

THEORETICAL HYDRODYNAMICS, L. M. Milne-Thomson. Classic exposition of the mathematical theory of fluid motion, applicable to both hydrodynamics and aerodynamics. Over 600 exercises. 768pp. 6⅛ x 9¼. 0-486-68970-0

OLD-TIME VIGNETTES IN FULL COLOR, Carol Belanger Grafton (ed.). Over 390 charming, often sentimental illustrations, selected from archives of Victorian graphics–pretty women posing, children playing, food, flowers, kittens and puppies, smiling cherubs, birds and butterflies, much more. All copyright-free. 48pp. 9¼ x 12¼. 0-486-27269-9

PERSPECTIVE FOR ARTISTS, Rex Vicat Cole. Depth, perspective of sky and sea, shadows, much more, not usually covered. 391 diagrams, 81 reproductions of drawings and paintings. 279pp. 5⅜ x 8½. 0-486-22487-2

DRAWING THE LIVING FIGURE, Joseph Sheppard. Innovative approach to artistic anatomy focuses on specifics of surface anatomy, rather than muscles and bones. Over 170 drawings of live models in front, back and side views, and in widely varying poses. Accompanying diagrams. 177 illustrations. Introduction. Index. 144pp. 8⅜ x11¼. 0-486-26723-7

GOTHIC AND OLD ENGLISH ALPHABETS: 100 Complete Fonts, Dan X. Solo. Add power, elegance to posters, signs, other graphics with 100 stunning copyright-free alphabets: Blackstone, Dolbey, Germania, 97 more–including many lower-case, numerals, punctuation marks. 104pp. 8⅛ x 11. 0-486-24695-7

THE BOOK OF WOOD CARVING, Charles Marshall Sayers. Finest book for beginners discusses fundamentals and offers 34 designs. "Absolutely first rate . . . well thought out and well executed."–E. J. Tangerman. 118pp. 7¾ x 10⅝. 0-486-23654-4

ILLUSTRATED CATALOG OF CIVIL WAR MILITARY GOODS: Union Army Weapons, Insignia, Uniform Accessories, and Other Equipment, Schuyler, Hartley, and Graham. Rare, profusely illustrated 1846 catalog includes Union Army uniform and dress regulations, arms and ammunition, coats, insignia, flags, swords, rifles, etc. 226 illustrations. 160pp. 9 x 12. 0-486-24939-5

WOMEN'S FASHIONS OF THE EARLY 1900s: An Unabridged Republication of "New York Fashions, 1909," National Cloak & Suit Co. Rare catalog of mail-order fashions documents women's and children's clothing styles shortly after the turn of the century. Captions offer full descriptions, prices. Invaluable resource for fashion, costume historians. Approximately 725 illustrations. 128pp. 8⅜ x 11¼. 0-486-27276-1

HOW TO DO BEADWORK, Mary White. Fundamental book on craft from simple projects to five-bead chains and woven works. 106 illustrations. 142pp. 5⅜ x 8.
0-486-20697-1

THE 1912 AND 1915 GUSTAV STICKLEY FURNITURE CATALOGS, Gustav Stickley. With over 200 detailed illustrations and descriptions, these two catalogs are essential reading and reference materials and identification guides for Stickley furniture. Captions cite materials, dimensions and prices. 112pp. 6½ x 9¼. 0-486-26676-1

EARLY AMERICAN LOCOMOTIVES, John H. White, Jr. Finest locomotive engravings from early 19th century: historical (1804–74), main-line (after 1870), special, foreign, etc. 147 plates. 142pp. 11⅜ x 8¼. 0-486-22772-3

LITTLE BOOK OF EARLY AMERICAN CRAFTS AND TRADES, Peter Stockham (ed.). 1807 children's book explains crafts and trades: baker, hatter, cooper, potter, and many others. 23 copperplate illustrations. 140pp. 4⁵/₈ x 6.
0-486-23336-7

VICTORIAN FASHIONS AND COSTUMES FROM HARPER'S BAZAR, 1867–1898, Stella Blum (ed.). Day costumes, evening wear, sports clothes, shoes, hats, other accessories in over 1,000 detailed engravings. 320pp. 9⅜ x 12¼.
0-486-22990-4

THE LONG ISLAND RAIL ROAD IN EARLY PHOTOGRAPHS, Ron Ziel. Over 220 rare photos, informative text document origin (1844) and development of rail service on Long Island. Vintage views of early trains, locomotives, stations, passengers, crews, much more. Captions. 8⅞ x 11¾. 0-486-26301-0

VOYAGE OF THE LIBERDADE, Joshua Slocum. Great 19th-century mariner's thrilling, first-hand account of the wreck of his ship off South America, the 35-foot boat he built from the wreckage, and its remarkable voyage home. 128pp. 5⅜ x 8½.
0-486-40022-0

TEN BOOKS ON ARCHITECTURE, Vitruvius. The most important book ever written on architecture. Early Roman aesthetics, technology, classical orders, site selection, all other aspects. Morgan translation. 331pp. 5⅜ x 8½. 0-486-20645-9

THE HUMAN FIGURE IN MOTION, Eadweard Muybridge. More than 4,500 stopped-action photos, in action series, showing undraped men, women, children jumping, lying down, throwing, sitting, wrestling, carrying, etc. 390pp. 7⅞ x 10⅝.
0-486-20204-6 Clothbd.

TREES OF THE EASTERN AND CENTRAL UNITED STATES AND CANADA, William M. Harlow. Best one-volume guide to 140 trees. Full descriptions, woodlore, range, etc. Over 600 illustrations. Handy size. 288pp. 4½ x 6⅜. 0-486-20395-6

GROWING AND USING HERBS AND SPICES, Milo Miloradovich. Versatile handbook provides all the information needed for cultivation and use of all the herbs and spices available in North America. 4 illustrations. Index. Glossary. 236pp. 5⅜ x 8½.
0-486-25058-X

BIG BOOK OF MAZES AND LABYRINTHS, Walter Shepherd. 50 mazes and labyrinths in all—classical, solid, ripple, and more—in one great volume. Perfect inexpensive puzzler for clever youngsters. Full solutions. 112pp. 8⅛ x 11. 0-486-22951-3

PIANO TUNING, J. Cree Fischer. Clearest, best book for beginner, amateur. Simple repairs, raising dropped notes, tuning by easy method of flattened fifths. No previous skills needed. 4 illustrations. 201pp. 5⅜ x 8½. 0-486-23267-0

HINTS TO SINGERS, Lillian Nordica. Selecting the right teacher, developing confidence, overcoming stage fright, and many other important skills receive thoughtful discussion in this indispensible guide, written by a world-famous diva of four decades' experience. 96pp. 5⅜ x 8½. 0-486-40094-8

THE COMPLETE NONSENSE OF EDWARD LEAR, Edward Lear. All nonsense limericks, zany alphabets, Owl and Pussycat, songs, nonsense botany, etc., illustrated by Lear. Total of 320pp. 5⅜ x 8½. (Available in U.S. only.) 0-486-20167-8

VICTORIAN PARLOUR POETRY: An Annotated Anthology, Michael R. Turner. 117 gems by Longfellow, Tennyson, Browning, many lesser-known poets. "The Village Blacksmith," "Curfew Must Not Ring Tonight," "Only a Baby Small," dozens more, often difficult to find elsewhere. Index of poets, titles, first lines. xxiii + 325pp. 5⅝ x 8¼. 0-486-27044-0

DUBLINERS, James Joyce. Fifteen stories offer vivid, tightly focused observations of the lives of Dublin's poorer classes. At least one, "The Dead," is considered a masterpiece. Reprinted complete and unabridged from standard edition. 160pp. 5³⁄₁₆ x 8¼. 0-486-26870-5

GREAT WEIRD TALES: 14 Stories by Lovecraft, Blackwood, Machen and Others, S. T. Joshi (ed.). 14 spellbinding tales, including "The Sin Eater," by Fiona McLeod, "The Eye Above the Mantel," by Frank Belknap Long, as well as renowned works by R. H. Barlow, Lord Dunsany, Arthur Machen, W. C. Morrow and eight other masters of the genre. 256pp. 5⅜ x 8½. (Available in U.S. only.) 0-486-40436-6

THE BOOK OF THE SACRED MAGIC OF ABRAMELIN THE MAGE, translated by S. MacGregor Mathers. Medieval manuscript of ceremonial magic. Basic document in Aleister Crowley, Golden Dawn groups. 268pp. 5⅜ x 8½. 0-486-23211-5

THE BATTLES THAT CHANGED HISTORY, Fletcher Pratt. Eminent historian profiles 16 crucial conflicts, ancient to modern, that changed the course of civilization. 352pp. 5⅜ x 8½. 0-486-41129-X

NEW RUSSIAN-ENGLISH AND ENGLISH-RUSSIAN DICTIONARY, M. A. O'Brien. This is a remarkably handy Russian dictionary, containing a surprising amount of information, including over 70,000 entries. 366pp. 4½ x 6⅛. 0-486-20208-9

NEW YORK IN THE FORTIES, Andreas Feininger. 162 brilliant photographs by the well-known photographer, formerly with *Life* magazine. Commuters, shoppers, Times Square at night, much else from city at its peak. Captions by John von Hartz. 181pp. 9¼ x 10¾. 0-486-23585-8

INDIAN SIGN LANGUAGE, William Tomkins. Over 525 signs developed by Sioux and other tribes. Written instructions and diagrams. Also 290 pictographs. 111pp. 6⅛ x 9¼. 0-486-22029-X

ANATOMY: A Complete Guide for Artists, Joseph Sheppard. A master of figure drawing shows artists how to render human anatomy convincingly. Over 460 illustrations. 224pp. 8⅜ x 11¼. 0-486-27279-6

MEDIEVAL CALLIGRAPHY: Its History and Technique, Marc Drogin. Spirited history, comprehensive instruction manual covers 13 styles (ca. 4th century through 15th). Excellent photographs; directions for duplicating medieval techniques with modern tools. 224pp. 8⅜ x 11¼. 0-486-26142-5

DRIED FLOWERS: How to Prepare Them, Sarah Whitlock and Martha Rankin. Complete instructions on how to use silica gel, meal and borax, perlite aggregate, sand and borax, glycerine and water to create attractive permanent flower arrangements. 12 illustrations. 32pp. 5⅜ x 8½. 0-486-21802-3

EASY-TO-MAKE BIRD FEEDERS FOR WOODWORKERS, Scott D. Campbell. Detailed, simple-to-use guide for designing, constructing, caring for and using feeders. Text, illustrations for 12 classic and contemporary designs. 96pp. 5⅜ x 8½. 0-486-25847-5

THE COMPLETE BOOK OF BIRDHOUSE CONSTRUCTION FOR WOOD-WORKERS, Scott D. Campbell. Detailed instructions, illustrations, tables. Also data on bird habitat and instinct patterns. Bibliography. 3 tables. 63 illustrations in 15 figures. 48pp. 5¼ x 8½. 0-486-24407-5

SCOTTISH WONDER TALES FROM MYTH AND LEGEND, Donald A. Mackenzie. 16 lively tales tell of giants rumbling down mountainsides, of a magic wand that turns stone pillars into warriors, of gods and goddesses, evil hags, powerful forces and more. 240pp. 5⅜ x 8½. 0-486-29677-6

THE HISTORY OF UNDERCLOTHES, C. Willett Cunnington and Phyllis Cunnington. Fascinating, well-documented survey covering six centuries of English undergarments, enhanced with over 100 illustrations: 12th-century laced-up bodice, footed long drawers (1795), 19th-century bustles, l9th-century corsets for men, Victorian "bust improvers," much more. 272pp. 5⅜ x 8¼. 0-486-27124-2

ARTS AND CRAFTS FURNITURE: The Complete Brooks Catalog of 1912, Brooks Manufacturing Co. Photos and detailed descriptions of more than 150 now very collectible furniture designs from the Arts and Crafts movement depict davenports, settees, buffets, desks, tables, chairs, bedsteads, dressers and more, all built of solid, quarter-sawed oak. Invaluable for students and enthusiasts of antiques, Americana and the decorative arts. 80pp. 6½ x 9¼. 0-486-27471-3

WILBUR AND ORVILLE: A Biography of the Wright Brothers, Fred Howard. Definitive, crisply written study tells the full story of the brothers' lives and work. A vividly written biography, unparalleled in scope and color, that also captures the spirit of an extraordinary era. 560pp. 6⅛ x 9¼. 0-486-40297-5

THE ARTS OF THE SAILOR: Knotting, Splicing and Ropework, Hervey Garrett Smith. Indispensable shipboard reference covers tools, basic knots and useful hitches; handsewing and canvas work, more. Over 100 illustrations. Delightful reading for sea lovers. 256pp. 5⅜ x 8½. 0-486-26440-8

FRANK LLOYD WRIGHT'S FALLINGWATER: The House and Its History, Second, Revised Edition, Donald Hoffmann. A total revision—both in text and illustrations—of the standard document on Fallingwater, the boldest, most personal architectural statement of Wright's mature years, updated with valuable new material from the recently opened Frank Lloyd Wright Archives. "Fascinating"—*The New York Times.* 116 illustrations. 128pp. 9¼ x 10¾. 0-486-27430-6

PHOTOGRAPHIC SKETCHBOOK OF THE CIVIL WAR, Alexander Gardner. 100 photos taken on field during the Civil War. Famous shots of Manassas Harper's Ferry, Lincoln, Richmond, slave pens, etc. 244pp. 10⅝ x 8¼. 0-486-22731-6

FIVE ACRES AND INDEPENDENCE, Maurice G. Kains. Great back-to-the-land classic explains basics of self-sufficient farming. The one book to get. 95 illustrations. 397pp. 5⅜ x 8½. 0-486-20974-1

A MODERN HERBAL, Margaret Grieve. Much the fullest, most exact, most useful compilation of herbal material. Gigantic alphabetical encyclopedia, from aconite to zedoary, gives botanical information, medical properties, folklore, economic uses, much else. Indispensable to serious reader. 161 illustrations. 888pp. 6½ x 9¼. 2-vol. set. (Available in U.S. only.) Vol. I: 0-486-22798-7 Vol. II: 0-486-22799-5

HIDDEN TREASURE MAZE BOOK, Dave Phillips. Solve 34 challenging mazes accompanied by heroic tales of adventure. Evil dragons, people-eating plants, blood-thirsty giants, many more dangerous adversaries lurk at every twist and turn. 34 mazes, stories, solutions. 48pp. 8¼ x 11. 0-486-24566-7

LETTERS OF W. A. MOZART, Wolfgang A. Mozart. Remarkable letters show bawdy wit, humor, imagination, musical insights, contemporary musical world; includes some letters from Leopold Mozart. 276pp. 5⅜ x 8½. 0-486-22859-2

BASIC PRINCIPLES OF CLASSICAL BALLET, Agrippina Vaganova. Great Russian theoretician, teacher explains methods for teaching classical ballet. 118 illustrations. 175pp. 5⅜ x 8½. 0-486-22036-2

THE JUMPING FROG, Mark Twain. Revenge edition. The original story of The Celebrated Jumping Frog of Calaveras County, a hapless French translation, and Twain's hilarious "retranslation" from the French. 12 illustrations. 66pp. 5⅜ x 8½. 0-486-22686-7

BEST REMEMBERED POEMS, Martin Gardner (ed.). The 126 poems in this superb collection of 19th- and 20th-century British and American verse range from Shelley's "To a Skylark" to the impassioned "Renascence" of Edna St. Vincent Millay and to Edward Lear's whimsical "The Owl and the Pussycat." 224pp. 5⅜ x 8½. 0-486-27165-X

COMPLETE SONNETS, William Shakespeare. Over 150 exquisite poems deal with love, friendship, the tyranny of time, beauty's evanescence, death and other themes in language of remarkable power, precision and beauty. Glossary of archaic terms. 80pp. $5\frac{3}{16}$ x 8¼. 0-486-26686-9

HISTORIC HOMES OF THE AMERICAN PRESIDENTS, Second, Revised Edition, Irvin Haas. A traveler's guide to American Presidential homes, most open to the public, depicting and describing homes occupied by every American President from George Washington to George Bush. With visiting hours, admission charges, travel routes. 175 photographs. Index. 160pp. 8¼ x 11. 0-486-26751-2

THE WIT AND HUMOR OF OSCAR WILDE, Alvin Redman (ed.). More than 1,000 ripostes, paradoxes, wisecracks: Work is the curse of the drinking classes; I can resist everything except temptation; etc. 258pp. 5⅜ x 8½. 0-486-20602-5

SHAKESPEARE LEXICON AND QUOTATION DICTIONARY, Alexander Schmidt. Full definitions, locations, shades of meaning in every word in plays and poems. More than 50,000 exact quotations. 1,485pp. 6½ x 9¼. 2-vol. set. Vol. 1: 0-486-22726-X Vol. 2: 0-486-22727-8

SELECTED POEMS, Emily Dickinson. Over 100 best-known, best-loved poems by one of America's foremost poets, reprinted from authoritative early editions. No comparable edition at this price. Index of first lines. 64pp. $5\frac{3}{16}$ x 8¼. 0-486-26466-1

THE INSIDIOUS DR. FU-MANCHU, Sax Rohmer. The first of the popular mystery series introduces a pair of English detectives to their archnemesis, the diabolical Dr. Fu-Manchu. Flavorful atmosphere, fast-paced action, and colorful characters enliven this classic of the genre. 208pp. $5\frac{3}{16}$ x 8¼. 0-486-29898-1

THE MALLEUS MALEFICARUM OF KRAMER AND SPRENGER, translated by Montague Summers. Full text of most important witchhunter's "bible," used by both Catholics and Protestants. 278pp. 6⅝ x 10. 0-486-22802-9

SPANISH STORIES/CUENTOS ESPAÑOLES: A Dual-Language Book, Angel Flores (ed.). Unique format offers 13 great stories in Spanish by Cervantes, Borges, others. Faithful English translations on facing pages. 352pp. 5⅜ x 8½. 0-486-25399-6

GARDEN CITY, LONG ISLAND, IN EARLY PHOTOGRAPHS, 1869–1919, Mildred H. Smith. Handsome treasury of 118 vintage pictures, accompanied by carefully researched captions, document the Garden City Hotel fire (1899), the Vanderbilt Cup Race (1908), the first airmail flight departing from the Nassau Boulevard Aerodrome (1911), and much more. 96pp. 8⅞ x 11¾. 0-486-40669-5

OLD QUEENS, N.Y., IN EARLY PHOTOGRAPHS, Vincent F. Seyfried and William Asadorian. Over 160 rare photographs of Maspeth, Jamaica, Jackson Heights, and other areas. Vintage views of DeWitt Clinton mansion, 1939 World's Fair and more. Captions. 192pp. 8⅞ x 11. 0-486-26358-4

CAPTURED BY THE INDIANS: 15 Firsthand Accounts, 1750-1870, Frederick Drimmer. Astounding true historical accounts of grisly torture, bloody conflicts, relentless pursuits, miraculous escapes and more, by people who lived to tell the tale. 384pp. 5⅜ x 8½. 0-486-24901-8

THE WORLD'S GREAT SPEECHES (Fourth Enlarged Edition), Lewis Copeland, Lawrence W. Lamm, and Stephen J. McKenna. Nearly 300 speeches provide public speakers with a wealth of updated quotes and inspiration–from Pericles' funeral oration and William Jennings Bryan's "Cross of Gold Speech" to Malcolm X's powerful words on the Black Revolution and Earl of Spenser's tribute to his sister, Diana, Princess of Wales. 944pp. 5⅜ x 8⅜. 0-486-40903-1

THE BOOK OF THE SWORD, Sir Richard F. Burton. Great Victorian scholar/adventurer's eloquent, erudite history of the "queen of weapons"–from prehistory to early Roman Empire. Evolution and development of early swords, variations (sabre, broadsword, cutlass, scimitar, etc.), much more. 336pp. 6⅛ x 9¼. 0-486-25434-8

AUTOBIOGRAPHY: The Story of My Experiments with Truth, Mohandas K. Gandhi. Boyhood, legal studies, purification, the growth of the Satyagraha (nonviolent protest) movement. Critical, inspiring work of the man responsible for the freedom of India. 480pp. 5⅜ x 8½. (Available in U.S. only.) 0-486-24593-4

CELTIC MYTHS AND LEGENDS, T. W. Rolleston. Masterful retelling of Irish and Welsh stories and tales. Cuchulain, King Arthur, Deirdre, the Grail, many more. First paperback edition. 58 full-page illustrations. 512pp. 5⅜ x 8½. 0-486-26507-2

THE PRINCIPLES OF PSYCHOLOGY, William James. Famous long course complete, unabridged. Stream of thought, time perception, memory, experimental methods; great work decades ahead of its time. 94 figures. 1,391pp. 5⅜ x 8½. 2-vol. set. Vol. I: 0-486-20381-6 Vol. II: 0-486-20382-4

THE WORLD AS WILL AND REPRESENTATION, Arthur Schopenhauer. Definitive English translation of Schopenhauer's life work, correcting more than 1,000 errors, omissions in earlier translations. Translated by E. F. J. Payne. Total of 1,269pp. 5⅜ x 8½. 2-vol. set. Vol. 1: 0-486-21761-2 Vol. 2: 0-486-21762-0

MAGIC AND MYSTERY IN TIBET, Madame Alexandra David-Neel. Experiences among lamas, magicians, sages, sorcerers, Bonpa wizards. A true psychic discovery. 32 illustrations. 321pp. 5⅜ x 8½. (Available in U.S. only.) 0-486-22682-4

THE EGYPTIAN BOOK OF THE DEAD, E. A. Wallis Budge. Complete reproduction of Ani's papyrus, finest ever found. Full hieroglyphic text, interlinear transliteration, word-for-word translation, smooth translation. 533pp. 6½ x 9¼.
0-486-21866-X

HISTORIC COSTUME IN PICTURES, Braun & Schneider. Over 1,450 costumed figures in clearly detailed engravings–from dawn of civilization to end of 19th century. Captions. Many folk costumes. 256pp. 8⅜ x 11¾. 0-486-23150-X

MATHEMATICS FOR THE NONMATHEMATICIAN, Morris Kline. Detailed, college-level treatment of mathematics in cultural and historical context, with numerous exercises. Recommended Reading Lists. Tables. Numerous figures. 641pp. 5⅜ x 8½.
0-486-24823-2

PROBABILISTIC METHODS IN THE THEORY OF STRUCTURES, Isaac Elishakoff. Well-written introduction covers the elements of the theory of probability from two or more random variables, the reliability of such multivariable structures, the theory of random function, Monte Carlo methods of treating problems incapable of exact solution, and more. Examples. 502pp. 5⅜ x 8½. 0-486-40691-1

THE RIME OF THE ANCIENT MARINER, Gustave Doré, S. T. Coleridge. Doré's finest work; 34 plates capture moods, subtleties of poem. Flawless full-size reproductions printed on facing pages with authoritative text of poem. "Beautiful. Simply beautiful."–*Publisher's Weekly*. 77pp. 9¼ x 12. 0-486-22305-1

SCULPTURE: Principles and Practice, Louis Slobodkin. Step-by-step approach to clay, plaster, metals, stone; classical and modern. 253 drawings, photos. 255pp. 8⅛ x 11.
0-486-22960-2

THE INFLUENCE OF SEA POWER UPON HISTORY, 1660–1783, A. T. Mahan. Influential classic of naval history and tactics still used as text in war colleges. First paperback edition. 4 maps. 24 battle plans. 640pp. 5⅜ x 8½. 0-486-25509-3

THE STORY OF THE TITANIC AS TOLD BY ITS SURVIVORS, Jack Winocour (ed.). What it was really like. Panic, despair, shocking inefficiency, and a little heroism. More thrilling than any fictional account. 26 illustrations. 320pp. 5⅜ x 8½.
0-486-20610-6

ONE TWO THREE . . . INFINITY: Facts and Speculations of Science, George Gamow. Great physicist's fascinating, readable overview of contemporary science: number theory, relativity, fourth dimension, entropy, genes, atomic structure, much more. 128 illustrations. Index. 352pp. 5⅜ x 8½. 0-486-25664-2

DALÍ ON MODERN ART: The Cuckolds of Antiquated Modern Art, Salvador Dalí. Influential painter skewers modern art and its practitioners. Outrageous evaluations of Picasso, Cézanne, Turner, more. 15 renderings of paintings discussed. 44 calligraphic decorations by Dalí. 96pp. 5⅜ x 8½. (Available in U.S. only.) 0-486-29220-7

ANTIQUE PLAYING CARDS: A Pictorial History, Henry René D'Allemagne. Over 900 elaborate, decorative images from rare playing cards (14th–20th centuries): Bacchus, death, dancing dogs, hunting scenes, royal coats of arms, players cheating, much more. 96pp. 9¼ x 12¼. 0-486-29265-7

MAKING FURNITURE MASTERPIECES: 30 Projects with Measured Drawings, Franklin H. Gottshall. Step-by-step instructions, illustrations for constructing handsome, useful pieces, among them a Sheraton desk, Chippendale chair, Spanish desk, Queen Anne table and a William and Mary dressing mirror. 224pp. 8⅛ x 11¼.
0-486-29338-6

NORTH AMERICAN INDIAN DESIGNS FOR ARTISTS AND CRAFTSPEOPLE, Eva Wilson. Over 360 authentic copyright-free designs adapted from Navajo blankets, Hopi pottery, Sioux buffalo hides, more. Geometrics, symbolic figures, plant and animal motifs, etc. 128pp. 8⅜ x 11. (Not for sale in the United Kingdom.)   0-486-25341-4

THE FOSSIL BOOK: A Record of Prehistoric Life, Patricia V. Rich et al. Profusely illustrated definitive guide covers everything from single-celled organisms and dinosaurs to birds and mammals and the interplay between climate and man. Over 1,500 illustrations. 760pp. 7½ x 10⅛.
0-486-29371-8

VICTORIAN ARCHITECTURAL DETAILS: Designs for Over 700 Stairs, Mantels, Doors, Windows, Cornices, Porches, and Other Decorative Elements, A. J. Bicknell & Company. Everything from dormer windows and piazzas to balconies and gable ornaments. Also includes elevations and floor plans for handsome, private residences and commercial structures. 80pp. 9⅜ x 12¼.   0-486-44015-X

WESTERN ISLAMIC ARCHITECTURE: A Concise Introduction, John D. Hoag. Profusely illustrated critical appraisal compares and contrasts Islamic mosques and palaces—from Spain and Egypt to other areas in the Middle East. 139 illustrations. 128pp. 6 x 9.
0-486-43760-4

CHINESE ARCHITECTURE: A Pictorial History, Liang Ssu-ch'eng. More than 240 rare photographs and drawings depict temples, pagodas, tombs, bridges, and imperial palaces comprising much of China's architectural heritage. 152 halftones, 94 diagrams. 232pp. 10¾ x 9⅞.
0-486-43999-2

THE RENAISSANCE: Studies in Art and Poetry, Walter Pater. One of the most talked-about books of the 19th century, *The Renaissance* combines scholarship and philosophy in an innovative work of cultural criticism that examines the achievements of Botticelli, Leonardo, Michelangelo, and other artists. "The holy writ of beauty."–Oscar Wilde. 160pp. 5⅜ x 8½.
0-486-44025-7

A TREATISE ON PAINTING, Leonardo da Vinci. The great Renaissance artist's practical advice on drawing and painting techniques covers anatomy, perspective, composition, light and shadow, and color. A classic of art instruction, it features 48 drawings by Nicholas Poussin and Leon Battista Alberti. 192pp. 5⅜ x 8½.
0-486-44155-5

THE MIND OF LEONARDO DA VINCI, Edward McCurdy. More than just a biography, this classic study by a distinguished historian draws upon Leonardo's extensive writings to offer numerous demonstrations of the Renaissance master's achievements, not only in sculpture and painting, but also in music, engineering, and even experimental aviation. 384pp. 5⅜ x 8½.
0-486-44142-3

WASHINGTON IRVING'S RIP VAN WINKLE, Illustrated by Arthur Rackham. Lovely prints that established artist as a leading illustrator of the time and forever etched into the popular imagination a classic of Catskill lore. 51 full-color plates. 80pp. 8⅜ x 11.
0-486-44242-X

HENSCHE ON PAINTING, John W. Robichaux. Basic painting philosophy and methodology of a great teacher, as expounded in his famous classes and workshops on Cape Cod. 7 illustrations in color on covers. 80pp. 5⅜ x 8½.   0-486-43728-0

CATALOG OF DOVER BOOKS

LIGHT AND SHADE: A Classic Approach to Three-Dimensional Drawing, Mrs. Mary P. Merrifield. Handy reference clearly demonstrates principles of light and shade by revealing effects of common daylight, sunshine, and candle or artificial light on geometrical solids. 13 plates. 64pp. 5⅜ x 8½. 0-486-44143-1

ASTROLOGY AND ASTRONOMY: A Pictorial Archive of Signs and Symbols, Ernst and Johanna Lehner. Treasure trove of stories, lore, and myth, accompanied by more than 300 rare illustrations of planets, the Milky Way, signs of the zodiac, comets, meteors, and other astronomical phenomena. 192pp. 8⅜ x 11. 0-486-43981-X

JEWELRY MAKING: Techniques for Metal, Tim McCreight. Easy-to-follow instructions and carefully executed illustrations describe tools and techniques, use of gems and enamels, wire inlay, casting, and other topics. 72 line illustrations and diagrams. 176pp. 8¼ x 10⅞. 0-486-44043-5

MAKING BIRDHOUSES: Easy and Advanced Projects, Gladstone Califf. Easy-to-follow instructions include diagrams for everything from a one-room house for bluebirds to a forty-two-room structure for purple martins. 56 plates; 4 figures. 80pp. 8¾ x 6⅜. 0-486-44183-0

LITTLE BOOK OF LOG CABINS: How to Build and Furnish Them, William S. Wicks. Handy how-to manual, with instructions and illustrations for building cabins in the Adirondack style, fireplaces, stairways, furniture, beamed ceilings, and more. 102 line drawings. 96pp. 8¾ x 6⅜. 0-486-44259-4

THE SEASONS OF AMERICA PAST, Eric Sloane. From "sugaring time" and strawberry picking to Indian summer and fall harvest, a whole year's activities described in charming prose and enhanced with 79 of the author's own illustrations. 160pp. 8¼ x 11. 0-486-44220-9

THE METROPOLIS OF TOMORROW, Hugh Ferriss. Generous, prophetic vision of the metropolis of the future, as perceived in 1929. Powerful illustrations of towering structures, wide avenues, and rooftop parks–all features in many of today's modern cities. 59 illustrations. 144pp. 8¼ x 11. 0-486-43727-2

THE PATH TO ROME, Hilaire Belloc. This 1902 memoir abounds in lively vignettes from a vanished time, recounting a pilgrimage on foot across the Alps and Apennines in order to "see all Europe which the Christian Faith has saved." 77 of the author's original line drawings complement his sparkling prose. 272pp. 5⅜ x 8½. 0-486-44001-X

THE HISTORY OF RASSELAS: Prince of Abissinia, Samuel Johnson. Distinguished English writer attacks eighteenth-century optimism and man's unrealistic estimates of what life has to offer. 112pp. 5⅜ x 8½. 0-486-44094-X

A VOYAGE TO ARCTURUS, David Lindsay. A brilliant flight of pure fancy, where wild creatures crowd the fantastic landscape and demented torturers dominate victims with their bizarre mental powers. 272pp. 5⅜ x 8½. 0-486-44198-9

Paperbound unless otherwise indicated. Available at your book dealer, online at **www.doverpublications.com**, or by writing to Dept. GI, Dover Publications, Inc., 31 East 2nd Street, Mineola, NY 11501. For current price information or for free catalogs (please indicate field of interest), write to Dover Publications or log on to **www.doverpublications.com** and see every Dover book in print. Dover publishes more than 500 books each year on science, elementary and advanced mathematics, biology, music, art, literary history, social sciences, and other areas.